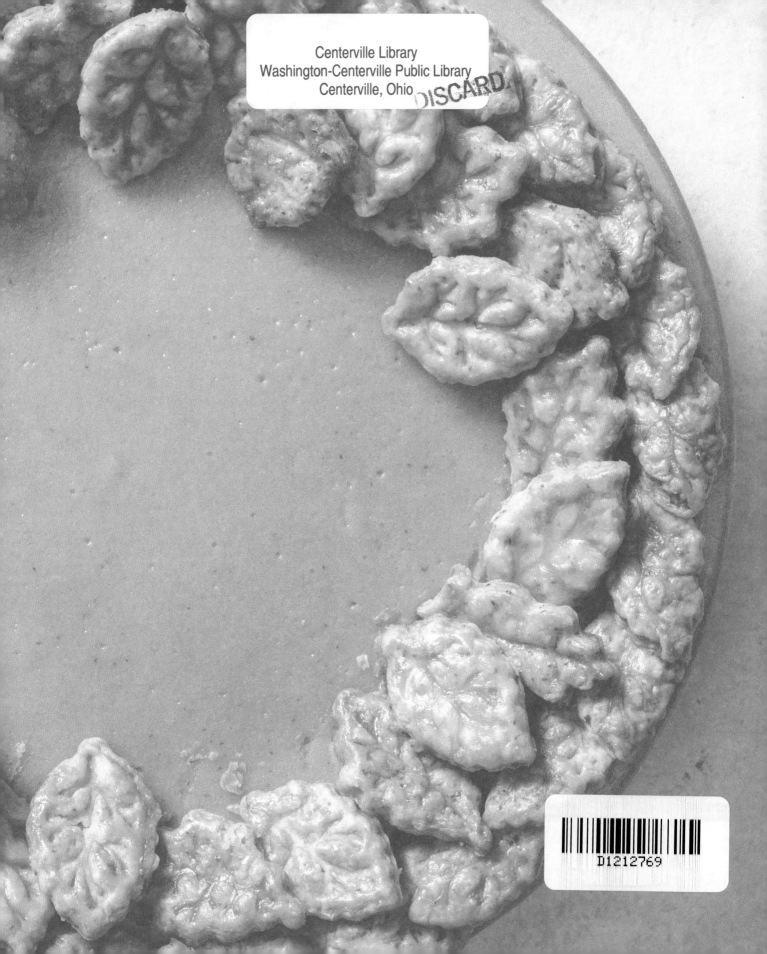

# ALSO BY AMERICA'S TEST KITCHEN

# PRAISE FOR AMERICA'S TEST KITCHEN TITLES

Selected as one of the 10 Best New Cookbooks of 2017
**THE LA TIMES** ON *THE PERFECT COOKIE*

"The editors at America's Test Kitchen pack decades of baking experience into this impressive volume of 250 recipes. . . . You'll find a wealth of keeper recipes within these pages."

**LIBRARY JOURNAL (STARRED REVIEW)** ON *THE PERFECT COOKIE*

"The book offers an impressive education for curious cake makers, new and experienced alike. A summation of 25 years of cake making at ATK, there are cakes for every taste."

**THE WALL STREET JOURNAL** ON *THE PERFECT CAKE*

Selected as the Cookbook Award Winner of 2017 in the Baking Category
**INTERNATIONAL ASSOCIATION OF CULINARY PROFESSIONALS (IACP)** ON *BREAD ILLUSTRATED*

"With 1,000 photos and the expertise of the America's Test Kitchen editors, this title might be the definitive book on bread baking."

**PUBLISHERS WEEKLY** ON *BREAD ILLUSTRATED*

"Cooks with a powerful sweet tooth should scoop up this well-researched recipe book for healthier takes on classic sweet treats."

**BOOKLIST** ON *NATURALLY SWEET*

"This book is a comprehensive, no-nonsense guide . . . a well-thought-out, clearly explained primer for every aspect of home baking."

**THE WALL STREET JOURNAL** ON *THE COOK'S ILLUSTRATED BAKING BOOK*

"The sum total of exhaustive experimentation . . . anyone interested in gluten-free cookery simply shouldn't be without it."

**NIGELLA LAWSON** ON *THE HOW CAN IT BE GLUTEN-FREE COOKBOOK*

"A one-volume kitchen seminar, addressing in one smart chapter after another the sometimes surprising whys behind a cook's best practices. . . . You get the myth, the theory, the science, and the proof, all rigorously interrogated as only America's Test Kitchen can do."

**NPR** ON *THE SCIENCE OF HOME COOKING*

"If there's room in the budget for one multicooker/Instant Pot cookbook, make it this one."

**BOOKLIST** ON *MULTICOOKER PERFECTION*

"Some books impress by the sheer audacity of their ambition. Backed up by the magazine's famed mission to test every recipe relentlessly until it is the best it can be, this nearly 900-page volume lands with an authoritative wallop."

**CHICAGO TRIBUNE** ON *THE COOK'S ILLUSTRATED COOKBOOK*

"The 21st-century *Fannie Farmer Cookbook* or *The Joy of Cooking*. If you had to have one cookbook and that's all you could have, this one would do it."

**CBS SAN FRANCISCO** ON *THE NEW FAMILY COOKBOOK*

"The go-to gift book for newlyweds, small families, or empty nesters."

**ORLANDO SENTINEL** ON *THE COMPLETE COOKING FOR TWO COOKBOOK*

"This book upgrades slow cooking for discriminating, 21st-century palates—that is indeed revolutionary."

**THE DALLAS MORNING NEWS** ON *SLOW COOKER REVOLUTION*

"Some 2,500 photos walk readers through 600 painstakingly tested recipes, leaving little room for error."

**ASSOCIATED PRESS** ON *THE AMERICA'S TEST KITCHEN COOKING SCHOOL COOKBOOK*

"This impressive installment from America's Test Kitchen equips readers with dozens of repertoire-worthy recipes. . . . This is a must-have for beginner cooks and more experienced ones who wish to sharpen their skills."

**PUBLISHERS WEEKLY (STARRED REVIEW)** ON *THE NEW ESSENTIALS COOKBOOK*

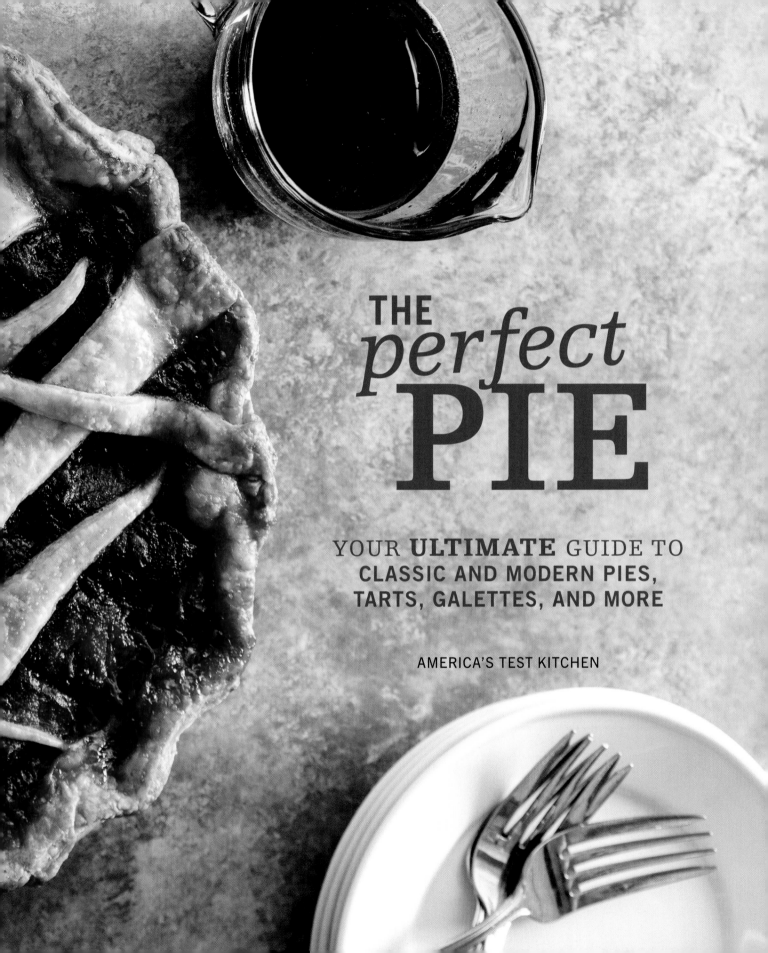

# THE perfect PIE

## YOUR **ULTIMATE** GUIDE TO CLASSIC AND MODERN PIES, TARTS, GALETTES, AND MORE

AMERICA'S TEST KITCHEN

Library of Congress Cataloging-in-Publication Data

Names: America's Test Kitchen (Firm), author.
Title: The perfect pie / America's Test Kitchen.
Description: Boston, MA : Americas Test Kitchen,
   [2019] | Includes index.
Identifiers: LCCN 2019019130 | ISBN 9781945256912
   (hardcover : alk. paper)
Subjects: LCSH: Pies. | LCGFT: Cookbooks.
Classification: LCC TX773 .P448 2019 | DDC 641.86/52--dc23
LC record available at https://lccn.loc.gov/2019019130

**AMERICA'S TEST KITCHEN**
21 Drydock Avenue, Boston, MA 02210

Manufactured in the United States of America
10 9 8 7 6 5 4 3 2 1

Distributed by Penguin Random House Publisher Services
Tel: 800.733.3000

**Pictured on front cover** Cape Gooseberry Elderflower Meringue Pie (page 122)

**Pictured on back cover** Chocolate-Cherry Pie Pops (page 226), Cookies and Cream Ice Cream Pie (page 331), Plum-Ginger Pie (page 112), Lavender Crème Brûlée Pie (page 79)

Editorial Director, Books **Elizabeth Carduff**

Executive Editor **Adam Kowit**

Executive Food Editor **Dan Zuccarello**

Deputy Food Editor **Stephanie Pixley**

Project Editor **Sacha Madadian**

Senior Editors **Leah Colins, Joseph Gitter, Sara Mayer, Russell Selander**

Associate Editor **Camila Chaparro**

Editorial Assistant **Brenna Donovan**

Art Director, Books **Lindsey Timko Chandler**

Deputy Art Director **Courtney Lentz**

Photography Director **Julie Bozzo Cote**

Photography Producer **Meredith Mulcahy**

Senior Staff Photographers **Steve Klise and Daniel J. van Ackere**

Staff Photographer **Kevin White**

Additional Photography **Keller + Keller and Carl Tremblay**

Food Styling **Catrine Kelty, Chantal Lambeth, Kendra McKnight, Ashley Moore, Marie Piraino, Elle Simone Scott, Kendra Smith, and Sally Staub**

Photoshoot Kitchen Team

Photo Team Manager **Timothy McQuinn**

Assistant Test Cooks **Sarah Ewald, Hannah Fenton, Jacqueline Gochenouer, Eric Haessler, and Jessica Rudolph**

Senior Manager, Publishing Operations **Taylor Argenzio**

Imaging Manager **Lauren Robbins**

Production and Imaging Specialists **Dennis Noble, Jessica Voas, and Amanda Yong**

Copy Editor **Elizabeth Wray Emery**

Proofreader **Jane Tunks Demel**

Indexer **Elizabeth Parson**

Chief Creative Officer **Jack Bishop**

Executive Editorial Directors **Julia Collin Davison and Bridget Lancaster**

# contents

# WELCOME TO AMERICA'S TEST KITCHEN

This book has been tested, written, and edited by the folks at America's Test Kitchen. Located in Boston's Seaport District in the historic Innovation and Design Building, it features 15,000 square feet of kitchen space, including multiple photography and video studios. It is the home of *Cook's Illustrated* magazine and *Cook's Country* magazine and is the workday destination for more than 60 test cooks, editors, and cookware specialists. Our mission is to test recipes over and over again until we understand how and why they work and until we arrive at the best version.

We start the process of testing a recipe with a complete lack of preconceptions, which means that we accept no claim, no technique, and no recipe at face value. We simply assemble as many variations as possible, test a half-dozen of the most promising, and taste the results blind. We then construct our own recipe and continue to test it, varying ingredients, techniques, and cooking times until we reach a consensus. As we like to say in the test kitchen, "We make the mistakes so you don't have to." The result, we hope, is the best version of a particular recipe, but we realize that only you can be the final judge of our success (or failure). We use the same rigorous approach when we test equipment and taste ingredients.

All of this would not be possible without a belief that good cooking, much like good music, is based on a foundation of objective technique. Some people like spicy foods and others don't, but there is a right way to sauté, there is a best way to cook a pot roast, and there are measurable scientific principles involved in producing perfectly beaten, stable egg whites. Our ultimate goal is to investigate the fundamental principles of cooking to give you the techniques, tools, and ingredients you need to become a better cook. It is as simple as that.

To see what goes on behind the scenes at America's Test Kitchen, check out our social media channels for kitchen snapshots, exclusive content, video tips, and much more. You can watch us work (in our actual test kitchen) by tuning in to *America's Test Kitchen* or *Cook's Country* on public television or on our websites. Download our award-winning podcast *Proof*, which goes beyond recipes to solve food mysteries (AmericasTestKitchen.com/proof), or listen in to test kitchen experts on public radio (SplendidTable.org) to hear insights that illuminate the truth about real home cooking. Want to hone your cooking skills or finally learn how to bake—with an America's Test Kitchen test cook? Enroll in one of our online cooking classes. And you can engage the next generation of home cooks with kid-tested recipes from America's Test Kitchen Kids.

However you choose to visit us, we welcome you into our kitchen, where you can stand by our side as we test our way to the best recipes in America.

facebook.com/AmericasTestKitchen
twitter.com/TestKitchen
youtube.com/AmericasTestKitchen
instagram.com/TestKitchen
pinterest.com/TestKitchen

AmericasTestKitchen.com
CooksIllustrated.com
CooksCountry.com
OnlineCookingSchool.com
AmericasTestKitchen.com/kids

# getting
# STARTED

# INTRODUCTION

Dessert pies as we know and define them today are a very American icon. For many of us, pie conjures homespun memories of rolling out dough, piling sweetened slices of seasonal fruit—maybe just-picked apples or farmers' market stone fruit—into passed-down pie plates, and baking a rustic pastry that fills the house with aromas of browned butter or spice. Or maybe you remember sitting at the diner counter, longingly staring up at plumes of whipped cream or meringue toppings higher than eye level.

We wanted to capture every pie memory and make new ones in our first book devoted to the art and science of pie and tart making. And as we baked our way through, we learned there was a lot of both. Conventional pie dough can be a pain to work with; we changed that. Fillings can be either soupy or overly gelled; we tailored our thickening methods to the pie at hand. And we took the tall-standing pies, the intricately-woven tops, and the barrier-breaking flavors out of the aspirational category and into the attainable. In short, we aggregated and built upon everything the test kitchen has learned about pie baking to not only engineer perfect pies but to carefully instruct you how to make them look and taste just so—and with ease.

Whichever kind of pie you find yourself wanting to make, and for whatever occasion, you'll find it here. You'll see standard favorites like Deep-Dish Apple Pie (with no gap between the fruit and top crust) or Pecan Pie (that isn't cloying) in our Mastering the Classics chapter. Beginning pie bakers will appreciate this chapter's approach: It sets you up for success with a photograph for each recipe step, so you know what your dough, filling, and topping should look like at every stage of the game. Build on those techniques to fashion the creamiest custard pies, elegant French tarts, treasured regional American pies, whimsical icebox pies and pie pops, and sheet-pan slab pies for a crowd (as many as 24 people). Bake with modern flavors in recipes like Chocolate-Tahini Tart (its ganache-slicked top is covered with a landscape of homemade sesame brittle), Crab Apple Rose Pie (with tart flavors from the overlooked backwoods apple), or Pear-Rosemary Muffin Tin Pies (there's browned butter and walnuts in there, too). You can also explore beyond-the-basic doughs to pair with your flavorful fillings—doughs made with nuts, herbs, or whole-grain flours. Shape those doughs with our guides to intricate crust patterns so your pies look as good as they taste (think: braids, ropes, and a herringbone lattice). We show you each bend and fold of these patterns so there's no ambiguity—anyone can make masterpieces.

Our foolproof recipes and clear instruction take away the intimidation factor. And so does this book's introductory chapter. We walk you through the common pie baking steps and ingredients, and suggest how to stock your pantry. But we'll also address the whys and hows: What makes pie dough flaky? How do you whip egg whites perfectly—and then spread and swirl them into a retro design? How do you slice the first piece of pie without it falling apart? The answers to these questions and the recipes in this book will help you make new pie memories, and we'll make sure they're sweet.

# PIE CHART: THE TOP TYPES OF PIE

The best pie chart has nothing to do with math. Here we chart some of the different categories of pies you'll find in this book. All come together to make your pie recipe collection complete.

# 1 DOUBLE-CRUST FRUIT PIE

These are the pies you bake after going to the orchard in the summer or fall. Buttery, flaky top and bottom crusts encase mounds of perfectly stewed fruit in these quintessential American pies. Because the top crust shields the filling, the juicy fruit usually requires a thickening agent such as ground tapioca or cornstarch to keep it from being too soupy. The most traditional crusts feature sliced vents for moisture to escape, although some fruit fillings, such as cherry and peach, require more evaporation and often sport lattice-woven crusts. You can brush the top crust with an egg wash and, if desired, sprinkle it with sugar. (For more information, see page 18.) Fruit pies take a full 4 hours to set up, so don't slice them too soon. If you want a warm slice of pie with ice cream, you can always heat up individual slices. (Here: Deep-Dish Apple Pie, page 28.)

# 2 CREAM PIE

Cream pies are filled with pastry cream—a cool, creamy, billowy custard that's cooked completely on the stove and then spread into a fully baked pie crust before the whole thing goes in the refrigerator to chill. These diner-style pies are frequently topped with whipped cream. (Here: Mocha Cream Pie, page 56.)

# 3 CUSTARD PIE

Custard pies feature an egg-thickened filling that's a bit firmer than pastry cream. A mixture of eggs, dairy, and sugar bakes until set within a single crust. Once cooled, the custard is a creamy, lightly eggy filling that coheres with the crust. A custard pie is done when the center still wobbles gently (165 degrees is typically the sweet spot for doneness). Overcooked custard pies can have rubbery, grainy fillings. Sometimes we cook the custard in a saucepan before adding it to the pie to give it a head start; this ensures it bakes quickly so the edges of the custard don't overcook before the center sets. The custard can be infused with just about any flavor you can dream up. (Here: Holiday Eggnog Custard Pie, page 76, sans whipped topping.)

# 4 MERINGUE PIE

These pies feature a lofty plume of whipped egg whites that adorns the filling like a fluffy, sweet cloud. The meringue, which we whip up in a stand mixer and then bake briefly on the pie to brown, usually tops a custard- or curd-filled pie, but we also whipped up elderflower-flavored meringue for a pie filled with Cape gooseberries (see page 122). Whipping the meringue until it just reaches stiff peaks (see page 21) ensures it doesn't weep, and anchoring the meringue to the edge of the crust keeps it from pulling away from the sides during broiling. (Here: Lemon Meringue Pie, page 66.)

# 5 TART

Tarts are an elegant subcategory of pie. The pastry, which is typically baked in a short-sided fluted pan, isn't flaky like a pie crust; instead it's sweet and has a closed crumb, reminiscent of shortbread. The filling for tarts is often creamy and rich and can be baked with the tart shell, like in Lemon Tart (page 154); added after, as with Fresh Fruit Tart (page 146); and sometimes topped with fruit, like in French Apple Tart (page 156). (Here: Fresh Fruit Tart, page 146.)

# 6 GALETTE

This pastry is a tart (it's open-faced), but it's also kind of like a pie in that it has a flaky crust and usually features a fruit filling that cooks during baking. It's made free-form (which is why we use the names free-form tart and galette interchangeably) on a baking sheet, so it's simple to pull together. Since the center is open, the fruit in these tarts essentially roasts, and their juices usually tighten up without the help of an additional thickener. (Here: Free-Form Fruit Tart with Plums and Raspberries, page 36.)

# 7 CHIFFON PIE

A chiffon pie has old-fashioned charm. Its filling feels much lighter than cream or custard pies—almost foamy—yet still satisfying. The mousse is supported by custard, meringue, or gelatin, or a combination. They're icebox pies that feature no-bake fillings (for the most part) that set up in the refrigerator. (Here: Grasshopper Pie, page 308.)

# 8 ICE CREAM PIE

This one is pretty self-explanatory—and pretty delicious. Ice cream (or sorbet or gelato) is softened, maybe combined with mix-ins, and spread into a prebaked cookie crust for a sundae in sliceable form. (Here: Cookies and Cream Ice Cream Pie, page 311.)

# CORE PIE-BAKING TECHNIQUES

This book covers pies of all kinds, from classic fruit- or custard-filled creations to meringue-topped marvels, and even those that serve as many as 24 people (see slab pies in the Pies Big and Small chapter). But while different types of pies require different methods to achieve the desired outcome, nearly all pie recipes have seven key steps in common: measuring, making the dough, rolling the dough, filling the pie, covering the pie, baking, and cooling and storing. In the photos below, we use our Deep-Dish Apple Pie (page 28) to illustrate each of these steps, as this recipe covers the most basic (but also most essential) techniques that apply to most pies. In the pages that follow, we'll dive deeper into these processes for a thorough explanation of why the proper execution of each one is important.

## MEASURING

It might sound obvious, but measuring—the first step to creating perfect pies—takes care: Baking is a science, and inexact measurements will yield inferior results. We provide weights for dry ingredients in our recipes and use a digital scale to weigh them; we strongly recommend you do, too. This is particularly important for dough; tenderness and flakiness depend on exacting proportions of fat, flour, and liquid. But if you're dead set on measuring these ingredients by volume, there's a way to increase your accuracy: the dip and sweep method.

Dip the measuring cup into the flour, sugar, or other dry ingredient and sweep away the excess with a straightedge object, such as the back of a butter knife.

For wet ingredients, we use a liquid measuring cup. To get an accurate reading, set the cup on a level surface and bend down to read the bottom of the concave arc at the liquid's surface—known as the meniscus line—at eye level. And for sticky ingredients, we recommend using an adjustable measuring cup (page 8). If you don't own one, spray a dry measuring cup with vegetable oil spray before filling it; when emptied, the liquid should slide right out of the cup.

## MAKING THE DOUGH

Not all dough recipes yield the same results. Sure, both pie and tart doughs contain similar ingredients—flour, butter (or another fat; see page 13), water, salt, and often some amount of sugar—but the proportions of each and the way you mix them dictate the texture of your crust. Here we describe some of the ways these factors can affect crust texture. Be sure not to overwork any dough during the mixing (or rolling) stages; this can lead to overdevelopment of gluten and crust that's tough or shrinks. **Note:** *You'll also want to reference the Pie and Tart Doughs chapter for start-to-finish steps for making, rolling, and molding different type of doughs.*

### for a flaky crust

Our Foolproof All-Butter Pie Dough (page 318) cuts easily under the side of your fork and encases pie filling (such as our example, apple) in layers of flakes; another flaky dough is our Classic Pie Dough (page 322), which includes both butter and vegetable shortening. Our all-butter dough is our go-to recommendation for *all* bakers because it's inventively formulated to achieve these characteristics no matter your skill level (and it's delicious). However, experienced pie makers might find our classic dough steps to be more familiar.

Regardless, in both recipes you mix the dry ingredients with the fat in the food processor, and some of the fat coats the flour. Then you bring the dough together into a rollable mass with water. Since a portion of the flour is coated with fat, that portion doesn't interact directly with the water; this fat barrier inhibits the flour proteins from forming a strong gluten network. Gluten gives baked goods structure, but too much structure means tough, hard-to-cut crust—it's a balancing act. The remaining fat that doesn't get combined disperses in small chunks. The purpose of these chunks? When the butter melts in the oven, it leaves small voids. Then, as water in the dough turns to steam, it expands the gaps and creates layers. So fat pockets precede flakes.

### for a sturdy crust

Another way to flakes is a French technique called *fraisage*. Here you briefly cut the butter into the flour and add some water, but then you use the heel of your hand to press the barely mixed dough firmly against the counter. As a result, the chunks of butter press into long, thin sheets that create lots of flaky layers when baked—without the faults created by spaces among the butter chunks in classic pie dough. This makes the dough sturdy enough to be baked free-form on a baking sheet (rather than in a pie plate) for free-form tarts and galettes—but still pleasant to eat. (See page 332 for more information on our Free-Form Tart Dough.)

### for a short crust

Flakes are fantastic, but sometimes we want a tender, slightly crumbly dough—something closer to shortbread—to serve as the base of a tart. Tart dough has a closed crumb and no flakes because the butter is fully incorporated into the flour. It's meant to be sweeter, but the sugar also further tenderizes the dough.

After you mix any dough according to the recipe, you gather it into a disk (or square for rectangular pies) and let it chill in the refrigerator. During this time, the dough becomes cohesive and the uncoated flour hydrates so the dough doesn't crumble when you roll it.

## ROLLING THE DOUGH

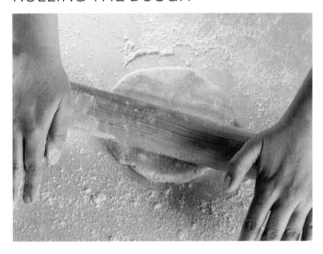

There are certain conditions that must be met for dough to roll out easily. First, the dough must be the right temperature. You don't want the butter to get too warm or it will melt into the dough and you'll lose your flake-forming pockets. But it must be malleable enough so you can roll the dough without it cracking. Letting the dough sit on the counter for about 10 minutes after chilling and then working confidently and quickly does the trick.

Dough can stick to the counter and tear; to prevent this, we flour the counter for most doughs. For very moist doughs, such as our Foolproof All-Butter Pie Dough (page 318), we flour the counter liberally. (A specific dough recipe will indicate if special treatment is required.) It's always best to roll dough in a single direction to create an even circle. Start at the middle of the dough disk, roll away from you, rotate the dough 90 degree (a bench scraper makes it easy to lift the dough from the counter and rotate it and can help if the dough begins to stick), and again roll away from you. Continue rolling in one direction and rotating the dough until it reaches your desired diameter.

## FILLING THE PIE

The dough might be the most intimidating part of a pie to tackle but what's inside counts, too—after all, a pie is named for its filling. We rarely just toss fruit with sugar or whisk together some wet ingredients. For most of our fillings, we've had the best success with some form of pretreatment. For our Deep-Dish Apple Pie, we learned that the apples would hold their shape during baking—and we could fit more apples into the pie—if we cooked them first (for more on the science of precooking apple pie fillings, see page 28). Custards bake more evenly when cooked on the stovetop first. (Note: Sometimes we dot the top of fruit pie fillings with a little butter for extra richness—you can leave this out to make many pie fillings vegan (see our recipe for Vegan Pie Dough on page 324).

### blind-baking the crust

For a double-crust fruit pie (such as our Deep-Dish Apple Pie), the filling goes directly into a chilled dough-lined pie plate; for a single-crust pie, however, we often partially or fully parbake (also known as blind-bake) the crust before filling it. This prevents the bottom crust from becoming saturated by the wet filling. Sometimes we make sure the crust is still warm from parbaking before we add something such as a custard; this helps the filling set quickly on the bottom to further sog-proof the crust (see Pumpkin Pie on page 38 for an example). When we're adding an already-cooked filling, such as pastry cream for diner-style pies (see Banana Cream Pie on page 50), or sorbet and gelato (see Coconut-Raspberry Gelato Pie on page 312), we fully bake and cool the single crust to serve as our vessel.

When blind-baking a single-crust pie, we line the dough with a double layer of aluminum foil and then fill it to the brim with pie weights (see page 323). The weights prevent the crust from shrinking (as its tendency is to contract inward) and eliminate puffing. Be sure to shield the dough edges with foil to prevent overbrowning, but don't enclose them completely; this will overinsulate them and steam the dough so it loses its shape. Plus, the foil could stick to the egg wash or dough.

## COVERING THE PIE

Our Deep-Dish Apple Pie has a homey, traditional top crust, with cutout air vents that allow just enough evaporation for the precooked filling. Other double-crust pies—such as juicy stone fruit or berry pies—require more moisture escape routes; in these cases, we choose a cutout or lattice crust. (For fancy ways to top your pie, see pages 134–142.) If you're covering the pie with a traditional top, you need only roll out another disk of pie dough and then transfer it to the pie following the steps on page 321. If you're working with a lattice or other decorative top, you roll out your second piece of dough into a rectangle, cut out dough strips as directed, and weave the strips before crimping the edges. Don't cut things too close: You want to leave an overhang for folding under and crimping, steps that seal the sides so they won't rip open during baking and that adhere the dough to the lip of the pie plate to help prevent slumping. (For more on crimping, see pages 130–133.) Sometimes we paint the top crust with an egg wash, which gives it nice color and sheen after baking. (For more on egg wash, see page 18.)

## BAKING

Your pie is now ready for the oven. For most pies, we recommend baking them on an aluminum foil–lined rimmed baking sheet, which has a few benefits. First, it ensures the bottom crust doesn't overbrown in the time it takes the filling to cook by providing some insulation. Second, it makes rotating the pie easy: It gives you something to hold on to, and there's no chance of marring the crimped edge with your bulky dish towel or potholder (the same goes for transferring the pie in and out of the oven). Finally, pies aren't the tidiest desserts: They can drip butter or egg wash; fruit juices can bubble up; and custard fillings may slosh over the sides. A lined baking sheet will catch all of this and make cleanup easy.

Sometimes pies go in the oven at a higher temperature and then we lower the heat. This sets the crust (so it doesn't get soggy) yet still allows the filling to cook gently. If at any point the edges or top of a pie appear to be browning too quickly, you can shield them lightly with aluminum foil.

How do you know when the pie is done baking if it's covered with a top crust? It depends on the pie. For fruit pies, judge by the color of the crust and if the filling is bubbling. A well-browned crust is more flavorful than a blond one, and it won't be doughy in the middle; if the filling is bubbling it has reached the boiling point, which means its thickener has been activated and its fruit cooked through. For custard and curd pies, we use an instant-read thermometer to ensure the filling is set and perfectly cooked—neither overcooked and rubbery nor undercooked and weepy.

## COOLING AND STORING

Pies are not for the impatient. Not only do they take some time to prepare (although, in this book, the methods are simple), they also need to cool completely. In fact, most pies require around 4 hours of cooling time. Pie is great warm, so why would you wait? The thickeners were activated in the oven, but the pie filling gels further with cooling. If you cut into a pie before it's set, the filling will pour out of the pie rather than slice cleanly. So while the wait may seem punishingly long, you can see below that you'll be sorry if you don't wait! If you want warm pie, simply heat up slices.

*Apple pie sliced after 1 hour.*  *Apple pie sliced after 4 hours.*

Where's the best place to store a pie, whether whole or left over? According to the U.S. Department of Agriculture (USDA), pies containing fillings with perishable ingredients such as eggs or dairy must be refrigerated once cool. But what about fruit pies? The USDA says they're food-safe at room temperature for up to two days because they contain plenty of sugar and acid, which retard bacteria growth. The refrigerator is fine for these pies, too, however. While cold typically hastens the staling of baked goods, the low moisture and high fat content of pie crust makes it resistant to staling in a way that leaner, moister items, such as breads, are not. If you don't have a pie carrier (see page 11), we've had luck overturning a large bowl over a pie plate.

# EQUIPMENT AND TOOLS

There are certain pieces of equipment that make pie baking easier (and more accurate). These are the basic tools you'll need and the specialty items you'll want.

## PREPARING PIES

### digital scale

We weigh dry ingredients to ensure consistent results. (This is especially important for pie dough.) We prefer digital scales for their readability and precision. Look for one that has a large weight range and that can be zeroed. The **OXO Good Grips 11 lb Food Scale with Pull Out Display** ($50) has clear buttons, and its display can be pulled out from the platform for easy viewing when weighing bulky items.

### dry measuring cups

While we much prefer to weigh our dry ingredients for baking, we understand that many will measure by volume. (And you'll still want a set of measuring cups for other purposes.) Look for heavy, well-constructed, evenly weighted stainless-steel models with easy-to-read measurement markings and long, straight handles. We use the very accurate **OXO Good Grips Stainless Steel Measuring Cups** ($20).

### liquid measuring cups

We turn to the industry-standard durable, accurate **Pyrex Measuring Cups** (in multiple sizes) for measuring milk, buttermilk, water, and coffee. We also like to whisk our wet ingredients together in these cups when a recipe calls for adding them gradually to the mixer.

### adjustable measuring cup

Sticky ingredients such as peanut butter and corn syrup can be difficult to measure and scrape out of liquid measuring cups. Enter: the adjustable-bottom liquid measuring cup. This style of measuring cup has a plunger-like bottom that you set to the correct measurement and then push up to extract the ingredient. Our favorite is the **KitchenArt Adjust-A-Cup Professional Series, 2-Cup** ($11).

### measuring spoons

We prefer a simple design that allows for a continuous, bump-free sweep into ingredient containers and sturdy stainless steel, which ingredients are less likely to cling to. We recommend **Cuisipro Stainless Steel 5-Piece Measuring Spoons** ($14).

### chef's knife

When you think of pie baking, a sharp-bladed chef's knife might not be the first tool that comes to mind. But this kitchen essential isn't just for savory cooking; lots of baking prep, such as chopping nuts and chocolate or slicing fruit, requires a good knife. We think the best chef's knife for this or any job is the inexpensive **Victorinox 8" Swiss Army Fibrox Pro Chef's Knife** ($39); it's been a test kitchen favorite for more than 20 years. We find that it maintains its edge long after its competitors have gone dull. Its textured grip feels secure for a wide range of hand sizes. You'll use it for everything.

### rasp-style grater

We flavor many pies with citrus zest or spices, so you'll want a rasp-style grater. This essential tool can also be used for other sweet kitchen tasks such as grating chocolate. Our top rasp-style grater is the **Microplane Premium Classic Zester/Grater** ($13); it came sharp, stayed sharp, and looked good as new after testing.

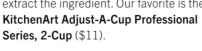

# WORKING WITH DOUGH

## food processor

We never make pie dough by hand anymore, and we don't recommend it: A food processor cuts ingredients into flour evenly so you're less likely to overwork your dough, and it does so efficiently so everything stays cold. And it's so useful in the kitchen, we can more than justify having one: In the context of pie alone, a food processor is ideal for chopping nuts with ease, making fruit purees, or smoothing out pumpkin and squash fillings. Look for a workbowl that has a capacity of at least 11 cups. With a powerful motor, responsive pulsing action, sharp blades, and a simple design, the **Cuisinart Custom 14 Cup Food Processor** ($169) aced our tests.

## ruler

Shaping dough rounds and rectangles to fit pie plates and baking sheets or cutting strips of dough for lattices to the right size ensures even baking and professional-looking results. A straight-sided ruler also gives you an edge to cut along. We use the **Empire 18-inch Stainless Steel Ruler** ($8.49). It's easy to read, use, and clean. The inches are divided into 32nds on one side and 16ths on the other.

## grater

One of the first steps to our gold-standard Foolproof All-Butter Pie Dough is grating a portion of the butter. We like the **Microplane Specialty Series 4-Sided Box Grater** ($30). This model frames four supersharp grating planes with tough plastic, making it easier to handle than other etched graters.

## rubber spatula

For scraping bowls, folding ingredients, mixing caramel, and smoothing fillings, you'll want the no-nonsense **Rubbermaid Professional 13½-Inch High-Heat Scraper** ($13) and the **Di Oro Living Seamless Silicone Spatula—Large** ($16). The large head on the Rubbermaid spatula makes it easy to properly fold ingredients; the Di Oro Living spatula is a good multi-purpose tool.

## rolling pin

There are many styles of rolling pins, but we like the classic French-style wood pins without handles. They come straight and tapered. We tend to reach for straight pins, which make achieving even dough thickness and rolling out larger disks and rectangles easy. The **J.K. Adams Plain Maple Rolling Dowel** ($16) has a gentle weight and a slightly textured surface for less sticking.

## bench scraper

This basic tool is handy for moving pie dough, lifting dough while you roll it, marking dough at intervals, and cutting dough into pieces. Our winner is the **Dexter-Russell 6" Dough Cutter/ Scraper—Sani Safe Series** ($11). It has a comfortable handle, and the deeply beveled edge cuts through dough quickly.

## kitchen shears

Once pie dough is placed in the pie plate, we trim the edge so the overhang isn't too thick and doughy when folded over. Our favorite shears are the **Kershaw Taskmaster Shears/Shun Multi-Purpose Shears** ($50), but if you're using your shears just for baking and not for cutting and butchering meat and poultry, our Best Buy, **J.A. Henckels International Take-Apart Kitchen Shears** ($15), are very good.

## pastry brush

We use a pastry brush to paint crusts with water or egg wash before they enter the oven or to dab jam over fruit tarts. With a thick head of uniformly sized bristles, the **Ateco 1.5" Flat Stainless Steel Ferrule Pastry Brush** ($11) picks up plenty of liquid and is agile.

## parchment paper

Lining your baking sheets with parchment paper is a simple way to keep dough from sticking when transferring dough rounds or strips in and out of the refrigerator or when baking free-form. We also spray parchment with vegetable oil spray and place it on top of custard pie fillings before chilling to prevent a skin from forming. If you bake a lot, order sheets that are already cut to fit 18 by 13-inch baking sheets: **King Arthur Flour Parchment Paper 100 Half-Sheets** ($19.95 per package).

## MAKING FILLINGS AND TOPPINGS

### whisk

Fat or skinny, tapered or short, with wires that twist at odd angles or sport a silicone coating, there seems to be a whisk for every facet of cooking. Could one all-purpose whisk tackle all of our pie filling needs? We tested 10 slim, tapered French-style models and skinny balloon whisks as they're best at getting into corners. What we found was that for an all-purpose whisk, we liked 10 moderately thin wires. Our favorite 10-wired whisk, the **OXO Good Grips 11" Balloon Whisk** ($10), features a grippy handle and lightweight frame for whipping.

### stand mixer

With its hands-free operation, numerous attachments, and strong mixing arm, a stand mixer is a worthwhile investment if you bake regularly. We can't imagine making meringue without it. Heft matters, as does a strong motor that doesn't give out when whipping for a long period of time. Our favorite stand mixer is the **KitchenAid Pro Line Series 7-Qt Bowl-Lift Stand Mixer** ($549.95). Our Best Buy is the **KitchenAid Classic Plus Stand Mixer** ($240).

### peeler

Every season delivers a fruit that's going to need to be peeled for pie—and we fit a lot of fruit in our pies. A peeler is also handy for making chocolate curls, if you like to adorn pies. Our favorite is the **Kuhn Rikon Original Swiss Peeler** ($5), which peels smoothly with minimal surface drag.

### instant-read thermometer

When it comes to sweet tasks, thermometers aren't just for candy making. They also take the temperature of a pastry cream, fruit curd, or caramel (check the temperature in various locations since it varies a bit from place to place in the pot), or judge the doneness of custard-based pies. A digital instant-read thermometer—rather than a slow-registering stick candy thermometer—will provide you with an accurate reading almost immediately; this is especially important with egg-based fillings, which can quickly overcook into a curdled mess. Thermometers with long probes easily reach into deep pots. The **ThermoWorks Thermapen Mk4** ($99) has every bell and whistle.

### small offset spatula

Smoothing pie surfaces or decorating with whipped cream is a lot easier (and neater) with a mini offset spatula. Our favorite is the **Wilton 9-inch Angled Spatula** ($5); it offers great control and is comfortable to use.

### piping sets

Floppy cloth pastry bags can stain or hold on to smells. Canvas bags tend to be too stiff. We prefer disposable plastic bags; they're easy to handle for neat pie decorating and effortless to clean. In addition, we consider six different tips essential to cover a range of decorating needs: #4 round, #12 round, #70 round, #103 petal, #2D large closed star, and #1M open star. You'll also want four couplers—plastic nozzles that adhere the tip to the bag. We like **Wilton** supplies.

## BAKING PIES

### oven thermometer

It's common for ovens to run hot or cold, which can lead to pies that are either overbaked or underbaked. The easiest way to accurately gauge oven temperature is with a thermometer. The **CDN Pro Accurate Oven Thermometer** ($4) has a clear display and attaches to the oven rack securely. Note that it's manufactured in two factories, so your model may not look exactly like the picture.

### pie plate

A pie plate is one of the most important items for perfect pie baking. While Pyrex and good ceramic dishes stand the test of time, the ultimate plate is the **Williams-Sonoma Goldtouch Nonstick Pie Dish** ($18.95). This golden-hued metal plate bakes crusts beautifully without overbrowning; even bottom crusts emerge crisp and flaky. Additionally, we liked this plate's nonfluted lip, which allowed for maximum crust-crimping flexibility. One minor drawback: The metal surface is susceptible to cuts and nicks, but we found that this didn't affect its performance—just be careful when slicing.

## muffin tin

Mini pies require mini vessels and the easiest choice for baking multiple small pies at once is a muffin tin. In addition to a light interior we like a muffin tin with a large rim, which makes it easy to move around. Our favorite is the **OXO Good Grips Non-Stick Pro 12-Cup Muffin Pan** ($24.99).

## tart pans

Shallow, fluted tart pans give a home baker's tarts a professional French-pastry look. The very best tart pan is the **Matfer Steel Non-Stick Fluted Tart Mold with Removable Bottom 9½"** ($30). It produces perfectly even golden-brown tarts with crisp, professional-looking edges. Its nonstick coating makes the transfer from pan to platter a cinch.

## aluminum foil

Aluminum foil is used a lot in pie baking in some very essential ways: It lines pie and tart shells before the pie weights go in for blind baking, it shields crusts from overbrowning, and it lines baking sheets to prevent a mess from bubbling pie fillings. You'll always want some on hand.

## ceramic pie weights

There are innovative substitutes for pie weights on the market, and many home bakers use rice or sugar or coins. We had our best success with the classic: pie weights. We like **Mrs. Anderson's Baking Ceramic Pie Weights** ($5); however, like with most sets, they come with just a cup of weights. We purchase four sets for 4 cups (more than 2 pounds of weights) to completely fill an aluminum foil–lined pie shell. With weights piled up and pressing firmly against the dough's walls, the edges of the pie shell remain high and the bottom turns out crisp, flaky, and golden brown.

## baking sheet

We bake nearly every pie or tart on a baking sheet to prevent overbrowned bottoms and for easy transfer to and from the oven. They also give us something to hold on to when rotating pies during baking so we don't mar crust edges. **Nordic Ware Baker's Half Sheet** ($14.97) performs flawlessly.

## cooling rack

Properly cooling a pie (often as long as 4 hours) is an essential step that shouldn't be overlooked. A good wire rack allows air to circulate all around the pie as it cools. The **Checkered Chef Cooling Rack** ($17) is our favorite and it's reinforced with an extra support bar that runs perpendicular to the three main bars.

## pie carrier

Traveling with a delicate pie can feel like tempting fate, but a good pie carrier can make the task easier and more secure. The **Prepworks Collapsible Party Carrier** ($28) is a nifty case. This collapsible plastic tote expands to accommodate even our tallest meringue-topped pies. Its large, nonskid base holds 8-, 9-, and 10-inch pies perfectly in place, even on bumpy car rides. Bonus: It comes with two molded inserts for deviled eggs, one of which can be flipped upside down and used as a second tier for transporting two shorter pies at once. Its one slight fault: The latches took a little finessing to secure properly.

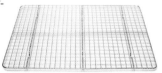

## pie server

Surprisingly, serving up a slice of pie isn't always the easiest part of pie baking. You can use a knife, but a pie server—essentially a pointed spatula—is specifically designed to cut, remove, and transport pie slices and should produce picturesque, intact pieces. The **OXO Steel Pie Server** ($10) is the best.

# THE PIE BUILDING BLOCKS: FLOUR, FATS, SWEETENERS, EGGS, THICKENERS

Like all baking, pie making is a science. But it doesn't have to be an intimidating process, especially once you understand the workings of the five common ingredients, most of which you probably stock regularly. These basic ingredients can be mixed and measured in countless ways to yield an incredible array of pies. Here's how we put the Big Five to work.

## FLOUR

Pie needs crust, so flour is arguably the most important ingredient for many pies. Flour gives baked goods structure, crumb, and texture, whether tough (bad), tender (good), or something in between (sometimes desired). While most of our pie dough recipes call for basic all-purpose flour, we make flavorful doughs with whole-grain flours, too. Different flours contain different amounts of protein; more protein leads to more gluten development, which translates to more structured pastries or, depending on the proporetion of other ingredients, tough, dense crusts. For that reason you won't see us using bread flour, which has the highest protein content of any white flour, in our pie crust recipes. Conversely, cake flour, with a low protein content, would give us crumbly crusts. Here are the flours we use in this book.

### all-purpose flour

All-purpose flour has a moderate protein content (10 to 11.7 percent, depending on the brand) and is by far the most versatile variety for baking. As mentioned on page 5, pie crust needs *some* structure provided by gluten; otherwise, it would be a poor levee for bubbling fillings and wouldn't hold a slice once cut. Gluten is also necessary for the dough to uphold flakes rather than just crumble. We develop our recipes with easy-to-find Gold Medal Unbleached All-Purpose Flour (10.5 percent protein). Pillsbury All-Purpose Unbleached Flour (also 10.5 percent protein) offers comparable results. If you use an all-purpose flour with a higher protein content (such as King Arthur Unbleached All-Purpose Flour, with 11.7 percent protein) in our recipes that call for all-purpose flour, the pastry might be a bit drier and denser.

### whole-grain flour

Whole-grain flour gives baked goods a distinctive flavor and texture because it's made from the entire wheat berry, unlike white flours, which are ground solely from the grain's endosperm. Whole-grain flour can be tricky to work with, though: It's high in protein (about 13 percent), yes, but it doesn't readily form gluten. The problem lies with the bran—the very thing that gives whole-grain flour its character. The fiber in bran has sharp edges that tend to cut the gluten strands; this means that a crust made with it is less likely to hold shatteringly crisp flakes. For that reason, we combine whole-grain flours with all-purpose flour in our pie doughs for the best balance of nutty flavor and good texture.

But while most recipes that combine whole-grain flour with white flour typically call for 40 percent or less whole-grain flour, we were able to flip the ratio in our variations for Foolproof All-Butter Pie Dough (page 318). That's because this novel recipe calls for coating a larger portion of the flour with butter than is typical to waterproof it; the second addition of flour does all of the gluten-forming work. (For more information, see page 318.) So in our variations we combine just the whole-grain flour with the butter in the first stage and reserve all the white flour for the second addition. We make this dough with whole-wheat flour (we use King Arthur Premium Whole Wheat Flour in the test kitchen) and rye flour (use light or medium in our recipe).

### storing flour

It's best to store all-purpose flour in the pantry, away from light and heat. Whole-grain flours contain more fat and quickly turn rancid at room temperature, so they should be stored in the freezer. Make sure to bring flour kept in the freezer to room temperature before using. To quickly accomplish this, spread the flour in a thin layer on a baking sheet and let it sit for about 30 minutes.

# FATS

You'll find a lot of butter in this book; its satisfyingly rich flavor makes for delicious pie crust, and it can bolster fillings and emulsify custards. While the latter uses are important, the nitty-gritty of fat, butter or otherwise, is on display most notably in the crust. As a general rule, the more fat in your crust, the more tender it will be—and it can be too tender: Fat coats the flour proteins, inhibiting their ability to form a strong gluten network.

Our go-to pie dough is our Foolproof All-Butter Pie Dough (page 318), which, of course, uses just butter for the fat. We love its flavor, flakes, and workability. We think it's the very best, but many seasoned pie bakers are used to combining butter and shortening (or lard). These doughs take some pie-baking intuition to execute as flawlessly—you have to have a feel for when you've processed them to just the right degree—but they too have their merits. Below we dive into butter, our favorite baking fat, and then discuss how other fats contribute to pie dough.

## use unsalted butter

Our recipes call for unsalted butter. That's because the amount of salt in salted butter varies from brand to brand. This is problematic for a couple of reasons: First, it makes it impossible to know how much salt to call for in a recipe. Second, salted butter contains more water than unsalted does, and the excess water can affect gluten development.

## plain, premium, and cultured butter

We use regular unsalted butter in all the pies in this book. We usually don't think high-fat butters are worth their higher price tag; Land O'Lakes Unsalted Sweet Butter has received top ratings in our taste tests for its clean dairy flavor. Regular supermarket butter contains about 82 percent fat or less. (The rest is mostly water, with some milk solids as well.) Premium butters, many of which are imported from Europe, have a slightly higher fat level—up to 86 percent. But in baking tests, we've had trouble telling the difference. Our favorite premium butter, Plugrá European-Style Unsalted Butter, is better saved for spreading on toast or for making croissants. Similarly, we leave cultured butter on the supermarket shelves when baking. Culturing, or fermenting, cream before churning it into butter builds tangy, complex flavors—which are lost when baked into pie crusts.

## storing butter

Butter can pick up off-flavors and turn rancid when kept in the refrigerator for longer than a month, as its fatty acids oxidize. For longer storage (up to 4 months), move it to the freezer. And because butter quickly picks up odors and flavors, we like to slip the sticks into a zipper-lock bag, whether it's stored in the refrigerator or in the freezer.

**THE OTHER FATS**

**Vegetable shortening** contains no water, so on its own this fat option creates an almost too-tender short crust with no flakes (not to mention zero flavor). But when you use a combination of shortening and chilled cubes of butter, you can make a very nice crust: The shortening coats the flour to encourage tenderness, while the cubes of butter create flake-forming pockets; this pairing is the key to success in our Classic Pie Dough (page 322). To illustrate the difference in how butter and shortening behave, we baked up one all-butter pie crust and one all-shortening pie crust. A cross-section shows the stark textural difference.

*Pie dough made with just butter is flaky.*

*Pie dough made with just shortening is short and dense.*

**Lard** is the fat of pie-baking past—and present if you're a traditionalist. But we don't include recipes that use it because supermarket lard has an unpleasant taste. Higher quality (but harder to find) leaf lard is a different story. It contains very little water so you could use it in place of the shortening in our Classic Pie Dough if you choose.

**Coconut oil** is the last fat we've come to associate with pie baking. This is our fat of choice for vegan pie doughs. We incorporate the coconut oil (at room temperature as it's very hard when chilled) much as we do butter in the fool-proof all-butter dough. The two additions of flour and fat make two grades of dough: one tender and rich due to its flour being coated in fat and one lean to offer structure that will hold any filling.

# SWEETENERS

As a sweet treat, pie fillings (and usually crusts) require sugar. Sweeteners come in many forms, from conventional white sugar to sticky-sweet honey or molasses. These are the sweeteners we use in this book.

## granulated sugar

White granulated sugar, made from either sugarcane or sugar beets, is the type of sugar used in our pie crusts (for a little flavor and browning) and most often in our pie fillings. It has a clean flavor and its evenly ground, loose texture allows it to dissolve quickly in fruit and custard fillings.

## confectioners' sugar

Also called powdered sugar, confectioners' sugar is the most finely ground sugar. It's commonly used for dusting finished pies and tarts, but it's also used for sweetening glazes such as the Earl Grey glaze on our Blueberry Earl Grey Pie (page 120) or icebox pie fillings like the one for our Peanut Butter Pie (page 307) because its fine texture can go undetected in raw applications and because it thickens and stabilizes these mixtures. You can approximate confectioners' sugar with this substitution: For 1 cup of confectioners' sugar, process 1 cup granulated sugar with 1 tablespoon cornstarch in a blender (not a food processor) until fine, 30 to 40 seconds.

## brown sugar

Brown sugar is granulated sugar that's been combined with molasses, giving it a deep caramel flavor. If important, an ingredient list will indicate light or dark brown sugar; if either can be used, we simply call for brown sugar. Store brown sugar in an airtight container to prevent it from drying out. (We pop in a Sugar Bears Inc. Brown Sugar Bear ($11), a clay bear that keeps the sugar soft.) If brown sugar does become hard, place it in a bowl with a slice of sandwich bread, cover, and microwave for 10 to 20 seconds to revive it.

To approximate 1 cup of light brown sugar, pulse 1 cup of granulated sugar with 1 tablespoon of mild molasses in a food processor until blended. Use 2 tablespoons of molasses for dark brown sugar. Brown sugar is so moist and clumpy that it must be packed into a measuring cup to get an accurate reading. To do this, use your fingers or the bottom of a smaller cup to tap and press the sugar into the cup.

## maple syrup

This syrup is made by boiling down sap from maple trees. It has a high moisture level, so you should refrigerate it not only to retain flavor but also to prevent microorganisms from growing. It will keep for six months to a year. For long-term storage, maple syrup can be kept in the freezer. If it crystalizes, a zap in the microwave will restore it.

# EGGS

Eggs are a baking essential. Their yolks and whites have different properties and serve different functions in pies: The yolks thicken creamy pastry cream, and the whites make marvelous meringues, from the meringue crust for our Chocolate Angel Pie (page 71) to tall toppings for Lemon Meringue Pie (page 66). And whole eggs give baked custards structure and finish pie crusts with sheen. Theoretically, eggs come in three grades (AA, A, and B), six sizes (from peewee to jumbo), and a rainbow of colors. But the only grade you'll find in a standard supermarket is grade A, the only colors brown and white, and the only sizes jumbo, extra-large, large, and medium. After extensive tasting, we could not discern any flavor differences among egg sizes or these two colors. For consistency's sake, however, the size of the eggs is important. Thus, in all of our recipes, we use large eggs.

## storing eggs

Properly stored eggs will last up to three months, but both the yolks and the whites will become looser and they'll begin to lose their structure-lending properties. To be sure your eggs are fresh, check the sell-by date on the carton. By law, the sell-by date must be no more than 30 days after the packing date. To ensure freshness, store eggs in the back of the refrigerator (the coldest area), not in the door (the warmest area), and keep them in the carton; it holds in moisture and protects the eggs from odors. Separated egg whites can be frozen, but in our tests we found that their whipping properties were a bit compromised.

## liquid egg whites

If you're tossing egg yolks when making recipes that call for egg whites only, you might think liquid whites are a better option. But we've found that in baked goods most liquid egg whites come up short—literally. The pasteurization process they undergo compromises the whites' structure; as a result, they can't achieve the same volume as fresh whites when whipped. While we'd rather use conventional whites from whole eggs, we have found Eggology 100% Egg Whites to be satisfactory.

## tempering

In our pastry cream and custard recipes, you'll notice that we don't just dump all the ingredients together before cooking. Instead, we heat the liquids in the recipe and then slowly incorporate a portion of them into the recipe's eggs before cooking everything together to the proper temperature. Conventional cooking wisdom says that tempering prevents the eggs from seizing up into tight curds by allowing them to warm up gradually. Tempering is essential but this isn't exactly why. Tempering works to prevent curdled custards because the addition of liquid dilutes the uncooked egg proteins, making it harder for them to link up and form firm clumps when heated. By tempering, you won't need a super-human wrist for the amount of whisking that would be needed during cooking to prevent tight bonds.

## THICKENERS

A common fear associated with fruit pie baking is that the filling will turn out soupy (and of course the opposite—an overly gelled brick—is a problem, too). That's where thick-eners come in; they work with fruit's juices to rein them in. (Additionally, eggs thicken cream and custard fillings.) Here are the thickeners we turn to and why.

### tapioca

Tapioca starch comes from the tropical root vegetable cassava, also called manioc or yuca. This neutral-tasting thickener can be an asset in fruit pies: It dissolves easily during baking—especially after it's been pulverized in a spice grinder—and preserves rather than dampens fresh fruit flavor (as other common thickeners can). That's it then, right? It sounds like the perfect thickener, and while it is our preferred choice in most cases, too much can make a filling gluey. Sometimes a pie benefits from a little bit of another thickener.

### pectin

Many fruits are naturally high in pectin. Pectin is a complex polysaccharide that acts as a sort of glue, binding mixtures when it comes into contact with liquid. The apple is one such fruit (in fact, we give the tapioca in our Blueberry Pie, page 30, a helping hand by incorporating shredded apple). Husk cherries are another. But that doesn't mean the natural pectin is released in amounts high enough to thicken fillings. Sometimes, as in our Cape Gooseberry Elderflower Meringue Pie (page 122), we'll bolster natural pectin with commercial pectin, which begins with apple or citrus extract and is chemically processed to produce a dry, powdered substance. Commercial pectin needs to be used in modest doses, however; it's acidic and can result in a puckering pie.

### cornstarch

When working with fruits (such as plums) that don't exude enough moisture for tapioca to dissolve in, we'll use corn-starch as a thickener. It's the perfect choice for the drier consistency desired in our Oregon Blackberry Pie (page 251). Because cornstarch is a pure starch, it is a more effective thickener than flour, which is only 75 percent starch. We've also found that flour can taste raw in fruit fillings.

# THE PIE PANTRY: STAPLES AND MISCELLANY

## MILK

When it comes to pie, milk is found most often in cream and custard fillings. Use whole milk in our pie recipes; the fat in whole milk lends the appropriate richness.

## CREAM

Cream is a custard standard as well. Using a combination of milk and cream allows us to achieve a custard with the exact level of richness we desire. Sometimes we're able to split the difference and use just half-and-half in a recipe. Cream also tops a lot of pies—in the form of whipped cream.

## VANILLA BEANS

When vanilla is really supposed to shine, as in our Vanilla Cream Pie (page 46) or our Apricot, Vanilla Bean, and Carda-mom Pie (page 114), we've found that beans impart deeper flavor than extract. We tested five vanilla beans, three mail-order and two from the supermarket. Although all samples were acceptable—including cheaper Spice Islands ($8.49 for two)—we recommend splurging on **McCormick Madagascar Vanilla Beans** ($15.99 for two) for their plump, seed-filled pods and complex caramel-like flavor.

**1** To remove the seeds from vanilla bean pods, first use a paring knife to cut the bean in half lengthwise.

**2** Scrape the seeds out of the bean with the blade of the knife.

## VANILLA EXTRACT

Vanilla extract rounds out the flavor of many custard fillings. It's sold in pure and imitation varieties. Which should you buy? If you want to buy just one bottle of extract for all kitchen tasks, our top choice is a real extract—real vanilla has around 250 flavor compounds compared with imitation vanilla's one, giving it a complexity tasters appreciated when we tried it in cooked applications and in cold, creamy desserts. Our favorite pure vanilla is Simply Organic Pure Vanilla Extract. But if you use vanilla only for baking, we have to admit there's not much of a difference between a well-made synthetic vanilla and the real thing (the flavor and aroma compounds in pure vanilla begin to bake off at higher temperatures, so the subtleties are lost). Our top-rated imitation vanilla, Baker's Imitation Vanilla Flavor, has a well-balanced and full vanilla flavor—and a budget-friendly price to boot.

## NUTS

We love the richness and texture nuts contribute to pies—in classics such as Pecan Pie (page 40) or in crunchy candied toppings for tarts like Chocolate-Hazelnut Raspberry Mousse Tart (page 187). We also grind them into flour and incorporate them into traditional pie doughs to add something special to pies such as Pecan Peach Pie (page 116) or Sour Cherry Hazelnut Pie (page 98).

### storing

All nuts are high in oil and will become rancid rather quickly. We store nuts in the freezer in zipper-lock bags. Frozen nuts will keep for months, and there's no need to defrost them before toasting or chopping. In fact, we call for frozen nuts in our pie dough recipes; they keep cool this way and don't turn to an oily paste during processing.

### nut varieties

Nut nomenclature can be confusing. Recipes may call for raw, roasted, blanched, slivered, or sliced nuts. If there is no descriptor in the ingredient list, raw is assumed. Roasted nuts have already been toasted but we rarely use these, as we like to control the degree of toasting ourselves. However, they're a good choice for peanuts because we like the flavor of salted peanuts, which are nearly always roasted. We often use blanched slivered almonds when grinding them for recipes such as the frangipane in our Poached Pear and Almond Tart (page 150) because the sweet nuts are stripped of their skins, which can add too much nuttiness or even bitterness to the delicate filling; the slivered nuts are also easier to grind than harder blanched whole almonds.

### skinning hazelnuts

The skins from hazelnuts can impart a bitter flavor and undesirable texture.

To remove the skins, simply rub the hot toasted nuts inside a clean dish towel.

## PEANUT BUTTER

Peanut butter makes its way into whimsical pies like the sweet-salty Caramel Turtle Icebox Pie (page 304) and our Peanut Butter and Concord Grape Pie (page 94). It comes salted and unsalted; in creamy, chunky, and even extra-chunky varieties; and conventional and natural. Natural peanut butter refers either to butters made simply from ground peanuts without added partially hydrogenated fats or emulsifiers (these butters exhibit natural oil separation and require stirring) or to those made with only ground peanuts and palm oil (these do not require stirring). We avoid varieties you need to stir as they make for oily fillings. And we like the flavor boost provided by salt. Our favorite creamy peanut butter is Skippy Peanut Butter.

## BAKING SPICES

The addition of spices is a great way to round out the flavor of a pie filling or to give it a bolder profile. We recommend following a few tips: Label spices with the purchase date; store them in a cool, dry place; and use within a year. Buy whole spices when you can and grind them in a coffee grinder devoted solely to this purpose; the flavors of preground spices fade fast. We use the following spices in our pie baking.

### cinnamon

Cinnamon is Americans' favorite baking spice; while basic versions abound, you can also choose from among bottles labeled Vietnamese or even Saigon. These specialty cinnamons command a higher price—up to about $4.00 per ounce, compared with as little as $0.90 per ounce for those with generic labeling. Does origin really matter? We found that cinnamons are indeed markedly different from each other. The Vietnamese cinnamons, for example, all fell on the spicier end of the spectrum, while the Indonesian cinnamons were mild. If you like a big, spicy flavor, we recommend springing for **Penzeys Vietnamese Cinnamon Ground**. At $4.09 per ounce, it was the most expensive product in our lineup, but it also had the highest percentage of volatile oils, which carry the flavor of cinnamon. If you prefer a milder spice, stick with less expensive cinnamons that make no claim to origin. Our favorite basic cinnamon is **Morton & Bassett Spices Ground Cinnamon**.

### nutmeg

Nutmeg is a hard, brown seed from a tropical tree that, when ground, offers a heady, potent aroma and flavor. We compared fresh with preground and found that for recipes in which nutmeg is a starring spice—such as our Holiday Eggnog Pie on page 76—grinding it yourself is important (we like to use a rasp-style grater for this task). But in foods with lots of spices, preground nutmeg is fine.

### cardamom

Fragrant cardamom comes in pods—either black or the more common green—and each holds many tiny seeds. Most of the highly aromatic flavors live in the seeds, which we grind ourselves for recipes such as Apricot, Vanilla Bean, and Cardamom Pie (page 114) rather than buying it preground.

### ground ginger

Ground ginger comes from the dried fresh root, but you can't substitute one for the other: fresh ginger has a floral flavor, while dry ginger is spicier. They also function differently in baking (fresh is moister). Our favorite is **Spice Islands Ground Ginger**.

### black peppercorns

While we generally associate this spice with savory applications, it makes an intriguing addition to spiced pies like Mulled Wine Quince Pie (page 108) where we steep peppercorns in the wine poaching liquid. The test kitchen's favorite peppercorns are **Tone's Whole Black Peppercorns**.

### lavender

Lavender is actually a relative of mint, and the dried buds lend sweets a pleasant floral quality. The key to using lavender successfully is restraint; we use a light hand in our Lavender Crème Brûlée Pie (page 79).

### cloves

Ground cloves are quite pungent, potent, and peppery, but the spice, in a small amount, is an important part of achieving the chai flavor profile for our Chai Blackberry Pie (page 128).

### allspice

Allspice is a complex winter baking spice that tastes like a blend of cinnamon, nutmeg, and clove. Allspice berries give the poaching liquid in Mulled Wine Quince Pie (page 108) great depth of flavor.

## HERBS

Herbs aren't the most common baking ingredient, but we use them like spices in some of our pies; their freshness and aroma make for complex desserts. Autumnal sage (processed so its leaves are imperceptible) pairs well with squash in Butternut Squash Pie with Browned Butter and Sage (page 102), candied thyme adds a pleasant herbal background flavor in Ricotta Lemon-Thyme Pie (page 74), and candied basil leaves finish off a beautiful summer strawberry galette (see page 170). We also include herbed pie doughs so you can pair herbs with your favorite filling recipes for extra flavor.

## COCONUT

Packaged coconut products all start as raw coconut meat that's then boiled, grated, and dried. Dried coconut comes in large flakes, shreds, or desiccated. There are two types of shredded coconut—sweetened and unsweetened. The dehydrated shreds are either immediately packaged and sold as unsweetened coconut or soaked in a liquid sugar solution and dried again to make sweetened coconut. We most often use the moister sweetened shredded coconut.

## SWEETENED CONDENSED MILK

Although 21st-century Americans have refrigerators and no longer need to rely on canned milk for safety, we still reach for sweetened condensed milk to make desserts such as Key Lime Pie (page 59) because it's sweet, thick, smooth, and resistant to curdling.

## GRAHAM CRACKERS

A graham cracker crust is probably the second most popular pie crust after a more traditional dough. It's commonly seen in icebox, ice cream, and cream pies, but it's also the base for our Summer Berry Pie (page 32). Our favorite is Keebler Grahams Crackers Original.

## OREOS

For fillings that go well with chocolate, we love a crust made with pulverized Oreo cookies. But everyone loves Oreos so they also find themselves in pies in various other ways: combined with vanilla ice cream for Cookies and Cream Ice Cream Pie (page 311) and made into a cookie streusel for Mississippi Mud Pie (page 284).

# FINISH YOUR CRUST

Choosing a crust—whether a puff pastry tart crust or a whole-grain pie dough—doesn't come down to simply picking a recipe. You also have to decide how to finish your crust's crimped edge (for a single-crust pie) or covered top (for a double-crust pie) before it goes into the oven—and your choice will determine the pie's surface appearance once baked. Below are the methods we use for finishing our crusts; you might find you have a favorite, or you might prefer to change things up every time. Note that a little egg wash goes a long way; you don't want your dough dripping wash and you should have some left once you're done painting.

## 1 FINISH-FREE

Crimp or top your pie and pop it in the oven: That's all this option requires. A plain pie crust has a rustic appearance once baked, sometimes with some attractive spotting. It has a matte finish and its browning comes solely from the fat and protein in the pie dough itself, not from any additions.

## 2 EGG WASH

Egg wash is a thinned egg mixture that you can lightly brush onto your pie before baking to enhance its golden color and give it a bit of sophisticated sheen. An egg-washed pie is inviting and convinces you the pastry is buttery and delicious before you even take a bite because it browns more than a finish-free pie. It's also nice to use an egg wash on a pie with intricate details, as it highlights any fork or spoon designs or intricate latticework. (For information, see pages 130–143.) Our egg wash involves lightly beating an egg with 1 tablespoon of water so it's thinned enough to distribute evenly and not so concentrated that it overbrowns. This is our go-to finishing technique.

## 3 WATER AND SUGAR

Sugar gives pies a little sparkle. Brushing the pie with some water before sprinkling on sugar helps the sugar adhere. A sugary crust also gets a pleasant exterior crackle, and some of the sugar caramelizes. It's nice to balance fillings that are a little tart, such as the one for Strawberry-Rhubarb Pie (page 127), with a sugar-sprinkled crust.

## 4 EGG WASH AND SUGAR

This luxe finish gives you the best of all worlds: sparkle and crackle but also golden browning for stunning display case–worthy pies. Both the sugar and the eggs encourage browning, so this will be the most burnished of the bunch. It's a good choice for quick-baking pies like hand pies because they finish baking before their tops can take on a lot of color; the egg-sugar wash boosts browning.

# WHIPPED TOPPING WHIMSY

Pies can be rustic, but they can also be showpieces—and the showiest of the bunch are those with a topping. We have a chapter of supplementary sauces and crunchy toppers that perk up pies (see the Toppings, Sauces, and More chapter), but whipped toppings are often the most whimsical. Here's how to have fun making pastry-case-perfect pies.

## WHIPPED CREAM

With little effort, the addition of whipped cream instantly makes dessert more fun. Some pies, such as cream pies, require it to solidify their identity, while others benefit from a dollop simply as an enhancement or creamy contrast to bolder, heavier ingredients. When you're whipping cream, make sure it's refrigerator-cold; the colder your cream, the more voluptuous it will be once whipped. A whipped cream topping is inviting no matter how it's applied, but we most often spread it attractively across the top of the pie—either with a small offset spatula or the back of a spoon for some decorative swoops. Sometimes we'll leave the edge of the filling exposed so you know what's inside. But we encourage you to get fancy, too.

STAR-PIPED TOP

SWIRLED TOP

### star-piped top

For whipped cream that plays a starring role, fit a pastry bag with a star tip of your desired size and fill the bag with whipped cream. Start around the edge of the pie and pipe in concentric circles until you reach the middle and have covered the whole pie. Hold the bag perpendicular to the surface of the pie, pipe out a small amount of whipped cream, and pull the bag straight away from the pie.

### swirled top

For rosette-like swirls of whipped cream, fit a pastry bag with a closed star tip of your desired size and fill the bag with whipped cream. Pipe out whipped cream while direct-ing the top in a circular motion, then stop piping and pull the bag straight away from the pie. You can leave as much or as little space as you like between each swirl.

## MERINGUE

Meringue—that sweet, shiny, fluffy confection—requires a little work, but its flavor and texture provide a beautiful contrast to tart, bright fillings such as those in Lemon Meringue Pie (page 66), Cape Gooseberry Elderflower Meringue Pie (page 122), and Key Lime Slab Pie (page 212). And the real appeal: Once baked briefly, the sugars and proteins in the egg-white mixture caramelize, brown, and highlight any decorative techniques. You can simply smooth it over the pie, but we like these two fun flourishes.

### spoon swoops

This is what you can expect to see in the shiniest dessert cases at diners and bakeries. It creates an appealing contrast between browned ridges and paler valleys. Using a rubber spatula, immediately distribute meringue evenly around the edge and then the center of pie, attaching meringue to the pie crust to prevent shrinking. Using the back of a spoon, create attractive swirls and peaks in the meringue, lifting the spoon quickly if you'd like taller, sharper peaks. Bake as directed.

SPOON SWOOPS

THE BEEHIVE

## the beehive

This retro look shows off impressively tall meringue and beautifully browned detail. Using a rubber spatula, immediately distribute meringue evenly around the edge, again attaching it to the crust and then the center of the pie, to prevent shrinking. Then, working quickly and using your spatula, smooth the meringue around the pie, spreading the meringue inward and upward to create a cone-like mound of meringue. Using the back of a spoon, make an indented swirl starting at the bottom of the pie and working your way up to the top. Bake as directed.

For our pie meringues, we pour hot sugar syrup into the whites as they are beaten (the Italian method) rather than simply beating egg whites with raw sugar (the French method). The hot syrup cooks the whites and helps transform them into a soft, smooth meringue that's stable enough to resist weeping during its short time in the oven. With a French meringue, the bottom portion often doesn't cook through and weeping is a greater possibility. Start with eggs straight from the fridge—these will separate more easily than eggs at room temperature. Be careful not to puncture the yolk as you separate the eggs. And use a scrupulously clean bowl as fat inhibits egg whites from whipping properly.

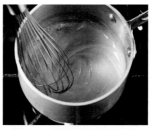

**1** Bring water and cornstarch to simmer in small saucepan and cook, whisking occasionally, until thickened and translucent, 1 to 2 minutes. Remove from heat; let cool slightly.

**2** Using stand mixer fitted with whisk attachment, whip egg whites, vanilla, and cream of tartar on medium-low speed until foamy, about 1 minute.

**3** Increase speed to medium-high and beat in sugar, 1 tablespoon at a time, until incorporated and mixture forms soft, billowy mounds.

**4** Add cornstarch mixture, 1 tablespoon at a time, and continue to beat to glossy, stiff peaks, 2 to 3 minutes.

# PIE TROUBLESHOOTING

Here are some common problems you may have experienced during pie baking—and how to fix them.

**problem** The dough doesn't roll out to symmetrical circle.

SOLUTION Make sure the dough isn't too cold. Rotate between turns.

**problem** The prebaked crust cracks.

SOLUTION Spackle the crust with scrap dough.

**problem** The crust shrinks or slumps.

SOLUTION Refrain from stretching the dough, chill before baking, and fill with pie weights, which stop slumping.

**problem** The first slice always falls apart.

SOLUTION Make 3 cuts before slicing. The extra cut allows for movement in the pie, making it easier to tidily wiggle out the first piece.

**problem** The edges brown too quickly.

SOLUTION Cover them lightly with aluminum foil.

**problem** The pie oozes filling.

SOLUTION Don't rush cooling or chilling.

**problem** The custard is pitted.

SOLUTION Don't combine the egg yolks with sugar in advance.

**problem** The whipped cream weeps.

SOLUTION Top just before serving.

**problem** The fruit filling is insipid.

SOLUTION Include the skins, which hold fruity tartness and colorful pigments.

# *mastering* THE CLASSICS

# SKILLET APPLE PIE

**Serves 6 to 8**

½ cup apple cider

⅓ cup maple syrup

2 tablespoons lemon juice

2 teaspoons cornstarch

⅛ teaspoon ground cinnamon (optional)

2 tablespoons unsalted butter

2½ pounds apples, peeled, cored, and cut into ½-inch-thick wedges

1 recipe single-crust pie dough (see pages 316–326)

2 teaspoons sugar

**WHY THIS RECIPE WORKS** Who says a pie needs to bake in a special plate—or even have a bottom crust? While we have a recipe for traditional deep-dish apple-packed pie worthy of a blue ribbon (see page 28), we wanted to expand the definition of perfect apple pie: It can come in a skillet, and it can be just about the easiest pie you can make. Unlike the filling for a double-crust pie, which needs to be juicy enough to flatter the fresh fruit but tight enough to keep the crust from becoming soggy, the filling for a skillet apple pie can be saucy. Apple cider provided resonant apple flavor and, when thickened with cornstarch, it yielded a juicy filling with just the right body. We used ⅓ cup of maple syrup to further sweeten the filling, and it complemented the natural sweetness of the apples without being cloying. Working in a heavy skillet allowed us to sauté the apples just long enough to caramelize them before we transferred the dough-topped pie to the oven for 20 minutes, where the crust developed a lovely deep brown hue. Cutting the dough into six pieces prior to baking allowed the crust to develop multiple crisp, flaky edges that contrasted with the saucy, caramelized, and tender apples. Use a combination of sweet, crisp apples such as Golden Delicious and firm, tart apples such as Cortland or Empire.

**1** Adjust oven rack to upper-middle position and heat oven to 500 degrees. Whisk cider, maple syrup, lemon juice, cornstarch, and cinnamon, if using, in bowl until smooth.

**2** Melt butter in 12-inch ovensafe skillet over medium-high heat. Add apples and cook, stirring 2 or 3 times, until apples begin to caramelize, about 5 minutes (do not fully cook apples).

**3** Off heat, add cider mixture and gently stir until apples are well coated. Set aside to cool slightly.

**4** Roll dough into 11-inch circle on floured counter. Loosely roll dough around rolling pin and gently unroll it onto apple filling.

**5** Brush dough with water and sprinkle evenly with sugar. Using sharp knife, gently cut dough into 6 pieces by making 1 vertical cut followed by 2 evenly spaced horizontal cuts (perpendicular to first cut).

**6** Bake until apples are tender and crust is deep golden brown, 15 to 20 minutes, rotating skillet halfway through baking. Let cool for 30 minutes; serve warm.

# DEEP-DISH APPLE PIE

**Serves 8**

1 recipe double-crust pie dough
(see pages 320–327)

2½ pounds Granny Smith apples,
peeled, cored, and sliced
¼ inch thick

2½ pounds Golden Delicious apples,
peeled, cored, and sliced
¼ inch thick

½ cup (3½ ounces) plus
1 tablespoon granulated
sugar, divided

¼ cup packed (1¾ ounces)
light brown sugar

½ teaspoon grated lemon zest
plus 1 tablespoon juice

¼ teaspoon table salt

⅛ teaspoon ground cinnamon

1 large egg, lightly beaten with
1 tablespoon water

**WHY THIS RECIPE WORKS** If you find yourself with a surplus of fruit after a fall apple-picking extravaganza, we recommend you enjoy them in a towering deep-dish pie. But this iconic pie can be tricky to get right, so our goal was to find solutions to the pitfalls: Unevenly cooked apples swimming in their own exuded juices atop a pale, soggy bottom crust and a large gap below the top crust are among common ones. We wanted each slice to be dense with juicy apples and framed by a buttery, flaky crust. Recipes call for many methods to tackle the apple filling, but we found that precooking allowed us to cram in lots of apples (a mix of tart and sweet); it also solved the shrinking problem and eliminated any excess liquid, thereby protecting the bottom crust. But why didn't the apples then turn to mush during baking? When apples are gently preheated, their pectin is converted to a heat-stable form that keeps them from becoming mushy when cooked further in the oven. In the end, our sky-high apple pie emerged golden brown and chock-full of tender apples, filling our kitchen with the homey, comforting aromas of autumn. Good choices for tart apples are Granny Smiths, Empires, or Cortlands; for sweet, we recommend Golden Delicious, Jonagolds, or Braeburns.

1 Roll 1 disk of dough into 12-inch circle on floured counter. Loosely roll dough around rolling pin and gently unroll it onto 9-inch pie plate, letting excess dough hang over edge. Ease dough into plate by gently lifting edge of dough with your hand while pressing into plate bottom with your other hand. Leave any dough that overhangs plate in place. Wrap dough-lined plate loosely in plastic wrap and refrigerate until firm, about 30 minutes. Roll other disk of dough into 12-inch circle on floured counter, then transfer to parchment paper–lined baking sheet; cover with plastic and refrigerate for 30 minutes.

2 Toss apples, ½ cup granulated sugar, brown sugar, lemon zest, salt, and cinnamon together in Dutch oven. Cover and cook over medium heat, stirring frequently, until apples are tender when poked with fork but still hold their shape, 15 to 20 minutes.

3 Spread apples and their juices on rimmed baking sheet and let cool completely, about 30 minutes.

4 Adjust oven rack to lowest position and heat oven to 425 degrees. Drain cooled apples thoroughly in colander set over bowl, reserving ¼ cup of juice. Stir lemon juice into reserved juice.

5 Spread apples into dough-lined plate, mounding them slightly in middle, and drizzle with lemon juice mixture. Loosely roll remaining dough round around rolling pin and gently unroll it onto filling.

6 Trim overhang to ½ inch beyond lip of plate. Pinch edges of top and bottom dough firmly together. Tuck overhang under itself; folded edge should be flush with edge of plate.

7 Crimp dough evenly around edge of plate. Cut four 2-inch slits in top of dough. Brush surface with egg wash and sprinkle evenly with remaining 1 tablespoon granulated sugar.

8 Place pie on aluminum foil–lined rimmed baking sheet and bake until crust is light golden brown, about 25 minutes. Reduce oven temperature to 375 degrees, rotate sheet, and continue to bake until juices are bubbling and crust is deep golden brown, 30 to 40 minutes longer. Let pie cool on wire rack until filling has set, about 4 hours. Serve.

# BLUEBERRY PIE

**SERVES 8**

| | |
|---|---|
| 1 | recipe double-crust pie dough (see pages 320–327) |
| 30 | ounces (6 cups) blueberries, divided |
| 1 | Granny Smith apple, peeled and shredded |
| ¾ | cup (5¼ ounces) sugar |
| 2 | tablespoons instant tapioca, ground |
| 2 | teaspoons grated lemon zest plus 2 teaspoons juice |
| | Pinch table salt |
| 2 | tablespoons unsalted butter, cut into ¼-inch pieces |
| 1 | large egg, lightly beaten with 1 tablespoon water |

**WHY THIS RECIPE WORKS** If the filling for blueberry pie doesn't gel, a sliced wedge can collapse into a soupy puddle topped by a sodden crust. But use too much thickener and cutting through the filling is like slicing through gummi bears. We wanted a pie with a firm, glistening filling full of fresh, bright flavor and still-plump berries. To thicken the pie, we favored tapioca because it didn't mute the fresh yet subtle blueberry flavor as cornstarch and flour did; but as with the other thickeners, too much made the filling stiff and congealed. Cooking and reducing half of the berries helped us cut down on the tapioca required, but not enough. A second inspiration came from a peeled and grated Granny Smith apple. Apples are high in pectin, a type of carbohydrate that acts as a thickener when cooked. Combined with a modest 2 tablespoons of instant tapioca, the apple helped the filling take on a soft, even consistency. We still needed a bit of moisture evaporation as more liquid was released during baking; cutouts atop the pie were a simple and attractive alternative to a more advanced lattice crust. This recipe was developed using fresh blueberries, but unthawed frozen blueberries will work as well. In step 2, cook half the frozen berries over medium-high heat, without mashing, until reduced to 1¼ cups, 12 to 15 minutes. Use the large holes of a box grater to shred the apple.

**1** Roll 1 disk of dough into 12-inch circle on floured counter. Loosely roll dough around rolling pin and gently unroll it onto 9-inch pie plate, letting excess dough hang over edge. Ease dough into plate by gently lifting edge of dough with your hand while pressing into plate bottom with your other hand. Leave any dough that overhangs plate in place. Wrap dough-lined plate loosely in plastic wrap and refrigerate until firm, about 30 minutes. Roll other disk of dough into 12-inch circle on floured counter. Using 1¼-inch round biscuit cutter, cut round from center of dough. Cut 6 more rounds from dough, 1½ inches from edge of center hole and equally spaced around center hole. Transfer dough to parchment paper–lined baking sheet; cover with plastic and refrigerate for 30 minutes.

**2** Place 3 cups blueberries in medium saucepan and set over medium heat. Using potato masher, mash blueberries several times to release juice. Continue to cook, stirring often and mashing occasionally, until about half of blueberries have broken down and mixture is thickened and reduced to 1½ cups, about 8 minutes; let cool slightly.

**3** Adjust oven rack to lowest position and heat oven to 400 degrees. Place apple in clean dish towel and wring dry. Transfer apple to large bowl and stir in sugar, tapioca, lemon zest and juice, salt, cooked blueberries, and remaining 3 cups uncooked blueberries until combined.

**4** Spread mixture into dough-lined plate and scatter butter over top.

**5** Loosely roll remaining dough round around rolling pin and gently unroll it onto filling. Trim overhang to ½ inch beyond lip of plate. Pinch edges of top and bottom dough firmly together. Tuck overhang under itself; folded edge should be flush with edge of plate.

**6** Crimp dough evenly around edge of plate. Brush surface with egg wash. Place pie on aluminum foil–lined rimmed baking sheet and bake until crust is light golden brown, about 25 minutes. Reduce oven temperature to 375 degrees, rotate sheet, and continue to bake until juices are bubbling and crust is deep golden brown, 35 to 50 minutes longer. Let pie cool on wire rack until filling has set, about 4 hours. Serve.

# SUMMER BERRY PIE

**Serves 8**

| | |
|---|---|
| 10 | ounces (2 cups) raspberries |
| 10 | ounces (2 cups) blackberries |
| 10 | ounces (2 cups) blueberries |
| ½ | cup (3½ ounces) sugar |
| 3 | tablespoons cornstarch |
| ⅛ | teaspoon table salt |
| 1 | tablespoon lemon juice |
| 1 | recipe Graham Cracker Crust (page 334), baked and cooled |
| 2 | tablespoons red currant or apple jelly |

**WHY THIS RECIPE WORKS** We feature many delicious fruit pies in this book, but this one, which captures the flavors of summer in a simple pat-in-the-pan crust, might be the easiest to make. There's no bouncy gelatin or dairy-heavy pudding here to overshadow the sweet-tart flavor of perfectly ripe berries. Rather, the filling is simply fresh whole berries piled on a puree of more berries that we cooked down with some sugar and just enough cornstarch to hold the filling together. A flavorful graham cracker crust provided the perfect complement to the bright mix of berries. The result was a pie that sliced neatly and had great berry texture and flavor. Tossing the whole berries with a bit of jelly gave them a beautiful sheen and contributed the perfect amount of sweetness. If you are short on one type of berry but have extras of another, you can always make up the difference with the extras. If blackberries are not available, use 3 cups each of raspberries and blueberries. When pureeing the berries, be sure to process them for a full minute; otherwise, they may not yield enough puree.

**1** Gently toss berries together in large bowl. Process 2½ cups berries in food processor until very smooth, about 1 minute (do not underprocess).

**2** Strain puree through fine-mesh strainer into small saucepan, pressing on solids to extract as much liquid as possible (you should have about 1½ cups); discard solids.

**3** Whisk sugar, cornstarch, and salt together in bowl, then whisk into strained puree. Bring puree mixture to boil, stirring constantly, and cook until thickened to the consistency of pudding, about 7 minutes. Off heat, stir in lemon juice and let cool slightly.

**4** Pour warm berry puree into cooled crust.

**5** Melt jelly in clean, dry small saucepan over low heat, then pour over remaining 3½ cups berries and toss to coat.

**6** Spread berries evenly over puree and lightly press them into puree. Cover pie loosely with plastic wrap and refrigerate until filling is chilled and set, at least 3 hours or up to 24 hours. Serve chilled or at room temperature.

# SWEET CHERRY PIE

**Serves 8**

1 recipe double-crust pie dough (see pages 320–327)

2 red plums, halved and pitted

2½ pounds fresh sweet cherries, pitted and halved

½ cup (3½ ounces) sugar

2 tablespoons instant tapioca, ground

1 tablespoon lemon juice

2 teaspoons bourbon (optional)

⅛ teaspoon table salt

⅛ teaspoon ground cinnamon (optional)

2 tablespoons unsalted butter, cut into ¼-inch pieces

1 large egg, lightly beaten with 1 teaspoon water

**WHY THIS RECIPE WORKS** Some think of sour cherries as pie cherries, and for good reason: Their soft, juicy flesh and bright, punchy flavor aren't dulled by oven heat or sugar. But sour cherry season is cruelly short and chances are the fresh cherries that are available to you are the sweet variety. Sweet cherries have a mellower flavor and firm, meaty flesh—traits that make them ideal for eating straight off the stem but don't translate well to baking. Our challenge: developing a recipe for sweet cherry pie with all the intense, jammy flavor and softened but still intact fruit texture of the best sour cherry pie. We started by supplementing our sweet cherries with chopped plums; their tartness helped balance the cherries' sweet flavor. To fix the texture problem, we cut the cherries in half to expose their sturdy flesh. This step encouraged the cherries to soften and give up some of their juices. We also pureed some of the cherries with the plums, straining out the skins, so the plum flesh wouldn't be noticeable and to help create a more cohesive filling. To keep the filling juicy, we turned to a traditional top crust rather than the lattice crust typically seen on cherry pie, which prevented too much moisture from evaporating. You can substitute 2 pounds of frozen sweet cherries for the fresh cherries. If you are using frozen fruit, measure it frozen, but let it thaw before filling the pie. If you don't thaw the fruit, you run the risk of partially cooked fruit and undissolved tapioca.

**1** Roll 1 disk of dough into 12-inch circle on floured counter. Loosely roll dough around rolling pin and gently unroll it onto 9-inch pie plate, letting excess dough hang over edge. Ease dough into plate by gently lifting edge of dough with your hand while pressing into plate bottom with your other hand. Leave any dough that overhangs plate in place. Wrap dough-lined plate loosely in plastic wrap and refrigerate until firm, about 30 minutes. Roll other disk of dough into 12-inch circle on floured counter, then transfer to parchment paper–lined rimmed baking sheet; cover with plastic and refrigerate until firm, about 30 minutes.

**2** Adjust oven rack to lowest position and heat oven to 400 degrees. Process plums and 1 cup cherries in food processor until smooth, about 1 minute, scraping down sides of bowl as needed.

**3** Strain puree through fine-mesh strainer into large bowl, pressing on solids to extract as much liquid as possible; discard solids. Stir remaining cherries; sugar; tapioca; lemon juice; bourbon, if using; salt; and cinnamon, if using, into strained puree. Let stand for 15 minutes.

**4** Spread cherry mixture with its juices into dough-lined plate and scatter butter over top. Loosely roll remaining dough round around rolling pin and gently unroll it onto filling. Trim overhang to ½ inch beyond lip of plate. Pinch edges of top and bottom dough firmly together. Tuck overhang under itself; folded edge should be flush with edge of plate. Crimp dough evenly around edge of plate.

**5** Cut eight 1-inch slits in top of dough. Brush surface with egg wash.

**6** Place pie on aluminum foil–lined rimmed baking sheet and bake until crust is light golden brown, about 30 minutes. Reduce oven temperature to 350 degrees, rotate sheet, and continue to bake until juices are bubbling and crust is deep golden brown, 35 to 50 minutes longer. Let pie cool on wire rack until filling has set, about 4 hours. Serve.

1

2

3

4

5

6

# FREE-FORM FRUIT TART WITH PLUMS AND RASPBERRIES

Serves 6

1 recipe Free-Form Tart Dough (page 332)

1 pound plums, halved, pitted, and cut into ½-inch wedges

5 ounces (1 cup) raspberries

¼ cup (1¾ ounces) plus 1 tablespoon sugar, divided

1 large egg, lightly beaten with 1 tablespoon water

**WHY THIS RECIPE WORKS** Rather than molded into a pie plate or tart pan, the round of dough for a free-form tart—what's known as a "galette" in France—is placed flat on a baking sheet and then folded around a generous fruit filling. These tarts taste like pie, but they are much easier to prepare. And while their assembly and appearance make them decidedly rustic, we think they also have a quiet elegance and intense beauty; the large window of juicy, bright fruit and the golden rim of pleated crust form an impressive display of seasonal bounty. The dough we developed for our free-form tarts results in an extra-flaky, crisp crust that surrounds the fruit with structure. (See page 332 for more information.) Because ripe summer fruit is a treat in itself, a modest ¼ cup of sugar was all our filling needed to enhance the fruit's natural sweetness. Some drips of fruit juice make a free-form tart appealing, but to prevent unsightly leaks or pastry damage we found it crucial to leave a small swath about ½ inch wide between the fruit and the edge of the tart to act as a barrier. We particularly love the pairing of earthy plums and bright raspberries, but we've included two additional combinations of stone fruit and berries. Taste the fruit before adding sugar; use less sugar if the fruit is very sweet, more if it is tart.

**1** Roll dough into 12-inch circle between 2 large sheets of floured parchment paper. (If dough sticks to parchment, gently loosen dough with bench scraper and dust parchment with additional flour.)

**2** Slide dough, still between parchment, onto rimmed baking sheet and refrigerate until firm, 15 to 30 minutes.

**3** Adjust oven rack to middle position and heat oven to 375 degrees. Gently toss plums, raspberries, and ¼ cup sugar together in bowl.

**4** Remove top sheet of parchment paper from dough. Mound fruit in center of dough, leaving 2½-inch border around edge of fruit.

**5** Fold outermost 2 inches of dough over fruit, pleating it every 2 to 3 inches as needed; be sure to leave ½-inch border of dough between fruit and edge of tart.

**6** Gently pinch pleated dough to secure, but do not press dough into fruit.

**7** Brush top and sides of dough lightly with egg wash and sprinkle with remaining 1 tablespoon sugar. Bake until crust is golden brown and fruit is bubbling, about 1 hour, rotating sheet halfway through baking.

**8** Let tart cool on baking sheet for 10 minutes. Using parchment, carefully slide tart onto wire rack and let tart cool until filling thickens, about 25 minutes. Serve slightly warm or at room temperature.

*Free-Form Fruit Tart with Apricots and Blackberries*
Substitute 1 pound apricots for plums and 1 cup blackberries for raspberries.

*Free-From Fruit Tart with Peaches and Blueberries*
Substitute 1 pound peaches for plums and 1 cup blueberries for raspberries.

# PUMPKIN PIE

**Serves 8**

1 recipe single-crust pie dough (see pages 316–326)

1 cup heavy cream

1 cup whole milk

3 large eggs plus 2 large yolks

1 teaspoon vanilla extract

1 (15-ounce) can unsweetened pumpkin puree

1 cup drained candied sweet potatoes or yams

¾ cup (5¼ ounces) sugar

¼ cup maple syrup

2 teaspoons grated fresh ginger

1 teaspoon table salt

½ teaspoon ground cinnamon

¼ teaspoon ground nutmeg

**WHY THIS RECIPE WORKS** Our pumpkin pie sets the standard: It's velvety smooth (not stodgy or dense), packed with pumpkin flavor (not diluted), and perfectly spiced (not like potpourri). Canned pumpkin puree contains flavor-muting moisture, so to eliminate some of the liquid and concentrate the pumpkin's flavor we cooked the puree with sugar and spices before whisking in heavy cream, milk, and eggs to enrich it. Working with this hot filling and a warm prebaked crust helped the custard firm up quickly in the oven and prevented it from soaking into the crust. For spices, we used ground nutmeg and cinnamon—just enough to provide warmth without being distracting—and added some fresh grated ginger to awaken the mix. This autumnal pie was better than most, but it still didn't taste distinctly like sugar pumpkins. Granulated sugar and maple syrup sweetened things, but, surprisingly, it was *another* vegetable that really put our pie's flavor over the top. The addition of mashed candied sweet potatoes actually made our filling taste more like pumpkin than when it was made from pumpkin puree alone. Starting the pie in a hot oven and then dropping the temperature partway through baking prevented curdling. If candied sweet potatoes or yams are unavailable, regular canned sweet potatoes or yams can be substituted. When the pie is properly baked, the center 2 inches of the pie should look firm but jiggle slightly.

1 Roll dough into 12-inch circle on floured counter. Loosely roll dough around rolling pin and gently unroll it onto 9-inch pie plate, letting excess dough hang over edge. Ease dough into plate by gently lifting edge of dough with your hand while pressing into plate bottom with your other hand.

2 Trim overhang to ½ inch beyond lip of plate. Tuck overhang under itself; folded edge should be flush with edge of plate. Crimp dough evenly around edge of plate. Wrap dough-lined plate loosely in plastic wrap and refrigerate until firm, about 30 minutes. Adjust oven rack to middle position and heat oven to 350 degrees.

3 Line chilled pie shell with double layer of aluminum foil, covering edges to prevent burning, and fill with pie weights. Bake on foil-lined rimmed baking sheet until edges are set and just beginning to turn golden, 25 to 30 minutes, rotating sheet halfway through baking.

4 Remove foil and weights, rotate sheet, and continue to bake crust until golden brown and crisp, 10 to 15 minutes longer. Transfer sheet to wire rack. (Crust must still be warm when filling is added.) Increase oven temperature to 400 degrees.

5 While crust is baking, whisk cream, milk, eggs and yolks, and vanilla together in bowl; set aside. Bring pumpkin, sweet potatoes, sugar, maple syrup, ginger, salt, cinnamon, and nutmeg to simmer in large saucepan over medium heat and cook, stirring constantly and mashing sweet potatoes against sides of saucepan, until thick and shiny, 15 to 20 minutes.

6 Remove saucepan from heat and whisk in cream mixture until fully incorporated.

7 Strain mixture through fine-mesh strainer into bowl, using back of ladle or spatula to press solids through strainer.

8 Whisk mixture, then, with pie still on sheet, pour into warm crust. Bake for 10 minutes. Reduce oven temperature to 300 degrees and continue to bake until edges of pie are set and center registers 175 degrees, 20 to 35 minutes longer, rotating sheet halfway through baking. Let pie cool completely on wire rack, about 4 hours. Serve.

# PECAN PIE

Serves 8

1 recipe single-crust pie dough (see pages 316–326)

6 tablespoons unsalted butter, cut into 1-inch pieces

1 cup packed (7 ounces) dark brown sugar

½ teaspoon table salt

3 large eggs

¾ cup light corn syrup

1 tablespoon vanilla extract

2 cups pecans, toasted and chopped fine

**WHY THIS RECIPE WORKS** Pecan pie is a classic for good reason—rich, buttery pecans mingle with a custardy, deeply flavored sugar filling in a crisp crust for an irresistible treat. That's the ideal, at least. Pecan pies are often overwhelmingly sweet and lacking in their namesake flavor. What's more, the custard often curdles and separates, resulting in a weepy filling that makes the bottom crust soggy and leathery. We tackled this classic pie's classic problems by using dark brown sugar rather than granulated for deeper flavor; we also reduced the amount, which helped tame the saccharine bite and also allowed the pecan flavor to shine. Some butter added a lush texture to the filling and underscored the richness of the pecans. After partially baking the crust, we found it important to add the hot filling to the warm pie crust to keep the crust from getting soggy. Melting the butter and cooking the filling over a simulated double-boiler was an easy way to maintain gentle heat and prevent the eggy filling from curdling. Finally, we avoided overbaking the pie—further insurance against curdling—by removing it from the oven when the center was still jiggly. As the pie cooled, the residual heat of the filling cooked the center through, so each slice of pie was silky and tender rather than marred by sugary curds. We recommend chopping the toasted pecans by hand.

1 Roll dough into 12-inch circle on floured counter. Loosely roll dough around rolling pin and gently unroll it onto 9-inch pie plate, letting excess dough hang over edge. Ease dough into plate by gently lifting edge of dough with your hand while pressing into plate bottom with your other hand. Trim overhang to ½ inch beyond lip of plate. Tuck overhang under itself; folded edge should be flush with edge of plate. Crimp dough evenly around edge of plate. Wrap dough-lined plate loosely in plastic wrap and refrigerate until firm, about 30 minutes. Adjust oven rack to lowest position and heat oven to 425 degrees.

2 Line chilled pie shell with double layer of aluminum foil, covering edges to prevent burning, and fill with pie weights. Bake on foil-lined rimmed baking sheet until pie dough looks dry and is pale in color, about 15 minutes. Remove foil and weights, rotate sheet, and continue to bake until crust is light golden brown, 4 to 7 minutes longer. Transfer sheet to wire rack. (Crust must still be warm when filling is added.)

3 While crust is baking, melt butter in heatproof bowl set over saucepan filled with 1 inch of barely simmering water, making sure that water does not touch bottom of bowl. Off heat, stir in sugar and salt until butter is absorbed.

4 Whisk in eggs, then corn syrup and vanilla, until smooth. Return bowl to saucepan and stir until mixture is shiny, hot to touch, and registers 130 degrees. Off heat, stir in pecans.

5 As soon as pie crust comes out of oven, adjust oven rack to lower-middle position and reduce oven temperature to 275 degrees. With pie still on sheet, pour pecan mixture into warm crust.

6 Bake until filling looks set but yields like gelatin when gently pressed with back of spoon, 50 minutes to 1 hour, rotating sheet halfway through baking. Let pie cool completely on wire rack, about 4 hours. Serve.

### Maple Pecan Pie

*Maple syrup yields a more custardy pie. Toasted walnuts can be substituted for the pecans. Use dark amber maple syrup here.*

Decrease butter to 4 tablespoons and pecans to 1½ cups. Substitute ½ cup granulated sugar for brown sugar and 1 cup maple syrup for corn syrup and vanilla.

# CHOCOLATE CREAM PIE

**Serves 8**

2½  cups half-and-half

⅓  cup (2⅓ ounces) sugar, divided

Pinch table salt

6  large egg yolks

2  tablespoons cornstarch

6  tablespoons unsalted butter, cut into 6 pieces

6  ounces semisweet or bittersweet chocolate, chopped fine

1  ounce unsweetened chocolate, chopped fine

1  teaspoon vanilla extract

1  recipe Chocolate Cookie Crust (page 335), baked and cooled

1  recipe Whipped Cream (page 340)

**WHY THIS RECIPE WORKS** A staple of the diner or deli dessert case, chocolate cream pie holds a lot of promise for chocolate fans, but it often fails to deliver. Gluey (rather than creamy) and overly sweet fillings can belie even the best-looking cream pies. We wanted a silky, voluptuous pie filling with well-balanced chocolate flavor somewhere between that of a milkshake (dairy-rich) and a melted candy bar (intensely chocolaty). We found we got the best filling by combining two different types of chocolate for deep, complex flavor: Bittersweet or semisweet chocolate provided the main chocolate hit, as well as creaminess, and intense unsweetened chocolate lent depth. Just 1 ounce of unsweetened chocolate may not seem like much, but it packs a punch that gives this pie great flavor. A set but ultrasilky custard requires a few simple key steps, and this pie was no exception: carefully tempering the egg mixture with the simmering dairy (to prevent overcooking the eggs), cooking the custard to 180 degrees (the point at which the custard is properly thickened but before it curdles), and, finally, whisking in cold butter so the filling emulsifies. Finally, rather than encasing our custard in a traditional pie dough, we spread it into a chocolate cookie crust to bring home the filling's chocolate flavor. Do not combine the egg yolks and sugar in advance of making the filling.

**1** Bring half-and-half, 3 tablespoons sugar, and salt to simmer in medium saucepan over medium heat, stirring occasionally. Whisk egg yolks, cornstarch, and remaining sugar in bowl until smooth.

**2** Slowly whisk 1 cup of warm half-and-half mixture into yolk mixture to temper, then slowly whisk tempered yolk mixture into remaining half-and-half mixture in saucepan.

**3** Whisking constantly, cook over medium heat until mixture is thickened and registers 180 degrees, 30 to 90 seconds (mixture should have consistency of thick pudding).

**4** Off heat, whisk in butter, semisweet chocolate, and unsweetened chocolate until completely smooth and melted. Stir in vanilla.

**5** Pour warm filling into cooled crust and spread into even layer. Spray piece of parchment paper with vegetable oil spray and press directly against surface of filling. Refrigerate until chilled and set, at least 4 hours or up to 24 hours.

**6** Spread whipped cream attractively over pie. Serve.

# cream, custard,
# AND CURD PIES

# VANILLA CREAM PIE

**Serves 8**

| | |
|---|---|
| 1 | recipe single-crust pie dough (see pages 316–326) |
| ½ | cup plus 2 tablespoons (4⅓ ounces) sugar |
| ¼ | cup (1 ounce) cornstarch |
| ⅛ | teaspoon table salt |
| ½ | cup evaporated milk |
| 5 | large egg yolks |
| 2 | cups whole milk |
| ½ | vanilla bean |
| 2 | tablespoons unsalted butter, cut into 2 pieces |
| 1–2 | teaspoons brandy |
| 1 | recipe Whipped Cream (page 340) |

**WHY THIS RECIPE WORKS** A crisp crust encasing cool, luscious pastry cream filling and a plume of whipped cream that seemingly lightens the richness of the ingredients below it: All of this makes cream pies a diner special. They're perfect after a greasy-spoon lunch, or as a satisfying after-dinner dessert. The most basic (in a good way) cream pie is probably vanilla. Aromatic vanilla gives the dairy-rich pastry cream a warm, fragrant flavor that will please just about anyone. To avoid common problems—such as a filling that's too stiff, soupy, gummy, or flat in flavor—we needed to determine the right cooking method, flavorings, and thickener that would guarantee a substantial yet velvety filling. As with most custards, we relied on egg yolks to help set the mixture while keeping the filling creamy and soft. In addition, a little cornstarch made it just thick and stiff enough to cut cleanly. Whole milk provided the essential dairy component, but it was a surprise ingredient—evaporated milk—that was key to our cream pie's success. With so much of the water removed from evaporated milk, it provided caramel undertones and dairy flavor without adding too much liquid, so the filling wasn't too loose. Brandy amplified the vanilla's warmth, and butter finished the filling with creamy richness. Billows of whipped cream were the perfect finishing touch.

**1** Roll dough into 12-inch circle on floured counter. Loosely roll dough around rolling pin and gently unroll it onto 9-inch pie plate, letting excess dough hang over edge. Ease dough into plate by gently lifting edge of dough with your hand while pressing into plate bottom with your other hand.

**2** Trim overhang to ½ inch beyond lip of plate. Tuck overhang under itself; folded edge should be flush with edge of plate. Crimp dough evenly around edge of plate. Wrap dough-lined plate loosely in plastic wrap and refrigerate until firm, about 30 minutes. Adjust oven rack to middle position and heat oven to 350 degrees.

**3** Line chilled pie shell with double layer of aluminum foil, covering edges to prevent burning, and fill with pie weights. Bake on foil-lined rimmed baking sheet until edges are set and just beginning to turn golden, 25 to 30 minutes, rotating sheet halfway through baking. Remove foil and weights, rotate sheet, and continue to bake crust until golden brown and crisp, 10 to 15 minutes longer. Transfer sheet to wire rack and let cool completely, about 45 minutes.

**4** Whisk sugar, cornstarch, and salt together in medium saucepan. Whisk in evaporated milk, followed by egg yolks, and finally milk, until smooth. Cut vanilla bean in half lengthwise. Using tip of paring knife, scrape out seeds, then combine vanilla bean and seeds with sugar mixture. Bring mixture to simmer and cook, whisking constantly, until mixture is thickened, smooth, and registers 180 degrees, 30 to 90 seconds. Off heat, whisk in butter and brandy. Let mixture cool, stirring often, for 5 minutes. Remove vanilla bean and pour warm filling into cooled crust, smoothing top with clean spatula into even layer. Spray piece of parchment paper with vegetable oil spray and press directly against surface of filling. Refrigerate until set, at least 4 hours or up to 24 hours. Spread whipped cream attractively over pie. Serve.

# COCONUT CREAM PIE

Serves 8

3 cups whole milk, divided

½ cup (3½ ounces) sugar

5 large egg yolks

5 tablespoons (1¼ ounces) cornstarch

¼ teaspoon table salt

¾ cup (2¼ ounces) sweetened shredded coconut, divided

½ teaspoon vanilla extract

1 recipe Coconut Cookie Crust (page 334), baked and cooled

1 recipe Whipped Cream (page 340)

**WHY THIS RECIPE WORKS** With its lofty profile, billowy whipped cream, and golden coconut topping, coconut cream pie is perhaps the queen of rotating glass dessert displays. Often this pie features a classic flaky crust, but in testing we fell in love with our coconut cookie crust for snappy, vanilla-scented, salty contrast—and, of course, extra coconut flavor. Beyond the crust, we wanted to find out how to pack maximum coconut flavor into this retro pie. Coconut milk was too subtle, while coconut extract had an artificial taste reminiscent of sunscreen. Folding sweetened shredded coconut into a milk custard gave us the clear yet restrained coconut flavor we wanted. A generous sprinkling of toasted coconut over the whipped cream topping dressed up our pie with an inviting garnish and provided welcome texture. Coconut is an iconic flavor, but it also plays well with others; since our pie was so good, we made a variation, combining coconut with the warm (and sunny) spices of turmeric, cinnamon, cardamom, and ginger for a play on the trendy, soothing tea drink that is known as golden milk. To toast the small measure of coconut evenly and with ease, we do so in the microwave—no burnt edges. Be sure to let the cookie crust cool completely before you begin making the filling—at least 30 minutes.

1 Whisk ¼ cup milk, sugar, egg yolks, cornstarch, and salt together in bowl. Bring remaining 2¾ cups milk to simmer in large saucepan over medium heat. Slowly whisk 1 cup of hot milk mixture into yolk mixture to temper, then slowly whisk tempered yolk mixture into remaining milk in saucepan. Cook over medium heat, whisking constantly, until mixture is thickened, bubbling, and registers 180 degrees, 30 to 90 seconds (mixture should have consistency of thick pudding). Strain mixture through fine-mesh strainer into clean bowl, then stir in ½ cup coconut and vanilla.

2 Pour filling into cooled crust, smoothing top with clean spatula into even layer. Spray piece of parchment paper with vegetable oil spray and press directly against surface of filling. Refrigerate until set, at least 4 hours or up to 24 hours.

3 Microwave remaining ¼ cup coconut on large plate until golden, about 2 minutes, stirring every 30 seconds; set aside to cool slightly, about 10 minutes. Once coconut is cooled, spread whipped cream attractively over pie and sprinkle with toasted coconut. Serve.

### Golden Milk Coconut Cream Pie
Add 1 teaspoon ground turmeric, ¾ teaspoon ground cinnamon, ½ teaspoon ground cardamom, and ¼ teaspoon ground ginger to milk in saucepan before bringing to simmer in step 1.

# BANANA CREAM PIE

Serves 8

1 recipe single-crust pie dough (see pages 316–326)

5 ripe bananas, divided

4 tablespoons unsalted butter, divided

2½ cups half-and-half

½ cup (3½ ounces) plus 2 tablespoons sugar

6 large egg yolks

¼ teaspoon table salt

3 tablespoons cornstarch

1 teaspoon vanilla extract

2 tablespoons orange juice

1 recipe Whipped Cream (page 340)

**WHY THIS RECIPE WORKS** Banana cream pie is a staple of slapstick comedy. Unfortunately, our first round of testing was no laughing matter. The creamiest versions were unsliceable, while those that produced the tidiest slices were starchy and gloppy—these pies were indeed best only for throwing. Six egg yolks and just 2 tablespoons of cornstarch—our usual thickeners for pastry cream—gave us a clean slice but limited the banana flavor to the layer of slices in the middle of the custard. We didn't want to use banana extract (artificial tasting) or liqueur (impractical), but adding mashed banana to the pastry cream itself resulted in a stodgy, runny, dull-colored cream. We decided to try infusing the custard for this pie with fresh banana. We steeped two sliced and sautéed (for extra flavor) bananas in the half-and-half and then strained them out so their solids didn't muddy our pie. And to slow the discoloration of the requisite layer of fresh banana slices, we tossed them in orange juice. With a creamy banana-boosted pastry cream, yellow sliced bananas, and a light and stable whipped cream, this pie will put a smile on your face. Peel and slice the bananas just before using to minimize browning.

---

**1** Roll dough into 12-inch circle on floured counter. Loosely roll dough around rolling pin and gently unroll it onto 9-inch pie plate, letting excess dough hang over edge. Ease dough into plate by gently lifting edge of dough with your hand while pressing into plate bottom with your other hand.

**2** Trim overhang to ½ inch beyond lip of plate. Tuck overhang under itself; folded edge should be flush with edge of plate. Crimp dough evenly around edge of plate. Wrap dough-lined plate loosely in plastic wrap and refrigerate until firm, about 30 minutes. Adjust oven rack to middle position and heat oven to 350 degrees.

**3** Line chilled pie shell with double layer of aluminum foil, covering edges to prevent burning, and fill with pie weights. Bake on foil-lined rimmed baking sheet until edges are set and just beginning to turn golden, 25 to 30 minutes, rotating sheet halfway through baking. Remove foil and weights, rotate sheet, and continue to bake crust until golden brown and crisp, 10 to 15 minutes longer. Transfer sheet to wire rack and let cool completely, about 45 minutes.

**4** Peel and slice 2 bananas ½ inch thick. Melt 1 tablespoon butter in medium saucepan over medium-high heat. Add sliced bananas and cook until they begin to soften, about 2 minutes. Add half-and-half, bring to boil, and cook for 30 seconds. Remove from heat, cover, and let sit for 40 minutes.

**5** Whisk sugar, egg yolks, and salt in large bowl until smooth. Whisk in cornstarch. Strain cooled half-and-half mixture through fine-mesh strainer into yolk mixture (do not press on bananas) and whisk until incorporated; discard cooked bananas.

**6** Transfer mixture to clean medium saucepan. Cook over medium heat, whisking constantly, until mixture is thickened and registers 180 degrees, 4 to 6 minutes (mixture should have the consistency of thick pudding). Off heat, whisk in vanilla and remaining 3 tablespoons butter. Transfer filling to bowl; spray piece of parchment paper with vegetable oil spray and press directly against surface of filling and let cool for about 1 hour.

**7** Peel and slice remaining 3 bananas ¼ inch thick and toss with orange juice. Whisk filling briefly, then spread half evenly over bottom of cooled crust. Arrange sliced bananas on filling. Spread remaining filling evenly on top.

**8** Refrigerate until set, at least 5 hours or up to 24 hours. Spread whipped cream attractively over pie. Serve.

### Chocolate—Peanut Butter Banana Cream Pie

Increase half-and-half to 2½ cups plus 1½ tablespoons, divided; use 2½ cups in pastry cream as directed. While pastry cream cools in step 6, combine 4 ounces chopped milk chocolate and remaining 1½ tablespoons half-and-half in bowl and microwave until melted, about 40 seconds, stirring halfway through microwaving. After tossing banana slices with juice in step 7, spread melted chocolate mixture evenly in bottom of empty baked pie shell and sprinkle with ⅓ cup chopped salted dry-roasted peanuts. Layer with filling and bananas as directed. Substitute Peanut Butter Whipped Cream (page 340) for Whipped Cream. Refrigerate pie until set as directed. Sprinkle topped pie with 2 tablespoons chopped salted dry-roasted peanuts before serving.

### Making Banana Pastry Cream

**1** Melt 1 tablespoon butter in medium saucepan over medium-high heat. Add sliced bananas and cook until they begin to soften, about 2 minutes.

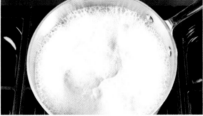

**2** Add half-and-half, bring to boil, and cook for 30 seconds.

**3** Whisk sugar, egg yolks, and salt in large bowl until smooth. Whisk in cornstarch.

**4** Strain cooled half-and-half mixture through fine-mesh strainer into yolk mixture (do not press on bananas) and whisk until incorporated; discard cooked bananas.

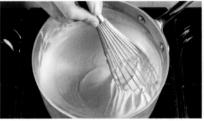

**5** Transfer mixture to clean medium saucepan. Cook over medium heat, whisking constantly, until mixture is thickened and registers 180 degrees, 4 to 6 minutes.

**6** Off heat, whisk in vanilla and remaining 3 tablespoons butter.

BANANA CREAM PIE

# BLACK BOTTOM PIE

**Serves 8**

⅔ cup (4⅔ ounces) sugar

2 cups half-and-half

4 teaspoons cornstarch

4 large egg yolks plus 1 large white

6 ounces semisweet chocolate, chopped fine

1 recipe Chocolate Cookie Crust (page 335), baked and cooled

3 tablespoons golden or light rum

2 tablespoons water, divided

1 teaspoon unflavored gelatin

¼ teaspoon cream of tartar

1 recipe Whipped Cream (page 340)

**WHY THIS RECIPE WORKS** Restaurant critic Duncan Hines (yes, *that* Duncan Hines) had his first slice of black bottom pie at an Oklahoma diner, and his rave review of the decadent trifecta of chocolate custard, rum chiffon, and whipped cream immediately put this luscious pie on the map. Most black bottom pie recipes take hours to make and include many parts—could we serve up this dreamy dessert without the fuss? A chocolate cookie crust was an easy, logical, and perfectly chocolaty base for the pie. The layers are where things start to get messy. Instead of making two separate mixtures for the custard, we made one large batch and whisked chopped semisweet chocolate into half of it for the chocolate layer. The second layer, the chiffon, required stability, and an added mixture of gelatin, rum, and water got us on track. For even more structure, we made a meringue-like frosting of sugar, egg white, water, and cream of tartar and folded it into the rum chiffon. Once set, that layer emerged from the refrigerator with a perfectly wobbly texture. It was easy to see why Duncan Hines was impressed with this pie of lush chocolate and rum layers topped with a cloud of sweetened whipped cream. To prevent the filling from overflowing the crust, add the final ½ cup of the rum layer after the filling has set for 20 minutes.

**1** Whisk ⅓ cup sugar, half-and-half, cornstarch, and egg yolks together in large saucepan. Cook over medium heat, stirring constantly, until mixture comes to boil, about 8 minutes.

**2** Divide hot custard evenly between 2 bowls. Whisk chocolate into custard in 1 bowl until smooth, then pour into cooled crust, smoothing top with clean spatula into even layer; refrigerate. Whisk rum and 1 tablespoon water together in third bowl. Sprinkle gelatin over rum mixture and let sit until gelatin softens, about 5 minutes. Stir gelatin mixture into bowl with plain custard and refrigerate, stirring occasionally, until mixture is wobbly but not set, about 20 minutes.

**3** Combine egg white, cream of tartar, ⅓ cup sugar, and remaining 1 tablespoon water in large heatproof bowl set over saucepan filled with ½ inch barely simmering water, making sure that water does not touch bottom of bowl. Using handheld mixer set at medium-high speed, beat egg white mixture until soft peaks form, about 2 minutes; remove bowl from heat and beat egg white mixture until very thick and glossy and cooled completely, about 3 minutes.

**4** Whisk cooled egg white mixture into chilled rum custard until smooth. Pour all but ½ cup rum chiffon into chocolate custard–filled pie crust, smoothing top with clean spatula into even layer. Refrigerate for 20 minutes, then top with remaining rum chiffon, smoothing top with clean spatula into even layer. Refrigerate until set, at least 4 hours or up to 24 hours. Spread whipped cream attractively over pie. Serve.

## Making Black Bottom Pie

**1** Whisk ⅓ cup sugar, half-and-half, cornstarch, and egg yolks together in saucepan. Cook over medium heat, stirring constantly, until mixture comes to boil, about 8 minutes.

**2** Divide hot custard evenly between 2 bowls.

**3** Whisk chocolate into custard in 1 bowl until smooth.

**4** Pour chocolate custard into cooled pie crust, smoothing top with clean spatula into even layer; refrigerate.

**5** Whisk rum and 1 tablespoon water together in third bowl. Sprinkle gelatin over rum mixture and let sit until gelatin softens, about 5 minutes.

**6** Stir gelatin mixture into bowl with plain custard and refrigerate, stirring occasionally, until mixture is wobbly but not set.

**7** With handheld mixer set at medium-high speed, beat egg white mixture in large bowl set over saucepan filled with ½ inch barely simmering water until soft peaks form, about 2 minutes.

**8** Remove bowl from heat and beat egg white mixture until very thick and glossy and cooled completely, about 3 minutes.

**9** Whisk cooled egg white mixture into chilled rum custard until smooth.

**10** Pour all but ½ cup rum chiffon into chocolate custard–filled pie crust, smoothing top with clean spatula into even layer; refrigerate for 20 minutes.

**11** Top with remaining rum chiffon, smoothing top with clean spatula into even layer; refrigerate until completely set, at least 4 hours or up to 24 hours.

**12** Spread whipped cream attractively over pie.

# MOCHA CREAM PIE

Serves 8

1 recipe single-crust pie dough (see pages 316–326)

2¾ cups whole milk

6 ounces milk chocolate, chopped

⅓ cup packed (2⅓ ounces) light brown sugar

¼ cup heavy cream

¼ cup instant espresso powder

3 tablespoons Dutch-processed cocoa powder

3 tablespoons cornstarch

¼ teaspoon table salt

½ teaspoon vanilla extract

1 recipe Whipped Cream (page 340)

1 recipe Candied Coffee Beans (page 345)

**WHY THIS RECIPE WORKS** For an adult-flavored spin on chocolate cream pie, we wanted to incorporate a jolt of java. To give the chocolate pudding filling an appropriate boost of coffee flavor, we added ¼ cup of espresso powder. But while the coffee flavor came through, this pie was bitter—we wanted grown-up, not harsh. Interestingly, switching from sophisticated dark chocolate to milder milk chocolate was the answer. The milk variety provided chocolate flavor and sweetness without underscoring the strong flavor of the coffee. With our rich filling settled, we tested crusts. An Oreo cookie crust, which we liked for our traditional Chocolate Cream Pie (page 42), actually overwhelmed the filling for this pie and dimmed the star of the show—the espresso. The buttery-rich but more neutral flavor of traditional pie dough was a better choice. In a nod to mocha coffee house drinks, we topped our pie with whipped cream. And for contrasting texture, visual appeal, and more coffee flavor, we sprinkled candied coffee beans on top.

1 Roll dough into 12-inch circle on floured counter. Loosely roll dough around rolling pin and gently unroll it onto 9-inch pie plate, letting excess dough hang over edge. Ease dough into plate by gently lifting edge of dough with your hand while pressing into plate bottom with your other hand.

2 Trim overhang to ½ inch beyond lip of plate. Tuck overhang under itself; folded edge should be flush with edge of plate. Crimp dough evenly around edge of plate. Wrap dough-lined plate loosely in plastic wrap and refrigerate until firm, about 30 minutes. Adjust oven rack to middle position and heat oven to 350 degrees.

3 Line chilled pie shell with double layer of aluminum foil, covering edges to prevent burning, and fill with pie weights. Bake on foil-lined rimmed baking sheet until edges are set and just beginning to turn golden, 25 to 30 minutes, rotating sheet halfway through baking. Remove foil and weights, rotate sheet, and continue to bake crust until golden brown and crisp, 10 to 15 minutes longer. Transfer sheet to wire rack and let cool completely, about 45 minutes.

4 Combine milk, chocolate, sugar, cream, espresso powder, cocoa, cornstarch, and salt in large saucepan. Bring to simmer over medium heat, whisking occasionally, then reduce heat to medium-low and cook, whisking constantly, until mixture is thickened, bubbling, and registers 180 degrees, 2 to 3 minutes (mixture should have consistency of thick pudding). Strain mixture through fine-mesh strainer into clean bowl, then stir in vanilla.

5 Pour filling into cooled crust, smoothing top with clean spatula into even layer. Spray piece of parchment paper with vegetable oil spray and press directly against surface of filling. Refrigerate until set, at least 4 hours or up to 24 hours. Spread whipped cream attractively over pie and sprinkle with candied coffee beans. Serve.

# KEY LIME PIE

Serves 8

4 large egg yolks

4 teaspoons grated lime zest plus
½ cup juice (5 limes)

1 (14-ounce) can sweetened
condensed milk

1 recipe Graham Cracker Crust
(page 334), baked and still warm

1 recipe Whipped Cream
(page 340)

**WHY THIS RECIPE WORKS** Key lime pie should remind us of the warm breezes of the Florida Keys. Unfortunately, when we're not on vacation it often disappoints us with its harsh, artificial flavor. We wanted a recipe for classic Key lime pie with fresh flavor and a silky filling. Traditional Key lime pie is usually not baked; instead, the combination of egg yolks, lime juice, and sweetened condensed milk firms up when chilled because the juice's acidity causes the proteins in the eggs and milk to bind. We found that just one simple swap—from the typical bottled, reconstituted lime juice to fresh lime juice and zest—gave us a pie that was pungent and refreshing, cool yet creamy, and very satisfying. We also discovered that while the pie filling will set without baking (most recipes call only for mixing and then chilling), it set much more nicely after being baked for just 15 minutes. These two seemingly minor adjustments to the classic recipe made all the difference. Despite this pie's name, we found that most tasters could not tell the difference between pies made with regular supermarket limes (called Persian limes) and true Key limes. Since Persian limes are easier to find and to juice we recommend using them instead.

1 Adjust oven rack to middle position and heat oven to 325 degrees. Whisk egg yolks, condensed milk, and lime zest and juice together in bowl. Cover mixture and let sit at room temperature until thickened, about 30 minutes.

2 Pour thickened filling into warm crust. Bake pie until center is firm but jiggles slightly when shaken, 15 to 20 minutes. Let pie cool slightly on wire rack, about 1 hour. Cover pie loosely with plastic wrap and refrigerate until filling is chilled and set, at least 3 hours or up to 24 hours. Spread whipped cream attractively over pie. Serve.

# BANOFFEE PIE

### SERVES 8

1 recipe single-crust pie dough
(see pages 316–326)

7 ounces soft caramels

¼ cup water

3 ripe but firm bananas, peeled
and sliced ½ inch thick

1½ cups heavy cream, chilled

2 tablespoons sugar

2 teaspoons instant espresso
powder or instant coffee powder

**WHY THIS RECIPE WORKS** The recipe name banoffee pie may sound strange at first, but it is actually just what you might think: banana and toffee pie! Add some drifts of espresso-flavored whipped cream over the bananas and caramel, and this British pie is universally appealing. Traditionally, the filling is prepared by boiling a can of condensed milk—yes, in the can—for hours until it caramelizes and thickens. For this multicomponent pie, we wanted something less time-consuming (and less dangerous). We turned to wrapped caramels, which we heated with some water to make a seductively smooth—not sticky—filling that contrasted beautifully with the crisp pastry. The rest was even easier: slicing some bananas and whipping some cream with a dash of espresso powder. Knowing that a superclean slice would highlight the three layers of our pie, we put it in the freezer for a couple of hours—just until chilled—so no layer got squashed. We like to use either Kraft Caramels or Brach's Milk Maid Caramels for this recipe, but any brand of soft caramels will do. (We found we needed about 26 caramels to equal 7 ounces.) For a more child-friendly version of this classic pie, omit the espresso powder and substitute with 1 teaspoon vanilla extract.

1 Roll dough into 12-inch circle on floured counter. Loosely roll dough around rolling pin and gently unroll it onto 9-inch pie plate, letting excess dough hang over edge. Ease dough into plate by gently lifting edge of dough with your hand while pressing into plate bottom with your other hand.

2 Trim overhang to ½ inch beyond lip of plate. Tuck overhang under itself; folded edge should be flush with edge of plate. Crimp dough evenly around edge of plate. Wrap dough-lined plate loosely in plastic wrap and refrigerate until firm, about 30 minutes. Adjust oven rack to middle position and heat oven to 350 degrees.

3 Line chilled pie shell with double layer of aluminum foil, covering edges to prevent burning, and fill with pie weights. Bake on foil-lined rimmed baking sheet until edges are set and just beginning to turn golden, 25 to 30 minutes, rotating sheet halfway through baking. Remove foil and weights, rotate sheet, and continue to bake crust until golden brown and crisp, 10 to 15 minutes longer. Transfer sheet to wire rack and let cool completely, about 45 minutes.

4 Cook caramels and water in small saucepan over medium-high heat, stirring occasionally, until melted and smooth, 8 to 10 minutes. Spread caramel evenly over bottom of cooled crust. Shingle banana slices in concentric rings on top of caramel. Cover pie with plastic and refrigerate until caramel is cold, at least 1 hour or up to 6 hours.

5 Two hours before serving, using stand mixer fitted with whisk attachment, whip cream, sugar, and espresso powder on medium speed until frothy, about 1 minute. Increase speed to high and whip until soft peaks form, 1 to 3 minutes. Spread whipped cream attractively over chilled pie, then freeze pie until whipped cream is very stiff but pie is not fully frozen, about 2 hours. (Do not let pie freeze completely.) Serve.

# LEMON CHESS PIE

Serves 8

1 recipe single-crust pie dough
(see pages 316–326)

5 large eggs

1¾ cups (12¼ ounces) plus
1 teaspoon sugar, divided

2 tablespoons cornmeal

1 tablespoon grated lemon zest
plus 3 tablespoons juice

¼ teaspoon table salt

8 tablespoons unsalted butter,
melted and cooled

**WHY THIS RECIPE WORKS** Some historians believe English settlers brought chess pie to the new world as early as the 17th century. Most likely originating from an archaic English spelling of cheese ("chese"), this word was used to signify the types of curds and custards commonly used in pies. Chess pie came to popularity in the South in the 1800s. It's made from everyday ingredients, namely lots of eggs (one recipe we found included 16), lots of sugar (that same recipe called for a pound), lots of butter, sometimes milk or cream, and, to thicken, flour, cornmeal, or a combination. Chess pies can be incredibly rich and sweet, so a popular variation, lemon chess pie, is the perfect recipe, the tart lemon balancing out everything else. To get the filling of this intense pie right, we combined 1¾ cups sugar (considerably less than the norm), 8 tablespoons of butter (for richness without greasiness), five eggs (for a set pie), and 1 tablespoon each of flour and cornmeal (to thicken). After testing various amounts of lemon juice and zest, we landed on 3 tablespoons of juice and 1 tablespoon of zest for a delicately tart flavor. After more testing, we found that pies made with cornmeal alone had a deeper flavor and got a particular crackly exterior that we loved; the flour had a raw flavor that we didn't. Out with the flour. To mix the custard, we thought modern technology might make things go faster. Sure, but it didn't make it better: The food processor aerated the mixture, making the baked filling foamy, so we stuck with an old-fashioned bowl and a whisk. Regular yellow cornmeal (not stone ground) works best here. Make the filling before baking the shell so the cornmeal has time to soften.

**1** Roll dough into 12-inch circle on floured counter. Loosely roll dough around rolling pin and gently unroll it onto 9-inch pie plate, letting excess dough hang over edge. Ease dough into plate by gently lifting edge of dough with your hand while pressing into plate bottom with your other hand.

**2** Trim overhang to ½ inch beyond lip of plate. Tuck overhang under itself; folded edge should be flush with edge of plate. Crimp dough evenly around edge of plate. Wrap dough-lined plate loosely in plastic wrap and refrigerate until firm, about 30 minutes. Adjust oven rack to middle position and heat oven to 350 degrees.

**3** Whisk eggs in large bowl until smooth. Slowly whisk in 1¾ cups sugar, cornmeal, lemon zest and juice, and salt until combined. Whisk in melted butter.

**4** Line chilled pie shell with double layer of aluminum foil, covering edges to prevent burning, and fill with pie weights. Bake on foil-lined rimmed baking sheet until edges are set and just beginning to turn golden, 25 to 30 minutes, rotating sheet halfway through baking. Remove foil and weights. (Crust must still be warm when filling is added.) Whisk filling to recombine. With pie still on sheet, transfer filling to hot crust and bake until filling's surface is light brown and center jiggles slightly when shaken, 35 to 40 minutes. Sprinkle with remaining 1 teaspoon sugar. Let pie cool completely on wire rack, about 4 hours. Serve.

# BUTTERSCOTCH CREAM PIE

Serves 8

1 recipe Whole-Wheat Single-Crust Pie Dough (page 318)

6 large egg yolks

2 tablespoons cornstarch

8 tablespoons unsalted butter, cut into ½-inch pieces

⅓ cup (2⅓ ounces) granulated sugar

⅓ cup packed (2⅓ ounces) dark brown sugar

2 tablespoons water

2 tablespoons light corn syrup

1 teaspoon lemon juice

¼ teaspoon table salt

1 cup heavy cream, divided

1½ cups whole milk

1 teaspoon vanilla extract

½ teaspoon dark rum (optional)

1 recipe Whipped Cream (page 340)

Flake sea salt

**WHY THIS RECIPE WORKS** Butterscotch cream pie often *looks* like butterscotch—a caramel color lightened by the creamy custard it tints—but it rarely tastes like the deep, buttery, brown sugar confection. Instead, it tastes artificial or too sweet, or simply falls flat. We wanted to fill a pastry crust (we particularly liked the nutty contrast of whole wheat) with the very best butterscotch pastry cream. We already knew how to make custards and puddings; it was the butterscotch itself that needed the work. For butterscotch custard with rich, bittersweet flavor, we made butterscotch sauce by cooking butter, brown and white sugars, corn syrup, lemon juice, and salt together into a deep, dark caramel—the darker the caramel (without burning), the more its flavor carried through the dairy. We made the process foolproof by first boiling the caramel to jump-start it and then reducing the heat to a low simmer; this approach provided a large window to take the temperature of our caramel and stop cooking it at the right moment. This pie was cool and creamy, but deep and rich-tasting with adult appeal—especially after a sprinkling of crunchy sea salt to enhance the pie's flavor. When taking the temperature of the caramel in step 4, tilt the saucepan and move the thermometer back and forth to equalize hot and cool spots. We like the flavor of whole-wheat pie dough in this recipe, but you can use any single-crust pie dough (see pages 316–326). You can omit the flake sea salt or substitute kosher salt if you prefer.

---

**1** Roll dough into 12-inch circle on floured counter. Loosely roll dough around rolling pin and gently unroll it onto 9-inch pie plate, letting excess dough hang over edge. Ease dough into plate by gently lifting edge of dough with your hand while pressing into plate bottom with your other hand.

**2** Trim overhang to ½ inch beyond lip of plate. Tuck overhang under itself; folded edge should be flush with edge of plate. Crimp dough evenly around edge of plate. Wrap dough-lined plate loosely in plastic wrap and refrigerate until firm, about 30 minutes. Adjust oven rack to middle position and heat oven to 350 degrees.

**3** Line chilled pie shell with double layer of aluminum foil, covering edges to prevent burning, and fill with pie weights. Bake on foil-lined rimmed baking sheet until edges are set and just beginning to turn golden, 25 to 30 minutes, rotating sheet halfway through baking. Remove foil and weights, rotate sheet, and continue to bake crust until golden brown and crisp, 10 to 15 minutes longer. Transfer sheet to wire rack and let cool completely, about 45 minutes.

**4** Whisk egg yolks and cornstarch together in bowl until smooth; set aside. Bring butter, granulated sugar, brown sugar, water, corn syrup, lemon juice, and salt to boil in large saucepan over medium-high heat. Cook, without stirring, until mixture is straw-colored, 4 to 6 minutes. Reduce heat to low and continue to cook, swirling saucepan occasionally, until caramel is color of dark peanut butter and registers 300 degrees, 12 to 16 minutes.

**5** Off heat, carefully stir in ¼ cup cream; mixture will bubble and steam. Whisk vigorously, being sure to scrape corners of saucepan, until mixture is completely smooth. Gradually whisk in remaining ¾ cup cream and milk, then bring to simmer over medium heat.

**6** Slowly whisk 1 cup hot caramel mixture into yolk mixture to temper, then slowly whisk tempered yolk mixture into remaining caramel mixture in saucepan. Cook, whisking constantly, until mixture is thickened, bubbling, and registers 180 degrees, 4 to 6 minutes (mixture should have consistency of thick pudding). Strain mixture through fine-mesh strainer into clean bowl, then stir in vanilla and rum, if using.

**7** Pour custard into cooled crust, smoothing top with clean spatula into even layer. Spray piece of parchment paper with vegetable oil spray and press directly against surface of filling. Refrigerate until set, at least 4 hours or up to 24 hours. Spread whipped cream attractively over pie and sprinkle with sea salt to taste. Serve.

# LEMON MERINGUE PIE

**Serves 8**

1 recipe single-crust pie dough
(see pages 316–326)

*filling*
1½ cups water

1 cup (7 ounces) sugar

¼ cup (1 ounce) cornstarch

⅛ teaspoon table salt

6 large egg yolks

1 tablespoon grated lemon zest
plus ½ cup juice (3 lemons)

2 tablespoons unsalted butter,
cut into 2 pieces

*meringue*
⅓ cup water

1 tablespoon cornstarch

4 large egg whites

½ teaspoon vanilla extract

¼ teaspoon cream of tartar

½ cup (3½ ounces) sugar

**WHY THIS RECIPE WORKS** When done just right, lemon meringue pie is a delight to eat. There's just one problem: The meringue is notoriously troublesome. It can shrink, bead, puddle, deflate, burn, sweat, break down, or turn rubbery. We wanted a pie with a rich, lemony filling that was soft but not runny and firm but not gelatinous—and we wanted it topped with a perfect, airy meringue, one that wouldn't break down and puddle on the bottom or "tear" on the top. We learned that the puddling underneath the meringue was from undercooking, while the beading on top was from overcooking. We discovered that if the filling—a standard, appropriately bracing lemon curd—is nice and hot when the meringue is applied, the underside of the meringue will cook properly. And if the oven temperature is relatively low, the top of the meringue won't overcook. Baking the pie in a relatively cool oven also produced the best-looking, most evenly baked meringue. To further stabilize the meringue and prevent weeping, we beat in a small amount of cornstarch. Make the pie crust, let it cool, and then begin work on the filling. As soon as the filling is made, cover it with greased parchment to keep it hot and then start working on the meringue topping. You want to add hot filling to the cooled pie crust and then apply the meringue topping and quickly get the pie into the oven.

1 Roll dough into 12-inch circle on floured counter. Loosely roll dough around rolling pin and gently unroll it onto 9-inch pie plate, letting excess dough hang over edge. Ease dough into plate by gently lifting edge of dough with your hand while pressing into plate bottom with your other hand.

2 Trim overhang to ½ inch beyond lip of plate. Tuck overhang under itself; folded edge should be flush with edge of plate. Crimp dough evenly around edge of plate. Wrap dough-lined plate loosely in plastic wrap and refrigerate until firm, about 30 minutes. Adjust oven rack to middle position and heat oven to 350 degrees.

3 Line chilled pie shell with double layer of aluminum foil, covering edges to prevent burning, and fill with pie weights. Bake on foil-lined rimmed baking sheet until edges are set and just beginning to turn golden, 25 to 30 minutes, rotating sheet halfway through baking. Remove foil and weights, rotate sheet, and continue to bake crust until golden brown and crisp, 10 to 15 minutes longer. Transfer sheet to wire rack and let cool completely, about 45 minutes. Reduce oven temperature to 325 degrees.

4 *for the filling* Bring water, sugar, cornstarch, and salt to simmer in large saucepan, whisking constantly. When mixture starts to turn translucent, whisk in egg yolks, two at a time. Whisk in lemon zest and juice and butter. Return mixture to brief simmer, then remove from heat. Spray piece of parchment paper with vegetable oil spray and press directly against surface of filling to keep warm and prevent skin from forming.

**5** *for the meringue* Bring water and cornstarch to simmer in small saucepan and cook, whisking occasionally, until thickened and translucent, 1 to 2 minutes. Remove from heat and let cool slightly.

**6** Using stand mixer fitted with whisk attachment, whip egg whites, vanilla, and cream of tartar on medium-low speed until foamy, about 1 minute. Increase speed to medium-high and beat in sugar, 1 tablespoon at a time, until incorporated and mixture forms soft, billowy mounds. Add cornstarch mixture, 1 tablespoon at a time, and continue to beat to glossy, stiff peaks, 2 to 3 minutes.

**7** Meanwhile, remove parchment from filling and return to very low heat during last minute or so of beating meringue (to ensure filling is hot).

**8** With pie still on sheet, pour warm filling into cooled crust. Using rubber spatula, immediately dollop meringue evenly around edge of crust, spreading meringue so it touches crust (this will prevent the meringue from shrinking), then fill in center with remaining meringue. Using back of spoon, create attractive swirls and peaks in meringue. Bake until meringue is light golden brown, about 20 minutes. Let pie cool on wire rack until filling has set, about 2 hours. Serve.

## Topping Lemon Meringue Pie

**1** Using rubber spatula, immediately dollop meringue evenly around edge of crust, attaching meringue to pie crust to prevent shrinking. Then fill in center of pie.

**2** Using back of spoon, create attractive swirls and peaks in meringue.

CHOCOLATE ANGEL PIE

# CHOCOLATE ANGEL PIE

**Serves 8**

## *filling*

- 9   ounces milk chocolate, chopped fine
- 5   ounces bittersweet chocolate, chopped fine
- 3   large egg yolks
- 1½   tablespoons sugar
- ½   teaspoon table salt
- ½   cup half-and-half
- 1¼   cups heavy cream, chilled

## *meringue crust*

- 1   tablespoon cornstarch, plus extra for pie plate
- ½   cup (3½ ounces) sugar
- 3   large egg whites
-    Pinch cream of tartar
- ½   teaspoon vanilla extract

- 1   recipe Whipped Cream (page 340)
-    Unsweetened cocoa powder

**WHY THIS RECIPE WORKS** An assortment of recipes going by the name angel pie first appeared in print in the 1920s, but it was only after World War II that the name was used for a meringue pie shell filled with creamy mousse and topped with whipped cream. And it was an instant hit. Rationing was at an end, so eggs and sugar were in plentiful supply, and a lavish dessert was in order—and we'd argue it still is. Ideally, chocolate angel pie should have a light, crisp meringue crust; a filling so chocolaty and satiny that it would put a truffle to shame; and plenty of whipped cream. But the mousse filling in older published versions of the recipe wasn't deeply chocolaty enough for our modern sensibilities, so we made a cooked custard for our filling instead. This allowed us to pack a whopping 14 ounces of chocolate into our filling, and as a bonus it ensured we didn't waste the yolks left over from the meringue crust. True meringue takes time, and we found that 2½ hours in the oven was necessary for the lightest, crispest crust. To prevent the crust from sticking to the pan, we relied on a double dose of cornstarch—in the egg whites and as a coating for the pie plate. Topped with whipped cream, this angelic pie certainly felt lavish—rich yet light as a cloud. Serve the pie within 3 hours of chilling.

---

**1** *for the filling* Microwave milk chocolate and bittersweet chocolate in large bowl at 50 percent power, stirring occasionally, until melted, 2 to 4 minutes.

**2** Whisk egg yolks, sugar, and salt together in bowl. Bring half-and-half to simmer in small saucepan over medium heat. Slowly whisk simmering half-and-half into egg yolk mixture in 2 additions to temper. Return half-and-half mixture to now-empty saucepan, reduce heat to low, and cook, whisking constantly, until mixture is thickened and registers 180 degrees, 30 seconds to 1 minute (mixture should have consistency of thick pudding). Stir half-and-half mixture into melted chocolate until combined. Let cool slightly, about 8 minutes.

**3** Using stand mixer fitted with whisk attachment, whip cream on medium-low speed until foamy, about 1 minute. Increase speed to high and whip until soft peaks form, 1 to 3 minutes.

**4** Using rubber spatula, gently fold one-third of whipped cream into cooled chocolate mixture. Gently fold in remaining whipped cream until no white streaks remain. Cover bowl tightly with plastic wrap and refrigerate for at least 3 hours or up to 24 hours.

**5** *for the meringue crust* Adjust oven rack to lower-middle position and heat oven to 275 degrees. Grease 9-inch pie plate and dust well with extra cornstarch, using pastry brush to distribute evenly. Combine sugar and 1 tablespoon cornstarch in bowl.

**6** Using stand mixer fitted with whisk attachment, whip egg whites and cream of tartar on medium-low speed until foamy, about 1 minute. Increase speed to medium-high and whip whites to soft, billowy mounds, about 1 minute. Gradually add sugar mixture and whip until glossy, stiff peaks form, 2 to 3 minutes. Add vanilla to meringue and whip until incorporated.

**7** Spread meringue in bottom of prepared plate, following contours of plate to completely cover bottom, sides, and edges. Bake for 1½ hours. Rotate plate, reduce oven temperature to 200 degrees, and bake until completely dried out, about 1 hour longer. (Meringue crust will rise above rim of plate; some cracking is OK.) Transfer plate to wire rack and let cool completely, about 30 minutes.

**8** Spoon cooled chocolate filling into cavity of cooled crust, using offset spatula to spread it evenly. Refrigerate until filling is set, at least 1 hour or up to 3 hours. Spread whipped cream attractively over pie. Dust with cocoa and serve.

## Making the Meringue Crust

**1** Grease 9-inch pie plate and dust well with cornstarch, using pastry brush to distribute evenly.

**2** Combine sugar and 1 tablespoon cornstarch in bowl.

**3** Whip egg whites and cream of tartar on medium-low speed until foamy, about 1 minute. Increase speed to medium-high and whip whites to soft, billowy mounds, about 1 minute.

**4** Gradually add sugar mixture and whip until glossy, stiff peaks form, 2 to 3 minutes. Add vanilla to meringue and whip until incorporated.

**5** Spread meringue in bottom of prepared plate, following contours of plate to completely cover bottom, sides, and edges.

**6** Bake for 1½ hours. Rotate plate, reduce oven temperature to 200 degrees, and bake until completely dried out, about 1 hour longer. Let cool completely.

# RHUBARB CUSTARD PIE

Serves 8

1 recipe double-crust pie dough (see pages 320–327)

1 cup (7 ounces) sugar

2 large eggs

2 tablespoons all-purpose flour

½ teaspoon table salt

1 pound rhubarb, trimmed, halved lengthwise, and chopped

**WHY THIS RECIPE WORKS** In a pie (or pretty much anywhere else), rhubarb is almost always associated with strawberry. But the pink-hued vegetable (yes, vegetable) is delicious in its own right and we thought it deserved star status. Sure, rhubarb is tangy and can be bitter, but that's what the sugar is for. And in this pie, we combine the rhubarb with a creamy, sweet custard; the custard's richness offers a welcome counterpoint to the sharp rhubarb. After assembling a simple custard (with a bit of flour to ensure stability), we stirred in pieces of chopped rhubarb and then poured our filling into a buttery double crust (which provided another foil for the bracing rhubarb). And magically, as the pie baked, the rhubarb separated itself from the custard and rose to the top so each slice presented a candy stripe. Sweet-tart, creamy, and rich, this pie will make you forget about the fruit. The slits in the top crust permit moisture evaporation, although you can use a lattice top if you'd prefer here.

---

**1** Roll 1 disk of dough into 12-inch circle on floured counter. Loosely roll dough around rolling pin and gently unroll it onto 9-inch pie plate, letting excess dough hang over edge. Ease dough into plate by gently lifting edge of dough with your hand while pressing into plate bottom with your other hand. Leave any dough that overhangs plate in place. Wrap dough-lined plate loosely in plastic wrap and refrigerate until firm, about 30 minutes. Roll other disk of dough into 12-inch circle on floured counter, then transfer to parchment paper–lined rimmed baking sheet; cover with plastic and refrigerate until firm, about 30 minutes.

**2** Adjust oven rack to lowest position and heat oven to 375 degrees. Whisk sugar, eggs, flour, and salt together in large bowl. Stir in rhubarb. Transfer filling to dough-lined pie plate.

**3** Loosely roll remaining dough round around rolling pin and gently unroll it onto filling. Trim overhang to ½ inch beyond lip of plate. Pinch edges of top and bottom dough firmly together. Tuck overhang under itself; folded edge should be flush with edge of plate. Crimp dough evenly around edge of plate. Cut four 1-inch slits near center of pie.

**4** Place pie on aluminum foil–lined rimmed baking sheet and bake until juices are bubbling and crust is golden brown, about 50 minutes, rotating sheet halfway through baking. Let pie cool on wire rack until filling has set, about 4 hours. Serve.

# RICOTTA LEMON-THYME PIE

Serves 8

1¼ pounds (2½ cups) whole-milk ricotta cheese

1 recipe Herb Single-Crust Pie Dough (page 318)

¾ cup heavy cream

1 cup (7 ounces) plus 1 tablespoon sugar, divided

2 large eggs plus 1 large yolk

2 teaspoons grated lemon zest plus 4 (2-inch) strips zest, sliced thin lengthwise

1 teaspoon vanilla extract

⅛ teaspoon table salt

12 sprigs fresh thyme

⅓ cup water

**WHY THIS RECIPE WORKS** Traditional ricotta pie consists of sweetened, rich, mildly cheesy ricotta for a filling that's reminiscent of a fine Italian cannoli. The Italian version of this pie is typically baked like a cheesecake, but we envisioned ours as the single-crust custard pie we are familiar with stateside. We started by pressing out all the excess water from the cheese to keep our pie crust from getting soggy. Next we amplified the richness of the cheese and smoothed out the custard by adding heavy cream. Two eggs plus a yolk gave the filling structure, and flavor additions of lemon zest and vanilla brightened the filling and added depth. To take this already flavorful pie to the next level, we incorporated thyme into the pie dough, which added an aromatic, slightly woodsy background note. For an attractive sugar-frosted topping, we candied some lemon peel and thyme sprig tips. We like the flavor of our herb pie dough in this recipe (be sure to use thyme for the herb), but you can use any single-crust pie dough (see pages 316–326). Our favorite ricotta is Belgioioso Ricotta con Latte Whole Milk Ricotta Cheese.

1 Line rimmed baking sheet with triple layer of paper towels. Spread ricotta on paper towels into even layer then cover with second triple layer of paper towels. Place second rimmed baking sheet on top and weight with several heavy cans. Let ricotta sit for at least 30 minutes or up to 2 hours. Discard top layer of paper towels, then transfer ricotta to food processor bowl.

2 Roll dough into 12-inch circle on floured counter. Loosely roll dough around rolling pin and gently unroll it onto 9-inch pie plate, letting excess dough hang over edge. Ease dough into plate by gently lifting edge of dough with your hand while pressing into plate bottom with your other hand.

3 Trim overhang to ½ inch beyond lip of plate. Tuck overhang under itself; folded edge should be flush with edge of plate. Crimp dough evenly around edge of plate. Wrap dough-lined plate loosely in plastic wrap and refrigerate until firm, about 30 minutes. Adjust oven rack to middle position and heat oven to 350 degrees.

4 Line chilled pie shell with double layer of aluminum foil, covering edges to prevent burning, and fill with pie weights. Bake on foil-lined rimmed baking sheet until edges are set and just beginning to turn golden, 25 to 30 minutes, rotating sheet halfway through baking. Remove foil and weights, rotate sheet, and continue to bake crust until golden brown and crisp, 10 to 15 minutes longer. Transfer sheet to wire rack. (Crust must still be warm when filling is added.) Increase oven temperature to 400 degrees.

**5** While crust bakes, process cream, ⅔ cup sugar, eggs and yolk, grated lemon zest, vanilla, and salt with ricotta in food processor until well combined and smooth, about 30 seconds. With pie still on sheet, pour mixture into warm crust, smoothing top with clean spatula into even layer. Bake until center of pie registers 160 degrees, 30 to 40 minutes. Let pie cool completely on wire rack, about 4 hours.

**6** Snip off and keep tender, pliable tips of thyme sprigs. (Save woody sprig parts for another use.) Cook ⅓ cup sugar and water in small saucepan over medium heat, stirring occasionally, until sugar is dissolved, about 1 minute. Add thinly sliced lemon zest and thyme sprig tips and bring to simmer. Cook until zest begins to soften, 3 to 7 minutes. Remove from heat and let cool completely, about 1 hour. Strain mixture through fine-mesh strainer, reserving simple syrup for another use. Transfer candied zest and thyme to wire rack set in rimmed baking sheet, separating clumps as needed. Let drain for 1 minute, then sprinkle with remaining 1 tablespoon sugar. Scatter candied zest and thyme decoratively over top of pie. Serve.

# HOLIDAY EGGNOG CUSTARD PIE

Serves 8

1 recipe single-crust pie dough (see pages 316–326)

⅔ cup (4⅔ ounces) sugar

3 large eggs

3 tablespoons cornstarch

¼ teaspoon ground cinnamon, divided

⅛ teaspoon ground nutmeg

⅛ teaspoon table salt

2 cups whole milk

1 cup heavy cream

2 tablespoons dark rum

1 recipe Brown Sugar and Bourbon Whipped Cream (page 340)

**WHY THIS RECIPE WORKS** For a delicious eggnog, three elements need to be in perfect balance: sweetness, richness, and the amount of alcohol. We wanted to strike that balance in a custard pie for a new take on this classic holiday drink. Adding cinnamon and nutmeg to our custard base gave it a subtle hint of spice, but in our opinion it wasn't truly eggnog without a little booze—just 2 tablespoons of dark rum added plenty of depth to our pie without overpowering it. To preserve the rum's flavor, we stirred it into the filling after heating and straining the custard. To top off our eggnog pie, we whipped up our Brown Sugar and Bourbon Whipped Cream. If you prefer your pie with a boozier punch, increase the rum to ¼ cup; if you prefer a nonalcoholic eggnog, you can omit the rum altogether and use regular Whipped Cream (page 340).

1 Roll dough into 12-inch circle on floured counter. Loosely roll dough around rolling pin and gently unroll it onto 9-inch pie plate, letting excess dough hang over edge. Ease dough into plate by gently lifting edge of dough with your hand while pressing into plate bottom with your other hand.

2 Trim overhang to ½ inch beyond lip of plate. Tuck overhang under itself; folded edge should be flush with edge of plate. Crimp dough evenly around edge of plate. Wrap dough-lined plate loosely in plastic wrap and refrigerate until firm, about 30 minutes. Adjust oven rack to middle position and heat oven to 350 degrees.

3 Line chilled pie shell with double layer of aluminum foil, covering edges to prevent burning, and fill with pie weights. Bake on foil-lined rimmed baking sheet until edges are set and just beginning to turn golden, 25 to 30 minutes, rotating sheet halfway through baking. Remove foil and weights, rotate sheet, and continue to bake crust until golden brown and crisp, 10 to 15 minutes longer. Transfer sheet to wire rack. (Crust must still be warm when filling is added.)

4 While crust bakes, whisk sugar, eggs, cornstarch, ⅛ teaspoon cinnamon, nutmeg, and salt together in bowl. Bring milk and cream to simmer in large saucepan over medium heat. Slowly whisk 1 cup of hot milk mixture into egg mixture to temper, then slowly whisk tempered egg mixture into remaining milk in saucepan. Cook over medium heat, whisking constantly, until mixture is thickened, bubbling, and registers 180 degrees, 30 to 90 seconds (custard should have consistency of thick pudding). Strain mixture through fine-mesh strainer into clean bowl, then stir in rum.

5 With pie still on sheet, pour custard into warm crust, smoothing top with clean spatula into even layer. Bake until center of pie registers 160 degrees, 14 to 18 minutes. Let pie cool completely on wire rack, about 4 hours. Spread whipped cream attractively over pie and dust with remaining ⅛ teaspoon cinnamon. Serve.

# LAVENDER CRÈME BRÛLÉE PIE

Serves 8

| | |
|---|---|
| 1 | recipe Lemon Single-Crust Pie Dough (page 318) |
| ⅔ | cup (4⅔ ounces) plus 3 tablespoons sugar, divided |
| 3 | large eggs |
| 3 | tablespoons cornstarch |
| ¼ | teaspoon table salt |
| 2 | cups whole milk |
| 1 | cup heavy cream |
| 2 | teaspoons dried lavender |
| 1 | teaspoon vanilla extract |
| 10–12 | candied violets (optional) |

**WHY THIS RECIPE WORKS** Crème brûlée, the light, silky custard with a crackly sugar top, is a mainstay on the dessert menu of fancy restaurants. We thought the textural contrast of the dessert would translate well to pie form, so we set out to develop a recipe for crème brûlée pie that would be practical for the home cook. For a creative twist, we skipped the traditional vanilla bean and instead infused our custard with lavender by steeping (and later straining) dried lavender blossoms in milk and cream. For the delicate sugar crust, we sprinkled sugar over the chilled custard pie and then torched it. We like the flavor of the lemon pie dough in this recipe, but you can use any single-crust pie dough (see pages 316–326). Do not use a broiler to caramelize the sugar crust. We love the pop of color candied violets add, but they are optional.

---

**1** Roll dough into 12-inch circle on floured counter. Loosely roll dough around rolling pin and gently unroll it onto 9-inch pie plate, letting excess dough hang over edge. Ease dough into plate by gently lifting edge of dough with your hand while pressing into plate bottom with your other hand.

**2** Trim overhang to ½ inch beyond lip of plate. Tuck overhang under itself; folded edge should be flush with edge of plate. Crimp dough evenly around edge of plate. Wrap dough-lined plate loosely in plastic wrap and refrigerate until firm, about 30 minutes. Adjust oven rack to middle position and heat oven to 350 degrees.

**3** Line chilled pie shell with double layer of aluminum foil, covering edges to prevent burning, and fill with pie weights. Bake on foil-lined rimmed baking sheet until edges are set and just beginning to turn golden, 25 to 30 minutes, rotating sheet halfway through baking. Remove foil and weights, rotate sheet, and continue to bake crust until golden brown and crisp, 10 to 15 minutes longer. Transfer sheet to wire rack. (Crust must still be warm when filling is added.)

**4** While crust bakes, whisk ⅔ cup sugar, eggs, cornstarch, and salt together in bowl. Bring milk, cream, and lavender to simmer in large saucepan over medium heat. Slowly whisk 1 cup of hot milk mixture into egg mixture to temper, then slowly whisk tempered egg mixture into remaining milk in saucepan. Cook over medium heat, whisking constantly, until custard is thickened, bubbling, and registers 180 degrees, 30 to 90 seconds (custard should have consistency of thick pudding). Strain mixture through fine-mesh strainer into clean bowl, then stir in vanilla.

**5** With pie still on sheet, pour custard into warm crust, smoothing top with clean spatula into even layer. Transfer pie to oven and bake until center of pie registers 160 degrees, 14 to 18 minutes. Let pie cool completely on wire rack, about 4 hours. Cover cooled pie loosely with plastic and refrigerate until chilled, at least 4 hours or up to 24 hours. Blot surface of pie dry with paper towels, then sprinkle evenly with remaining 3 tablespoons sugar. Using torch, evenly caramelize sugar until deep golden brown. Sprinkle with candied violets, if using. Serve.

# ORANGE-CHOCOLATE CUSTARD PIE

Serves 8

1 recipe single-crust pie dough (see pages 316–326)

⅔ cup (4⅔ ounces) sugar

3 large eggs

3 tablespoons cornstarch

1 tablespoon grated orange zest plus 1½ tablespoons juice

⅛ teaspoon table salt

2 cups whole milk

1 cup heavy cream

1 teaspoon vanilla extract

6 ounces bittersweet chocolate, chopped fine

1 recipe Orange Whipped Cream (page 340)

Chocolate shavings

**WHY THIS RECIPE WORKS** Citrusy, sweet orange cuts through the richness of chocolate, making the two flavors a beloved pairing that's hard to beat. We wanted to showcase this great combination in an impressive custard pie. But instead of merely adding some orange essence to chocolate cream filling, we decided to make a two-layer custard that would fill our pie shell with a stripe of chocolate and one of orange. The best way to do this was to cook one orange-scented custard, divide it in half, and add melted bittersweet chocolate to one half. We layered the more buoyant orange custard over the chocolate custard and baked the pie until just set. Topping the pie with orange-flavored whipped cream and shaved chocolate highlighted the flavors of the custards. Use a vegetable peeler to scrape chocolate shavings from a block of chocolate.

1  Roll dough into 12-inch circle on floured counter. Loosely roll dough around rolling pin and gently unroll it onto 9-inch pie plate, letting excess dough hang over edge. Ease dough into plate by gently lifting edge of dough with your hand while pressing into plate bottom with your other hand.

2  Trim overhang to ½ inch beyond lip of plate. Tuck overhang under itself; folded edge should be flush with edge of plate. Crimp dough evenly around edge of plate. Wrap dough-lined plate loosely in plastic wrap and refrigerate until firm, about 30 minutes. Adjust oven rack to middle position and heat oven to 350 degrees.

3  Line chilled pie shell with double layer of aluminum foil, covering edges to prevent burning, and fill with pie weights. Bake on foil-lined rimmed baking sheet until edges are set and just beginning to turn golden, 25 to 30 minutes, rotating sheet halfway through baking. Remove foil and weights, rotate sheet, and continue to bake crust until golden brown and crisp, 10 to 15 minutes longer. Transfer sheet to wire rack. (Crust must still be warm when filling is added.)

4  While crust bakes, whisk sugar, eggs, cornstarch, orange zest and juice, and salt together in bowl. Bring milk and cream to simmer in large saucepan over medium heat. Slowly whisk 1 cup of hot milk mixture into egg mixture to temper, then slowly whisk tempered egg mixture into remaining milk in saucepan. Cook over medium heat, whisking constantly, until mixture is thickened, bubbling, and registers 180 degrees, 30 to 90 seconds (mixture should have consistency of thick pudding). Strain mixture through fine-mesh strainer into clean bowl, then stir in vanilla. Transfer 1½ cups custard to second bowl; whisk in chocolate until smooth.

5  With pie still on sheet, pour chocolate mixture into warm crust, smoothing top with clean spatula into even layer. Gently pour remaining custard over chocolate layer, smoothing top with clean spatula into even layer. Bake until center of pie registers 160 degrees, 14 to 18 minutes. Let pie cool completely on wire rack, about 4 hours. Spread whipped cream attractively over pie and sprinkle with chocolate shavings. Serve.

# CHOCOLATE CHESS PIE

**Serves 8**

1 recipe single-crust pie dough
   (see pages 316–326)

2 tablespoons unsalted butter,
   cut into 12 pieces

3 ounces unsweetened chocolate,
   chopped

1½ cups (10½ ounces) plus
   1 teaspoon sugar, divided

3 tablespoons all-purpose flour

½ teaspoon table salt

4 large eggs plus 2 large yolks

¼ cup heavy cream

1½ teaspoons vanilla extract

**WHY THIS RECIPE WORKS** Our Lemon Chess Pie (page 63) is delicious and balanced, and the flavor is a typical one in this family of Southern custard pies. For a second chess pie, we wanted to go in a less common but more luxurious direction by introducing smooth, silky chocolate. Melted unsweetened chocolate (rather than cocoa powder) and cream (instead of buttermilk or too-thick evaporated milk, which we found in some recipes) lent the right amount of richness, while four eggs plus two additional yolks created a silky, creamy texture. Unlike our lemon version, we didn't need the cornmeal crunch in this lush, elegant chess pie, so we used 3 tablespoons of flour to help bind the ingredients and ensure neat slicing. (The starchiness we detected from flour in the lemon chess was absent here with all that creamy melted bar chocolate.) We baked this pie in a moderate 325-degree oven to yield a soft but fully cooked custard. An even coat of granulated sugar over the top provided a crunchy textural contrast to the rich, fudgy filling.

1 Roll dough into 12-inch circle on floured counter. Loosely roll dough around rolling pin and gently unroll it onto 9-inch pie plate, letting excess dough hang over edge. Ease dough into plate by gently lifting edge of dough with your hand while pressing into plate bottom with your other hand.

2 Trim overhang to ½ inch beyond lip of plate. Tuck overhang under itself; folded edge should be flush with edge of plate. Crimp dough evenly around edge of plate. Wrap dough-lined plate loosely in plastic wrap and refrigerate until firm, about 30 minutes. Adjust oven rack to middle position and heat oven to 425 degrees.

3 Line chilled pie shell with double layer of aluminum foil, covering edges to prevent burning, and fill with pie weights. Bake on foil-lined rimmed baking sheet until pie dough looks dry and is pale in color, about 15 minutes. Remove parchment and weights and continue to bake until center begins to look opaque and slightly drier, 3 to 6 minutes. Transfer sheet to wire rack and let cool completely, about 45 minutes.

4 Reduce oven temperature to 325 degrees. Microwave butter and chocolate in bowl at 50 percent power, stirring occasionally, until melted, about 2 minutes. Whisk 1½ cups sugar, flour, and salt in second bowl until combined. Whisk eggs and yolks, cream, and vanilla into sugar mixture until combined. Whisk chocolate mixture into sugar-egg mixture until fully incorporated and no streaks remain.

5 With pie still on sheet, pour filling into cooled crust and sprinkle remaining 1 teaspoon sugar evenly over filling. Bake until center of pie is just set and registers 180 degrees, 35 to 40 minutes, rotating sheet halfway through baking. (Slight crust will have formed on top.) Let pie cool completely on wire rack, about 4 hours. Serve. (Pie can be refrigerated for up to 4 days. Bring to room temperature before serving.)

# PASSION FRUIT CURD PIE

**Serves 8**

1¼ pounds passion fruit, halved

1¼ cups water

¾ cup (5¼ ounces) plus 1½ teaspoons sugar, divided

6 large egg yolks

⅓ cup (1⅓ ounces) cornstarch

⅛ teaspoon table salt

2 tablespoons unsalted butter, cut into 2 pieces

½ cup heavy cream

½ teaspoon vanilla extract

½ cup raspberry jam

1 recipe Coconut Cookie Crust (page 334), baked and cooled

5 ounces (1 cup) raspberries

¼ cup (¾ ounce) sweetened shredded coconut, toasted

**WHY THIS RECIPE WORKS** Maybe you're not familiar with passion fruit pie (or with passion fruit at all!), but you should be: Passion fruit packs a tropical punch that, even in the middle of winter, transports us to the beach on a hot, sunny day. We made a smooth passion fruit curd to fill our pie with just the right balance of sweet, tangy, and rich. To complement this special fruit, we had to choose our components carefully—nothing too sour or cloyingly sweet. Our coconut cookie crust gave a subtle nod to the tropics, as did toasted coconut sprinkled on top. But we still needed something to make the passion fruit flavor really pop, and raspberries provided just the right sweet-sour balance. A schmear of raspberry jam beneath the curd and some puckery fresh raspberries on top were the perfect combination. You can substitute ½ cup frozen passion fruit puree, thawed, for the fresh in this recipe (skip step 1).

1 Scrape pulp (including seeds) from passion fruit into bowl of food processor. Pulse until seeds are separated from pulp, about 4 pulses. Strain puree through fine-mesh strainer into bowl, discarding solids. Measure out ½ cup puree, reserving any remaining for another use.

2 Whisk water, ¾ cup sugar, ½ cup puree, egg yolks, cornstarch, and salt together in large saucepan until combined. Cook over medium-low heat, stirring constantly with rubber spatula, until mixture thickens slightly and registers 170 degrees, 5 to 10 minutes. Off heat, whisk in butter until smooth. Strain curd through clean fine-mesh strainer into large bowl, cover with plastic wrap, and refrigerate until chilled, about 1½ hours.

3 Using stand mixer fitted with whisk attachment, whip cream, vanilla, and remaining 1½ teaspoons sugar on medium-low speed until foamy, about 1 minute. Increase speed to high and whip until soft peaks form, 1 to 3 minutes. Gently whisk one-third whipped cream into chilled puree mixture until lightened. Using rubber spatula, gently fold in remaining whipped cream until homogeneous. Spread raspberry jam evenly over cooled crust, then top with curd mixture, smoothing with clean spatula into even layer. Refrigerate until set, at least 8 hours or up to 24 hours. Arrange raspberries decoratively on top of pie and sprinkle with coconut. Serve.

# upping
# YOUR GAME

# SALTED CARAMEL APPLE PIE

**Serves 8**

| | |
|---|---|
| 1 | recipe single-crust pie dough (see pages 316–326) |
| 1½ | cups (10½ ounces) plus 2 tablespoons sugar, divided |
| 3 | large eggs |
| ¼ | cup (1 ounce) cornstarch |
| 2 | tablespoons white miso |
| ½ | teaspoon vanilla extract |
| ¼ | teaspoon table salt |
| 2 | tablespoons water |
| 1 | cup heavy cream, divided |
| 1½ | cups whole milk |
| 3 | Fuji, Gala, or Golden Delicious apples, cored, quartered, and sliced very thin lengthwise |
| 2 | tablespoons lemon juice |
| | Flake sea salt |

**WHY THIS RECIPE WORKS** A chewy caramel-coated apple on a stick is a whimsical fall orchard or county fair treat, but the combination of caramel with apples is a winning one in many dessert forms. We wanted to create a grown-up pie that brought together apples and flavorful salted caramel. Instead of stewing the fruit in a double crust, we reimagined our apple slices and used them as a fancy garnish to a caramel custard pie. We made the salted caramel filling by whisking basic custard components into homemade caramel. A surprising ingredient—white miso—deepened the flavor of the caramel dramatically so it stood out from the dairy. The miso's savory quality also prevented our caramel custard filling from being too sweet. To adorn the custard, we softened thin apple slices with sugar and a little lemon juice so they could be bent and formed into beautiful roses that made our pie look like an edible bouquet. Carefully tilt the saucepan to pool the caramel to get a more consistent temperature reading. For best results, use a mandoline to slice the apples paper-thin.

**1** Roll dough into 12-inch circle on floured counter. Loosely roll dough around rolling pin and gently unroll it onto 9-inch pie plate, letting excess dough hang over edge. Ease dough into plate by gently lifting edge of dough with your hand while pressing into plate bottom with your other hand.

**2** Trim overhang to ½ inch beyond lip of plate. Tuck overhang under itself; folded edge should be flush with edge of plate. Crimp dough evenly around edge of plate. Wrap dough-lined plate loosely in plastic wrap and refrigerate until firm, about 30 minutes. Adjust oven rack to middle position and heat oven to 350 degrees.

**3** Line chilled pie shell with double layer of aluminum foil, covering edges to prevent burning, and fill with pie weights. Bake on foil-lined rimmed baking sheet until edges are set and just beginning to turn golden, 25 to 30 minutes, rotating sheet halfway through baking. Remove foil and weights, rotate sheet, and continue to bake crust until golden brown and crisp, 10 to 15 minutes longer. Transfer sheet to wire rack. (Crust must still be warm when filling is added.)

**4** Whisk ¾ cup sugar, eggs, cornstarch, miso, vanilla, and table salt together in bowl; set aside. Bring ¾ cup sugar and water to boil in large saucepan over medium-high heat. Cook, without stirring, until mixture is straw-colored, 4 to 6 minutes. Reduce heat to low and continue to cook, swirling saucepan occasionally, until caramel is amber-colored and registers 360 to 370 degrees, 2 to 5 minutes.

**5** Off heat, carefully stir in ¼ cup cream; mixture will bubble and steam. Whisk vigorously, being sure to scrape corners of saucepan, until mixture is completely smooth, at least 30 seconds. Gradually whisk in remaining ¾ cup cream and milk, then bring to simmer over medium heat. Slowly whisk 1 cup hot caramel mixture into egg mixture to temper then slowly whisk tempered egg mixture into remaining caramel mixture in saucepan. Cook, whisking constantly, until mixture is thickened and bubbling and registers 180 degrees, 4 to 6 minutes (mixture should have consistency of thick pudding). Strain mixture through fine-mesh strainer into clean bowl.

**6** With pie still on sheet, pour filling into warm crust, smoothing top with clean spatula into even layer. Bake until center of pie registers 160 degrees, 14 to 18 minutes. Let pie cool completely on wire rack, about 4 hours.

**7** Before serving, combine apple slices, remaining 2 tablespoons sugar, and lemon juice in bowl. Microwave until apples are pliable, about 2 minutes, stirring halfway through microwaving. Drain apples then transfer to paper towel–lined sheet and pat dry with paper towels. Shingle 5 apple slices, peel side out, overlapping each slice by about ½ inch on cutting board or counter. Starting at 1 end, roll up slices to form rose shape; place in center of pie. Repeat, arranging apple roses decoratively over top of pie. Sprinkle with sea salt and serve.

## Making Apple Rosettes

**1** Combine apple slices, 2 tablespoons sugar, and lemon juice in bowl. Microwave until apples are pliable, about 2 minutes, stirring halfway through microwaving.

**2** Drain apples and pat dry with paper towels. Shingle 5 apple slices, peel side out, overlapping each slice by about ½ inch.

**3** Starting at 1 end, roll up slices to form rose shape.

SALTED CARAMEL APPLE PIE

PUMPKIN PRALINE PIE

# PUMPKIN PRALINE PIE

Serves 8

1   recipe single-crust pie dough
    (see pages 316–326)

*filling*
1   (15-ounce) can unsweetened
    pumpkin puree
¾   cup packed (5¼ ounces) dark
    brown sugar
2   teaspoons ground cinnamon
1   teaspoon ground ginger
½   teaspoon ground allspice
½   teaspoon table salt
    Pinch ground cloves
1   cup evaporated milk
3   large eggs
2   teaspoons vanilla extract

*topping*
1   cup pecans, chopped fine
½   cup packed (3½ ounces) dark
    brown sugar
    Pinch table salt
2   teaspoons dark corn syrup
1   teaspoon vanilla extract
2   teaspoons granulated sugar

**WHY THIS RECIPE WORKS** Pumpkin praline pie combines the best features of two holiday favorites: It has the spiced custard of a pumpkin pie and the praline-like chew of a pecan pie. We cooked our filling on the stovetop to evaporate excess moisture; this ensured our pie would have enough structure to support a substantial topping. For the praline, we tossed chopped pecans with sugar and a smidgen of corn syrup—just enough to make the topping clump like streusel. We wanted cohesiveness between the praline and the filling, so we thought we'd add the topping a few minutes before the center was set; unfortunately, the topping caused the filling to buckle under its weight. Instead, we turned to a visual cue that bothers many bakers: cracking around the edge of the custard. Usually the sign of a problem, the cracking here was the cue that our filling was set enough to add the topping. After just 10 more minutes of baking, the praline became a crisp contrast to the smooth custardy filling.

---

**1** Roll dough into 12-inch circle on floured counter. Loosely roll dough around rolling pin and gently unroll it onto 9-inch pie plate, letting excess dough hang over edge. Ease dough into plate by gently lifting edge of dough with your hand while pressing into plate bottom with your other hand.

**2** Trim overhang to ½ inch beyond lip of plate. Tuck overhang under itself; folded edge should be flush with edge of plate. Crimp dough evenly around edge of plate. Wrap dough-lined plate loosely in plastic wrap and refrigerate until firm, about 30 minutes. Adjust oven rack to middle position and heat oven to 425 degrees.

**3** Line chilled pie shell with double layer of aluminum foil, covering edges to prevent burning, and fill with pie weights. Bake on rimmed baking sheet until pie dough looks dry and is pale in color, about 15 minutes. Remove foil and weights and continue to bake crust until light golden brown, 4 to 7 minutes longer. Transfer to wire rack. (Crust must still be warm when filling is added.) Reduce oven temperature to 350 degrees.

**4** *for the filling* Process pumpkin, sugar, cinnamon, ginger, allspice, salt, and cloves in food processor until smooth, about 1 minute. Transfer mixture to large saucepan and cook over medium-high heat until sputtering and thickened, about 4 minutes. Off heat, whisk evaporated milk into pumpkin mixture, then whisk in eggs and vanilla. With pie still on sheet, pour filling into warm crust. Bake until filling is puffed and cracked around edges and center barely jiggles when pie is shaken, about 35 minutes.

**5** *for the topping* While pie is baking, toss pecans, brown sugar, and salt together in bowl. Add corn syrup and vanilla, using your fingers to ensure that ingredients are well blended. Scatter topping evenly over puffed filling. Sprinkle with granulated sugar. Bake until pecans are fragrant and topping is bubbling around edges, about 10 minutes. Let pie cool completely on wire rack, about 4 hours. Serve.

## Baking Pumpkin Praline Pie

**1** Pour filling into warm pie crust.

**2** Bake until filling is puffed and cracked around edges and center barely jiggles when pie is shaken, about 35 minutes.

**3** While pie is baking, toss pecans, brown sugar, and salt together in bowl.

**4** Add corn syrup and vanilla, using your fingers to ensure that ingredients are well blended.

**5** Scatter topping evenly over filling.

**6** Sprinkle with granulated sugar.

**7** Bake until pecans are fragrant and topping is bubbling around edges, about 10 minutes.

**8** Let pie cool completely on wire rack, about 4 hours. Serve.

# PEANUT BUTTER AND CONCORD GRAPE PIE

**Serves 8**

1   recipe Nut Single-Crust Pie Dough (page 318)

*peanut butter mousse*

½   cup (2 ounces) confectioners' sugar

½   cup creamy peanut butter

4   ounces cream cheese, softened

2   tablespoons plus ½ cup heavy cream, divided

*grape filling*

1   cup (7 ounces) granulated sugar, divided

2   tablespoons low- or no-sugar-needed fruit pectin

1½   pounds Concord grapes, stemmed

1   teaspoon lemon zest plus 1 tablespoon juice

¼   teaspoon table salt

1   recipe Peanut Butter Whipped Cream (page 340)

1   recipe Candied Nuts (page 345)

**WHY THIS RECIPE WORKS** When we think about grape flavor, the profile of one special grape, the Concord grape, usually comes to mind. But while they have the deepest flavor, they're not typically eaten out of hand: Tough skins and seeds don't make them the most appealing of snacks. When transformed into jams, compotes, or fruit fillings, however, this seasonal grape's flavor is bold and delicious. We wanted to take the beloved combination of peanut butter and grape jelly and create a dessert spin on the classic sandwich. We made a thick grape filling by cooking down the fruit and then straining out the solids before reducing the juice further. We filled a peanutty pie crust with peanut butter mousse and then topped it with this deep-flavored jelly. We now had our peanut butter and our jelly, but the grape layer was really prominent so we decided to incorporate more peanut butter. A peanut butter whipped cream added a pleasantly light layer and candied peanuts gave the creamy pie some welcome crunch. Look for grapes that are firm, plump, and securely attached to their stems. For fruit pectin we recommend both Sure-Jell for Less or No Sugar Needed Recipes and Ball RealFruit Low or No-Sugar Needed Pectin. We like the extra layer of peanut butter flavor our nut dough made with peanuts gives this pie, but you can use any single-crust pie dough (see pages 316–326). Use peanuts in the candied nuts.

---

**1** Roll dough into 12-inch circle on floured counter. Loosely roll dough around rolling pin and gently unroll it onto 9-inch pie plate, letting excess dough hang over edge. Ease dough into plate by gently lifting edge of dough with your hand while pressing into plate bottom with your other hand.

**2** Trim overhang to ½ inch beyond lip of plate. Tuck overhang under itself; folded edge should be flush with edge of plate. Crimp dough evenly around edge of plate. Wrap dough-lined plate loosely in plastic wrap and refrigerate until firm, about 30 minutes. Adjust oven rack to middle position and heat oven to 350 degrees.

**3** Line chilled pie shell with double layer of aluminum foil, covering edges to prevent burning, and fill with pie weights. Bake on foil-lined rimmed baking sheet until edges are set and just beginning to turn golden, 25 to 30 minutes, rotating sheet halfway through baking. Remove foil and weights, rotate sheet, and continue to bake crust until golden brown and crisp, 10 to 15 minutes longer. Transfer sheet to wire rack and let cool completely, about 45 minutes.

**4** *For the peanut butter mousse* Using stand mixer fitted with whisk attachment, whip sugar, peanut butter, cream cheese, and 2 tablespoons cream on low speed until combined, about 1 minute. Increase speed to medium-high and whip until fluffy, about 1 minute. Transfer to large bowl; set aside.

**5** In now-empty mixer bowl, whip remaining ½ cup cream on medium-low speed until foamy, about 1 minute. Increase speed to high and whip until stiff peaks form, 1 to 3 minutes. Gently fold whipped cream into peanut butter mixture in 2 additions until no white streaks remain. Spoon filling into cooled crust and spread into even layer with spatula. Refrigerate until set, about 1 hour.

**6** *For the grape filling* While mousse chills, whisk ¼ cup sugar and pectin together in bowl; set aside. Bring grapes to simmer in large saucepan over high heat. Off heat, coarsely mash grapes with potato masher. Return to simmer over medium-high heat and cook until grapes have softened and pulp has separated from skins, about 5 minutes.

**7** Working in batches, strain grapes through fine-mesh strainer into large bowl, pressing firmly on solids to extract as much liquid as possible (you should have about 1¼ cups); discard solids. Return strained grape juice to now-empty saucepan. Bring grape juice, remaining ¾ cup sugar, lemon zest and juice, and salt to boil over medium-high heat. Whisk in pectin mixture, return to boil, and cook for 1 minute, whisking constantly. Let cool off heat until just warm, about 30 minutes. Slowly pour filling over peanut butter mousse, spreading into even layer with rubber spatula. Refrigerate until filling is set, about 2 hours. Spread whipped cream attractively over pie and sprinkle with candied nuts. Serve.

## Making Candied Nuts

**1** Line baking sheet with parchment paper.

**2** Bring all ingredients to boil in medium saucepan over medium heat.

**3** Cook, stirring constantly, until water evaporates and sugar appears dry, opaque, and somewhat crystallized and evenly coats nuts, about 5 minutes.

**4** Reduce heat to low and continue to stir nuts until sugar is amber-colored, about 2 minutes longer.

**5** Transfer nuts to prepared sheet and spread into even layer. Let cool completely, about 10 minutes.

PEANUT BUTTER AND
CONCORD GRAPE PIE

SOUR CHERRY—HAZELNUT PIE

# SOUR CHERRY–HAZELNUT PIE

**Serves 8**

1    recipe Nut Double-Crust Pie Dough (page 320)

1    cup (7 ounces) sugar

1    teaspoon grated lemon zest plus 2 teaspoons juice

¼    cup instant tapioca, ground

⅛    teaspoon table salt

2    pounds fresh sour cherries, pitted

3    tablespoons hazelnut liqueur (optional)

1    large egg, lightly beaten with 1 tablespoon water

**WHY THIS RECIPE WORKS** With their refreshingly tart, complex flavor and vibrant ruby red color, sour cherries make a brilliant summertime pie filling. We have a recipe for Sweet Cherry Pie (page 34) since the season for sour cherries is so short, but we thought this classic deserved a place in our recipe collection. We left all of the pitted cherries whole in our pie; they baked down to a tender and juicy filling that really highlighted the fruit. A full cup of sugar balanced the cherries' tartness. To make this pie extra special, we added hazelnut liqueur to our filling; the nuttiness was a round counterpoint to the bracing berries. To take that flavor profile further, we used our hazelnut pie dough for a sweet-tart, rich summer treat. Use a spice grinder to grind the tapioca. We like the flavor of our nut dough made with hazelnuts here, but you can use any double-crust pie dough (see pages 320–327). Any of the top crusts on pages 134–142 will allow for enough evaporation to ensure a perfect slice. The method here produces a standard lattice top.

---

**1** Roll 1 disk of dough into 12-inch circle on floured counter. Loosely roll dough around rolling pin and gently unroll it into 9-inch pie plate, letting excess dough hang over edge. Ease dough into plate by gently lifting edge of dough with your hand while pressing into plate bottom with your other hand. Leave any dough that overhangs plate in place. Wrap dough-lined plate loosely in plastic wrap and refrigerate until firm, about 30 minutes.

**2** Roll other piece of dough into 13 by 10½-inch rectangle on floured counter, then transfer to parchment paper–lined rimmed baking sheet; cover loosely with plastic and refrigerate until firm, about 30 minutes.

**3** Using pizza wheel, fluted pastry wheel, or paring knife, trim ¼ inch dough from long sides of rectangle, then cut lengthwise into eight 1¼-inch-wide strips. Cover loosely with plastic and refrigerate until firm, about 30 minutes. Adjust oven rack to middle position and heat oven to 400 degrees.

**4** Whisk sugar, lemon zest, tapioca, and salt together in large bowl. Stir in cherries, lemon juice, and hazelnut liqueur, if using, and let sit for 15 minutes. Spread cherry mixture into dough-lined plate.

**5** Remove dough strips from refrigerator; if too stiff to be workable, let sit at room temperature until softened slightly but still very cold. Space 4 strips evenly across top of pie, parallel to counter edge. Fold back first and third strips almost completely. Lay 1 strip across pie, perpendicular to second and fourth strips, keeping it snug to folded edges of dough strips, then unfold first and third strips over top. Fold back second and fourth strips and add second perpendicular strip, keeping it snug to folded edge. Unfold second and fourth strips over top. Repeat weaving remaining strips evenly across pie, alternating between folding back first and third strips and second and fourth strips to create lattice pattern. Shift strips as needed so they are evenly spaced over top of pie. (If dough becomes too soft to work with, refrigerate pie and dough strips until firm.)

**6** Trim overhang to ½ inch beyond lip of plate. Pinch edges of bottom crust and lattice strips together firmly to seal. Tuck overhang under itself; folded edge should be flush with edge of plate. Crimp dough evenly around edge of plate. (If dough is very soft, refrigerate for 10 minutes before baking.) Brush surface with egg wash.

**7** Place pie on aluminum foil–lined rimmed baking sheet and bake until crust is light golden, 20 to 25 minutes. Reduce oven temperature to 350 degrees and continue to bake until juices are bubbling and crust is deep golden brown, 30 to 50 minutes longer. Let pie cool on wire rack until filling has set, about 4 hours. Serve.

## CHERRY PITTERS

You can pit cherries by hand, but a cherry pitter can save lots of time. And they're not a one-hit wonder: These gadgets can also be used to pit olives. A mechanism drives a dowel through the stem end of a cherry and pushes the pit out the bottom. Our favorite is the **Chef'n QuickPit Cherry Pitter** ($9.99). It resembles a plastic toy gun: Just pull the trigger to plunge the straight, moderately thick dowel into the cherry pit. It's easy to insert, stabilize, and remove the cherries, and while this pitter wasn't quite as neat, quick, or accurate as a contained version that pitted multiple cherries at once, many testers preferred its more compact profile and simpler operation.

If you don't have a cherry pitter, we've had luck setting the cherry on the mouth of an empty wine bottle and using a straw to push the pit through. The hollow end of the straw helps it grip the pit, and the narrow opening of the wine bottle (a beer bottle would work, too) holds the cherry in place while the pit is pushed through. The bottle catches the pits and juices, making cleanup easy.

# GINGER CRANBERRY-PEAR STREUSEL PIE

Serves 8

1 recipe single-crust pie dough (see pages 316–326)

3 pounds ripe but firm Bartlett or Bosc pears, peeled, halved, cored, and sliced ¼ inch thick

½ cup (3½ ounces) granulated sugar, divided

¾ cup (3¾ ounces) all-purpose flour

¼ cup packed (1¾ ounces) light brown sugar

2 tablespoons crystallized ginger, chopped

¾ teaspoon ground ginger

⅛ teaspoon table salt

5 tablespoons unsalted butter, melted

8 ounces (2 cups) fresh or thawed frozen cranberries

1 teaspoon grated fresh ginger

**WHY THIS RECIPE WORKS** Ripe pears are filled with floral, honey-flavored juices that stream from the fruit when you take a bite. Those same juices also stream out of a pie when you try to make one with pears—much more so than with the other fall fruit, apples. We wanted a pear pie, perked up with complementary flavors, that wasn't a watery mess. Microwaving the pears with some sugar released excess liquid. We knew a lattice crust could help increase evaporation, but we decided to make a streusel; it too would allow for evaporation, but it would also provide a nice textural contrast to the soft fruit. Baking the pie on the bottom rack further encouraged evaporation. By adding a little extra sugar, we were able to distribute 2 cups of cranberries throughout our pie without puckering. And for an alluring final component, we added 1 teaspoon of grated fresh ginger. Some ground ginger and chewy bits of crystallized ginger in the topping tied the components of our seasonal pie together.

---

1 Roll dough into 12-inch circle on floured counter. Loosely roll dough around rolling pin and gently unroll it onto 9-inch pie plate, letting excess dough hang over edge. Ease dough into plate by gently lifting edge of dough with your hand while pressing into plate bottom with your other hand.

2 Trim overhang to ½ inch beyond lip of plate. Tuck overhang under itself; folded edge should be flush with edge of plate. Crimp dough evenly around edge of plate. Wrap dough-lined plate loosely in plastic wrap and refrigerate until firm, about 30 minutes. Adjust oven rack to lowest position and heat oven to 400 degrees.

3 Toss pears with 2 tablespoons granulated sugar in large bowl. Microwave, covered, until pears turn translucent and release their juices, 4 to 8 minutes, stirring once halfway through microwaving. Uncover and let cool completely, about 30 minutes.

4 Combine flour, brown sugar, crystallized ginger, ground ginger, salt, and 2 tablespoons granulated sugar in bowl. Stir in melted butter until mixture is completely moistened; let sit for 10 minutes.

5 Combine cranberries, fresh ginger, and remaining ¼ cup granulated sugar in food processor and pulse until cranberries are coarsely chopped, about 5 pulses. Drain pears and discard liquid. Return pears to now-empty bowl and add cranberry mixture, stirring to combine. Spread mixture into dough-lined plate. Sprinkle topping over pear mixture, breaking apart any large clumps. Place pie on aluminum foil–lined rimmed baking sheet and bake until juices are bubbling and topping is deep golden brown, 45 to 55 minutes, rotating sheet halfway through baking. Let pie cool on wire rack until filling has set, about 4 hours. Serve.

# BUTTERNUT SQUASH PIE WITH BROWNED BUTTER AND SAGE

Serves 8

1    recipe Herb Single-Crust Dough (page 318)

8    tablespoons unsalted butter, cut into 8 pieces

1    teaspoon minced fresh sage

30   ounces butternut squash, peeled, seeded, and cut into 1-inch pieces (5 cups)

1    teaspoon table salt

1    teaspoon grated fresh ginger

¼    teaspoon ground nutmeg

¾    cup packed (5¼ ounces) brown sugar

¾    cup heavy cream

⅔    cup whole milk

2    large eggs plus 2 large yolks

1    teaspoon vanilla extract

**WHY THIS RECIPE WORKS** Pumpkin isn't the only winter squash that works in desserts—slightly earthier butternut is a lovely autumn alternative to the pie norm. To make this pie unique from its cousin, we incorporated browned butter for nutty richness. Mincing some sage and cooking it with the butter before adding it to the filling allowed this classic fall herb to subtly infuse the pie without being too prominent. For even more sage flavor we like to use our herb dough, here made with sage, but you can use any single-crust pie dough (see pages 316–326). If you want to top your pie with cutouts like in the photo, make a double crust so you have enough dough (see page 143 for more information).

1 Roll dough into 12-inch circle on floured counter. Loosely roll dough around rolling pin and gently unroll it onto 9-inch pie plate, letting excess dough hang over edge. Ease dough into plate by gently lifting edge of dough with your hand while pressing into plate bottom with your other hand.

2 Trim overhang to ½ inch beyond lip of plate. Tuck overhang under itself; folded edge should be flush with edge of plate. Crimp dough evenly around edge of plate. Wrap dough-lined plate loosely in plastic wrap and refrigerate until firm, about 30 minutes. Adjust oven rack to middle position and heat oven to 350 degrees.

3 Melt butter and sage in 8-inch skillet over medium-high heat. Continue to cook, swirling skillet occasionally, until butter is dark golden brown and has nutty aroma, about 2 minute; set aside. Microwave squash in covered bowl until very soft and easily pierced with fork, 15 to 18 minutes, stirring halfway through microwaving. Carefully uncover, allowing steam to escape away from you, then drain squash; transfer to food processor. Add browned butter, salt, ginger, and nutmeg and process until smooth, about 1 minute, scraping down sides of bowl as needed. Transfer to large saucepan and set aside.

4 Line chilled pie shell with double layer of aluminum foil, covering edges to prevent burning, and fill with pie weights. Bake on foil-lined rimmed baking sheet until edges are set and just beginning to turn golden, 25 to 30 minutes, rotating sheet halfway through baking. Remove foil and weights, rotate sheet, and continue to bake crust until golden brown and crisp, 10 to 15 minutes longer. Transfer to wire rack. (Crust must still be warm when filling is added.)

5 Meanwhile, cook squash mixture and sugar in saucepan over medium heat until thick, shiny, and reduced to 2½ cups, 10 to 15 minutes, stirring constantly. Return squash mixture to now-empty processor bowl, add cream, milk, eggs and yolks, and vanilla, and process until well combined and smooth, about 15 seconds. Transfer filling to warm crust. Reduce oven temperature to 300 degrees and bake until edges of pie are set but center jiggles slightly and registers 160 degrees, 25 to 35 minutes. Let pie cool completely on wire rack, about 4 hours. Serve.

# APPLE-CRANBERRY PIE

Serves 8

8 ounces (2 cups) fresh or frozen cranberries

¼ cup orange juice

1 cup (7 ounces) plus 1 tablespoon sugar, divided

½ teaspoon ground cinnamon, divided

½ teaspoon table salt, divided

¼ cup water

1 tablespoon cornstarch

3½ pounds Golden Delicious apples peeled, cored, and sliced ¼ inch thick

1 recipe double-crust pie dough (see pages 320–327)

1 large egg, lightly beaten with 1 tablespoon water

**WHY THIS RECIPE WORKS** The best apple pies strike a perfect balance of sweet and tart flavors as well as tender and crisp textures. Cranberries seem like they would make an ideal addition to this classic fall dessert, but the tart fruit disturbs that balance: The cranberries can overwhelm the apples and they also shed a lot of liquid. Still, we wanted to find a way to successfully combine these two fruits. Tossing tart whole cranberries with also-tart apples made us wince. Cooking down the cranberries (think cranberry sauce) helped, but their flavor still overwhelmed the apples—you wouldn't know it was apple pie! Using only sweet apples rather than a combination of sweet and tart varieties helped tame the tartness, but the apples' subtle flavor failed to come through. The solution? Don't combine the two fruits. We arranged the cooked cranberries and the apples in two layers within the pie: cranberries on the bottom, apples on top. Now the flavor of both elements came through loud and clear. In our Deep-Dish Apple Pie (page 28), we learned that precooking the apples made them firmer in the baked pie, but here we wanted to avoid stovetop cooking since we were already cooking the cranberry mixture. Luckily, 10 minutes in the microwave (and a bit of cornstarch) did the trick.

1 Bring cranberries, orange juice, ½ cup sugar, ¼ teaspoon cinnamon, and ¼ teaspoon salt to boil in medium saucepan. Cook, stirring occasionally and pressing cranberries against side of pot, until cranberries have completely broken down and juices have thickened to jam-like consistency (wooden spoon scraped across bottom should leave clear trail that doesn't fill in), 10 to 12 minutes. Off heat, stir in water and let cool completely, about 30 minutes.

2 Meanwhile, mix ½ cup sugar, remaining ¼ teaspoon cinnamon, remaining ¼ teaspoon salt, and cornstarch in large bowl. Add apples and toss to combine. Microwave, covered, stirring with rubber spatula every 3 minutes, until apples are just starting to turn translucent around edges and liquid is thick and glossy, 10 to 14 minutes. Let cool completely, about 30 minutes. (Fillings can be refrigerated separately for up to 2 days.)

3 While fillings cool, adjust oven rack to lowest position and heat oven to 425 degrees. Roll 1 disk of dough into 12-inch circle on floured counter. Loosely roll dough around rolling pin and gently unroll it onto 9-inch pie plate, letting excess dough hang over edge. Ease dough into plate by gently lifting edge of dough with your hand while pressing into plate bottom with your other hand. Leave any dough that overhangs plate in place. Wrap dough-lined plate loosely in plastic wrap and refrigerate until firm, about 30 minutes. Roll other disk of dough into 12-inch circle on floured counter, then transfer to parchment paper–lined rimmed baking sheet; cover with plastic and refrigerate for 30 minutes.

**4** Spread cooled cranberry mixture into even layer in dough-lined plate. Spread apple mixture on top, mounding it slightly in center. Loosely roll remaining dough round around rolling pin and gently unroll it onto filling. Trim overhang to ½ inch beyond lip of plate. Pinch edges of top and bottom crusts firmly together. Tuck overhang under itself; folded edge should be flush with edge of plate. Crimp dough evenly around edge of plate. Cut four 2-inch slits in top of dough. Brush surface with egg wash and sprinkle evenly with remaining 1 tablespoon sugar.

**5** Place pie on aluminum foil–lined rimmed baking sheet and bake until crust is light golden brown, about 25 minutes. Reduce oven temperature to 375 degrees, rotate sheet, and continue to bake until juices are bubbling and crust is deep golden brown, 30 to 40 minutes longer. Let pie cool on wire rack until filling has set, about 4 hours. Serve.

# CRAB APPLE ROSE PIE

Serves 8

1 recipe double-crust pie dough (see pages 320–327)

3 pounds crab apples, cored and chopped coarse

1½–1¾ cups (10½–12¼ ounces) sugar

¼ teaspoon table salt

1 tablespoon rose water

2 tablespoons unsalted butter, cut into ¼-inch pieces

1 large egg, lightly beaten with 1 tablespoon water

**WHY THIS RECIPE WORKS** Puckeringly tart crab apples are no longer limited to backyards and backwoods; these days they pop up at farmers' markets and orchards throughout the fall. We set out to highlight these overlooked apples in a unique, delicious pie. A crab apple pie is a bit more tart than traditional apple pie, but it's also more complex in flavor and offers a welcome variation on the standard. Additionally, crab apples have high levels of pectin, which helps the filling set and makes for an easy-to-slice pie. Since crab apples are so small, we opted to leave the skins on to make prep easier; the bright red skins also contributed a beautiful rosy hue to the filling. A tablespoon of aromatic rose water added a floral undertone that brought out the apples' complexity. We don't recommend using an apple corer to core the crab apples; instead, cut around the core using a sharp knife. Crab apples can range from sweet-tart to incredibly sour; use more or less sugar depending on the flavor of your crab apples. Any of the top crusts on pages 134–142 will allow for enough evaporation to ensure a perfect slice. The method here produces a standard lattice top; for the braided strips shown in the photo, see page 137.

1 Roll 1 disk of dough into 12-inch circle on floured counter. Loosely roll dough around rolling pin and gently unroll it onto 9-inch pie plate, letting excess dough hang over edge. Ease dough into plate by gently lifting edge of dough with your hand while pressing into plate bottom with your other hand. Leave any dough that overhangs plate in place. Wrap dough-lined plate loosely in plastic wrap and refrigerate until firm, about 30 minutes.

2 Roll other piece of dough into 13 by 10½-inch rectangle on floured counter, then transfer to parchment paper–lined rimmed baking sheet; cover loosely with plastic and refrigerate until firm, about 30 minutes.

3 Using pizza wheel, fluted pastry wheel, or paring knife, trim ¼ inch dough from long sides of rectangle, then cut lengthwise into eight 1¼-inch-wide strips. Cover loosely with plastic and refrigerate until firm, about 30 minutes.

4 Toss apples, sugar, and salt together in Dutch oven. Cover and cook over medium heat, stirring frequently, until apples are tender when poked with fork but still hold their shape, 10 to 15 minutes. Spread apples and their juices on second rimmed baking sheet and let cool completely, about 30 minutes.

5 Drain cooled apples thoroughly in colander then combine drained apples and rose water in bowl. Spread apples into dough-lined plate and scatter butter over top. Adjust oven rack to middle position and heat oven to 400 degrees.

**6** Remove dough strips from refrigerator; if too stiff to be workable, let sit at room temperature until softened slightly but still very cold. Space 4 strips evenly across top of pie, parallel to counter edge. Fold back first and third strips almost completely. Lay 1 strip across pie, perpendicular to second and fourth strips, keeping it snug to folded edges of dough strips, then unfold first and third strips over top. Fold back second and fourth strips and add second perpendicular strip, keeping it snug to folded edge. Unfold second and fourth strips over top. Repeat weaving remaining strips evenly across pie, alternating between folding back first and third strips and second and fourth strips to create lattice pattern. Shift strips as needed so they are evenly spaced over top of pie. (If dough becomes too soft to work with, refriger-ate pie and dough strips until firm.)

**7** Trim overhang to ½ inch beyond lip of plate. Pinch edges of bottom crust and lattice strips together firmly to seal. Tuck overhang under itself; folded edge should be flush with edge of plate. Crimp dough evenly around edge of plate. (If dough is very soft, refrigerate for 10 minutes before baking.) Brush surface with egg wash.

**8** Place pie on aluminum foil–lined rimmed baking sheet and bake until crust is light golden, 20 to 25 minutes. Reduce oven temperature to 350 degrees, rotate sheet, and continue to bake until juices are bubbling and crust is deep golden brown, 30 to 50 minutes longer. Let pie cool on wire rack until filling has set, about 4 hours. Serve.

# MULLED WINE QUINCE PIE

Serves 8

4 (2-inch) strips orange zest

3 bay leaves

1 cinnamon stick

1 teaspoon allspice berries

¼ teaspoon black peppercorns

1 (750-ml) bottle red wine

2 cups water

1¼ cups (8¾ ounces) sugar, divided

3 pounds quinces, peeled, halved, and cored

1 recipe double-crust pie dough (see pages 320–327)

½ cup dried cherries

¼ teaspoon table salt

1 large egg, lightly beaten with 1 tablespoon water

**WHY THIS RECIPE WORKS** The fall and winter fruit known as quince has a flavor somewhere between a pear and an apple, but it's quite tart when raw—sometimes even downright astringent—and has hard, dry flesh. However, when cooked into desserts, jams, pastes, or compotes, quinces soften and become something much more unique and appealing than their uncooked counterparts. We wanted to showcase the flavor of quinces in a sophisticated pie with strong seasonal appeal. Instead of just slicing the quinces and tossing the hard fruit in the pie, we poached them first; this step not only softened the fruit to the perfect texture, but the poaching liquid infused it with flavor. We chose red wine as our medium for its deep, round flavor and dramatic hue. Taking a cue from a wintertime favorite, mulled wine, we added spices and some floral citrus zest. We mashed half of the poached quinces and sliced the other half; quinces are a pectin powerhouse so this technique was enough to create pie that set up without an additional thickener. We combined the quinces with a bit of the cooking liquid and some dried cherries, which underscored the fruity tartness of the wine. It's important to be fastidious when coring quinces, as the core remains tough even after cooking. Use a good-quality medium-bodied wine, such as a Côtes du Rhône or Pinot Noir, for this pie. If you don't have cheesecloth, substitute a triple layer of disposable coffee filters. Any of the top crusts on pages 134–142 will work with this pie. The method here produces a standard lattice top; for the free-form shapes shown in the photo, see page 139.

1 Place orange zest, bay leaves, cinnamon, allspice, and peppercorns in triple layer of cheesecloth and tie closed with kitchen twine. Bring wine, water, ¾ cup sugar, and spice bundle to simmer in Dutch oven over medium-high heat, whisking to dissolve sugar. Add quinces and return to simmer. Reduce heat to medium-low and cook, covered, stirring occasionally, until quince is easily pierced with fork, about 2 hours.

2 While quinces cook, roll 1 disk of dough into 12-inch circle on floured counter. Loosely roll dough around rolling pin and gently unroll it onto 9-inch pie plate, letting excess dough hang over edge. Ease dough into plate by gently lifting edge of dough with your hand while pressing into plate bottom with your other hand. Leave any dough that overhangs plate in place. Wrap dough-lined plate loosely in plastic wrap and refrigerate until firm, about 30 minutes.

3 Roll other piece of dough into 13 by 10½-inch rectangle on floured counter, then transfer to parchment paper–lined rimmed baking sheet; cover loosely with plastic and refrigerate until firm, about 30 minutes.

4 Using pizza wheel, fluted pastry wheel, or paring knife, trim ¼ inch dough from long sides of rectangle, then cut lengthwise into eight 1¼-inch-wide strips. Cover loosely with plastic and refrigerate until firm, about 30 minutes. Adjust oven rack to middle position and heat oven to 400 degrees.

**5** Off heat, discard spice bundle from pot. Using slotted spoon, transfer 4 quince halves to large bowl and mash into coarse paste with potato masher. Transfer remaining quince halves to cutting board and let sit until cool enough to handle, about 10 minutes (reserve cooking liquid). Cut quinces in half lengthwise then slice ¼-inch thick crosswise. Add sliced quinces, ½ cup reserved cooking liquid, remaining ½ cup sugar, cherries, and salt to mashed quince mixture in bowl, stirring to combine. Spread quince filling into dough-lined plate.

**6** Remove dough strips from refrigerator; if too stiff to be workable, let sit at room temperature until softened slightly but still very cold. Space 4 strips evenly across top of pie, parallel to counter edge. Fold back first and third strips almost completely. Lay 1 strip across pie, perpendicular to second and fourth strips, keeping it snug to folded edges of dough strips, then unfold first and third strips over top. Fold back second and fourth strips and add second perpendicular strip, keeping it snug to folded edge. Unfold second and fourth strips over top. Repeat weaving remaining strips evenly across pie, alternating between folding back first and third strips and second and fourth strips to create lattice pattern. Shift strips as needed so they are evenly spaced over top of pie. (If dough becomes too soft to work with, refrigerate pie and dough strips until firm.)

**7** Trim overhang to ½ inch beyond lip of plate. Pinch edges of bottom crust and lattice strips together firmly to seal. Tuck overhang under itself; folded edge should be flush with edge of plate. Crimp dough evenly around edge of plate. (If dough is very soft, refrigerate for 10 minutes before baking.) Brush surface with egg wash.

**8** Place pie on aluminum foil–lined rimmed baking sheet and bake until crust is light golden, 20 to 25 minutes. Reduce oven temperature to 350 degrees, rotate sheet, and continue to bake until juices are bubbling and crust is deep golden brown, 30 to 50 minutes longer. Let pie cool on wire rack until filling has set, about 4 hours.

**9** Once pie is cooled, bring Dutch oven with remaining poaching liquid to boil over medium-high heat. Reduce until sauce has consistency of maple syrup and measures about ¾ cup, 15 to 20 minutes. Let cool slightly, about 20 minutes. Serve pie, passing sauce separately.

**POACHING FRUIT**

If we precook fruit before filling a pie, it's typically by means of sautéing, stewing, or microwaving. But poaching is an excellent way to soften fruit that needs to be broken down a bit before baking, and it provides an opportunity to infuse the fruit with additional flavor. This technique uses liquid—in this case, red wine—which simmers just enough (the temperature is kept between 160 and 180 degrees) so that small bubbles break at the surface. This is a gentle way to cook fruit without making it mushy. The poaching liquid is often seasoned with aromatics that reach the fruit in an exchange of flavors between the food and the liquid; here we use classic mulling ingredients to bring the warmth and coziness of mulled wine to our winter fruit pie. As the wine adds a lot of flavor to the pie and also becomes a sauce, you want to use one you'd enjoy drinking.

PLUM-GINGER PIE

# PLUM-GINGER PIE

Serves 8

1 recipe Whole-Grain Double-Crust Pie Dough (page 320)

¾ cup (5¼ ounces) sugar

3 tablespoons cornstarch

2 teaspoons grated lemon zest plus 1 tablespoon juice

1 teaspoon grated fresh ginger

¼ teaspoon ground ginger

¼ teaspoon table salt

2½ pounds plums, halved, pitted, and cut into ¼-inch-thick wedges

1 large egg, lightly beaten with 1 tablespoon water

**WHY THIS RECIPE WORKS** Plum pies have a problem: They're either a mushy disappointment or a dense brick of overcooked, dried-out, leathery fruit. We wanted tender bites of plum in a fresh but slightly jammy filling. Leaving the skins on the plums and cutting them into ¼-inch-thick slices resulted in perfectly cooked fruit and filling. Plums, while plenty juicy, release less liquid during baking than fruit such as blueberries or cherries, so using tapioca for the thickener gave our filling a slightly sticky quality; cornstarch was a much better choice. Another key step to nailing our pie's texture was letting the filling sit for 15 minutes before adding it to the pie shell; this drew out some of the plums' juices which ensured that the cornstarch was evenly absorbed and eliminated any clumps of thickener. A bit of spicy, tangy ginger complemented the sweetness of the plums. We think our whole-grain pie crust made with whole-wheat flour pairs particularly well with this filling, but you can use any double-crust pie dough (see pages 320–327). Any of the top crusts on pages 134–142 will allow for enough evaporation to ensure a perfect slice. The method here produces a standard lattice top; for the herringbone lattice crust shown in the photo, see page 140.

**1** Roll 1 disk of dough into 12-inch circle on floured counter. Loosely roll dough around rolling pin and gently unroll it into 9-inch pie plate, letting excess dough hang over edge. Ease dough into plate by gently lifting edge of dough with your hand while pressing into plate bottom with your other hand. Leave any dough that overhangs plate in place. Wrap dough-lined plate loosely in plastic wrap and refrigerate until firm, about 30 minutes.

**2** Roll other piece of dough into 13 by 10½-inch rectangle on floured counter, then transfer to parchment paper–lined rimmed baking sheet; cover loosely with plastic and refrigerate until firm, about 30 minutes.

**3** Using pizza wheel, fluted pastry wheel, or paring knife, trim ¼ inch dough from long sides of rectangle, then cut lengthwise into eight 1¼-inch-wide strips. Cover loosely with plastic and refrigerate until firm, about 30 minutes. Adjust oven rack to middle position and heat oven to 400 degrees.

**4** Whisk sugar, cornstarch, lemon zest, fresh ginger, ground ginger, and salt together in large bowl. Stir in plums and lemon juice and let sit for 15 minutes. Spread plum mixture into dough-lined plate.

**5** Remove dough strips from refrigerator; if too stiff to be workable, let sit at room temperature until softened slightly but still very cold. Space 4 strips evenly across top of pie, parallel to counter edge. Fold back first and third strips almost completely. Lay 1 strip across pie, perpendicular to second and fourth strips, keeping it snug to folded edges of dough strips, then unfold first and third strips over top. Fold back second and fourth strips and add second perpendicular strip, keeping it snug to folded edge. Unfold second and fourth strips over top. Repeat weaving remaining strips evenly across pie, alternating between folding back first and third strips and second and fourth strips to create lattice pattern. Shift strips as needed so they are evenly spaced over top of pie. (If dough becomes too soft to work with, refrigerate pie and dough strips until firm.)

**6** Trim overhang to ½ inch beyond lip of plate. Pinch edges of bottom crust and lattice strips together firmly to seal. Tuck overhang under itself; folded edge should be flush with edge of plate. Crimp dough evenly around edge of plate. (If dough is very soft, refrigerate for 10 minutes before baking.) Brush surface with egg wash.

**7** Place pie on aluminum foil–lined rimmed baking sheet and bake until crust is light golden, 20 to 25 minutes. Reduce oven temperature to 350 degrees, rotate sheet, and continue to bake until juices are bubbling and crust is deep golden brown, 30 to 50 minutes longer. Let pie cool on wire rack until filling has set, about 4 hours. Serve.

## ALL ABOUT FRESH GINGER

Fresh ginger adds spice, brightness, and complexity to many desserts; here are some tips for making the most of it.

**Grate It** If you're incorporating ginger into a dessert, you're likely grating it, but its fibrous texture can be distracting when coarsely grated or minced. The best method for grating ginger is with a rasp-style grater. (Our favorite is the **Microplane Premium Classic Zester/Grater**, $13.)

**Store It** A nub of ginger can be wrapped in plastic wrap and stored in the refrigerator for a few days, but for prolonged storage (after all, when do you ever go through the amount you bring home from the store?), we typically freeze ginger. We've also found you can submerge pieces of ginger in vodka. Fresh ginger contains enzymes that break down its starch and pectin over time. This mostly flavorless alcohol inhibits these enzymes, as does freezing, so ginger stored via either method will maintain its firm texture.

**Toss It (or Not)** Sometimes ginger can't be saved. Maybe you forgot about that nub in the refrigerator. After a few weeks, it will start to shrivel; at this point, the ginger flavor will not be very potent and it would be hard to know how much extra to use in the recipe.

Sometimes during refrigerator storage, ginger will take on a blue-gray color; this is because it becomes less acidic over time. Should you toss this pigmented ginger? While the flavor may be ever so slightly less piercing, blue ginger is perfectly safe to use and eat.

# APRICOT, VANILLA BEAN, AND CARDAMOM PIE

Serves 8

1    recipe Whole-Grain Double-Crust Pie Dough (page 320)

1    vanilla bean

1    cup (7 ounces) sugar

3    tablespoons cornstarch

1    teaspoon grated lemon zest plus 1 tablespoon juice

¼    teaspoon ground cardamom

¼    teaspoon table salt

2½    pounds apricots, halved, pitted, and cut into ½-inch-thick wedges

1    large egg, lightly beaten with 1 tablespoon water

**WHY THIS RECIPE WORKS** Apricots are a wonderful summertime treat: Their sweet flavor is balanced with an undertone of musky tartness that makes them taste like a sophisticated cousin to the peach. We wanted to create a pie that showcased this distinctive fruit. Cornstarch tightened our filling but didn't thicken it so much that we lost the meaty texture of the apricots. The unique flavor of apricots called for an equally unique flavor profile. Vanilla bean heightened the floral notes of the apricots and rounded out their flavor, while a touch of earthy cardamom highlighted the apricots' subtle tang. To make our pie stand out further, we paired it with a rye pie dough. The nuttiness of our whole-grain pie dough made with rye flour pairs well with the bright filling, but you can use any double-crust pie dough (see pages 320–327). Any of the top crusts on pages 134–142 will allow for enough evaporation to ensure a perfect slice. The method here produces a standard lattice top; for the cutout crust shown in the photo, see page 136.

---

**1** Roll 1 disk of dough into 12-inch circle on floured counter. Loosely roll dough around rolling pin and gently unroll it onto 9-inch pie plate, letting excess dough hang over edge. Ease dough into plate by gently lifting edge of dough with your hand while pressing into plate bottom with your other hand. Leave any dough that overhangs plate in place. Wrap dough-lined plate loosely in plastic wrap and refrigerate until firm, about 30 minutes.

**2** Roll other piece of dough into 13 by 10½-inch rectangle on floured counter, then transfer to parchment paper–lined rimmed baking sheet; cover loosely with plastic and refrigerate until firm, about 30 minutes.

**3** Using pizza wheel, fluted pastry wheel, or paring knife, trim ¼ inch dough from long sides of rectangle, then cut lengthwise into eight 1¼-inch-wide strips. Cover loosely with plastic and refrigerate until firm, about 30 minutes. Adjust oven rack to middle position and heat oven to 400 degrees.

**4** Cut vanilla bean in half lengthwise. Using tip of paring knife, scrape out seeds. Whisk vanilla bean seeds, sugar, cornstarch, lemon zest, cardamom, and salt together in large bowl. Stir in apricots and lemon juice and let sit for 15 minutes. Spread apricot mixture into dough-lined plate.

**5** Remove dough strips from refrigerator; if too stiff to be workable, let sit at room temperature until softened slightly but still very cold. Space 4 strips evenly across top of pie, parallel to counter edge. Fold back first and third strips almost completely. Lay 1 strip across pie, perpendicular to second and fourth strips, keeping it snug to folded edges of dough strips, then unfold first and third strips over top. Fold back second and fourth strips and add second perpendicular strip, keeping it snug to folded edge. Unfold second and fourth strips over top. Repeat weaving remaining strips evenly across pie, alternating between folding back first and third strips and second and fourth strips to create lattice pattern. Shift strips as needed so they are evenly spaced over top of pie. (If dough becomes too soft to work with, refrigerate pie and dough strips until firm.)

**6** Trim overhang to ½ inch beyond lip of plate. Pinch edges of bottom crust and lattice strips together firmly to seal. Tuck overhang under itself; folded edge should be flush with edge of plate. Crimp dough evenly around edge of plate. (If dough is very soft, refrigerate for 10 minutes before baking.) Brush surface with egg wash.

**7** Place pie on aluminum foil–lined rimmed baking sheet and bake until crust is light golden, 20 to 25 minutes. Reduce oven temperature to 350 degrees, rotate sheet, and continue to bake until juices are bubbling and crust is deep golden brown, 30 to 50 minutes longer. Let pie cool on wire rack until filling has set, about 4 hours. Serve.

# PECAN PEACH PIE

Serves 8

1 recipe Nut Double-Crust Pie Dough (page 320)

3 pounds ripe but firm peaches, peeled, halved, pitted, and cut into 1-inch pieces

½ cup (3½ ounces) plus 2 tablespoons sugar, divided

1 teaspoon grated lemon zest plus 1 tablespoon juice

⅛ teaspoon table salt

2 tablespoons low- or no-sugar-needed fruit pectin

¼ teaspoon ground cinnamon

Pinch ground nutmeg

1 tablespoon cornstarch

1 large egg, lightly beaten with 1 tablespoon water

**WHY THIS RECIPE WORKS** Eaten out of hand, a juicy peach is one of summer's greatest pleasures. Incorporate peaches into a pie, however, and what you get is a soupy mess. We needed to corral the moisture exuded by this juicy fruit. For most pies one of the following techniques does the trick: macerating or cooking the fruit, adding a thickener, or supplementing the fruit's natural pectin. We discovered that with peaches we had to use all three. First, we macerated the peaches to draw out its juices. Second, we used both cornstarch and pectin (the latter of which we cooked with some of the peach liquid) to bind our filling; this gave us a clear, silky filling without the gumminess or gelatinous texture that larger amounts of either one alone produced. If your peaches are too soft to withstand the pressure of a peeler, cut a shallow X in the bottom of the fruit, blanch them in a pot of simmering water for 15 seconds, and then shock them in a bowl of ice water before peeling. For fruit pectin we recommend both Sure-Jell for Less or No Sugar Needed Recipes and Ball RealFruit Low or No-Sugar Needed Pectin. We like the richness and Southern flair that our nut pie dough made with pecans contributes, but you can use any double-crust pie dough (see pages 320–327). Any of the top crusts on pages 134–142 will allow for enough evaporation to ensure a perfect slice. The method here produces a standard lattice top; for the free-from lattice shown in the photo, see page 138.

**1** Roll 1 disk of dough into 12-inch circle on floured counter. Loosely roll dough around rolling pin and gently unroll it onto 9-inch pie plate, letting excess dough hang over edge. Ease dough into plate by gently lifting edge of dough with your hand while pressing into plate bottom with your other hand. Leave any dough that overhangs plate in place. Wrap dough-lined plate loosely in plastic wrap and refrigerate until firm, about 30 minutes.

**2** Roll other piece of dough into 13 by 10½-inch rectangle on floured counter, then transfer to parchment paper–lined rimmed baking sheet; cover loosely with plastic and refrigerate until firm, about 30 minutes.

**3** Using pizza wheel, fluted pastry wheel, or paring knife, trim ¼ inch dough from long sides of rectangle, then cut lengthwise into eight 1¼-inch-wide strips. Cover loosely with plastic and refrigerate until firm, about 30 minutes. Adjust oven rack to middle position and heat oven to 400 degrees.

**4** Toss peaches, ½ cup sugar, lemon zest and juice, and salt in bowl and let sit for at least 30 minutes or up to 1 hour. Combine pectin, cinnamon, nutmeg, and remaining 2 tablespoons sugar in small bowl; set aside. Measure out 1 cup peach pieces and mash with fork to coarse paste. Drain remaining peach pieces through colander set in bowl, reserving ½ cup peach juice. Return peach pieces to now-empty bowl and toss with cornstarch.

**5** Whisk reserved peach juice and pectin mixture together in 12-inch skillet. Cook over medium heat, stirring occasionally, until thickened slightly and pectin is dissolved (liquid should become less cloudy), 3 to 5 minutes. Transfer peach-pectin mixture and peach paste to bowl with peach pieces and stir to combine. Spread peach mixture into dough-lined plate.

**6** Remove dough strips from refrigerator; if too stiff to be workable, let sit at room temperature until softened slightly but still very cold. Space 4 strips evenly across top of pie, parallel to counter edge. Fold back first and third strips almost completely. Lay 1 strip across pie, perpendicular to second and fourth strips, keeping it snug to folded edges of dough strips, then unfold first and third strips over top. Fold back second and fourth strips and add second perpendicular strip, keeping it snug to folded edge. Unfold second and fourth strips over top. Repeat weaving remaining strips evenly across pie, alternating between folding back first and third strips and second and fourth strips to create lattice pattern. Shift strips as needed so they are evenly spaced over top of pie. (If dough becomes too soft to work with, refrigerate pie and dough strips until firm.)

**7** Trim overhang to ½ inch beyond lip of plate. Pinch edges of bottom crust and lattice strips together firmly to seal. Tuck overhang under itself; folded edge should be flush with edge of plate. Crimp dough evenly around edge of plate. (If dough is very soft, refrigerate for 10 minutes before baking.) Brush surface with egg wash.

**8** Place pie on aluminum foil–lined rimmed baking sheet and bake until crust is light golden, 20 to 25 minutes. Reduce oven temperature to 350 degrees, rotate sheet, and continue to bake until juices are bubbling and crust is deep golden brown, 30 to 50 minutes longer. Let pie cool on wire rack until filling has set, about 4 hours. Serve.

## Making the Peach Filling

**1** Toss peaches, ½ cup sugar, lemon zest and juice, and salt in bowl; let sit for at least 30 minutes. Combine pectin, cinnamon, nutmeg, and remaining sugar in small bowl.

**2** Measure out 1 cup peach pieces and mash with fork to coarse paste.

**3** Drain remaining peach pieces through colander set in bowl, reserving ½ cup peach juice.

**4** Return peach pieces to now-empty bowl and toss with cornstarch.

**5** Whisk reserved peach juice and pectin mixture together in 12-inch skillet. Cook over medium heat, stirring occasionally, until thickened slightly and pectin is dissolved, 3 to 5 minutes.

**6** Transfer peach-pectin mixture and peach paste to bowl with peach pieces and stir to combine.

BLUEBERRY EARL GREY PIE

# BLUEBERRY EARL GREY PIE

Serves 8

1  recipe double-crust pie dough
   (see pages 320–327)
1  large egg, lightly beaten with
   1 tablespoon water

*filling*

30  ounces (6 cups) blueberries,
    divided
¾  cup (5¼ ounces) granulated
   sugar
2  tablespoons instant tapioca,
   ground
2  teaspoons Earl Grey tea leaves,
   ground
⅛  teaspoon grated orange zest
   Pinch table salt
1  Granny Smith apple, peeled
   and shredded
2  tablespoons unsalted butter,
   cut into ¼-inch pieces

*glaze*

2  tablespoons milk
1  teaspoon Earl Grey tea leaves,
   ground
1  cup (4 ounces) confectioners'
   sugar

**WHY THIS RECIPE WORKS**  The sweet, almost earthy flavor of blueberries is great on its own (see our foolproof Blueberry Pie on page 30), but those qualities also make them a perfect match for tea. We liked the citrusy, slightly musky flavor of Earl Grey paired with blueberry. Grinding it and adding it to the filling—along with just a touch of orange zest to reinforce its citrus notes—added a comforting, floral note to an already stellar pie. But we didn't stop there. We elevated this better-than-the-rest blueberry pie even further with a finishing drizzle of glaze that we made by steeping tea in some milk before whisking in the confectioners' sugar. The tea-toned stripes of glaze looked beautiful atop a burnished lattice crust. Use a spice grinder to grind the tea and tapioca. Use the large holes of a box grater to shred the apple. Any of the top crusts on pages 134–142 will allow for enough evaporation to ensure a perfect slice. The method here produces a standard lattice top. The strips in the photo are 2 inches wide.

1  Roll 1 disk of dough into 12-inch circle on floured counter. Loosely roll dough around rolling pin and gently unroll it into 9-inch pie plate, letting excess dough hang over edge. Ease dough into plate by gently lifting edge of dough with your hand while pressing into plate bottom with your other hand. Leave any dough that overhangs plate in place. Wrap dough-lined plate loosely in plastic wrap and refrigerate until firm, about 30 minutes.

2  Roll other piece of dough into 13 by 10½-inch rectangle on floured counter, then transfer to parchment paper–lined rimmed baking sheet; cover loosely with plastic and refrigerate until firm, about 30 minutes.

3  Using pizza wheel, fluted pastry wheel, or paring knife, trim ¼ inch dough from long sides of rectangle, then cut lengthwise into eight 1¼-inch-wide strips. Cover loosely with plastic and refrigerate until firm, about 30 minutes.

4  *For the filling*  Place 3 cups blueberries in medium saucepan and set over medium heat. Using potato masher, mash blueberries several times to release juice. Continue to cook, stirring often and mashing occasionally, until about half of blueberries have broken down and mixture is thickened and reduced to 1½ cups, about 8 minutes; let cool slightly. Adjust oven rack to middle position and heat oven to 400 degrees.

5  Whisk sugar, tapioca, tea, orange zest, and salt together in large bowl. Place shredded apple in clean dish towel and wring dry. Stir apple, remaining 3 cups blueberries, and cooked blueberries into sugar mixture. Spread mixture into dough-lined pie plate and scatter butter over top.

6  Remove dough strips from refrigerator; if too stiff to be workable, let sit at room temperature until softened slightly but still very cold. Space 4 strips evenly across top of pie, parallel to counter edge. Fold back first and third strips almost completely. Lay 1 strip across pie, perpendicular to second and fourth strips, keeping it snug to folded edges of dough strips, then unfold first and third strips over top. Fold back second and fourth strips and add second

perpendicular strip, keeping it snug to folded edge. Unfold second and fourth strips over top. Repeat weaving remaining strips evenly across pie, alternating between folding back first and third strips and second and fourth strips to create lattice pattern. Shift strips as needed so they are evenly spaced over top of pie. (If dough becomes too soft to work with, refrigerate pie and dough strips until firm.)

**7** Trim overhang to ½ inch beyond lip of plate. Pinch edges of bottom crust and lattice strips together firmly to seal. Tuck overhang under itself; folded edge should be flush with edge of plate. Crimp dough evenly around edge of plate. (If dough is very soft, refrigerate for 10 minutes before baking.) Brush surface with egg wash.

**8** Place pie on aluminum foil–lined rimmed baking sheet and bake until crust is light golden, 20 to 25 minutes. Reduce oven temperature to 350 degrees, rotate sheet, and continue to bake until juices are bubbling and crust is deep golden brown, 30 to 50 minutes longer. Let pie cool on wire rack until filling has set, about 4 hours.

**9** *For the glaze* Once pie is cooled, combine milk and tea in bowl. Microwave until steaming, about 30 seconds. Let cool completely, about 10 minutes. Whisk sugar into milk mixture until smooth; let sit until thick but pourable, about 10 minutes. Drizzle glaze attractively over top of cooled pie. Let glaze set for 10 minutes before serving.

## Glazing the Pie

**1** Combine milk and tea in bowl and microwave until steaming. Let cool completely, about 10 minutes.

**2** Whisk sugar into milk mixture until smooth.

**3** Let sit until thick but pourable, about 10 minutes.

**4** Drizzle glaze attractively over top of cooled pie. Let glaze set for 10 minutes before serving.

# CAPE GOOSEBERRY ELDERFLOWER MERINGUE PIE

**Serves 8`**

1 recipe single-crust pie dough
(see pages 316–326)

*filling*
¾ cup (5¼ ounces) sugar, divided

3 tablespoons low- or no-sugar-needed fruit pectin

2½ pounds Cape gooseberries, husks and stems removed, rinsed well, and dried, divided

1 teaspoon grated lemon zest plus ¼ cup juice (2 lemons)

¼ teaspoon table salt

*meringue*
⅓ cup water

2½ teaspoons cornstarch

3 large egg whites

½ teaspoon vanilla extract

¼ teaspoon cream of tartar

⅓ cup (2⅓ ounces) sugar

2½ tablespoons elderflower liqueur (optional)

**WHY THIS RECIPE WORKS** Cape gooseberries may be a mystery to you—after all, they're hiding in a papery skin when you buy them. And you might know them as husk cherries depending on where in the country you live, but this relative of the tomatillo (no, this pie doesn't taste anything like salsa) is a fantastic fruit, one which tastes slightly tropical with a bit of acidity and notes of pine. Like tomatillos, they're filled with seeds, which might seem troublesome for a pie, but fear not: Once these berries cook, their seeds become so soft they're almost imperceptible. Their great flavor is not the only reason they're a perfect pie filling: They're also very high in pectin so they thicken the filling nicely. But as with most pies, natural pectin wasn't quite enough on its own, so we added some additional pectin for a glossy filling that could support a unique topping—elderflower meringue—without spilling out upon slicing. The crown of meringue brought out the floral qualities of the fruit and provided a delicate counterpoint to their acidity. For fruit pectin, we recommend both Sure-Jell for Less or No Sugar Needed Recipes and Ball RealFruit Low or No-Sugar Needed Pectin. Look for berries that are mostly golden (some underripe fruit will add a bit of tartness), with dry, clean husks.

---

**1** Roll dough into 12-inch circle on floured counter. Loosely roll dough around rolling pin and gently unroll it onto 9-inch pie plate, letting excess dough hang over edge. Ease dough into plate by gently lifting edge of dough with your hand while pressing into plate bottom with your other hand.

**2** Trim overhang to ½ inch beyond lip of plate. Tuck overhang under itself; folded edge should be flush with edge of plate. Crimp dough evenly around edge of plate. Wrap dough-lined plate loosely in plastic wrap and refrigerate until firm, about 30 minutes. Adjust oven rack to middle position and heat oven to 350 degrees.

**3** Line chilled pie shell with double layer of aluminum foil, covering edges to prevent burning, and fill with pie weights. Bake on foil-lined rimmed baking sheet until edges are set and just beginning to turn golden, 25 to 30 minutes, rotating sheet halfway through baking. Remove foil and weights and transfer sheet to wire rack. (Crust must still be warm when filling is added.)

**4** *For the filling* Meanwhile, whisk ¼ cup sugar and pectin together in bowl; set aside. Bring 2 pounds gooseberries, lemon zest and juice, salt, and remaining ½ cup sugar to boil in large saucepan over medium-high heat. Off heat, using potato masher, coarsely mash fruit, leaving some berries intact. Return to boil over medium-high heat and cook until slightly thickened, about 20 minutes, stirring often.

**5** Whisk pectin mixture and remaining 8 ounces gooseberries into saucepan. Return to boil and cook for 1 minute, whisking constantly. With pie still on sheet, transfer filling to warm crust, spreading into even layer with rubber spatula. Bake until edge of crust is golden, 20 to 25 minutes.

**6** *For the meringue* While pie bakes, bring water and cornstarch to simmer in small saucepan over medium-high heat and cook, whisking occasionally, until thickened and translucent, 1 to 2 minutes. Remove from heat and let cool slightly.

**7** Using stand mixer fitted with whisk attachment, whip egg whites, vanilla, and cream of tartar on medium-low speed until foamy, about 1 minute. Increase speed to medium-high and beat in sugar, 1 tablespoon at a time, until incorporated and mixture forms soft, billowy mounds. Add cornstarch mixture and elderflower liqueur, if using, 1 tablespoon at a time, and continue to beat to glossy, stiff peaks, 2 to 3 minutes.

**8** While pie is still hot, use rubber spatula to distribute meringue attractively over top of filling, spreading meringue so it touches crust (this will prevent the meringue from shrinking). (See page 21.) Return pie to oven and bake until meringue is light golden brown, about 20 minutes. Let pie cool on wire rack until filling has set, about 4 hours. Serve.

# RED CURRANT AND FIG PIE

Serves 8

1   recipe double-crust pie dough (see pages 320–327)

¾   cup (5¼ ounces) sugar

2   tablespoons instant tapioca, ground

1   teaspoon grated orange zest plus 2 tablespoons juice

⅛   teaspoon table salt

1½   pounds fresh red currants, divided

1   pound fresh figs, stemmed and cut into ¼-inch wedges

1   large egg, lightly beaten with 1 tablespoon water

**WHY THIS RECIPE WORKS** Red currants have a clear tartness and a flavor more complex than that of other berries. Although their season at the farmers' market is short, we wanted to capture their distinctive flavor in a special pie. For a thickened, jammy filling (and to make sure it wasn't overly seedy or peel-filled) we cooked down some of the berries and strained them through a fine-mesh strainer; we stirred the remaining berries in whole. Some orange zest and juice complemented their flavor and ensured it remained bright after cooking. But we thought the berries' intense flavor could use some taming and their texture some breaking up with the addition of another fruit. Fresh figs are in season at the same time and added a meatiness and caramel sweetness that made this filling exceptionally unique. Use a spice grinder to grind the tapioca. Any of the top crusts on pages 134–142 will allow for enough evaporation to ensure a perfect slice. The method here produces a standard lattice top; for the cutout crust shown in the photo, see page 136.

1  Roll 1 disk of dough into 12-inch circle on floured counter. Loosely roll dough around rolling pin and gently unroll it into 9-inch pie plate, letting excess dough hang over edge. Ease dough into plate by gently lifting edge of dough with your hand while pressing into plate bottom with your other hand. Leave any dough that overhangs plate in place. Wrap dough-lined plate loosely in plastic wrap and refrigerate until firm, about 30 minutes.

2  Roll other piece of dough into 13 by 10½-inch rectangle on floured counter, then transfer to parchment paper–lined rimmed baking sheet; cover loosely with plastic and refrigerate until firm, about 30 minutes.

3  Using pizza wheel, fluted pastry wheel, or paring knife, trim ¼ inch dough from long sides of rectangle, then cut lengthwise into eight 1¼-inch-wide strips. Cover loosely with plastic and refrigerate until firm, about 30 minutes. Adjust oven rack to middle position and heat oven to 400 degrees.

4  Whisk sugar, tapioca, orange zest, and salt together in large bowl; set aside. Bring 1 pound currants to simmer in large saucepan over medium-high heat. Off heat, coarsely mash currants with potato masher. Return to simmer over medium-high heat and cook until currants are softened, about 3 minutes.

5  Strain currants through fine-mesh strainer set over bowl with sugar mixture, pressing firmly on solids to extract as much liquid and pulp as possible; discard solids. Stir in figs, orange juice, and remaining 8 ounces currants and let sit for 15 minutes. Spread currant mixture into dough-lined plate.

**6** Remove dough strips from refrigerator; if too stiff to be workable, let sit at room temperature until softened slightly but still very cold. Space 4 strips evenly across top of pie, parallel to counter edge. Fold back first and third strips almost completely. Lay 1 strip across pie, perpendicular to second and fourth strips, keeping it snug to folded edges of dough strips, then unfold first and third strips over top. Fold back second and fourth strips and add second perpendicular strip, keeping it snug to folded edge. Unfold second and fourth strips over top. Repeat weaving remaining strips evenly across pie, alternating between folding back first and third strips and second and fourth strips to create lattice pattern. Shift strips as needed so they are evenly spaced over top of pie. (If dough becomes too soft to work with, refrigerate pie and dough strips until firm.)

**7** Trim overhang to ½ inch beyond lip of plate. Pinch edges of bottom crust and lattice strips together firmly to seal. Tuck overhang under itself; folded edge should be flush with edge of plate. Crimp dough evenly around edge of plate. (If dough is very soft, refrigerate for 10 minutes before baking.) Brush surface with egg wash.

**8** Place pie on aluminum foil–lined rimmed baking sheet and bake until crust is light golden, 20 to 25 minutes. Reduce oven temperature to 350 degrees, rotate sheet, and continue to bake until juices are bubbling and crust is deep golden brown, 30 to 50 minutes longer. Let pie cool on wire rack until filling has set, about 6 hours. Serve.

# STRAWBERRY-RHUBARB PIE

Serves 8

1    recipe double-crust pie dough (see pages 320–327)

2    pounds rhubarb, trimmed and cut into ½-inch pieces (7 cups)

1¼   cups (8¾ ounces) sugar plus 3 tablespoons, divided

1    pound strawberries, hulled, halved if less than 1 inch, quartered if more than 1 inch (3 to 4 cups)

3    tablespoons instant tapioca, ground

**WHY THIS RECIPE WORKS** Strawberries and rhubarb aren't the perfect couple you might think they are. The trouble lies not in their differences, but in a similarity: Both are loaded with water. During baking, all this water heats up and causes the rhubarb to blow out, releasing its moisture into the filling and collapsing into mush, while the strawberries become bloated. To fix these problems, we microwaved the rhubarb with sugar to draw out some liquid and then stirred in a portion of the strawberries into the warm liquid to soften; we then cooked the liquid down with the remaining strawberries to make a jam that we folded into the filling. This allowed us to use less thickener and more fruit than most pies for an intense filling that was chunky and softly gelled. Brushing the dough with water and sprinkling it with a generous amount of sugar gave it a crackly finish.

1   Roll 1 disk of dough into 12-inch circle on floured counter. Loosely roll dough around rolling pin and gently unroll it onto 9-inch pie plate, letting excess dough hang over edge. Ease dough into plate by gently lifting edge of dough with your hand while pressing into plate bottom with your other hand. Leave any dough that overhangs plate in place. Wrap dough-lined plate loosely in plastic wrap and refrigerate until firm, about 30 minutes. Roll other disk of dough into 12-inch circle on floured counter, then transfer to parchment paper–lined rimmed baking sheet; cover loosely with plastic and refrigerate until firm, about 30 minutes.

2   While dough chills, combine rhubarb and 1¼ cups sugar in bowl and microwave for 1½ minutes. Stir and continue to microwave until sugar is mostly dissolved, about 1 minute longer. Stir in 1 cup strawberries and set aside for 30 minutes, stirring once halfway through. Drain rhubarb mixture in fine-mesh strainer set over large saucepan. Return drained rhubarb mixture to bowl; set aside. Add remaining strawberries to rhubarb liquid and cook over medium-high heat until strawberries are very soft and mixture is reduced to 1½ cups, 10 to 15 minutes. Mash berries with fork (mixture does not have to be smooth). Add strawberry mixture and tapioca to drained rhubarb mixture and stir to combine; set aside.

3   Adjust oven rack to lowest position and heat oven to 425 degrees. Spread filling into dough-lined plate. Loosely roll remaining dough round around rolling pin and gently unroll it onto filling. Trim overhang to ½ inch beyond lip of plate. Pinch edges of top and bottom crusts firmly together. Tuck overhang under itself; folded edge should be flush with edge of plate. Crimp dough evenly around edge of plate. Cut eight 2-inch slits in top of dough. Brush surface thoroughly with water and sprinkle with remaining 3 tablespoons sugar.

4   Place pie on aluminum foil–lined rimmed baking sheet and bake until crust is set and begins to brown, about 25 minutes, Rotate pie and reduce oven temperature to 375 degrees; continue to bake until crust is deep golden brown and filling is bubbling, 30 to 40 minutes longer. Let pie cool on wire rack until filling has set, about 4 hours. Serve.

# CHAI BLACKBERRY PIE

Serves 8

1 recipe double-crust pie dough (see pages 320–327)

1 cup (7 ounces) sugar

5 tablespoons (1¼ ounces) cornstarch

1 teaspoon grated lemon zest plus 2 tablespoons juice

¼ teaspoon table salt

¼ teaspoon ground cardamom

¼ teaspoon ground cinnamon

⅛ teaspoon ground cloves

⅛ teaspoon ground ginger

Pinch pepper

1¾ pounds (5⅔ cups) blackberries

1 large egg, lightly beaten with 1 tablespoon water

**WHY THIS RECIPE WORKS** Blackberries are big, bold berries, and they boast a musky sweetness and some tartness that allow them to stand up to big flavors. Warm spices aren't just for fall fruits, and we loved the idea of pairing them with blackberries. We decided to spice up our blackberries with classic chai spices: cardamom, cinnamon, clove, and ginger, plus a pinch of black pepper to accentuate all the others. Some lemon zest and juice added welcome brightness. Any of the top crusts on pages 134–142 will allow for enough evaporation to ensure a perfect slice. The method here produces a standard lattice top; for the free-form lattice shown in the photo, see page 138.

---

**1** Roll 1 disk of dough into 12-inch circle on floured counter. Loosely roll dough around rolling pin and gently unroll it into 9-inch pie plate, letting excess dough hang over edge. Ease dough into plate by gently lifting edge of dough with your hand while pressing into plate bottom with your other hand. Leave any dough that overhangs plate in place. Wrap dough-lined plate loosely in plastic wrap and refrigerate until firm, about 30 minutes.

**2** Roll other piece of dough into 13 by 10½-inch rectangle on floured counter, then transfer to parchment paper–lined rimmed baking sheet; cover loosely with plastic and refrigerate until firm, about 30 minutes.

**3** Using pizza wheel, fluted pastry wheel, or paring knife, trim ¼ inch dough from long sides of rectangle, then cut lengthwise into eight 1¼-inch-wide strips. Cover loosely with plastic and refrigerate until firm, about 30 minutes. Adjust oven rack to middle position and heat oven to 400 degrees.

**4** Whisk sugar, cornstarch, lemon zest, salt, cardamom, cinnamon, cloves, ginger, and pepper together in large bowl. Stir in blackberries and lemon juice and let sit for 15 minutes. Spread blackberry mixture into dough-lined plate.

**5** Remove dough strips from refrigerator; if too stiff to be workable, let sit at room temperature until softened slightly but still very cold. Space 4 strips evenly across top of pie, parallel to counter edge. Fold back first and third strips almost completely. Lay 1 strip across pie, perpendicular to second and fourth strips, keeping it snug to folded edges of dough strips, then unfold first and third strips over top. Fold back second and fourth strips and add second perpendicular strip, keeping it snug to folded edge. Unfold second and fourth strips over top. Repeat weaving remaining strips evenly across pie, alternating between folding back first and third strips and second and fourth strips to create lattice pattern. Shift strips as needed so they are evenly spaced over top of pie. (If dough becomes too soft to work with, refrigerate pie and dough strips until firm.)

**6** Trim overhang to ½ inch beyond lip of plate. Pinch edges of bottom crust and lattice strips together firmly to seal. Tuck overhang under itself; folded edge should be flush with edge of plate. Crimp dough evenly around edge of plate. (If dough is very soft, refrigerate for 10 minutes before baking.) Brush surface with egg wash.

**7** Place pie on aluminum foil–lined rimmed baking sheet and bake until crust is light golden, 20 to 25 minutes. Reduce oven temperature to 350 degrees, rotate sheet, and continue to bake until juices are bubbling and crust is deep golden brown, 30 to 50 minutes longer. Let pie cool on wire rack until filling has set, about 4 hours. Serve.

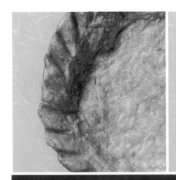

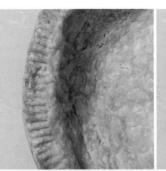

# *crust edge* DESIGNS

The filling is on full display in a single-crust pie, but that doesn't mean you shouldn't have fun with the crust. Surrounding the filling with a decorative edge results in a very put-together pie. We've written every single-crust pie recipe in this book with simple language for the most classic crimping style, but we encourage you to use these guides and choose one of our favorite techniques to finish your crust edges with flair. With a photo and description explaining every step, your pie is guaranteed to come out of the oven looking as good as it did when it went in. If you find your thumbs, fork, pen, or spoon sticking to the dough, coat them with flour before proceeding.

## CLASSIC CRIMPING

Master the classic crimp, and your pies will always look homemade yet neat and professional. We default to smaller crimps, but you can make more rustic-looking, wider scallops by using your knuckle or thumb in place of your index finger. See an example of this on our Peanut Butter and Concord Grape Pie (page 94).

### Crimping with Your Fingers

**1** Rest your thumb and index finger on 1 side of dough edge. Press dough in between thumb and index finger using your other index finger.

**2** Shift thumb and index finger directly next to crimp and repeat pressing dough. Repeat crimping evenly around edge of pie.

# FORK CRIMPING

We love this edge sealing style because it's very simple to do, but there's also a number of unexpected ways you can use a fork. Try alternating directions to mimic our Red Currant and Fig Pie (page 124) or overlapping indentations like in our Buttermilk Pie (page 258).

## Crimping with a Fork

**1** Press tines of fork into edge of dough, using even and firm pressure, to flatten dough against rim of pie plate.

**2** Repeat pressing fork into dough evenly around edge of pie.

# SCALLOPED SPOON EDGE

Created with a spoon, this scalloped edge looks superfestive and takes little effort to complete. We prefer to use a teaspoon for this edging, but you can use any size spoon— or mix and match.

## Making a Scalloped Edge

**1** Invert spoon so rounded side faces up. Line up tip of spoon with inside edge of lip of plate with spoon handle facing out. Press spoon firmly into dough to leave behind indentation.

**2** Shift spoon so that tip is halfway between inside and outside edge of lip of plate with spoon handle facing out and press firmly into dough to leave behind second indentation.

**3** Repeat pressing spoon into dough evenly around edge of pie.

# ROPE EDGE

This twisted-looking edge can make pies look elegant, elevated, and even a bit nautical. Many techniques are overly complicated and require twisting with your fingers. We got a clean look just by pressing in a pen. You can make an even easier look-alike by scoring the edge of the pie with the flat edge of a butter knife (see our Strawberry-Rhubarb Pie on page 127). Chill the dough for 10 minutes before shaping the edge so you won't flatten it too much; if you're moving slowly, return the pie to the refrigerator to chill halfway through crimping.

## Making a Rope Edge

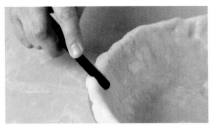

**1** Using ¼-inch-wide pen, firmly press body of pen at 45-degree angle to edge of plate into chilled dough.

**2** Repeat pressing pen into dough evenly around edge of pie, leaving ½ inch between each mark.

# CUTOUT EDGE

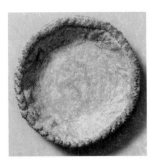

This edge gives the baker an opportunity to tell the story of a pie. Is it a holiday pie? Maybe it's for a birthday? Whatever the occasion, there's likely a cookie cutter to match. Avoid cutouts larger than 1 inch in diameter as they slump over the edge during baking. Attaching the cutouts with water prevents them from falling into the pie during baking; you also need to press them firmly into the edge. Here we use the scraps from a single-crust recipe. For more freedom to decorate, make a double-crust recipe, as a single-crust may not yield enough for more intricate edges. Roll the second disk to a 12-inch diameter and use it for the cutouts.

## Making a Cutout Edge

**1** Using small cookie cutters no larger than 1 inch wide, cut as many shapes as desired. Transfer to parchment paper–lined rimmed baking sheet, cover loosely with plastic wrap, and refrigerate for 30 minutes.

**2** Brush edge of dough with water.

**3** Attach cutouts by pressing firmly into edge. Repeat to cover edge of dough, overlapping as desired.

# BRAIDED EDGE

Adding a braided edge to your pie shows you went the extra mile. Braid the strips tightly for the neatest, narrowest braids, and refrigerate the dough if it starts to soften. This edge requires a double-crust pie dough; roll the piece for the braid into a 13 by 11-inch rectangle and then trim to a 13 by 10½-inch rectangle. These instructions are for a single-crust pie; if you're adding a braided edge to a double-crust pie (you will need more dough), as in our Apricot, Vanilla Bean, and Cardamom Pie (page 114), press the top and bottom crust firmly together before applying the braids to seal the pie shut and ensure the edge won't be too thick.

## Making a Braided Edge

**1** Cut 13 by 10½-inch dough rectangle into nine 13-inch-long by ½-inch-wide strips. (Save remaining dough for another use.) Chill for 30 minutes.

**2** Working with 3 strips at a time (and refrigerating remaining dough strips while you work), arrange side by side on counter, perpendicular to counter edge, then firmly pinch tops of strips together to seal.

**3** Lift and place right dough strip over center dough strip as close to top as possible. Lift and place left dough strip over center dough strip as close to top as possible. Repeat braiding dough strips tightly until you reach bottom of braid.

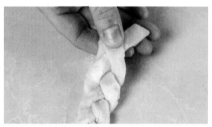

**4** Firmly pinch ends of strips together to secure braid. Return to sheet and chill while braiding remaining strips. (You should have total of 3 braids.)

**5** Brush edge of dough with water.

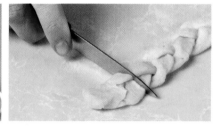

**6** Working with 1 braid at a time, trim and discard pinched ends of braids.

**7** Gently transfer braid to edge of dough, pressing on braid firmly to secure.

**8** Repeat with remaining braids, trimming and overlapping edges of braids as needed.

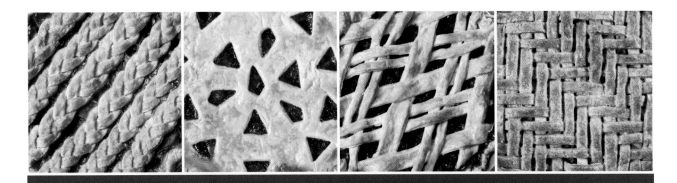

# *top crust*
# DESIGNS

Each double-crust pie in this chapter is an opportunity to show off a different style of top crust. A lattice or cutout crust allows the proper amount of moisture to evaporate from a fruit pie for the perfect fruit-to-juice ratio. And they're simply beautiful, with the bubbly fruit peeking through buttery, golden strips and shapes of crust. We've written every double-crust recipe in this chapter with the basic lattice crust technique, but we encourage you to use these guides and choose one of your favorite designs. With a photo and description explaining every step, not only will you understand how to weave without fear, but you're guaranteed to get pies that come out of the oven looking as good as they did when they went in.

## BASIC LATTICE

This is the classic lattice crust treatment that creates a woven window to the fruit below and allows for moisture evaporation. You can cut your dough strips wider or smaller than indicated here for a tighter (see page 119) or looser (see page 118) look. The wider the dough strips, the less weaving you'll need to do; if you're in a rush or are a beginner, try 2-inch-wide dough strips. For the neatest lattice, take care when cutting the dough rectangle; mark the top and bottom edges of the dough at 1¼-inch intervals (or however wide you'd like your strips) using a bench scraper or a paring knife and then cut along the edge of a ruler, connecting corresponding top and bottom marks.

## Making a Basic Lattice

**1** Cut 13 by 10-inch dough rectangle into eight 13-inch-long by 1¼-inch-wide strips. Chill for 30 minutes.

**2** Fill chilled dough-lined pie plate. Space 4 strips evenly across top of pie, parallel to counter edge.

**3** Fold back first and third strips almost completely.

**4** Lay 1 strip across pie, perpendicular to second and fourth strips, keeping it snug to folded edges of dough strips.

**5** Unfold first and third strips over top of perpendicular dough strip.

**6** Fold back second and fourth strips and add second perpendicular strip, keeping it snug to folded edge. Unfold second and fourth strips over top.

**7** Repeat weaving remaining strips evenly across pie, alternating between folding back first and third strips and second and forth strips to create lattice pattern.

**8** Trim overhang to ½ inch beyond lip of plate, then pinch edges of bottom crust and lattice strips together firmly to seal. Tuck overhang under itself.

**9** Crimp dough evenly around edge of plate.

# CUTOUT CRUST

You can find cutouts in our Blueberry Pie (page 30) top crust, but this method allows you to take the concept further for more intricate designs. For the neatest cutout top crust, we've found it best to roll out your top crust as normal and then use a pie plate as a guide to make an even circle to place on top of the pie. You can use any shape cookie cutter to produce whatever design you can dream up. Be sure to leave at least ¾ inch between each cutout and to leave a 1-inch border around the edge or you may end up with tearing. This design works best with a fruit filling that doesn't need to be mounded. You can save the dough from the cutouts and add them to the top crust for another layer of design; brush the bottom of each cutout with water and press gently but firmly to seal them to the dough before chilling.

## Making a Cutout Crust

**1** Roll 1 disk of dough into 12-inch circle on floured counter. Invert 9-inch pie plate over center of dough round and run paring knife around edge to cut out circle; transfer circle to parchment paper–lined rimmed baking sheet and chill for 30 minutes.

**2** Use cookie cutter to cut out shapes from chilled crust in attractive design, leaving 1-inch border around edge and at least ¾ inch between each cutout. Chill dough round for 30 minutes.

**3** Fill chilled dough-lined plate. Brush edges of dough with water, then place chilled top crust over top of filling.

**4** Using index and middle fingers or palm of hand, pinch bottom and top crusts firmly together around edge of plate to seal.

**5** Tuck overhang under itself; folded edge should be flush with edge of plate. Crimp dough evenly around edge of plate.

# BRAIDED STRIPS

This showstopping alternative to a top crust shows off your pie dough skills while also showing off plenty of the pie filling. You can vary the width of the dough strips to create fewer thicker braids or more skinnier braids, or alternate braid widths. This technique can take some time, so be sure to keep dough strips you're not working with in the refrigerator. We prefer the look of tightly braided dough strips as they retain their shape better during baking.

### Making a Braided Crust

**1** Cut 13 by 10-inch dough rectangle into eighteen 13-inch-long by ½-inch-wide strips. Chill for 30 minutes.

**2** Working with 3 strips at a time (and refrigerating remaining dough strips while you work), arrange side by side on counter, perpendicular to counter edge, then firmly pinch tops of strips together to seal.

**3** Lift and place right dough strip over center dough strip as close to top as possible. Lift and place left dough strip over center dough strip as close to top as possible. Repeat braiding dough strips tightly until you reach bottom of braid.

**4** Firmly pinch ends of strips together to secure braid. Return to sheet and chill while braiding remaining strips. (You should have a total of 6 braids.)

**5** Fill chilled dough-lined pie plate. Arrange chilled braids evenly over top of filling, then trim overhang to ½ inch beyond lip of plate.

**6** Pinch braids and bottom crust together firmly to seal. Tuck overhang under itself; folded edge should be flush with edge of plate. Crimp dough evenly around edge of plate.

# FREE-FORM LATTICE

Make a masterpiece with this customizable top crust. The instructions below will produce a pie similar to the design of our Pecan Peach Pie (page 116), but you can change up the design in a number of ways. Try using a combination of wide and narrow dough strips, placing two narrow strips side by side to act as one larger strip, using fluted and straight cutting edges, or building your lattice on a diagonal instead of the standard perpendicular setup (as below); or use a combination of braids and dough strips with different cutting styles (see our Chai Blackberry Pie on page 128 for more inspiration).

## Making a Free-Form Lattice

**1** Cut 13 by 10-inch dough rectangle into six 13-inch-long by 1-inch-wide strips and eight 13-inch-long by ½-inch-wide strips. Chill for 30 minutes.

**2** Fill chilled dough-lined plate. Treating 2 thin strips as 1 double strip and alternating between 1 single and 1 double strip, arrange 3 single strips and 2 double strips over top of filling. Rotate plate so strips are parallel to counter edge.

**3** Fold back first and third dough strips almost completely from right to left. Lay one single strip positioned as close to edge of plate and folded edges of single strips as possible, and at 45-degree angle to second strip. Unfold first and third strips over top.

**4** Fold back both double strips from right to left until they reach diagonal strip (strips will not be folded back to the same point). Lay 1 double strip across pie at 45 degree angle to first and third strips but parallel to first diagonal strip. Unfold double strips over top.

**5** Fold back first, third, and fifth dough strips and repeat weaving pattern with remaining dough strips, alternating between single and double strips.

**6** Trim overhang to ½ inch beyond lip of plate, then pinch bottom crust and lattice strips together firmly to seal. Tuck overhang under itself; folded edge should be flush with edge of plate. Crimp dough evenly around edge of plate.

# FREE-FORM SHAPES

This elegant alternative to a woven lattice is deceptively simple, and there's a lot of room for artistic imagination. You can cut whatever shapes you like from the dough; we like the dramatic angular look of long triangles. It's important to anchor at least one side of each shape to the dough, and not to overlap more than two shapes, or the top crust will bake up doughy. Unlike the other decorative pie tops, this design doesn't require trimming the dough rectangle before proceeding with the steps. The instructions below will produce a pie design similar to our Mulled Wine Quince Pie (page 108), but you can use whatever shapes you can think of, or you can even use a cookie cutter (see Pear-Butterscotch Slab Pie on page 206).

## Making Free-Form Shapes

**1** Cut 13 by 10½-inch dough rectangle into two 10½-inch-long by ½-inch-wide triangles, two 10½-inch-long by 1-inch-wide triangles, and two 10½-inch-long by 3-inch-wide triangles. Chill for 30 minutes.

**2** Fill chilled dough-lined pie plate. Arrange chilled dough triangles decoratively over top of filling, with 1 end of each triangle placed at least ½ inch beyond edge of plate and overlapping each triangle no more than once.

**3** Trim overhang to ½ inch beyond lip of plate, then pinch edges of bottom crust and triangles together firmly to seal.

**4** Tuck overhang under itself; folded edge should be flush with edge of plate. Crimp dough evenly around edge of plate.

# HERRINGBONE LATTICE CRUST

This beautiful herringbone lattice may seem dizzying, but accomplishing it isn't difficult once you understand the pattern; it's all a matter of working in threes. This can be achieved with wider or smaller dough strips, but wider strips will result in a less detailed pattern. You can leave space between the lattice to show off the filling. (Note that you won't need as many strips if you space them farther apart.) This technique takes time, so be sure to keep dough strips you're not working with in the refrigerator and return the pie and strips to the refrigerator as needed. Readjust the strips as needed. Rolling the dough to a larger 16½ by 10-inch rectangle (and then trimming ¼ inch off the short sides) ensures the dough wil be thin enough to bake up crisp despite all the overlapping.

---

## Making a Herringbone Lattice

**1** Cut 16 by 10-inch dough rectangle into thirty-two 10-inch-long by ½-inch wide strips. Chill for 30 minutes.

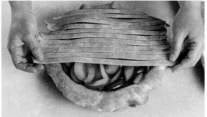

**2** Fill chilled dough-lined plate. Space 16 strips across top of pie, leaving no space in between each strip, parallel to counter edge.

**3** Starting with dough strip farthest from counter edge, fold back first strip halfway from right to left.

**4** Skip next 3 strips, then fold back following 3 strips halfway from right to left. (Continue alternating between skipping 3 strips and folding back 3 strips until you reach bottom of pie.)

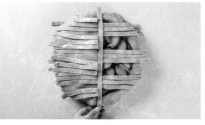

**5** Lay 1 strip across pie, perpendicular to unfolded dough strips, keeping it snug to edge of folded dough strips.

**6** Unfold dough strips over top of perpendicular strip.

**7** Starting from top, fold back top 2 strips halfway from right to left. Repeat skipping and folding back every 3 dough strips until you reach bottom of pie. Add perpendicular strip and unfold dough strips over top.

**8** Starting from top, fold back top 3 strips. Repeat skipping and folding back every 3 dough strips until you reach bottom of pie. Add perpendicular strip and unfold dough strips over top.

**9** Starting from top, skip first strip. Fold back next 3 strips, then skip following 3 strips. Repeat folding back and skipping every 3 dough strips until you reach bottom of pie. Add perpendicular strip and unfold dough strips over top.

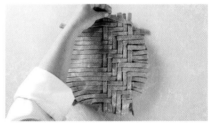

**10** Starting from top, skip top 2 strips. Repeat folding back and skipping every 3 dough strips until you reach bottom of pie. Add perpendicular strip and unfold dough strips over top.

**11** Starting from top, skip top 3 strips. Repeat folding back and skipping every 3 dough strips until you reach bottom of pie. Add perpendicular strip and unfold dough strips over top.

**12** Starting from top, fold back top strip. Repeat skipping and folding back every 3 dough strips until you reach bottom of pie. Add perpendicular strip and unfold dough strips over top.

**13** Starting from top, fold back top 2 strips. Repeat skipping and folding back every 3 dough strips until you reach bottom of pie. Add perpendicular strip and unfold dough strips over top. (This perpendicular strip should sit on the far right edge of pie.)

**14** Starting from top of pie, skip top 3 strips then fold back following 3 strips from left to right. Repeat skipping and folding every 3 dough strips until you reach bottom of pie. Add perpendicular strip and unfold dough strips over top.

**15** Starting from top, skip top 2 strips. Repeat folding back and skipping every 3 dough strips until you reach bottom of pie. Add perpendicular strip and unfold dough strips over top.

**16** Starting from top, skip first strip. Repeat folding back and skipping every 3 dough strips until you reach bottom of pie. Add perpendicular strip and unfold dough strips over top.

**17** Starting from top, fold back top 3 strips. Repeat skipping and folding back every 3 dough strips until you reach bottom of pie. Add perpendicular strip and unfold dough strips over top.

**18** Starting from top, fold back top 2 strips. Repeat skipping and folding back every 3 dough strips until you reach bottom of pie. Add perpendicular strip and unfold dough strips over top.

**19** Starting from top, fold back top strip. Repeat skipping and folding back every 3 dough strips until you reach bottom of the pie. Add perpendicular strip and dough strips over top.

**20** Starting from top, skip top 3 strips. Repeat folding back and skipping every 3 dough strips until you reach bottom of pie. Add perpendicular strip and unfold dough strips over top.

**21** Starting from top, skip top 2 strips. Repeat folding back and skipping every 3 dough strips until you reach bottom of pie. Add perpendicular strip and unfold dough strips over top. (This perpendicular strip should sit on far left edge of pie.)

**22** Pinch bottom crust and lattice strips together firmly to seal. Using paring knife, trim any excess dough flush to edge of plate. Brush surface with egg wash before baking.

# IMPORTANT TIPS FOR DECORATING WITH DOUGH

**The refrigerator is your best friend.** There are chilling steps built into every crust design, from a traditional double crust to the most intricate of lattice-woven tops. But you can also turn to the refrigerator whenever you need or want to. Dough should be firm but malleable during these decorating processes: You don't want butter to melt as your dough will be misshapen, the design won't stay, and overhandled dough won't be flaky once baked. However, you also don't want dough strips to be too cold. You need to do a lot of folding and too-cold dough may crack, ruining your design. The more pie you bake, the easier it will be to get a feel for the perfect dough temperature and texture.

**Stay put.** The easiest way to track your progress on any design is for you, the pie maker, to stay in one place and to instead move the pie plate as needed. When crimping an edge, rotate the pie plate as you go; if you try to move, the crimps will come out crooked. When weaving lattice strips, don't move around the counter; if you stay in the same position vis-à-vis the pie, you'll remember which strips one and three are versus two and four.

**Flour as needed.** If dough sticks to your fingers (or to any implement) while you're working, dip them in a little flour so you can continue working with your hands.

**Save your scraps.** We have included very specific designs here, but once you understand how dough works, you can play with it as you like. Any extra dough can be used to make further flourishes. Check out the dough bow on our Chai Blackberry Pie (page 128) or the rosettes on our Crab Apple Rose Pie (page 106). You can also bake your scrap dough (much like individual cookies) and place shapes on the surface of cooled custard pies like our Butternut Squash Pie with Browned Butter and Sage (page 102). While your pie cools, brush dough cutouts with egg wash and bake them on a parchment paper–lined rimmed baking sheet in a 350-degree oven until they're deep golden brown, 8 to 10 minutes. Have fun! Those scraps also come in handy when accidents happen. Patch dough cracks and breaks with these bits.

**Use an egg wash.** We don't always use egg wash (for more on wash options, see page 18), but we like it when applying more intricate edging or designs as it highlights those designs, as with the spoon edge or the free-form shapes.

**Roll out a larger rectangle.** We always roll out our dough to a rectangle size slightly larger than what we need (usually that means a 13 by 10½-inch rectangle) and then trim ¼ inch from the long sides so that our strips are straight and neat.

# *elegant* TARTS

# FRESH FRUIT TART

**Serves 8**

| | |
|---|---|
| 1 | recipe tart dough (see pages 328–331) |
| ⅓ | cup (2 ounces) white baking chips |
| ¼ | cup heavy cream |
| 1 | teaspoon grated lime zest plus 2 tablespoons juice |
| | Pinch table salt |
| 6 | ounces (¾ cup) mascarpone cheese, room temperature |
| 2 | ripe peaches, peeled |
| 20 | ounces (4 cups) blackberries, blueberries, and raspberries |
| ⅓ | cup apricot preserves |

**WHY THIS RECIPE WORKS** A fresh fruit tart is a showpiece of bakery pastry cases, from Europe to the United States and beyond. With its fluted crust and artful arrangement of mixed fruits glistening with glaze, this stunning dessert conveys a sense of occasion. But it's definitely a project and sometimes—at little fault of the baker's—instead of neat, elegant wedges you wind up with shards of pastry oozing messy fruit and a juice-stained filling. We wanted to modernize this tart so each slice would live up to its beautiful ideal. Traditional pastry cream is delicious but we knew it wasn't practical here; it simply isn't sturdy enough to support the layer of fruit. Instead, we swapped it for a lush, full-bodied filling that was firm enough to slice cleanly and was just as tasty: a mix of mascarpone cheese, melted white baking chips, and lime zest and juice. Arranging thinly sliced peaches in lines radiating from the center of the tart to its outer edge created cutting guides between which we arranged the berries. These guides ensured that we could slice the tart into neat portions without marring the fruit. A glaze of apricot preserves and lime juice brightened the fruit and gave the tart a polished, professional look. This recipe calls for extra berries to account for any bruising. Ripe, unpeeled nectarines can be substituted for the peaches, if desired. Use white baking chips here and not white bar chocolate, which contains cocoa butter and will result in a loose filling. Use a light hand when applying the glaze; too much force will dislodge the fruit. If the glaze begins to solidify while you're working, microwave it for 5 to 10 seconds.

1  Roll dough into 11-inch circle on floured counter, then transfer to parchment paper–lined rimmed baking sheet; cover loosely with plastic wrap and refrigerate until firm but pliable, about 10 minutes.

2  Loosely roll dough around rolling pin and gently unroll it onto 9-inch tart pan with removable bottom, letting excess dough hang over edge. Ease dough into pan by gently lifting edge of dough with your hand while pressing into corners and fluted sides of pan with your other hand. Run rolling pin over top of pan to remove any excess dough. Wrap loosely in plastic, place on large plate, and freeze until fully chilled and firm, about 30 minutes. (Dough-lined tart pan can be frozen for up to 1 month.) Adjust oven rack to middle position and heat oven to 375 degrees.

3  Line chilled tart shell with double layer of aluminum foil and fill with pie weights. Bake on foil-lined rimmed baking sheet until tart shell is golden and set, about 30 minutes, rotating sheet halfway through baking. Remove foil and weights and continue to bake tart shell until it is fully baked and golden, 5 to 10 minutes longer. Transfer sheet to wire rack and let cool completely, about 1 hour.

4  Microwave baking chips, cream, lime zest, and salt in bowl, stirring every 10 seconds, until baking chips are melted, 30 seconds to 1 minute. Whisk in one-third of mascarpone, then whisk in lime juice and remaining mascarpone until smooth. Spread filling evenly over bottom of cooled tart shell.

**5** Place 1 peach, stem side down, on cutting board. Placing knife just to side of pit, cut down to remove 1 side of peach. Turn peach 180 degrees and cut off opposite side. Cut off remaining 2 sides. Place pieces cut side down and slice ¼ inch thick. Repeat with second peach. Select best 24 slices.

**6** Evenly space 8 berries around outer edge of tart. Using berries as guide, arrange 8 sets of 3 peach slices in filling, slightly overlapping slices with rounded sides up, starting at center and ending on right side of each berry. Arrange remaining berries in attractive pattern between peach slices, covering as much of filling as possible and keeping fruit in even layer.

**7** Microwave preserves in small bowl until fluid, 20 to 30 seconds. Strain mixture through fine-mesh strainer into bowl. Using pastry brush, gently dab mixture over fruit, avoiding crust. Refrigerate tart for 30 minutes.

**8** Remove outer ring of tart pan, slide thin metal spatula between tart and tart pan bottom, and carefully slide tart onto serving platter or cutting board. Let tart sit at room temperature for 15 minutes. Using peaches as guide, cut tart into wedges along markings and serve. (Tart can be refrigerated for up to 24 hours. If refrigerated for more than 1 hour, let tart sit at room temperature for 1 hour before serving.)

## Decorating Fresh Fruit Tart

**1** Evenly arrange 8 berries around outer edge of tart.

**2** Arrange 8 sets of 3 overlapping peach slices from center to edge of tart on right side of each berry.

**3** Arrange remaining berries in attractive pattern between peach slices.

**4** Continue filling in fruit in even layer to cover filling.

POACHED PEAR AND
ALMOND TART

# POACHED PEAR AND ALMOND TART

**Serves 10 to 12**

## poached pears

| | |
|---|---|
| 1 | (750-ml) bottle white wine |
| 2⁄3 | cup (4 2⁄3 ounces) sugar |
| 5 | (2-inch) strips lemon zest plus 2 tablespoons juice |
| 1 | cinnamon stick |
| 15 | black peppercorns |
| 3 | cloves |
| 1⁄8 | teaspoon table salt |
| 1⁄2 | vanilla bean (optional) |
| 4 | ripe but firm Bosc or Bartlett pears (8 ounces each), peeled, halved, and cored |

## filling

| | |
|---|---|
| 1 | cup slivered almonds |
| 1⁄2 | cup (3 1⁄2 ounces) sugar |
| 1⁄8 | teaspoon table salt |
| 1 | large egg plus 1 large white |
| 1⁄2 | teaspoon almond extract |
| 1⁄2 | teaspoon vanilla extract |
| 6 | tablespoons unsalted butter, cut into 6 pieces and softened |
| 1 | recipe tart dough (see pages 328–331) |
| 1⁄4 | cup apple jelly |

**WHY THIS RECIPE WORKS** Sliced poached pears, fanned atop light, nutty frangipane (a sweetened, custardy paste of ground almonds) and contained within a sweet crust is a stunning classic French tart. That beauty, unsurprisingly, requires a time investment, so we wanted to make sure we created the most flavorful—and foolproof—version of this tart to make it worthwhile. In this tart, the process of poaching doesn't just tenderize the pears; it perfumes them with flavor that complements the almond filling. White wine spiced with a cinnamon stick, black peppercorns, whole cloves, and a vanilla bean created our fragrant poaching liquid. For the frangipane, we processed blanched slivered almonds in a food processor with sugar; incorporating the sugar at this point allowed us to grind the almonds until superfine without the risk of them becoming a greasy almond butter. We made sure to dry the pears before setting them on the frangipane; otherwise, their moisture made the dessert sticky and wet. The finishing touch of a jelly glaze gave the pears a beautiful sheen. The flesh near the stem of a perfectly ripe but firm pear should give slightly when gently pressed. We like the bright, crisp flavor of pears poached in Sauvignon Blanc. Chardonnay-poached pears have a deeper, oakier flavor that we also like.

---

**1** *for the poached pears* Adjust oven rack to middle position and heat oven to 350 degrees. Combine wine, sugar, lemon zest and juice, cinnamon stick, peppercorns, cloves, and salt in large saucepan. If using, cut vanilla bean in half lengthwise, then, using tip of paring knife, scrape out seeds and add seeds and pod to saucepan. Bring mixture to simmer, stirring occasionally to dissolve sugar. Slide pear halves into simmering wine mixture. Return to simmer, then reduce heat to low, cover, and cook pears, covered, turning them occasionally, until tender and skewer can be inserted into pear with very little resistance, about 10 minutes. Off heat, let pears cool in liquid, partially covered, until pears have turned translucent and are cool enough to handle, about 1 hour. (Pears and liquid can be refrigerated for up to 3 days; transfer to bowl, let cool completely, and cover before refrigerating.)

**2** *for the filling* Pulse almonds, sugar, and salt in food processor until finely ground, about 25 pulses. Continue to process until nut mixture is as finely ground as possible, about 10 seconds. Add egg and white, almond extract, and vanilla and process until combined, about 10 seconds. Add butter and process until no lumps remain, about 20 seconds, scraping down bowl as needed. (Filling can be refrigerated for up to 3 days. Let filling stand at room temperature until softened, about 10 minutes, stirring 3 or 4 times, before using.)

**3** Roll dough into 11-inch circle on floured counter, then transfer to parchment paper–lined rimmed baking sheet; cover loosely with plastic wrap and refrigerate until firm but pliable, about 10 minutes.

**4** Loosely roll dough around rolling pin and gently unroll it onto 9-inch tart pan with removable bottom, letting excess dough hang over edge. Ease dough into pan by gently lifting edge of dough with your hand while pressing into corners and fluted sides of pan with your other hand. Run rolling pin over top of pan to remove any excess dough. Wrap loosely in plastic, place on large plate, and freeze until fully chilled and firm, about 30 minutes. (Dough-lined tart pan can be frozen for up to 1 month.) Adjust oven rack to middle position and heat oven to 375 degrees.

**5** Line chilled tart shell with double layer of aluminum foil and fill with pie weights. Bake on foil-lined rimmed baking sheet until tart shell is golden and set, about 30 minutes, rotating sheet halfway through baking. Remove foil and weights. Transfer sheet to wire rack and let cool completely, about 1 hour. Reduce oven temperature to 350 degrees.

**6** Spread filling evenly over bottom of cooled tart shell. Remove pears from poaching liquid and pat dry with paper towels. Cut 1 poached pear half crosswise into ⅜-inch slices, leaving pear half intact on cutting board (do not separate slices). Pat dry again with paper towels to absorb excess moisture. Discard first 4 slices

from narrow end of sliced pear half. Slide spatula under sliced pear and, steadying it with your hand, slide pear off spatula onto center of tart. Cut and dry another pear half. Slide spatula under pear and gently press pear to fan slices toward narrow end. Slide fanned pear half onto filling, narrow end toward center, almost touching center pear. Repeat slicing, fanning, and placing remaining pear halves, spacing them evenly and making flower petal pattern around center pear.

**7** Bake tart on sheet until crust is deep golden brown and almond filling is puffed, browned, and firm to the touch, about 45 minutes, rotating sheet halfway through baking. Transfer sheet to wire rack and let tart cool for 10 minutes.

**8** Melt jelly in small saucepan over medium-high heat, stirring occasionally to smooth out lumps. Using pastry brush, gently dab jelly over fruit, avoiding crust. Let tart cool completely, about 2 hours. Remove outer ring of tart pan, slide thin metal spatula between tart and tart pan bottom, and carefully slide tart onto serving platter or cutting board. Serve.

## Assembling Poached Pear and Almond Tart

**1** Cut 1 poached pear half crosswise into ⅜-inch slices. Pat dry with paper towels to absorb excess moisture.

**2** Discard first 4 slices from narrow end of sliced pear half. Slide offset spatula under sliced pear and, steadying it with 1 hand, slide pear off spatula onto center of frangipane-filled tart.

**3** Cut and dry second pear half. Slide spatula under pear and gently press pear to fan slices toward narrow end. Slide fanned pear half onto frangipane, narrow end toward center, almost touching center pear. Repeat with remaining pear halves, spacing them evenly and making flower petal pattern around center pear.

# EASY BERRY TART

Serves 4 to 6

1 (9½ by 9-inch) sheet puff pastry, thawed

2 teaspoons sugar

⅛ teaspoon ground cinnamon

4 ounces cream cheese, softened

½ cup plus 2 tablespoons strawberry jelly, divided

1 teaspoon vanilla extract

15 ounces (3 cups) blackberries, blueberries, and raspberries

**WHY THIS RECIPE WORKS** We love our Fresh Fruit Tart (page 146), and it's an elegant classic. But making tart dough from scratch and arranging berries with precision aren't always possible when you're preparing other components of a summertime party. Not to worry: A tart featuring gleaming summer berries atop a creamy filling and crisp crust can easily come together with help from the grocery store. Instead of making our own pastry, we used frozen puff pastry—it proved strong enough to support the filling, and folding in the edges of the pastry before baking created a barrier to keep the fruit in place. For the filling, we combined softened rich cream cheese with bright strawberry jelly. The jelly not only sweetened the cheese and bolstered berry flavor, it also thinned the cream cheese to a silky pastry cream consistency—no cooking required. To prevent the bottom of our tart shell from becoming soggy under the weight of our filling, we sprinkled sugar (combined with fragrant cinnamon) over the pastry before baking; this formed a moisture barrier that kept the crust nice and crisp beneath the cream cheese. To thaw frozen puff pastry, let it sit either in the refrigerator for 24 hours or on the counter for 30 minutes to 1 hour.

**1** Adjust oven rack to upper-middle position and heat oven to 425 degrees. Line rimmed baking sheet with parchment paper. Unfold thawed pastry onto baking sheet and brush ½-inch border along edges of pastry with water. Fold long edges of pastry over by ½ inch, then fold short edges over by ½ inch. Working lengthwise, lightly score outer edge of all folded edges with paring knife. Poke dough all over with fork.

**2** Combine sugar and cinnamon and sprinkle mixture over inside of tart shell. Bake until pastry and sugar are deep golden brown, 15 to 22 minutes. Transfer sheet to wire rack and let tart shell cool completely, about 1 hour.

**3** While tart shell is baking, stir cream cheese, 2 tablespoons jelly, and vanilla in bowl until smooth. Refrigerate until ready to use. (Mixture can be refrigerated for up to 2 days. Let mixture stand at room temperature until softened and stir well before using.)

**4** Spread cream cheese mixture evenly over bottom of cooled tart shell. Place remaining ½ cup jelly in large bowl and microwave until fluid, about 30 seconds. Add berries to bowl and toss gently until coated with jelly. Spoon berries over cream cheese mixture and refrigerate until jelly is set, at least 1 hour or up to 4 hours. Let sit at room temperature for 30 minutes before serving.

# LEMON TART

Serves 8 to 10

1   recipe tart dough
     (see pages 328–331)

2   large eggs plus 7 large yolks

1   cup (7 ounces) granulated sugar

¼   cup grated lemon zest plus
     ⅔ cup juice (4 lemons)

     Pinch table salt

4   tablespoons unsalted butter,
     cut into 4 pieces

3   tablespoons heavy cream

     Confectioners' sugar

**WHY THIS RECIPE WORKS** Shiny lemon filling and buttery crust: These are the two components of a classic lemon tart. But despite the tart's minimal ingredients, lemon curd can be tricky to get right. It can easily slip over the edge of perfectly sweet into cloying, or its tartness can grab at your throat; it can be gluey or eggy or, even worse, metallic-tasting. We wanted a proper tart, one with a filling that's baked with the tart shell (rather than spread into a finished, prebaked shell) for a cohesive finish. For just enough sweetness to offset the lemons' acidity, we used 3 parts sugar to 2 parts lemon juice, while a whopping ¼ cup of floral lemon zest provided well-rounded citrus flavor. To achieve a curd that was creamy and dense with a vibrant hue, we used a combination of whole eggs and egg yolks. We cooked the curd and then strained it and stirred in a lick of cream just before baking to ensure a smooth, light texture. Once the lemon curd ingredients have been combined, cook it immediately; otherwise, its finished texture will be grainy.

**1** Roll dough into 11-inch circle on floured counter, then transfer to parchment paper–lined rimmed baking sheet; cover loosely with plastic wrap and refrigerate until firm but pliable, about 10 minutes.

**2** Loosely roll dough around rolling pin and gently unroll it onto 9-inch tart pan with removable bottom, letting excess dough hang over edge. Ease dough into pan by gently lifting edge of dough with your hand while pressing into corners and fluted sides of pan with your other hand. Run rolling pin over top of pan to remove any excess dough. Wrap loosely in plastic, place on large plate, and freeze until fully chilled and firm, about 30 minutes. (Dough-lined tart pan can be frozen for up to 1 month.) Adjust oven rack to middle position and heat oven to 375 degrees.

**3** Line chilled tart shell with double layer of aluminum foil and fill with pie weights. Bake on foil-lined rimmed baking sheet until tart shell is golden and set, about 30 minutes, rotating sheet halfway through baking. Remove foil and weights and transfer sheet to wire rack. (Tart shell must still be warm when filling is added.)

**4** Whisk eggs and yolks together in medium saucepan. Whisk in granulated sugar until combined, then whisk in lemon zest and juice and salt. Add butter and cook over medium-low heat, stirring constantly, until mixture thickens slightly and registers 170 degrees, about 5 minutes. Immediately pour mixture through fine-mesh strainer into bowl. Stir in cream.

**5** Pour warm lemon filling into warm tart shell. Bake tart on sheet until filling is shiny and opaque and center jiggles slightly when shaken, 10 to 15 minutes, rotating sheet halfway through baking.

**6** Let tart cool completely on sheet on wire rack, about 2 hours. Remove outer ring of tart pan, slide thin metal spatula between tart and tart pan bottom, and carefully slide tart onto serving platter or cutting board. Dust with confectioners' sugar. Serve.

# FRENCH APPLE TART

Serves 8

1 recipe tart dough
(see pages 328–331)

10 large Golden Delicious apples
(8 ounces each), peeled and
cored

3 tablespoons unsalted butter,
divided

1 tablespoon water

½ cup apricot preserves

¼ teaspoon table salt

**WHY THIS RECIPE WORKS** French apple tart is a visually stunning centerpiece dessert that's little more than, well, apples—half of which are cooked down to an applesauce-like mixture—and pastry. But such simplicity means that imperfections are hard to hide. For intense fruit flavor, we packed our tart with a whopping 5 pounds of Golden Delicious apples; we found this variety broke down easily to make the puree. To concentrate the apple flavor, we cooked the puree until it measured about 2 cups. A little butter enriched the lean filling. For a beautiful presentation—and even more apple flavor—we parcooked apple slices until they were just pliable and arranged them on top of the tart in beautiful concentric circles to form a flower-like design. A thin coat of preserves and a final run under the broiler provided a caramelized finish. If you don't have a potato masher, you can puree the apples in a food processor. You may have extra apple slices after arranging the apples in step 8. To ensure that the outer ring of the pan releases easily from the tart, avoid getting apple puree and apricot glaze on the edge of the crust. The tart is best served the day it is assembled.

1 Roll dough into 11-inch circle on floured counter, then transfer to parchment paper–lined rimmed baking sheet; cover loosely with plastic wrap and refrigerate until firm but pliable, about 10 minutes.

2 Loosely roll dough around rolling pin and gently unroll it onto 9-inch tart pan with removable bottom, letting excess dough hang over edge. Ease dough into pan by gently lifting edge of dough with your hand while pressing into corners and fluted sides of pan with your other hand. Run rolling pin over top of pan to remove any excess dough. Wrap loosely in plastic, place on large plate, and freeze until fully chilled and firm, about 30 minutes. (Dough-lined tart pan can be frozen for up to 1 month.) Adjust oven rack to middle position and heat oven to 375 degrees.

3 Line chilled tart shell with double layer of aluminum foil and fill with pie weights. Bake on wire rack set in rimmed baking sheet until tart shell is golden and set, about 30 minutes, rotating sheet halfway through baking. Remove foil and weights; set aside.

4 Cut 5 apples lengthwise into quarters and cut each quarter lengthwise into 4 slices. Melt 1 tablespoon butter in 12-inch skillet over medium heat. Add apple slices and water and toss to combine. Cover and cook, stirring occasionally, until apples begin to turn translucent and are slightly pliable, 3 to 5 minutes. Transfer apples to large plate, spread into single layer, and set aside to cool. Do not clean skillet.

5 Microwave apricot preserves in small bowl until fluid, about 30 seconds. Strain preserves through fine-mesh strainer into bowl, reserving solids. Set aside 3 tablespoons strained preserves for brushing tart.

**6** Cut remaining 5 apples into ½-inch-thick wedges. Melt remaining 2 tablespoons butter in now-empty skillet over medium heat. Add remaining apricot preserves, reserved apricot solids, apple wedges, and salt. Cover and cook, stirring occasionally, until apples are very soft, about 10 minutes.

**7** Mash apples to puree with potato masher. Continue to cook, stirring occasionally, until puree is reduced to 2 cups, about 5 minutes.

**8** Spread filling evenly over bottom of tart shell. Select 5 thinnest slices of sautéed apple and set aside. Starting at outer edge of crust, arrange remaining slices, tightly overlapping, in concentric circles. Bend reserved slices to fit in center. Bake tart, still on wire rack set in sheet, on lower rack for 30 minutes. Remove tart from oven and heat broiler.

**9** While broiler heats, warm reserved preserves in microwave until fluid, about 20 seconds. Brush evenly over surface of apples, avoiding tart crust. Broil tart, checking every 30 seconds and turning as necessary, until apples are attractively caramelized, 1 to 3 minutes. Let tart cool on wire rack for 1½ hours. Remove outer ring of tart pan, slide thin metal spatula between tart and tart pan bottom, and carefully slide tart onto serving platter or cutting board. Serve.

## Topping French Apple Tart

**1** Starting at outer edge of crust, arrange apple slices, tightly overlapping, in concentric circles.

**2** Bend reserved slices to fit in center. Bake tart, still on sheet, on lower rack for 30 minutes.

**3** After baking for 30 minutes, brush warmed preserves evenly over surface of apples, avoiding tart crust.

**4** Broil tart, checking every 30 seconds and turning as necessary, until apples are attractively caramelized, 1 to 3 minutes. Let tart cool on wire rack for 1½ hours.

CLASSIC APPLE
TARTE TATIN

# CLASSIC APPLE TARTE TATIN

Serves 8

1 recipe tart dough
(see pages 328–331)

8 tablespoons unsalted butter

¾ cup (5¼ ounces) sugar

⅛ teaspoon table salt

6 large Granny Smith apples
(8 ounces each), peeled,
cored, and quartered

Crème fraîche

**WHY THIS RECIPE WORKS** Burnished, buttery, caramelized wedges of apple shine like jewels atop tarte Tatin, the classic French dessert with a reputation for being notoriously difficult to execute. After all, it involves arranging dough over (perfectly cooked) apples in a smoking-hot skillet of caramel and, once baked, inverting the tart. Many home bakers are reluctant to attempt it—burned fingers and apples that stubbornly cling to the sticky caramel-slicked pan are common woes—but, in reality, turning out the ideal tarte Tatin doesn't require the finesse of a French chef. To start, we melted butter in a skillet and then sprinkled sugar evenly over the bottom of the pan before arranging the apples; this approach meant we could avoid making a caramel in advance because the caramel formed right in the pan. Chilling the dough before placing it over the caramelized apples avoided a melty skillet mess and resulted in a tart with clean edges once flipped. Our stick-free tart was easy to flip out once we loosened the edges with a paring knife. And if some apples did stick, there was no need to sweat it: We simply popped them back into place and covered the tart with the sweet juices left in the pan for gleam. Crème fraîche is a traditional accompaniment, but you can serve the tart with vanilla ice cream or Yogurt Whipped Cream (page 340) in place of the crème fraîche if you prefer.

**1** Roll dough into 11-inch circle on floured counter, then transfer to parchment paper–lined rimmed baking sheet; cover loosely with plastic wrap and refrigerate until fully chilled and firm, about 30 minutes. Adjust oven rack to upper-middle position and heat oven to 375 degrees.

**2** Melt butter in 10-inch ovensafe nonstick skillet over medium heat. Off heat, sprinkle sugar and salt evenly over surface, then arrange apples cut side down in tight pinwheel around edge of skillet, overlapping as needed. Arrange remaining apples cut side down in center of skillet.

**3** Place skillet over high heat and cook until butter mixture is amber-colored, about 10 minutes. Off heat, using paring knife or fork, flip apples browned side up, rearranging into tight pinwheel as needed. Return skillet to high heat and cook for 5 minutes.

**4** Off heat, carefully transfer chilled dough to skillet, centering over top of apples. Being careful of hot skillet, gently fold excess dough up against skillet wall. Transfer skillet to oven and bake until crust is golden brown, about 25 minutes. Transfer skillet to wire rack and let cool for 20 minutes.

**5** Run paring knife around edge of crust to loosen. Using dish towels or potholders, carefully place serving platter on top of skillet, and, holding platter and skillet firmly together, invert tart onto serving platter. Transfer any apples that stick to skillet to tart and drizzle any remaining juices in skillet over top. Serve with crème fraîche.

## Making Classic Apple Tarte Tatin

**1** Roll dough into 11-inch circle on floured counter, then transfer to parchment paper–lined rimmed baking sheet; cover with plastic wrap and refrigerate until dough is fully chilled and firm, about 30 minutes.

**2** Melt butter in 10-inch ovensafe nonstick skillet over medium heat. Off heat, sprinkle sugar and salt evenly over surface.

**3** Arrange apples cut side down in tight pinwheel around edge of skillet, overlapping as needed.

**4** Arrange remaining apples cut side down in center of skillet.

**5** Cook over high heat until butter mixture is amber-colored, about 10 minutes. Off heat, flip apples browned side up, rearranging into tight pinwheel. Return skillet to high heat and cook for 5 minutes.

**6** Carefully transfer chilled dough to skillet, centering over top of apples. Transfer skillet to oven and bake until crust is golden brown, about 25 minutes. Transfer skillet to wire rack and let cool for 20 minutes.

**7** Run paring knife around edge of crust to loosen.

**8** Using dish towels or potholders, carefully place serving platter on top of skillet, and, holding platter and skillet firmly together, invert tart onto serving platter.

**9** Transfer any apples that stick to skillet to tart and drizzle any remaining juices in skillet over top.

# PEACH TARTE TATIN

Serves 8

1    recipe single-crust pie dough (see pages 316–326)

3    tablespoons unsalted butter, softened

½    cup (3 ½ ounces) plus 2 tablespoons sugar

¼    teaspoon table salt

2    pounds ripe but firm peaches, peeled, quartered, and pitted

1    tablespoon bourbon (optional)

**WHY THIS RECIPE WORKS** We wanted to put a summery spin on our Classic Apple Tarte Tatin (page 160), and figured we could substitute peaches for the apples. But peaches produced a cloying tart that was awash in juice; this soft fruit would require a different approach. To make peaches work, we started by cooking them in the skillet for slightly less time. We also decided to use pie crust instead of tart crust, as its flaky texture was a better match for the delicate peaches. Once baked, we poured off the excess juice before inverting our tart. Then we reduced the juices with a bit of bourbon and brushed the mixture over the peaches. Firm peaches are important here, as they hold their shape when cooked. Yellow peaches are preferable to white peaches. When pouring off the liquid in step 4, the peaches may shift; shake the skillet to redistribute them.

1  Invert rimmed baking sheet and place sheet of parchment paper or waxed paper on top. Roll dough into 10-inch circle on floured counter. Loosely roll dough around rolling pin and gently unroll it onto prepared sheet. Working around circumference, fold ½ inch of dough under itself and pinch to create 9-inch round with raised rim. Cut three 2-inch slits in center of dough and refrigerate until needed.

2  Adjust oven rack to middle position and heat oven to 400 degrees. Smear butter over bottom of 10-inch ovensafe skillet. Sprinkle ½ cup sugar over butter and shake skillet to distribute sugar in even layer. Sprinkle salt over sugar. Arrange peaches in circular pattern around edge of skillet, nestling fruit snugly. Tuck remaining peaches into center, squeezing in as much fruit as possible (it is not necessary to maintain circular pattern in center).

3  Place skillet over high heat and cook, without stirring fruit, until juice is released and turns from pink to deep amber, 8 to 12 minutes. (If necessary, adjust skillet's placement on burner to even out hot spots and encourage even browning.) Off heat, carefully slide prepared dough over fruit, making sure dough is centered and does not touch edge of skillet. Brush dough lightly with water and sprinkle with remaining 2 tablespoons sugar. Transfer skillet to oven and bake until crust is very well browned, 30 to 35 minutes. Transfer skillet to wire rack set in rimmed baking sheet and let cool for 20 minutes.

4  Place inverted plate on top of crust. With 1 hand firmly securing plate, carefully tip skillet over bowl to drain juice (skillet handle may still be hot). When all juice has been transferred to bowl, return skillet to wire rack, remove plate, and shake skillet firmly to redistribute peaches. Off heat, carefully invert tart onto plate, then slide tart onto wire rack. (If peaches have shifted during unmolding, gently nudge them back into place with spoon.)

5  Pour juice into now-empty skillet (handle may be hot). Stir in bourbon, if using, and cook over high heat, stirring constantly, until mixture is dark and thick and starting to smoke, 2 to 3 minutes. Return mixture to bowl and let cool until mixture is consistency of honey, 2 to 3 minutes. Brush mixture over peaches. Let tart cool for at least 20 minutes. Serve.

# EASY PEAR TARTE TATIN

Serves 6 to 8

1 (9½ by 9-inch) sheet puff
   pastry, thawed

*pears*
8 tablespoons unsalted butter

¾ cup (5¼ ounces) sugar

2 pounds Anjou or Bartlett pears,
   peeled, quartered, and cored

*whipped sour cream*
1 cup heavy cream

½ cup sour cream

2 tablespoons pear liqueur, such
   as Poire Williams (optional)

**WHY THIS RECIPE WORKS** You can tell we like a tarte Tatin, and while we had apple and peach versions perfected (see pages 160–163), we wanted one more to satisfy our craving for caramelized fruit in a buttery crust. But this time, we thought we'd create something for a weeknight that didn't require masterfully flipping pastry onto a platter. We first baked a sheet of store-bought puff pastry to a beautiful golden brown. While the pastry baked in the oven, we cooked pears in a skillet until they were browned and tender. We then spooned the pears over the pastry, arranging them in three even rows and leaving a ½-inch border around the outside of the pastry. We served the whole thing with whipped sour cream. This easy tarte Tatin was really good, but for a bit more flavor we decided to make a sauce, stirring some of the sour cream topping into the caramelized pear juices left in the pan to make a quick caramel. To get this recipe on the table in a flash, peel the pears while the oven preheats and the pastry thaws, and then bake the pastry while the pears are caramelizing. To thaw frozen puff pastry, let it sit either in the refrigerator for 24 hours or on the counter for 30 minutes to 1 hour. If the pastry rises unevenly during baking, press it flat immediately after removing it from the oven.

**1** Adjust oven rack to middle position and heat oven to 400 degrees. Line rimmed baking sheet with parchment paper. Place puff pastry on parchment, poke dough all over with fork, and bake until golden brown and puffed, 10 to 12 minutes. Transfer crust to serving platter or cutting board.

**2** *for the pears* Meanwhile, melt butter in 12-inch skillet over high heat. Off heat, sprinkle sugar evenly over surface, then arrange pears in skillet so they are all resting flat side down. Return skillet to high heat and cook until juices in pan turn rich amber color, about 15 minutes. Using tongs, turn pears over to the other flat side. Cook pears for 8 minutes longer.

**3** *for the topping* Using stand mixer fitted with whisk attachment, whip heavy cream and sour cream on medium-low speed until foamy, about 1 minute. Increase speed to high and whip until soft peaks form, 1 to 3 minutes. Add liqueur, if using, and whip until stiff peaks form.

**4** Using tongs, remove pear quarters from pan one at a time and place in 3 overlapping horizontal rows on baked crust. Spoon about three-quarters of pan juices over top of pears. (You can use pastry brush to dab some of liquid onto edges of pastry). Whisk 2 tablespoons whipped sour cream topping into liquid left in pan.

**5** Cut tart in half vertically down center, and then horizontally into 3 or 4 rows (to serve 6 or 8, respectively). Transfer portions to individual plates and top each with a dollop of whipped sour cream and a drizzle of pan sauce. Serve immediately.

# ALL ABOUT TART TYPES

For the purpose of this book, we consider tarts to be a type of pie. But tarts themselves have interesting subcategories too. They're not just the fluted French pastries you see in bakery cases, and they're filled with more than just fruit. Here are the major types of tarts we cover in this chapter and some basics about each.

## THE PUFF PASTRY TART

Puff pastry tarts are deliciously deceitful: Their many flaky layers and golden, elegant puffed appearance give the impression that they are difficult to execute. But they're the easiest tarts of the bunch if you start with store-bought frozen puff pastry. Thaw the pastry, roll it to the proper dimensions, and then the tart's only as hard as what you fill it with. Make a creamy base for fruit with just cream cheese and jam in our Easy Berry Tart (page 153), or roast plums with a lacquering sauce and set them on a mascarpone-lemon filling as in Roasted Plum and Mascarpone Tart (page 173).

**The crust** Frozen puff pastry.

**The filling** Fruit is a classic. Puff pastry shells also play nicely with creamy, whipped, or mousse fillings—the pastry is sturdy enough to support them, and the plush fillings provide a pleasing contrast to the crisp crust.

**The equipment** A rolling pin (see page 9) for rolling the premade dough, a paring knife for scoring the edges, a fork for docking the dough, a baking sheet (see page 11) for baking.

**Special tip** Make a platform for holding filling.

**1** Roll dough to desired dimensions. (Sometimes we'll divide dough in half to make 2 tarts.)

**2** Poke dough all over with fork.

**3** Brush with egg wash.

**4** Once crust is baked, use tip of paring knife to cut ½-inch-wide border around top edge of pastry (being careful not to cut through to bottom).

**5** Press center down with your fingertips and then fill.

Neat fluted edges created by a special tart pan and a layer (or more) of luxe filling make up these sleek and impressive tarts, appropriate for special occasions. They comprise some of the most classic tarts, including Fresh Fruit Tart (page 146), Lemon Tart (page 154), Rich Chocolate Tart (page 192), and more.

**The crust** A shortbread-like sweet pastry crust. We offer recipes for a classic, plus chocolate and nut tart doughs that you can experiment with in any recipe that calls for "1 recipe tart dough."

**The equipment** A rolling pin (see page 9) for rolling the tart dough, a tart pan (see page 11), pie weights (see page 11) for blind-baking the tart shell, a small offset spatula (see page 10) for spreading the filling, a baking sheet (see page 11) for baking the tart on.

**Special tip** Get the tart to the table in one piece.

**1** Once tart is cool, place your hand on base and remove outer ring of tart pan.

**2** Slide thin metal spatula between tart and tart pan bottom (we like to use a large offset spatula, which fits under the entire tart), and carefully slide tart onto serving platter or cutting board.

While the French word *galette* refers to essentially any round tart-like pastry, when we use the term *galette* in this book, we mean a free-form tart: a tart made from flaky dough that's easy-breezy in its construction when compared with a double-crust fruit pie. Simply roll the dough into a round, fill, and fold over the edges before baking. Its open face makes it beautiful.

**The crust** Buttery pie dough. (We use a method called *fraisage* to make this dough sturdier than our other pie doughs; for more information, see page 332.)

**The filling** Galettes are ideal for fruit; the extra-open space allows excess juices to evaporate and the fruit to essentially roast, which concentrates its flavor. The fruit's bright colors look good too.

**The equipment** A rolling pin (see page 9) for rolling dough disk, a baking sheet (see page 11) for baking.

**Special tip** Fold with finesse for a perfect pleated look.

**1** Fold outermost 2 inches of dough over fruit, pleating every 2 to 3 inches as needed.

**2** Gently pinch pleated dough to secure, but do not press dough into fruit.

# JAM SECRET

No matter the type of tart you're making, in addition to the fruit, nuts, or chocolate fillings there's a secret weapon that appears in many recipes: fruit jams, jellies, or preserves. A brush of one of them over fresh berries on tarts gives the fruit jewels luster. For this purpose, we typically use apricot preserves for their bright flavor and neutral amber color. A spread of apple jelly over the pears in Poached Pear and Almond Tart (page 150) complements rather than competes with the pears' flavor while giving the pear fans flair. Sometimes we apply confitures before baking. The apricot preserves on our French Apple Tart (page 156) help the apple petals achieve browning under the broiler; we microwave and then strain the preserves here for sleek sheen. Jam can help fruit taste more like itself all year round, as is the case with the strawberry jam in Strawberry Galette with Candied Basil and Balsamic (page 170), and it can lighten the texture and sweeten the flavor of creamy tart fillings as in our Easy Berry Tart (page 153). Finally, for a simple tart filling, jams or preserves can be the star ingredient. Freshened with a little lemon juice, preserves (we chose raspberry) are the traditional filling for Linzertorte (page 178).

# FREE-FORM APPLE TART

Serves 6

1 recipe Free-Form Tart Dough (page 332)

1 pound Granny Smith apples, peeled, cored, and sliced ¼ inch thick

1 pound McIntosh apples, peeled, cored, and sliced ¼ inch thick

½ cup (3½ ounces) plus 1 tablespoon sugar, divided

1 tablespoon lemon juice

⅛ teaspoon ground cinnamon

**WHY THIS RECIPE WORKS** Our French Apple Tart (page 156) has a buttoned-up elegance; it's the black tie attire of the elegant party. A free-form apple tart, with its display of roasted apples filling the open window of dough, is more laid-back but every bit as beautiful. A mix of Granny Smith and McIntosh apples, sliced thin, gave us complex flavor, and just ½ cup of sugar, a bit of lemon juice, and a pinch of cinnamon perfected the filling. We stacked the apples in a ring and then filled the ring with yet more apples to give the finished tart a neater, fuller appearance than if we had just casually piled the apples in the center as we often do with galettes. Finally, we folded and pleated the edge of the dough around the apples before baking the tart until golden brown. To prevent the tart from leaking, it is crucial to leave a ½-inch-wide border of dough around the fruit. We like to serve this tart with Caramel Sauce (page 341).

**1** Roll dough into 12-inch circle between 2 large sheets of floured parchment paper. (If dough sticks to parchment, gently loosen dough with bench scraper and dust parchment with additional flour.) Slide dough, still between parchment, onto rimmed baking sheet and refrigerate until firm, 15 to 30 minutes.

**2** Adjust oven rack to lower-middle position and heat oven to 375 degrees. Toss apples, ½ cup sugar, lemon juice, and cinnamon together in large bowl. Stack some apple slices into circular wall around dough, leaving 2½-inch border around edge. Fill in middle of tart with remaining apples. Fold outermost 2 inches of dough over fruit, pleating it every 2 to 3 inches as needed; be sure to leave ½-inch border of dough between fruit and edge of tart. Gently pinch pleated dough to secure, but do not press dough into fruit.

**3** Brush top and sides of dough lightly with water and sprinkle with remaining 1 tablespoon sugar. Bake until crust is golden brown and apples are tender, about 1 hour, rotating sheet halfway through baking.

**4** Let tart cool on baking sheet for 10 minutes. Using parchment, carefully slide tart onto wire rack and let tart cool until juices have thickened, about 25 minutes. Serve slightly warm or at room temperature.

## Arranging the Apples

**1** Stack some apple slices into circular wall around dough, leaving 2½-inch border around edge of fruit.

**2** Fill middle of tart with remaining apples. Fold outermost 2 inches of dough over fruit, pleating it every 2 to 3 inches.

# STRAWBERRY GALETTE WITH CANDIED BASIL AND BALSAMIC

Serves 6 to 8

## galette

- 1 recipe Free-Form Tart Dough (page 332)
- ⅓ cup strawberry jam
- ¼ cup (1¾ ounces) plus 1 tablespoon sugar, divided
- ¼ teaspoon table salt
- 1½ tablespoons cornstarch
- 1½ pounds strawberries, hulled and halved (5 cups)

## garnishes

- ½ cup balsamic vinegar
- 1½ teaspoons sugar, divided
  Vegetable oil spray
- ¼ cup fresh basil leaves
- 1 teaspoon coarsely ground pepper

**WHY THIS RECIPE WORKS** Whereas pie fillings run the gamut from custards and creams to fruit, chocolate, and nuts, galettes typically feature fruit alone. There's a good reason for this: The exposed fruit does more than just meld into a cohesive filling—it roasts! This deepens the flavor of the fruit and evaporates moisture quickly, so there's usually no need for an added thickener. But we discovered strawberries are an exception. We followed the method of our other galettes and what came from the oven was a watery mess severely lacking in strawberry flavor. We'd need a thickener of some kind. Tossing cornstarch with the berries did the trick, and incorporating some strawberry jam intensified the berry flavor while adding viscosity. This tart was beautifully fresh, but its flavor was further elevated by a drizzle of balsamic glaze made by reducing vinegar with some sugar: The balsamic' acidity heightened the flavor of the strawberries while its woodsy fruitiness deepened it. Some ground black pepper provided sharp contrast. And to gild the lily, we finished with some sugared basil leaves that took less than 2 minutes to candy in the microwave. We love these garnishes, but you could substitute 1 tablespoon chopped fresh basil for all of them if you prefer.

---

**1** *for the galette* Roll dough into 12-inch circle between 2 large sheets of floured parchment paper. (If dough sticks to parchment, gently loosen dough with bench scraper and dust parchment with additional flour.) Slide dough, still between parchment, onto rimmed baking sheet and refrigerate until firm, 15 to 30 minutes.

**2** Adjust oven rack to lower-middle position and heat oven to 375 degrees. Microwave jam, ¼ cup sugar, and salt in large bowl until warm, about 30 seconds. Whisk in cornstarch. Add strawberries and gently toss to coat. Mound fruit in center of chilled dough, leaving 2-inch border around edge. Fold outermost 2 inches of dough over fruit, pleating it every 2 to 3 inches as needed. Gently pinch pleated dough to secure, but do not press dough into fruit.

**3** Brush top and sides of dough lightly with water and sprinkle with remaining 1 tablespoon sugar. Bake until crust is deep golden brown and fruit is bubbling, 1 hour to 1 hour 10 minutes. Let tart cool on baking sheet for 10 minutes. Using parchment, carefully slide tart onto wire rack and let cool until just warm, about 30 minutes.

**4** *for the garnishes* While tart cools, bring vinegar and 1 teaspoon sugar to simmer in 8-inch skillet over medium heat. Cook until vinegar is reduced to 2 tablespoons, 5 to 7 minutes; set aside to cool slightly, about 5 minutes. Line large plate with parchment and lightly spray with oil spray. Arrange basil in single layer on plate, then lightly spray with oil spray and sprinkle evenly with remaining ½ teaspoon sugar. Microwave until bright green and crisp, about 90 seconds; transfer to paper towel–lined plate to cool completely, about 5 minutes. Serve tart, topping with basil and pepper and drizzling with balsamic reduction.

## Candying Basil Leaves

**1** Line large plate with parchment and lightly spray with oil spray. Arrange basil in single layer on plate, then lightly spray with oil spray.

**2** Sprinkle evenly with ½ teaspoon sugar.

**3** Microwave until bright green and crisp, about 90 seconds; transfer to paper towel–lined plate to cool completely, about 5 minutes.

# ROASTED PLUM AND MASCARPONE TART

Serves 6 to 8

12 ounces (1½ cups) mascarpone cheese, room temperature

2 tablespoons confectioners' sugar

1 teaspoon grated lemon zest plus ½ teaspoon juice

1 (9½ by 9-inch) sheet puff pastry, thawed

1 large egg, lightly beaten with 1 tablespoon water

3 tablespoons unsalted butter, divided

6 ripe but firm plums, halved and pitted

¾ cup dry white wine

¼ cup dried currants

¼ cup (1¾ ounces) granulated sugar

1 teaspoon fresh thyme leaves, divided

⅛ teaspoon table salt

**WHY THIS RECIPE WORKS** It's easy to love fruit that's sweetened just the right amount and surrounded by pastry. While a conventional pie's top crust shields fruit and traps moisture for a perfectly cooked, luscious texture, there's also something incredibly appealing about the richly caramelized exterior of roasted fruit that you don't get in a double-crust pie. So for this elegant puff pastry tart, we first roasted the fruit—we chose plums, which gain great complexity from roasting—before adding it to a baked shell for an easy-to-assemble multilayer tart. We jump-started the process by searing the plums in butter before transferring the skillet to a hot oven for 10 minutes. We deglazed the pan with white wine, adding sugar, thyme, and currants to create a lacquering sauce. For a rich, plush filling that tied the components together, we incorporated creamy, lightly sweetened mascarpone cheese flavored with a little lemon zest. To thaw frozen puff pastry, let it sit either in the refrigerator for 24 hours or on the counter for 30 minutes to 1 hour. Be gentle when stirring the mascarpone in step 1; stirring aggressively can cause the cheese to become too loose or even break.

---

**1** Adjust oven rack to middle position and heat oven to 425 degrees. Gently stir mascarpone, confectioners' sugar, and lemon zest together in bowl until combined, then cover with plastic wrap and refrigerate until ready to serve.

**2** Roll pastry into 14 by 10-inch rectangle on floured counter and transfer to parchment paper–lined rimmed baking sheet. Poke dough all over with fork, then brush surface with egg wash. Bake until puffed and golden brown, 12 to 15 minutes, rotating sheet halfway through baking.

**3** Using tip of paring knife, cut ½-inch-wide border around top edge of pastry (being careful not to cut through to bottom), then press center down with your fingertips. Transfer tart shell to wire rack and let cool completely, about 30 minutes.

**4** Melt 2 tablespoons butter in 12-inch ovensafe skillet over medium-high heat. Place plum halves cut side down in skillet and cook, without moving, until plums are beginning to brown, about 3 minutes. Transfer skillet to oven and roast for 5 minutes. Flip plums cut side up and continue to roast until fork easily pierces fruit, about 5 minutes.

**5** Remove skillet from oven and transfer plums to plate. Being careful of hot skillet handle, whisk in wine, currants, granulated sugar, ½ teaspoon thyme, and salt. Bring to vigorous simmer over medium-high heat, whisking to scrape up any browned bits, and cook until sauce has consistency of maple syrup and measures about ½ cup, 3 to 5 minutes. Off heat, stir in lemon juice. Let cool slightly, about 10 minutes.

**6** Spread mascarpone mixture evenly over cooled tart shell, avoiding raised border, then arrange plums over top. Drizzle with sauce and sprinkle with remaining ½ teaspoon thyme. Serve.

# SABLÉ BRETON TART WITH CRANBERRY CURD

**Serves 6 to 8**

## tart

1½  cups (7½ ounces) all-purpose flour

¼  teaspoon table salt

10  tablespoons unsalted butter, softened

6  tablespoons (2⅔ ounces) granulated sugar

1  large egg

1  teaspoon vanilla extract

## curd

6  ounces (1½ cups) fresh or frozen cranberries

½  cup (3½ ounces) granulated sugar

1  teaspoon grated orange zest plus 2 tablespoons juice

Pinch table salt

1  large egg plus 1 large yolk

4  tablespoons unsalted butter, cut into ½-inch pieces and chilled

5  ounces (1 cup) blackberries, halved lengthwise

2½  ounces (½ cup) blueberries

Fresh mint leaves, torn

Confectioners' sugar

**WHY THIS RECIPE WORKS** *Sablés Bretons* are buttery cookies from Brittany, traditionally made with the region's famous salted butter. *Sablé* is French for "sandy," and it's the shortbread-like cookies' sandy texture that sets them apart. It's become popular to bake sablé dough into a tart and serve it as an elegant composed dessert. Sablé doughs typically eschew whole eggs in favor of just the yolk, which minimizes the moisture content so that the granulated sugar in the dough doesn't fully dissolve—this is how the sandy texture is achieved. But when we tried baking the test kitchen's recipe for sablé cookie dough into a tart, we hit some obstacles: First, the very low-moisture dough was hard to roll out and press into a tart pan. Second, we couldn't slice the baked tart cleanly—sandy meant excessively crumbly! We switched to a whole egg, and the small increase in moisture allowed for much easier shaping while the additional protein from the egg white gave the dough just enough structure to achieve clean slices. However, we didn't want to lose the sandy texture, so to keep some of the sugar crystals dry despite the added moisture we didn't fully emulsify the egg into the batter—just a quick mix with the wet ingredients sufficed. A vibrant-hued cranberry curd was a lovely accompaniment to this cookie-tart hybrid; it cut through the buttery richness. Thanks to cranberries' high pectin content, they produced a thick, silky curd with half the eggs that are usually required, so the cranberry flavor remained bracing. We added a little orange to emphasize the bright, aromatic flavor of the berries. Halving the blackberries makes the fruit more homogeneous in size.

---

**1** *for the tart*  Whisk flour and salt together in bowl; set aside. Using stand mixer fitted with paddle, beat butter and sugar on medium-high speed until pale and fluffy, about 3 minutes. Add egg and vanilla and beat until combined. Reduce speed to low, add flour mixture, and beat until just combined, scraping down bowl as needed. Press dough with spatula until dough sticks together in cohesive mass. Form dough into 5-inch disk, wrap in plastic wrap, and refrigerate for at least 2 hours or up to 2 days. Let chilled dough sit on counter to soften slightly, about 10 minutes, before rolling. (Wrapped dough can be frozen for up to 1 month. If frozen, let dough thaw completely in refrigerator.)

**2** *for the curd*  Cook cranberries, granulated sugar, orange zest and juice, and salt in medium saucepan over medium-low heat until cranberries have softened, 5 to 8 minutes. Mash with potato masher until cranberries are completely broken down, then strain through fine-mesh strainer into bowl, pressing on solids with rubber spatula to extract as much puree as possible (you should have about ⅓ cup). Discard solids and refrigerate cranberry puree until cooled, about 10 minutes. Wipe saucepan clean with paper towels.

**3** Return cooled cranberry puree to clean saucepan and whisk in egg and yolk. Cook over medium-low heat, stirring constantly with rubber spatula, until mixture is thickened and registers 170 degrees, 3 to 5 minutes. Off heat, whisk in butter until smooth. Transfer curd to clean bowl, press plastic directly on surface of curd, and refrigerate for at least 1½ hours. (Curd can be refrigerated for up to 3 days.) Adjust oven rack to middle position and heat oven to 300 degrees.

**4** Spray 9-inch tart pan with removable bottom with vegetable oil spray. Roll dough between 2 large sheets of plastic into 9-inch circle. Remove top sheet of plastic and gently flip dough into prepared tart pan. Press dough into even layer in pan to edge of pan, discarding remaining plastic. (Do not push dough up sides of tart pan.) Bake on rimmed baking sheet until puffed and golden, 50 to 55 minutes, rotating sheet halfway through baking. Let tart cool completely on sheet on wire rack, about 1 hour.

**5** Remove outer metal ring of tart pan, slide thin metal spatula between tart and tart pan bottom, and carefully slide tart onto serving platter or cutting board. Spread cranberry curd over top of tart, leaving ½-inch border around edge. Arrange blackberries and blueberries decoratively over top, sprinkle with mint, and dust with confectioners' sugar. Serve.

## Making the Sablé Breton Tart

**1** Roll dough between 2 large sheets of plastic into 9-inch circle.

**2** Remove top sheet of plastic and gently flip into prepared tart pan.

**3** Press dough into even layer in pan, discarding remaining plastic.

**4** Bake on rimmed baking sheet until puffed and golden, 50 to 55 minutes, rotating pan halfway through baking. Let cool completely on sheet on wire rack.

**5** Remove outer metal ring of tart pan, slide thin metal spatula between tart and pan bottom, and carefully slide tart onto serving platter.

**6** Spread cranberry curd over top of tart, leaving ½-inch border around edge.

**7** Arrange berries decoratively over top.

**8** Dust with confectioners' sugar.

SABLÉ BRETON TART WITH
CRANBERRY CURD

LINZERTORTE

# LINZERTORTE

Serves 10 to 12

## tart dough

| | |
|---|---|
| 1 | large egg |
| 1 | teaspoon vanilla extract |
| 1 | cup hazelnuts, toasted and skinned |
| ½ | cup plus 2 tablespoons (4⅓ ounces) granulated sugar |
| ½ | cup whole blanched almonds |
| ½ | teaspoon table salt |
| 1 | teaspoon grated lemon zest |
| 1½ | cups (7½ ounces) all-purpose flour |
| ½ | teaspoon ground cinnamon |
| ⅛ | teaspoon ground allspice |
| 12 | tablespoons unsalted butter, cut into ½-inch pieces and chilled |

## filling

| | |
|---|---|
| 1¼ | cups raspberry preserves |
| 1 | tablespoon lemon juice |
| 1 | tablespoon heavy cream |
| 1½ | teaspoons turbinado or Demerara sugar (optional) |

**WHY THIS RECIPE WORKS** The components of a Linzertorte couldn't be easier to prepare. A buttery nut-enhanced crust comes together easily in the food processor, and the raspberry jam filling is something you buy. Making this holiday tart look special is what takes precision. The hazelnut-and-almond-enriched dough is extra-delicate, so we simply pat it into the tart pan in pieces rather than rolling it. As for the lattice, we cut the strips on parchment paper so we could use the parchment to transfer the soft strips to the jam-filled tart, peeling the paper back as we placed the strips. A brush of cream and a sprinkling of turbinado sugar gave the golden-brown tart glitter and glow. Make sure to buy blanched almonds and to use an 11-inch tart pan here. You will have some extra dough when cutting out the lattice strips; we suggest cutting out a few extra lattice strips as backup (they are delicate and could break). If the dough becomes too soft while forming the lattice, refrigerate it for 15 minutes before continuing. The Linzertorte may be served at room temperature the day it is baked, but it's at its best after a night in the refrigerator.

**1** *for the tart dough* Whisk egg and vanilla together in bowl. Process hazelnuts, sugar, almonds, and salt in food processor until very finely ground, 45 to 60 seconds. Add lemon zest and pulse to combine, about 5 pulses. Add flour, cinnamon, and allspice and pulse to combine, about 5 pulses. Scatter butter over top and pulse until mixture resembles coarse cornmeal, about 15 pulses. With processor running, add egg mixture and continue to process until dough just comes together, about 12 seconds longer.

**2** Transfer dough to counter and form into cohesive mound. Divide dough in half and form each half into 5-inch disk. (If not using immediately, wrap disks tightly in plastic wrap and refrigerate for up to 2 days. Let chilled dough sit on counter until soft and malleable, about 1 hour, before using.)

**3** Tear 1 disk into walnut-size pieces, then pat pieces into 11-inch tart pan with removable bottom, pressing dough into corners and ¾ inch up sides of pan. Cover dough with plastic and smooth out any bumps using bottom of measuring cup. Set pan on large plate and freeze until firm, about 30 minutes.

**4** Roll second disk into 12-inch square between 2 large sheets of floured parchment paper. (If dough sticks to parchment, gently loosen and lift sticky area with bench scraper and dust parchment with additional flour.) Slide dough, still between parchment, onto rimmed baking sheet and refrigerate until firm, about 15 minutes. Remove top layer of parchment and trim edges of dough to form perfect square, then cut ten ¾-inch-wide strips, cutting through underlying parchment. Cover with parchment and freeze until dough is fully chilled and firm, about 20 minutes.

**5** Meanwhile, adjust oven rack to middle position and heat oven to 350 degrees. Set dough-lined tart pan on rimmed baking sheet. Spray 1 side of double layer of aluminum foil with vegetable oil spray. Press foil, greased side down, into frozen tart shell, covering edges to prevent burning, and fill with pie weights. Bake until tart shell is golden brown and set, about 30 minutes, rotating sheet halfway through baking. Remove foil and weights, transfer sheet to wire rack, and let cool completely, about 1 hour.

**6** *for the filling* Stir raspberry preserves and lemon juice together in bowl. Spread filling evenly over bottom of cooled tart shell. Pick up 1 strip of dough by parchment ends, then flip it over onto tart, positioning it near edge of pan. Remove parchment strip and trim ends of dough strip by pressing down on top edge of pan; reserve all dough scraps. Place 2 more strips parallel to first, spacing them evenly so that one is across center and

other is near opposite edge of pan. Rotate pan 90 degrees, then place 3 more strips spacing as with first three. Rotate pan 90 degrees again, then place 2 strips across pan, spaced evenly between first three. Rotate pan again and complete lattice by placing last 2 strips between second set of three. Use small scraps of dough to fill in crust around edges between lattice strips. Top of crust should be just below top of pan.

**7** Gently brush lattice strips with cream and sprinkle with sugar, if using. Bake on sheet until crust is deep golden brown, about 50 minutes. Let tart cool completely on sheet on wire rack, about 2 hours. Remove outer ring of tart pan, slide thin metal spatula between tart and tart pan bottom, and carefully slide tart onto serving platter or cutting board. Serve or refrigerate overnight.

## Making the Lattice Top

**1** Pick up 1 strip of dough by parchment ends, then flip it over onto tart, positioning it near edge of pan. Remove parchment strip and trim ends of dough strip by pressing down on top edge of pan.

**2** Place 2 more strips parallel to first, spacing them evenly so that one is across center and other is near opposite edge of pan.

**3** Rotate pan 90 degrees, then place 3 more strips spacing as with first three.

**4** Rotate pan 90 degrees again, then place 2 strips across pan, spaced evenly between first three.

**5** Rotate pan again and complete lattice by placing last 2 strips between second set of three.

**6** Use small scraps of dough to fill in crust around edges between lattice strips.

# BAKED RASPBERRY TART

**Serves 8 to 10**

1     recipe tart dough
       (see page 328)

6     tablespoons unsalted butter

1     large egg plus 1 large white

½     cup (3½ ounces) plus
       1 tablespoon sugar

¼     teaspoon table salt

1     teaspoon vanilla extract

¼     teaspoon grated lemon zest
       plus 1½ teaspoons juice

1     teaspoon kirsch or framboise
       (optional)

2     tablespoons Wondra flour

2     tablespoons heavy cream

10    ounces (2 cups) raspberries

**WHY THIS RECIPE WORKS** Rich custard tempers tart raspberries in this balanced, crowd-pleasing tart. We started with a simple butter, egg, sugar, and flour batter for the filling, deepening its flavor by browning the butter for a hint of nuttiness. Lemon zest brightened our custard, and fruity kirsch accented the raspberries. Using one whole egg plus an additional egg white ensured that the filling would have a nicely firm yet creamy consistency appropriate for this elegant tart. And substituting instant flour (Wondra) for all-purpose produced a smooth and silky (rather than starchy) texture. We arranged the raspberries in the bottom of our tart shell and simply poured the filling on top. The filling baked up golden brown around the sweet-tart berries. Wondra is an instant flour sold in canisters in the baking aisle. To minimize waste, reserve the egg white left from making the tart pastry for use in the filling. If your raspberries are very tart or very sweet, adjust the amount of sugar in the filling by about a tablespoon or so. This tart is best eaten the day it is made.

---

**1** Roll dough into 11-inch circle on floured counter, then transfer to parchment paper–lined rimmed baking sheet; cover loosely with plastic wrap and refrigerate until firm but pliable, about 10 minutes.

**2** Loosely roll dough around rolling pin and gently unroll it onto 9-inch tart pan with removable bottom, letting excess dough hang over edge. Ease dough into pan by gently lifting edge of dough with your hand while pressing into corners and fluted sides of pan with your other hand. Run rolling pin over top of pan to remove any excess dough. Wrap loosely in plastic, place on large plate, and freeze until fully chilled and firm, about 30 minutes. (Dough-lined tart pan can be frozen for up to 1 month.) Adjust oven rack to middle position and heat oven to 375 degrees.

**3** Line chilled tart shell with double layer of aluminum foil and fill with pie weights. Bake on foil-lined rimmed baking sheet until tart shell is golden and set, about 30 minutes, rotating sheet halfway through baking. Remove foil and weights and transfer sheet to wire rack.

**4** Melt butter in small saucepan over medium heat, swirling occasionally, until butter is browned and releases nutty aroma, about 7 minutes; transfer to bowl and let cool slightly.

**5** Whisk egg and white together in bowl, then vigorously whisk in sugar and salt until light-colored, about 1 minute. Whisk in browned butter until combined. Whisk in vanilla, lemon zest and juice, and kirsch, if using. Whisk in Wondra. Whisk in cream until thoroughly combined.

**6** Distribute raspberries in single tightly packed layer in bottom of tart shell. Pour filling mixture evenly over raspberries. Bake tart on sheet until fragrant, filling is set (does not jiggle when shaken) and bubbling lightly around edges, and surface is puffed and deep golden brown, about 30 minutes, rotating sheet halfway through baking.

**7** Let tart cool completely on sheet on wire rack, about 2 hours. Remove outer ring of tart pan, slide thin metal spatula between tart and tart pan bottom, and carefully slide tart onto serving platter or cutting board. Serve. (Cooled tart can be wrapped loosely with plastic wrap and kept at room temperature for up to 4 hours before serving.)

**Baked Blackberry Tart**
Substitute 10 ounces blackberries for raspberries.

**Baked Blueberry-Raspberry Tart**
Replace 5 ounces raspberries with 5 ounces blueberries.

# FIG, CHERRY, AND WALNUT TART

Serves 8 to 10

1 recipe tart dough
  (see pages 328–331)

6 ounces dried Turkish or
  Calimyrna figs, stemmed
  and quartered

1 cup water

½ cup brandy

1 tablespoon grated orange zest

12 ounces frozen sweet cherries,
   thawed, drained, and chopped

1 cup walnuts, toasted and
  chopped

**WHY THIS RECIPE WORKS** Fig-walnut tart is an Italian dessert featuring fresh figs in a tender pastry crust. But sweet, delicate figs are highly perishable and have a relatively short growing season. To re-create this sophisticated tart with more accessible ingredients, we turned to dried fruit. We rehydrated dried figs before baking so they wouldn't end up tough and leathery; adding brandy and orange zest to the soaking liquid infused the figs with complementary flavors. Traditionally, halved or quartered figs are arranged in the crust before baking, but since we were using dried figs we opted to process them to a smooth puree before adding toasted chopped walnuts for crunchy texture. However, the processed figs felt a bit heavy in our delicate tart shell, so we decided to add a bright and juicy element. Cherries and figs are a winning combination, so we thawed, drained, and chopped frozen cherries and stirred them into the processed figs with the walnuts. The cherries broke up the texture of our filling and added a welcome freshness. You can use Black Mission figs if you can't find Turkish or Calimyrna figs.

**1** Roll dough into 11-inch circle on floured counter, then transfer to parchment paper–lined rimmed baking sheet; cover loosely with plastic wrap and refrigerate until firm but pliable, about 10 minutes.

**2** Loosely roll dough around rolling pin and gently unroll it onto 9-inch tart pan with removable bottom, letting excess dough hang over edge. Ease dough into pan by gently lifting edge of dough with your hand while pressing into corners and fluted sides of pan with your other hand. Run rolling pin over top of pan to remove any excess dough. Wrap loosely in plastic, place on large plate, and freeze until fully chilled and firm, about 30 minutes. (Dough-lined tart pan can be frozen for up to 1 month.) Adjust oven rack to middle position and heat oven to 375 degrees.

**3** Line chilled tart shell with double layer of aluminum foil and fill with pie weights. Bake on foil-lined rimmed baking sheet until tart shell is golden and set, about 30 minutes, rotating sheet halfway through baking. Remove foil and weights and transfer sheet to wire rack.

**4** Combine figs, water, brandy, and orange zest in small saucepan and simmer over medium-low heat until figs are softened and beginning to break down, 15 to 20 minutes. Transfer mixture to food processor and process until smooth, about 15 seconds. Transfer fig puree to large bowl and stir in chopped cherries and walnuts. Spread fig mixture evenly over bottom of tart shell. Bake tart on sheet until crust is golden brown and filling is set, 25 to 30 minutes, rotating sheet halfway through baking.

**5** Let tart cool completely on sheet on wire rack, about 2 hours. Remove outer ring of tart pan, slide thin metal spatula between tart and tart pan bottom, and carefully slide tart onto serving platter or cutting board. Serve.

# RUSTIC WALNUT TART

**Serves 8 to 10**

1   **recipe tart dough
(see pages 328–331)**

½   **cup packed (3½ ounces)
light brown sugar**

⅓   **cup light corn syrup**

4   **tablespoons unsalted butter,
melted and cooled**

1   **tablespoon bourbon or dark rum**

2   **teaspoons vanilla extract**

½   **teaspoon table salt**

1   **large egg**

1¾   **cups walnuts, chopped coarse**

**WHY THIS RECIPE WORKS** This elegant nut tart is as satisfying as a pecan pie but more refined in appearance (it's sleek and more about the nuts than the custard) and in flavor (rich, earthy walnuts make the tart decidedly more adult). Despite its sophistication, this tart is surprisingly easy to prepare thanks to a very simple filling. We started with a pecan pie filling base but swapped in the walnuts, reduced the amount of sugar, and added a hefty amount of vanilla as well as a hit of bourbon (you could also use rum). The liquor cut the sweetness and intensified the flavor of the nuts. The modest amount of filling allowed the buttery tart crust to shine so it was more than just a vessel. We love walnuts for this tart, but you can substitute pecans if desired. We like to serve this tart with Brown Sugar and Bourbon Whipped Cream (page 340).

1  Roll dough into 11-inch circle on floured counter, then transfer to parchment paper–lined rimmed baking sheet; cover loosely with plastic wrap and refrigerate until firm but pliable, about 10 minutes.

2  Loosely roll dough around rolling pin and gently unroll it onto 9-inch tart pan with removable bottom, letting excess dough hang over edge. Ease dough into pan by gently lifting edge of dough with your hand while pressing into corners and fluted sides of pan with your other hand. Run rolling pin over top of pan to remove any excess dough. Wrap loosely in plastic, place on large plate, and freeze until fully chilled and firm, about 30 minutes. (Dough-lined tart pan can be frozen for up to 1 month.) Adjust oven rack to middle position and heat oven to 375 degrees.

3  Line chilled tart shell with double layer of aluminum foil and fill with pie weights. Bake on foil-lined rimmed baking sheet until tart shell is golden brown and set, about 30 minutes, rotating sheet halfway through baking. Remove foil and weights and continue to bake tart shell until it is fully baked and golden, 5 to 10 minutes longer. Transfer sheet to wire rack and let cool completely, about 1 hour.

4  Whisk sugar, corn syrup, butter, bourbon, vanilla, and salt in large bowl until sugar dissolves. Whisk in egg until combined. Pour filling evenly into cooled tart shell and sprinkle with walnuts. Bake tart on sheet until filling is set and walnuts begin to brown, 30 to 40 minutes, rotating sheet halfway through baking.

5  Let tart cool completely on sheet on wire rack, about 2 hours. Remove outer ring of tart pan, slide thin metal spatula between tart and tart pan bottom, and carefully slide tart onto serving platter or cutting board. (Tart can be refrigerated for up 2 days; bring to room temperature before serving.)

# CHOCOLATE-HAZELNUT RASPBERRY MOUSSE TART

**Serves 6 to 8**

12½ ounces (2½ cups) raspberries, divided

⅓ cup (2⅓ ounces) sugar

1½ ounces cream cheese, cut into ½-inch pieces and softened

⅔ cup heavy cream

1 (9½ by 9-inch) sheet puff pastry, thawed

1 large egg, lightly beaten with 1 tablespoon water

⅓ cup Nutella

1 recipe Candied Nuts (page 345)

Shaved chocolate

**WHY THIS RECIPE WORKS** The sleek elegance inherent in tarts of all types—the low profile and delicate components—means any tart impresses no matter how simple it is to execute. Take this one: It's quick and doesn't require you to make dough from scratch, but it's filled with pretty pink mousse; packed with bright berry flavor; and complemented by nutty, sophisticated candied hazelnuts. Mousse doesn't have to be an egg white–whipping affair, but the usual shortcut method of folding raspberry puree into whipped cream didn't work here—it was too loose for a tart. Adding more cream would only dull the flavor, so instead we tried cooking the puree to a thick jam, but the mousse lost its brightness. The solution came in the form of another dairy product: cream cheese, which added body and tang. We loved pairing raspberry with hazelnuts, but we wanted even more nut flavor. No one complained when we added a slick of Nutella under the mousse. To thaw frozen puff pastry, let it sit either in the refrigerator for 24 hours or on the counter for 30 minutes to 1 hour. Use hazelnuts in the candied nuts.

1 Adjust oven rack to middle position and heat oven to 425 degrees. Using potato masher, mash 1½ cups raspberries and sugar in medium saucepan until raspberries are completely broken down. Cook mixture over medium-low until thickened slightly, about 5 minutes, stirring occasionally.

2 Off heat, whisk in cream cheese until well combined. Strain raspberry mixture through fine-mesh strainer into bowl, pressing on solids with rubber spatula to extract as much puree as possible. Discard solids and refrigerate puree until cooled, about 10 minutes.

3 Using stand mixer fitted with whisk attachment, whip cream on medium-low speed until foamy, about 1 minute. Increase speed to medium-high and whip until stiff peaks form, 1 to 3 minutes. Gently whisk one-third of whipped cream into chilled raspberry puree until lightened. Using rubber spatula, gently fold in remaining whipped cream until homogeneous. Refrigerate until ready to serve. (Mousse can be refrigerated for up to 24 hours.)

4 Roll pastry into 14 by 10-inch rectangle on floured counter. Cut in half lengthwise and transfer to parchment paper–lined rimmed baking sheet (you should have two 14 by 5-inch rectangles). Poke dough all over with fork and brush surface with egg wash. Bake until puffed and golden brown, 12 to 15 minutes, rotating sheet halfway through baking.

5 Using tip of paring knife, cut ½-inch-wide border around top edge of each tart shell (being careful not to cut through to bottom), then press center down with your fingertips. Transfer tart shells to wire rack and let cool completely, about 30 minutes.

6 Divide Nutella between cooled tart shells and, avoiding raised border, spread into even layer. Repeat with raspberry mixture. Top with remaining 1 cup raspberries, candied hazelnuts, and shaved chocolate. Serve.

# CRANBERRY-PECAN TART

Serves 8 to 10

1 recipe tart dough
(see pages 328–331)

¼ cup water

1 cup (7 ounces) sugar

⅔ cup heavy cream

3 tablespoons unsalted butter,
cut into ½-inch pieces

½ teaspoon lemon juice

½ teaspoon vanilla extract

⅛ teaspoon table salt

6 ounces (1½ cups) fresh or
thawed frozen cranberries

1¼ cups pecans, toasted and
chopped coarse

**WHY THIS RECIPE WORKS** A rich, buttery tart crust filled with caramel-coated nuts and bursts of fresh fruit is sophisticated perfection. We particularly like the combination of pecans and cranberries, as the tartness of the cranberries cuts through the richness and sweetness of the pecans. Many cranberry-pecan tarts call for a pecan pie–like filling. Instead, we made a simple caramel with sugar and water and then added cream and butter to soften it up. To brighten the flavor of our caramel, we added a touch of lemon juice along with a little vanilla, and then we folded in the nuts and cranberries before baking it all in our crust to set the texture.

1 Roll dough into 11-inch circle on floured counter, then transfer to parchment paper–lined rimmed baking sheet; cover loosely with plastic wrap and refrigerate until firm but pliable, about 10 minutes.

2 Loosely roll dough around rolling pin and gently unroll it onto 9-inch tart pan with removable bottom, letting excess dough hang over edge. Ease dough into pan by gently lifting edge of dough with your hand while pressing into corners and fluted sides of pan with your other hand. Run rolling pin over top of pan to remove any excess dough. Wrap loosely in plastic, place on large plate, and freeze until fully chilled and firm, about 30 minutes. (Dough-lined tart pan can be frozen for up to 1 month.) Adjust oven rack to middle position and heat oven to 375 degrees.

3 Line chilled tart shell with double layer of aluminum foil and fill with pie weights. Bake on foil-lined rimmed baking sheet until tart shell is golden and set, about 30 minutes, rotating sheet halfway through baking. Remove foil and weights and transfer sheet to wire rack.

4 Reduce oven temperature to 325 degrees. Pour water into medium saucepan, then pour sugar into center of pan (don't let it reach pan sides). Gently stir sugar with clean spatula to wet it thoroughly. Bring mixture to boil over medium-high heat and cook, without stirring, until sugar has dissolved completely and liquid has faint golden color and registers 300 degrees, 6 to 10 minutes.

5 Reduce heat to medium-low and continue to cook, stirring occasionally, until mixture turns dark amber and registers 350 degrees, 1 to 3 minutes. Off heat, slowly whisk in cream until combined (mixture will bubble and steam vigorously). Stir in butter, lemon juice, vanilla, and salt until combined. Add cranberries and pecans and stir gently until evenly distributed and thoroughly coated in caramel. Pour filling into tart shell. Bake tart on sheet until filling is bubbling and nearly set (it should jiggle slightly when shaken), 25 to 30 minutes.

6 Let tart cool completely on sheet on wire rack, about 2 hours. Remove outer ring of tart pan, slide thin metal spatula between tart and tart pan bottom, and carefully slide tart onto serving platter or cutting board. Serve. (Tart can be wrapped loosely with plastic and kept at room temperature for up to 4 hours.)

# RASPBERRY STREUSEL TART

Serves 8

1½ cups (7½ ounces) all-purpose flour

½ cup (3½ ounces) granulated sugar

¼ teaspoon table salt

12 tablespoons unsalted butter, cut into 12 pieces and softened, divided

½ cup (1½ ounces) old-fashioned rolled oats

½ cup sliced almonds, toasted

3 tablespoons packed brown sugar

¾ cup raspberry jam

7½ ounces (1½ cups) raspberries, divided

1 tablespoon lemon juice

**WHY THIS RECIPE WORKS** Our raspberry streusel tart is at once rustic and elegant. Made in a round springform pan for easy release, it strikes a perfect balance between the bright, tangy filling and rich, buttery crust, and both the base and topping are made from a single dough. We knew this tart would need a sturdy bottom crust so the jam wouldn't seep into it, but it also needed a topping that was light and would adhere to the filling. The key to achieving these two textures with one dough mixture was butter. A butter-rich shortbread made a supportive bottom crust; we then rubbed even more butter into the same dough, along with oats, nuts, and brown sugar, for an easy streusel topping. Combining fresh raspberries with raspberry jam made for a fresh-tasting fruit filling. Adding a dash of lemon juice brightened the filling further. Do no substitute quick or instant oats in this recipe. If the raspberries taste very tart, add an extra tablespoon or two of granulated sugar to the filling.

1 Adjust oven rack to middle position and heat oven to 375 degrees. Grease 9-inch springform pan.

2 Using stand mixer fitted with paddle, mix flour, granulated sugar, and salt on low speed until combined. Add 10 tablespoons butter, 1 piece at a time, and mix until mixture resembles wet sand, 1 to 2 minutes. Set aside ½ cup mixture for topping.

3 Sprinkle remaining mixture into prepared pan and press firmly into even, compact layer using bottom of dry measuring cup. Use back of spoon to press and smooth edges. Bake until fragrant and beginning to brown, about 15 minutes. Let tart shell cool slightly while making topping and filling.

4 Mix reserved flour mixture with oats, almonds, and brown sugar in bowl. Add remaining 2 tablespoons butter and pinch mixture between fingers into hazelnut-size clumps.

5 Mash jam, ½ cup raspberries, and lemon juice with fork to coarse puree in small bowl. Spread berry mixture evenly over warm crust, then top with remaining 1 cup raspberries. Sprinkle streusel topping over raspberries. Bake until filling is bubbling and topping is deep golden brown, 22 to 25 minutes, rotating pan halfway through baking. Let tart cool completely in pan, about 2 hours. (Tart can be kept at room temperature for up to 8 hours.)

6 To unmold tart, remove sides of pan and slide thin metal spatula between crust and pan bottom to loosen, then slide tart onto serving platter or cutting board. Serve.

# RICH CHOCOLATE TART

Serves 10 to 12

1 recipe tart dough
(see pages 328–331)

*filling*

9 ounces bittersweet chocolate, chopped fine

1¼ cups heavy cream

½ teaspoon instant espresso powder

¼ teaspoon table salt

4 tablespoons unsalted butter, sliced thin and softened

2 large eggs, room temperature

*glaze*

3 tablespoons heavy cream

1 tablespoon light corn syrup

2 ounces bittersweet chocolate, chopped fine

1 tablespoon hot water

**WHY THIS RECIPE WORKS** To us, the real draw of a rich chocolate tart is its simple confidence: The best versions boast a flawlessly smooth, truffle-like texture; unadulterated chocolate flavor; and a sophisticated polish. As chocolate is the sole filling, we wanted a custard-style mixture here: one that would be dense and rich, but not as dense as ganache; and plush, so we could eat more than a couple of bites. The ganache we saved for a thin glaze to give the top a pristine sheen. The tart can be garnished with chocolate curls or with a flaky coarse sea salt, such as Maldon. Chocolate pairs well with so many flavors that we also wanted to give our tart an intriguing variation. Chocolate and peanut butter are a classic combination but we wanted something distinctly grown-up, so we turned to nutty tahini. Its slight bitterness allowed its flavor to come through all that chocolate. A topping of sesame seed brittle enforced the sesame flavor and made for a stunning geometric finish to this artistic tart.

---

**1** Roll dough into 11-inch circle on floured counter, then transfer to parchment paper–lined rimmed baking sheet; cover loosely with plastic wrap and refrigerate until firm but pliable, about 10 minutes.

**2** Loosely roll dough around rolling pin and gently unroll it onto 9-inch tart pan with removable bottom, letting excess dough hang over edge. Ease dough into pan by gently lifting edge of dough with your hand while pressing into corners and fluted sides of pan with your other hand. Run rolling pin over top of pan to remove any excess dough. Wrap loosely in plastic, place on large plate, and freeze until fully chilled and firm, about 30 minutes. (Dough-lined tart pan can be frozen for up to 1 month.) Adjust oven rack to middle position and heat oven to 375 degrees.

**3** Line chilled tart shell with double layer of aluminum foil and fill with pie weights. Bake on foil-lined rimmed baking sheet until tart shell is golden brown and set, about 30 minutes, rotating sheet halfway through baking. Remove foil and weights and continue to bake tart shell until it is fully baked and golden, 5 to 10 minutes longer. Transfer sheet to wire rack and let cool completely, about 1 hour.

**4** *for the filling* Reduce oven temperature to 250 degrees. Place chocolate in large bowl. Bring cream, espresso powder, and salt to simmer in small saucepan over medium heat, whisking to dissolve espresso powder and salt, then pour over chocolate. Cover and let sit until chocolate is softened, about 5 minutes, then whisk to combine. Whisk in butter until smooth, then add eggs and whisk until combined and glossy.

**5** Pour filling into cooled tart shell and spread into even layer with rubber spatula, popping any large bubbles with toothpick. Bake until edge of filling is just set but center jiggles slightly and very faint cracks appear on surface, 30 to 35 minutes. Let tart cool completely on sheet on wire rack, about 2 hours. Refrigerate, uncovered, until filling is chilled and set, at least 3 hours. (Tart can be refrigerated for up to 18 hours.)

**6** *for the glaze* Remove tart from refrigerator and let sit at room temperature for 30 minutes. Bring cream and corn syrup to simmer in small saucepan over medium heat, stirring occasionally. Off heat, add chocolate, cover, and let sit until chocolate is softened, about 5 minutes. Whisk to combine, then whisk in hot water (glaze should be homogeneous, shiny, and pourable). Working quickly, pour glaze onto center of tart and tilt tart to allow glaze to run to edge. Pop any large bubbles with toothpick. Let sit at room temperature until glaze is set, at least 1 hour or up to 3 hours.

**7** Remove outer ring of tart pan, slide thin metal spatula between tart and tart pan bottom, and carefully slide tart onto serving platter or cutting board. Serve.

### Chocolate-Tahini Tart

*Be mindful of how you plan to cut the tart when arranging the brittle over top.*

In the filling, reduce cream to ¾ cup and chocolate to 5 ounces. Add ¼ cup sugar to saucepan with espresso powder in step 4, whisking until sugar is dissolved. Add ¾ cup tahini to saucepan with butter in step 4, whisking until smooth. Arrange 1 recipe Sesame Brittle (page 345) over finished tart before serving.

# BLOOD ORANGE AND CHOCOLATE TART

Serves 10 to 12

1 recipe Chocolate Tart Dough
(page 328)

*ganache*
¾ cup heavy cream

1 teaspoon grated blood orange
zest

¼ teaspoon table salt

4 ounces bittersweet chocolate,
chopped

3 tablespoons unsalted butter,
softened

½ teaspoon vanilla extract

*jelly*
1 teaspoon unflavored gelatin

1 teaspoon grated blood orange
zest plus 1 cup juice (4 oranges),
divided

½ cup (3½ ounces) sugar

¼ teaspoon table salt

1 blood orange

**WHY THIS RECIPE WORKS** Chocolate tart dough and a silky ganache are deeply chocolaty complementary foundations, but the star of this refined tart is a simple jewel-toned layer of jelly that consists of nothing more than fresh blood orange zest and juice, sugar, salt, and gelatin. For the clearest jelly, be sure to strain the orange juice with a fine-mesh strainer and discard any pulp.

1 Roll dough into 11-inch circle on floured counter, then transfer to parchment paper–lined rimmed baking sheet; cover loosely with plastic wrap and refrigerate until firm but pliable, about 10 minutes.

2 Loosely roll dough around rolling pin and gently unroll it onto 9-inch tart pan with removable bottom, letting excess dough hang over edge. Ease dough into pan by gently lifting edge of dough with your hand while pressing into corners and fluted sides of pan with your other hand. Run rolling pin over top of pan to remove any excess dough. Wrap loosely in plastic, place on large plate, and freeze until fully chilled and firm, about 30 minutes. (Dough-lined tart pan can be frozen for up to 1 month.) Adjust oven rack to middle position and heat oven to 375 degrees.

3 Line chilled tart shell with double layer of aluminum foil and fill with pie weights. Bake on foil-lined rimmed baking sheet until tart is set and fragrant, about 30 minutes, rotating sheet halfway through baking. Remove foil and weights and continue to bake 5 minutes longer. Transfer sheet to wire rack and let cool completely, about 30 minutes.

4 *for the ganache* Bring cream, orange zest, and salt to simmer in small saucepan over medium heat. Off heat, add chocolate, cover, and let sit until chocolate is softened, about 5 minutes, then whisk to combine. Whisk in butter and vanilla until smooth. Pour filling into cooled tart shell, spreading into even layer with rubber spatula. Refrigerate, uncovered, until filling is chilled and set, at least 2 hours or up to 2 days.

5 *for the jelly* Sprinkle gelatin over ¼ cup orange juice in bowl and let sit until gelatin softens, about 5 minutes. Cook orange zest and remaining ¾ cup juice, sugar, and salt in small saucepan over medium-low heat just until sugar dissolves, about 3 minutes, whisking occasionally. Off heat, add softened gelatin and whisk until dissolved. Strain mixture through fine-mesh strainer into bowl and let cool for 15 minutes; discard solids. Slowly pour orange mixture evenly over tart. Refrigerate until jelly is set, about 3 hours. (Tart can be refrigerated for up to 24 hours.)

6 Remove outer ring of tart pan, slide thin metal spatula between tart and tart pan bottom, and carefully slide tart onto serving platter or cutting board. Just before serving, cut away peel and pith from orange. Holding fruit over bowl, use paring knife to slice between membranes to release segments. Arrange orange segments attractively in pinwheel in center of tart. Serve.

# CHOCOLATE, MATCHA, AND POMEGRANATE TART

Serves 8 to 10

1   recipe tart dough
    (see pages 328–331)

*chocolate filling*
2 ½   cups plus 1 tablespoon water,
      divided

4   cups ice cubes

5⅓   ounces bittersweet chocolate
      (70 percent cacao or higher),
      chopped

3   tablespoons plus 1 teaspoon
    granulated sugar

¼   teaspoon kosher salt

*matcha whipped cream*
1   cup heavy cream

½   cup (2 ounces) confectioners'
    sugar

¼   teaspoon kosher salt

1   tablespoon plus 1 teaspoon
    matcha, divided

⅓   cup pomegranate seeds

**WHY THIS RECIPE WORKS** The flavors of this stunning tart are amazingly complex: bittersweet, tart, and herbaceous. There's a buttery tart shell, green tea–spiked whipped cream, and pomegranate seeds, but the sleeper hit is the layer of chocolate ganache. We employ a technique that French chemist Hervé This developed in the 1990s. He created a dairy-free chocolate Chantilly, or whipped chocolate, by melting chocolate with an abundant amount of water and then whipping it to achieve a mousse-like texture. Without the cream found in a normal Chantilly to mute the flavor, the result is something intensely chocolaty and decadent. For our ganache mixture, we melted the chocolate in water with a little sugar before rapidly cooling the mixture over an ice bath to partially crystallize the cocoa butter, form a stable emulsion, and trap a small amount of air. The result? An intense hit of creamy dark chocolate that could compete with the pleasantly strong flavor and umami notes of the matcha. Be sure to use chocolate containing 70 percent cacao or higher; using chocolate with a lower cacao percentage will result in a loose, grainy chocolate layer. You can make your tart look like the one in the photograph by transferring the matcha whipped cream to a piping bag fitted with ½-inch tip and piping small balls in concentric circles over the surface of the chocolate layer.

**1** Roll dough into 11-inch circle on lightly floured counter. Loosely roll dough around rolling pin and gently unroll it onto rimmed baking sheet, cover with plastic wrap, and refrigerate until firm but pliable, about 10 minutes.

**2** Loosely roll dough around rolling pin and gently unroll it onto 9-inch tart pan with removable bottom, letting excess dough hang over edge. Lift dough and gently press it into corners and fluted sides of pan. Run rolling pin over top of pan to remove any excess dough. Wrap loosely in plastic, place on large plate, and freeze until dough is fully chilled and firm, about 30 minutes. (Dough-lined tart pan can be frozen for up to 1 month.) Adjust oven rack to middle position and heat oven to 375 degrees.

**3** Line chilled tart shell with double layer of aluminum foil and fill with pie weights. Bake on foil-lined rimmed baking sheet until tart shell is golden brown and set, about 30 minutes, rotating sheet halfway through baking. Remove foil and weights and continue to bake tart shell until it is fully baked and golden, 5 to 10 minutes longer. Transfer sheet to wire rack and let cool completely, about 1 hour.

**4** *for the chocolate filling* Combine 2 cups water and ice cubes in large bowl to make ice bath. Place chocolate, remaining ½ cup plus 1 tablespoon water, sugar, and salt in metal or glass bowl over saucepan of simmering water. Cook, stirring frequently with rubber spatula, until chocolate is fully melted and smooth, about 5 minutes. Transfer bowl to ice bath and chill, stirring constantly, until mixture is slightly thickened and registers between

75 and 80 degrees, 30 to 60 seconds. Remove bowl from ice bath and continue to stir 30 seconds longer. Transfer filling to cooled tart shell and tap baking sheet lightly on counter to release air bubbles; refrigerate tart until set, about 1 hour. (Tart can be wrapped in plastic wrap and refrigerated for up to 24 hours.)

**5** *for matcha whipped cream* Using stand mixer fitted with whisk attachment, whip cream, sugar, and salt on high speed until soft peaks form. Add 1 tablespoon matcha, reduce speed to medium, and whip until stiff peaks form. Remove tart from refrigerator. Remove outer ring of tart pan, slide thin metal spatula between tart and tart pan bottom, and carefully slide tart onto serving platter or cutting board. Spread whipped cream evenly over chocolate layer. Using fine-mesh strainer, dust tart with remaining 1 teaspoon matcha. Sprinkle with pomegranate seeds. Serve.

# *pies*
# BIG AND SMALL

# APPLE SLAB PIE

Serves 18 to 24

2 recipes Slab Pie Dough (page 336)

3½ pounds Granny Smith apples, peeled, cored, and sliced ¼ inch thick

3½ pounds Golden Delicious apples, peeled, cored, and sliced ¼ inch thick

1 cup (7 ounces) granulated sugar

½ teaspoon table salt

6 tablespoons instant tapioca, ground

2 teaspoons ground cinnamon

5 tablespoons lemon juice (2 lemons), divided

1 tablespoon unsalted butter, softened

1¼ cups (5 ounces) confectioners' sugar

**WHY THIS RECIPE WORKS** Slab pie is a feat of baking ingenuity. The impressively large pie is prepared in a baking sheet rather than in a pie plate and can be cut into 24 easy-to-pick-up squares, making pie a big-party possibility. As with other fruit slabs, the filling for apple slab pie is thickened to a consistency that ensures neat slicing. And slab pie's flat top is perfect for holding a sweet glaze. But rolling out the dough to cover both the bottom and top of this mammoth pie is not without challenges. We increased the proportions of our all-butter pie dough to create a large-scale recipe specifically for slab pies. Rather than roll the dough into really big rectangles that were bound to tear as we transferred them to the pan, we rolled out four smaller rectangles (two for the bottom crust and two for the top), overlapping them slightly and sealing them at their seams with water. Tapioca thickened the filling, but another helpful step was tossing the apples with sugar and letting them sit until some of their juices drained. Not wanting that flavor to go to waste; we reduced the apple juice and stirred it into our confectioners' sugar–based glaze. Good choices for tart apples are Granny Smiths, Empires, or Cortlands; for sweet, we recommend Golden Delicious, Jonagolds, or Braeburns. You will need two 18 by 13-inch rimmed baking sheets for this recipe. You can toss the apple mixture in step 4 in two bowls if it doesn't fit in one.

1 Line rimmed baking sheet with parchment paper. Roll each dough square into 16 by 11-inch rectangle on floured counter; stack on prepared sheet, separated by additional sheets of parchment. Cover loosely with plastic wrap and refrigerate until dough is firm but still pliable, about 10 minutes.

2 Using parchment as sling, transfer 2 chilled dough rectangles to counter; discard parchment. Spray second rimmed baking sheet with vegetable oil spray. Starting at short side of 1 dough rectangle, loosely roll around rolling pin, then gently unroll over half of long side of prepared sheet, leaving about 2 inches of dough overhanging 3 edges. Repeat with second dough rectangle, unrolling it over empty side of sheet and overlapping first dough rectangle by ½ inch.

3 Ease dough into sheet by gently lifting edges of dough with your hand while pressing into sheet bottom with your other hand. Brush overlapping edge of dough rectangles with water and press to seal. Cover loosely with plastic and refrigerate until dough is firm, about 30 minutes.

4 Meanwhile, adjust oven racks to lower-middle and lowest positions and heat oven to 375 degrees. Toss apples, granulated sugar, and salt together in large bowl. Let sit, tossing occasionally, until apples release their juices, about 30 minutes.

5 Working in batches, drain apples thoroughly in colander set over bowl; transfer to another large bowl. Reserve ¾ cup of juice; discard remaining juice. Whisk tapioca and cinnamon together in small bowl, then add to apples along with 3 tablespoons lemon juice and toss to combine. Spread apple mixture evenly over chilled dough-lined sheet.

**6** Using parchment as sling, transfer remaining 2 dough rectangles to counter; discard parchment. Overlap longer sides of dough rectangles by ½ inch, then brush overlapping edge with water and press to seal. Starting at short side of joined dough rectangle, loosely roll dough around rolling pin, then gently unroll over top of filling, starting at short side of sheet.

**7** Trim overhang to ½ inch beyond edge of sheet. Pinch edges of top and bottom dough firmly together. Tuck overhang under itself; folded edge should rest on edge of sheet. Crimp dough evenly around edge of sheet. Cut 2-inch slits at 2-inch intervals in top of dough.

**8** Place large sheet of aluminum foil directly on lower rack (to catch any bubbling juices). Place pie on upper rack and bake until crust is deep golden brown and juices are bubbling, 1 to 1¼ hours, rotating sheet halfway through baking. Let pie cool on wire rack until filling has set, about 2 hours.

**9** While pie is cooling, bring reserved apple juice to simmer in small saucepan over medium heat and cook until thickened and reduced to ¼ cup, about 6 minutes. Off heat, stir in butter and remaining 2 tablespoons lemon juice. Let mixture cool slightly, about 10 minutes, then whisk in confectioners' sugar until combined. Brush glaze evenly over pie and let sit for 10 minutes. Serve.

# PEACH SLAB PIE

**Serves 18 to 24**

2    recipes Slab Pie Dough
    (page 336)

1    cup (7 ounces) sugar

⅓    cup instant tapioca, ground

½    teaspoon ground cinnamon

¼    teaspoon table salt

⅛    teaspoon ground nutmeg

6    pounds ripe but firm peaches,
    peeled, halved, pitted, and
    sliced ½ inch thick

2    teaspoons grated lemon zest
    plus 2 tablespoons juice

1    large egg, lightly beaten with
    1 tablespoon water

**WHY THIS RECIPE WORKS**  Peach pie—with its sweet, juicy, tender peaches encased in a buttery crust, just begging for a scoop of vanilla ice cream—is the epitome of summer desserts. But this sweet reward isn't without work, usually requiring precooking the fruit and using multiple thickeners to prevent a soupy mess. The larger surface area of our peach slab pie gives it a leg up on pies baked in a traditional pie plate because it allows for more moisture evaporation, particularly when topped with a lattice crust (which was easy to make on the rectangle pie). Tossing the peaches with plenty of ground tapioca ensured the filling held together. While slab pies have a thinner layer of filling compared with regular pies, we didn't skimp on the fruit; cutting the peaches into slices rather than chunks allowed us to fit 6 pounds of peaches in an even layer. If your peaches are too soft to peel with a peeler, cut a shallow X in the bottom of the fruit, blanch them in a pot of simmering water for 15 seconds, and then shock them in a bowl of ice water before peeling. You will need two 18 by 13-inch rimmed baking sheets for this recipe. You can toss the peach mixture in step 6 in two bowls if it doesn't fit in one.

---

**1**  Line rimmed baking sheet with parchment paper. Roll 2 dough squares into 16 by 11-inch rectangles on floured counter; stack on prepared sheet, separated by second sheet of parchment. Cover loosely with plastic wrap and refrigerate until dough is firm but still pliable, about 10 minutes.

**2**  Line second rimmed baking sheet with parchment. Roll 1 dough square into 15 by 12-inch rectangle and remaining 1 dough square into 20 by 9-inch rectangle on floured counter; stack on prepared sheet, separated by second sheet of parchment. Cover loosely with plastic and refrigerate until dough is firm but still pliable, about 10 minutes.

**3**  Using parchment as sling, transfer chilled 16 by 11-inch dough rectangles to counter; discard parchment. Wipe sheet clean with paper towels and spray with vegetable oil spray. Starting at short side of 1 dough rectangle, loosely roll around rolling pin, then gently unroll over half of long side of prepared sheet, leaving about 2 inches of dough overhanging 3 edges. Repeat with second dough rectangle, unrolling it over empty side of sheet and overlapping first dough rectangle by ½ inch.

**4**  Ease dough into sheet by gently lifting edges of dough with your hand while pressing into sheet bottom with your other hand. Brush overlapping edge of dough rectangles with water and press to seal. Cover loosely with plastic and refrigerate until firm, about 30 minutes.

**5**  Using parchment as sling, transfer remaining 2 dough rectangles to counter. Using ruler and pizza wheel, fluted pastry wheel, or paring knife, cut smaller dough rectangle into seven 15-inch-long by 1½-inch-wide strips and larger dough rectangle into five 20-inch-long by 1½-inch-wide strips. Return strips to sheet, still on parchment. Cover loosely with plastic and refrigerate until firm, about 30 minutes.

**6** Meanwhile, adjust oven racks to lower-middle and lowest positions and heat oven to 375 degrees. Whisk sugar, tapioca, cinnamon, salt, and nutmeg together in large bowl. Add peaches and lemon zest and juice and toss to combine. Spread peach mixture evenly over dough-lined sheet.

**7** Remove dough strips from refrigerator; if too stiff to be workable, let sit at room temperature until softened slightly but still very cold. Space long dough strips evenly across length of pie. Fold first, third, and fifth strips back halfway from right to left. Lay 1 short dough strip across pie, perpendicular to second and fourth strips, keeping it snug to folded edges of dough strips, then unfold first, third, and fifth strips over top. Fold back second and forth strips in same direction, stopping just before vertical strip. Lay second short dough strip over top of first, third, and fifth strips, keeping it snug to folded edges. Unfold strips.

**8** Repeat process, weaving 2 more short dough strips over half of pie, until you reach edge of sheet, then repeat on opposite half of pie. Shift short dough strips as needed so they are evenly spaced over top of pie. (If dough becomes too soft to work with, refrigerate pie and dough strips until firm.)

**9** Trim overhang to ½ inch beyond edge of sheet. Pinch edges of bottom crust and lattice strips firmly together. Tuck overhang under itself; folded edge should rest on rim of sheet. Crimp dough evenly around edge of sheet. Brush surface with egg wash.

**10** Place large sheet of aluminum foil directly on lower rack (to catch any bubbling juices). Place pie on upper rack and bake until crust is deep golden brown and juices are bubbling, 1 hour to 1¼ hours, rotating sheet halfway through baking. Let pie cool on wire rack until filling has set, about 2 hours. Serve.

## Making the Lattice Top for Peach Slab Pie

**1** Space long dough strips evenly across length of pie. Fold first, third, and fifth strips back halfway from right to left.

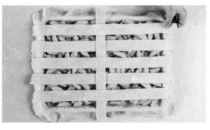

**2** Lay 1 short dough strip across pie, perpendicular to second and fourth strips, keeping it snug to folded edges of dough strips, then unfold first, third, and fifth strips over top.

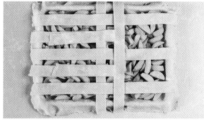

**3** Fold back second and forth strips in same direction, stopping just before vertical strip. Lay second short dough strip over top of first, third, and fifth strips, keeping it snug to folded edges. Unfold strips.

**4** Repeat process, weaving 2 more short dough strips over half of pie, until you reach edge of sheet.

**5** Repeat on opposite half of pie. Shift short dough strips as needed so they are evenly spaced over top of pie.

**6** Trim overhang to ½ inch beyond edge of sheet. Pinch edges of bottom crust and lattice strips firmly together. Tuck overhang under itself and crimp.

PEACH SLAB PIE

# PEAR-BUTTERSCOTCH SLAB PIE

**Serves 18 to 24**

2 recipes Slab Pie Dough (page 336)

7 pounds ripe but firm Bosc pears, peeled, halved, cored, and sliced ¼ inch thick

¼ cup (1¾ ounces) sugar

½ teaspoon table salt

¼ cup instant tapioca, ground

1 teaspoon ground cinnamon

¼ teaspoon ground cloves

¼ teaspoon ground star anise

2 recipes Butterscotch Sauce (page 342), divided

1 large egg, lightly beaten with 1 tablespoon water

**WHY THIS RECIPE WORKS** When it comes to fall desserts, pears are the neglected siblings of apples, with apple concoctions far outnumbering those where pears are the star. But pears can be more than just poached, and we set out to develop a beautiful slab pie featuring the other fall fruit. Firm but ripe Bosc pears gave our filling the best texture and didn't make the crust soggy. We matched the floral sweetness of the pears with a trio of warm spices (and not your average apple pie spices)—cinnamon, cloves, and star anise—and then drizzled our fruit filling with rich, buttery, vanilla-scented butterscotch. This pear slab pie was unique and deserved an appealing topper, so we covered it with pie dough cutouts—we loved the autumnal look of fall leaves (though you could choose another cutter). The cutouts were a simple alternative to a lattice crust but similarly ensured that moisture would evaporate during baking. With extra butterscotch sauce served on the side of our pear slab pie, no one will miss the apples. If you can't find ground star anise, you can grind your own, or substitute five-spice powder. You will need two 18 by 13-inch rimmed baking sheets for this recipe. You can toss the pear mixture in step 5 in two bowls if it doesn't fit in one. We prefer to use 3-inch cookie cutters for this recipe, but you can use whatever size and shape you prefer. When placing the cutouts on the pie, be sure to leave space for evaporation and don't overlap more than 2 cutouts.

1 Line rimmed baking sheet with parchment paper. Roll each dough square into 16 by 11-inch rectangle on floured counter; stack on prepared sheet, separated by additional sheets of parchment. Cover loosely with plastic wrap and refrigerate until dough is firm but still pliable, about 10 minutes.

2 Using parchment as sling, transfer 2 chilled dough rectangles to counter; discard parchment. Spray second rimmed baking sheet with vegetable oil spray. Starting at short side of 1 dough rectangle, loosely roll around rolling pin, then gently unroll over half of long side of prepared sheet, leaving about 2 inches of dough overhanging 3 edges. Repeat with second dough rectangle, unrolling it over empty side of sheet and overlapping first dough piece by ½ inch.

3 Ease dough into sheet by gently lifting edges of dough with your hand while pressing into sheet bottom with your other hand. Brush overlapping edge of dough rectangles with water and press to seal. Trim overhang to ½ inch beyond edge of sheet. Tuck overhang under itself; folded edge should rest on edge of sheet. Crimp dough evenly around edge of sheet. Cover loosely with plastic and refrigerate until firm, about 30 minutes.

4 Using parchment as sling, transfer remaining 2 dough rectangles to counter. Using cookie cutters, cut as many shapes from dough rectangles as you can. Reserve dough scraps for another use. Return cutouts to sheet, still on parchment, and cover loosely with plastic. Refrigerate until firm, about 30 minutes.

**5** Meanwhile, adjust oven racks to lower-middle and lowest positions and heat oven to 375 degrees. Toss pears, sugar, and salt together in large bowl. Let sit, tossing occasionally, until pears release their juices, about 30 minutes.

**6** Working in batches, drain pears thoroughly in colander, discarding juices; transfer to large bowl and discard juices. Whisk tapioca, cinnamon, cloves, and star anise together in small bowl, then add to pears and toss to combine. Spread pear mixture evenly over chilled dough-lined sheet, then drizzle evenly with 1 cup butterscotch sauce. Arrange cutouts evenly over fruit, being careful not to overlap more than 2 cutouts. Brush cutouts with egg wash.

**7** Place large sheet of aluminum foil directly on lower rack (to catch any bubbling juices). Place pie on upper rack and bake until crust is deep golden brown and juices are bubbling, 1 hour to 1 hour 10 minutes, rotating sheet halfway through baking. Let pie cool on wire rack until filling has set, about 2 hours. Serve, passing remaining butterscotch sauce separately.

---

### Decorating Pear-Butterscotch Slab Pie with Cutouts

**1** Using cookie cutters, cut as many shapes from dough rectangles as you can. Reserve dough scraps for another use.

**2** Return cutouts to sheet, still on parchment, and cover loosely with plastic. Refrigerate until firm, about 30 minutes.

**3** Arrange cutouts evenly over fruit, being careful not to overlap more than 2 cutouts.

**4** Brush cutouts with egg wash.

# NECTARINE AND RASPBERRY SLAB GALETTE

**Serves 18 to 24**

| 1 | recipe Slab Pie Dough (page 336) |
|---|---|
| 3¼ | pounds ripe but firm nectarines, halved, pitted, and sliced ½ inch thick |
| 12½ | ounces (2½ cups) raspberries |
| ½ | cup (3½ ounces) plus 1 tablespoon sugar, divided |
| ¼ | teaspoon table salt |

**WHY THIS RECIPE WORKS** At the height of summer, fruit galettes are a simple yet beautiful way to showcase the season's bounty. While galettes are typically free-form circular creations (see our Free-Form Fruit Tart with Plums and Raspberries on page 36, for example), we formed an extra-large galette in a baking sheet. The expansive surface highlighted the beauty of the exposed fruit, which was framed like stained glass by just a few inches of crust. Baking the galette on the lower-middle rack until the crust was deep golden brown helped crisp up the bottom. And the large surface area of the sheet meant the fruit juices evaporated readily and thickened enough on their own after cooking so we didn't need a thickener. You will need one 18 by 13-inch rimmed baking sheet for this recipe. You can toss the fruit mixture in step 4 in two bowls if it doesn't fit in one.

**1** Line rimmed baking sheet with parchment paper. Roll each dough square into 16 by 11-inch rectangle on floured counter; stack on prepared sheet, separated by second sheet of parchment. Cover loosely with plastic wrap and refrigerate until dough is firm but still pliable, about 10 minutes.

**2** Using parchment as sling, transfer chilled dough rectangles to counter; discard parchment. Wipe sheet clean with paper towels and spray with vegetable oil spray. Starting at short side of 1 dough rectangle, loosely roll around rolling pin, then gently unroll over half of long side of prepared sheet, leaving about 2 inches of dough overhanging 3 edges. Repeat with second dough rectangle, unrolling it over empty side of sheet and overlapping first dough piece by ½ inch.

**3** Ease dough into sheet by gently lifting edges of dough with your hand while pressing into sheet bottom with your other hand. Brush overlapping edge of dough rectangles with water and press to seal. Leave any dough that overhangs sheet in place. Cover loosely with plastic and refrigerate until firm, about 30 minutes.

**4** Adjust oven racks to lower-middle and lowest positions and heat oven to 375 degrees. Gently toss nectarines, raspberries, ½ cup sugar, and salt together in bowl. Spread nectarine mixture evenly over chilled dough-lined sheet. Fold overhanging dough over filling, pleating corners, trimming excess dough as needed, and pinching overlapping edges to secure. (If dough is too stiff to fold, let stand at room temperature until pliable.) Brush dough with water and sprinkle evenly with remaining 1 tablespoon sugar.

**5** Place large sheet of aluminum foil directly on lower rack (to catch any bubbling juices). Place galette on upper rack and bake until crust is deep golden brown and fruit is bubbling, about 1 hour, rotating sheet halfway through baking. Let galette cool on wire rack until filling has set, about 2 hours. Serve.

# TRIPLE BERRY SLAB PIE WITH GINGER-LEMON STREUSEL

**Serves 18 to 24**

1    recipe Slab Pie Dough
     (page 336)

*streusel*

1½   cups (7½ ounces) all-purpose
     flour

½    cup packed (3½ ounces) light
     brown sugar

½    cup crystallized ginger,
     chopped fine

¼    cup (1¾ ounces) granulated
     sugar

1    tablespoon ground ginger

1    teaspoon grated lemon zest

¼    teaspoon table salt

10   tablespoons unsalted butter,
     melted and cooled

*filling*

1    cup (7 ounces) granulated sugar

6    tablespoons instant tapioca,
     ground

1    teaspoon grated lemon zest

¼    teaspoon table salt

1¼   pounds (4 cups) blackberries

1¼   pounds (4 cups) blueberries

1¼   pounds (4 cups) raspberries

**WHY THIS RECIPE WORKS** Our berry slab pie is guaranteed to elicit oohs and aahs before the first slice is even cut. And no one will know it's a cinch to prepare. We started by tossing no-prep berries—blueberries, raspberries, and blackberries—with sugar, lemon zest, and tapioca for the filling. Instead of applying a top crust, which would hide the beautiful berry hues and trap moisture, we sprinkled on a streusel that we flavored liberally with more lemon zest as well as some crystallized ginger; the topping added fresh and zingy pops of flavor to the sweet, bright berries peeking through. You will need one 18 by 13-inch rimmed baking sheet for this recipe. You can toss the berry mixture in step 5 in two bowls if it doesn't fit in one.

---

**1** Line rimmed baking sheet with parchment paper. Roll each dough square into 16 by 11-inch rectangle on floured counter; stack on prepared sheet, separated by second sheet of parchment. Cover loosely with plastic wrap and refrigerate until dough is firm but still pliable, about 10 minutes.

**2** Using parchment as sling, transfer chilled dough rectangles to counter; discard parchment. Wipe sheet clean with paper towels and spray with vegetable oil spray. Starting at short side of 1 dough rectangle, loosely roll around rolling pin, then gently unroll over half of long side of prepared sheet, leaving about 2 inches of dough overhanging 3 edges. Repeat with second dough rectangle, unrolling it over empty side of sheet and overlapping first dough piece by ½ inch.

**3** Ease dough into sheet by gently lifting edges of dough with your hand while pressing into sheet bottom with your other hand. Brush overlapping edge of dough rectangles with water and press to seal. Trim overhang to ½ inch beyond edge of sheet. Tuck overhang under itself; folded edge should rest on edge of sheet. Crimp dough evenly around edge of sheet. Cover loosely with plastic and refrigerate until firm, about 30 minutes.

**4** *For the streusel* Meanwhile, adjust oven racks to lower-middle and lowest positions and heat oven to 375 degrees. Combine flour, brown sugar, crystallized ginger, granulated sugar, ground ginger, lemon zest, and salt in bowl. Stir in melted butter until mixture is completely moistened; let sit for 10 minutes.

**5** *For the filling* Whisk sugar, tapioca, lemon zest, and salt together in large bowl. Add blackberries, blueberries, and raspberries and gently toss to combine. Spread berry mixture evenly over chilled dough-lined sheet. Sprinkle streusel evenly over fruit, breaking apart any large chunks. Place large sheet of aluminum foil directly on lower rack (to catch any bubbling juices). Place pie on upper rack and bake until crust and streusel are deep golden brown and juices are bubbling, 45 minutes to 1 hour, rotating sheet halfway through baking. Let pie cool on wire rack until filling has set, about 2 hours. Serve.

# KEY LIME MERINGUE SLAB PIE

Serves 18 to 24

*crust*

**24** whole graham crackers, broken into 1-inch pieces

**½** cup sugar

**16** tablespoons unsalted butter, melted and cooled

*filling*

**12** large egg yolks

**3** cups sweetened condensed milk

**3** tablespoons grated lime zest plus 1½ cups juice (12 limes)

*meringue*

**⅔** cup water

**2** tablespoons cornstarch

**8** large egg whites

**1** teaspoon vanilla extract

**½** teaspoon cream of tartar

**1** cup (7 ounces) sugar

**2** teaspoons grated lime zest

**WHY THIS RECIPE WORKS** Meringue-topped pies are showstoppers, particularly when presented in the large format of slab pie. For a stunning spin on traditional Key lime pie, we topped the sweet-tart lime filling (made with lime juice, sweetened condensed milk, and egg yolks) with peaks of fluffy meringue instead of the more traditional whipped cream. But the sugary meringue made the pie toothachingly sweet. Cutting back on the condensed milk and including generous amounts of lime juice and zest in the filling restored balance. We baked the filling for a short time in a relatively cool oven until it was set; the hot filling helped cook the underside of the meringue once it was applied. A sprinkle of lime zest on the finished slab hinted at what was below the billowy meringue. A stiff metal spatula works well for evening out graham cracker crumbs in baking sheet corners. Despite this pie's name, we found that most tasters could not tell the difference between pies made with regular supermarket limes (called Persian limes) and true Key limes. Since Persian limes are easier to find and to juice we recommend using them instead. Though we prefer fresh lime juice, you may also use bottled lime juice in this recipe. You will need three (14-ounce) cans of sweetened condensed milk to make the filling. It is important that the crust still be warm when the filling is added in step 4.

---

**1** *For the crust* Adjust oven rack to middle position and heat oven to 325 degrees. Process graham cracker pieces and sugar in food processor to fine, even crumbs, about 30 seconds. Sprinkle melted butter over crumbs and pulse to incorporate, about 5 pulses.

**2** Spray rimmed baking sheet with vegetable oil spray. Using bottom of dry measuring cup, press crumbs into even layer on bottom and up sides of sheet. Bake until crust is fragrant and beginning to brown, 12 to 18 minutes; transfer to wire rack. (Crust must still be warm when filling is added.)

**3** *For the filling* Meanwhile, whisk egg yolks, condensed milk, and lime zest and juice together in bowl. Let sit at room temperature until thickened, about 30 minutes.

**4** *For the meringue* Bring water and cornstarch to simmer in small saucepan over medium-high heat and cook, whisking occasionally, until thickened and translucent, 1 to 2 minutes. Remove from heat and let cool slightly.

**5** Using stand mixer fitted with whisk attachment, whip egg whites, vanilla, and cream of tartar on medium-low speed until foamy, about 1 minute. Increase speed to medium-high and beat in sugar, 1 tablespoon at a time, until incorporated and mixture forms soft, billowy mounds, about 1 minute. Add cornstarch mixture, 1 tablespoon at a time, and continue to beat until glossy, stiff peaks form, 2 to 3 minutes. Set meringue aside.

**6** Spread thickened filling evenly into warm pie crust. Bake for 7 minutes, then remove from oven.

**7** Using rubber spatula, immediately dollop meringue evenly around edge of crust, spreading meringue so it touches crust (this will prevent the meringue from shrinking), then fill in center with remaining meringue. Using back of spoon, create attractive swirls and peaks in meringue. Return sheet to oven and bake until meringue is light golden brown, about 15 minutes, rotating sheet halfway through baking. Let pie cool on wire rack until filling has set, about 2 hours. Sprinkle lime zest evenly over top before serving.

## Topping Key Lime Meringue Slab Pie

**1** Using rubber spatula, immediately dollop meringue evenly around edge of crust, spreading meringue so it touches crust.

**2** Fill in center with remaining meringue.

**3** Return sheet to oven and bake until meringue is light golden brown, about 15 minutes, rotating sheet halfway through baking.

**4** Sprinkle lime zest evenly over top before serving.

KEY LIME MERINGUE
SLAB PIE

# PEAR-ROSEMARY MUFFIN TIN PIES

**Serves 10**

1   recipe double-crust pie dough
    (see pages 320–327)

*filling*

2½  pounds ripe but firm Bosc pears,
    peeled, halved, cored, and cut
    into ½-inch pieces

3   tablespoons packed brown
    sugar, divided

¼   teaspoon table salt

1   tablespoon instant tapioca,
    ground

¾   teaspoon minced fresh rosemary

*streusel*

⅔   cup (3⅓ ounces) all-purpose
    flour

½   cup walnuts, chopped fine

6   tablespoons packed
    (2⅔ ounces) brown sugar

½   teaspoon table salt

6   tablespoons unsalted butter

**WHY THIS RECIPE WORKS** These individual pear pies—made in a muffin tin—capture all the scents and flavors of fall in a few bites. We were delighted by the pairing of fragrant, piney rosemary with the sweet, honey-like flavor of Bosc pears in our simple filling, which we thickened with ground tapioca and sweetened with a hint of brown sugar. Precooking the pears removed excess moisture that might otherwise bubble over in the muffin tin cups; it also reduced the fruit's volume, allowing us to pack the entire dough cup with filling. We topped the pies with a walnut streusel brought together by browned butter. This streusel added a subtle savory note to the sweet pears, and its nutty aroma permeated the kitchen before we even put the pies in the oven. While a muffin tin was perfect for creating mini pies, the middle pies were insulated by the surrounding ones and emerged from the oven soggy and soft on the bottom. After testing various options, we found that leaving the middle two muffin cups empty was the most reliable approach to ensure all of our pies had consistently browned, flaky bottoms. Be sure to spray both the muffin tin cups and the surface between cups with vegetable oil spray to prevent sticking.

---

**1** Line rimmed baking sheet with parchment paper. Roll each dough piece into 16 by 11-inch rectangle on floured counter; stack on prepared sheet, separated by second sheet of parchment. Cover loosely with plastic wrap and refrigerate until dough is firm but still pliable, about 10 minutes.

**2** Spray outer cups of 12-cup muffin tin as well as surface in between cups with vegetable oil spray. Using parchment as sling, transfer chilled dough rectangles to counter. Using 5-inch round biscuit or cookie cutter, cut 5 rounds from each dough rectangle. Reserve dough scraps for another use. Return rounds to sheet, still on parchment, and cover loosely with plastic. Refrigerate until firm but still pliable, about 10 minutes.

**3** Center 1 dough round over outer muffin tin cup. Using your fingers, press center of dough into bottom of cup, then press dough into corners and against sides, smoothing out any overlapping creases. (You should have about ½-inch dough overhanging rim of cup.) Fold overhang over itself; fold edge over rim of cup to rest on surface of muffin tin. Repeat with remaining 9 dough rounds and outer muffin tin cups. (If dough rounds become too soft to work with, refrigerate tin and rounds until firm.) Cover and refrigerate muffin tin until dough is firm, about 30 minutes.

**4** *For the filling* Toss pears, 1 tablespoon sugar, and salt together in bowl. Microwave until pears soften slightly and release their juices, 6 to 8 minutes, stirring once halfway through microwaving. Drain pears thoroughly in colander set over bowl; discard juices and return pears to now-empty bowl. Let pears cool completely, about 30 minutes.

**5** *For the streusel* Meanwhile, adjust oven rack to lower-middle position and heat oven to 375 degrees. Whisk flour, walnuts, sugar, and salt together in medium bowl. Melt butter in 10-inch skillet over medium-high heat and cook, swirling skillet constantly, until butter is browned and has nutty aroma, 3 to 5 minutes. Stir butter into flour mixture until completely moistened.

**6** Whisk remaining 2 tablespoons sugar, tapioca, and rosemary together in small bowl. Add to pears and toss to combine. Divide pear mixture evenly among dough-lined cups. Sprinkle streusel evenly over fruit, breaking apart any large clumps. Bake until crusts are deep golden brown and juices are bubbling, 35 to 45 minutes, rotating muffin tin halfway through baking. Transfer muffin tin to wire rack and let pies cool for 10 minutes. Run paring knife around edges of pies, transfer to wire rack, and let cool until filling has set, about 2 hours. Serve.

## Making Pear-Rosemary Muffin Tin Pies

**1** Center 1 dough round over outer muffin tin cup.

**2** Using your fingers, press center of dough into bottom of cup.

**3** Press dough into corners and against sides, smoothing out any overlapping creases. (You should have about ½-inch dough overhanging rim of cup.)

**4** Fold overhang over itself.

**5** Fold edge over rim of cup to rest on surface of muffin tin.

**6** Divide pear mixture evenly among dough-lined cups. Sprinkle streusel evenly over fruit, breaking apart any large clumps.

# BLUEBERRY HAND PIES

Serves 8

1 pound (3¼ cups) fresh or frozen blueberries

½ cup (3½ ounces) plus 1 tablespoon sugar, divided

1 teaspoon grated lemon zest

¼ teaspoon table salt

¼ teaspoon ground cinnamon

1 tablespoon cornstarch

1 tablespoon water

2 (9½ by 9-inch) sheets puff pastry, thawed

1 large egg, lightly beaten with 1 tablespoon water

**WHY THIS RECIPE WORKS** Compared with traditional pies, small hand pies are incredibly versatile and a justifiable treat at any time. They're portable (and made to be eaten out of hand); perfect for parties, picnics, or on the go; and can easily cross over from dessert to sweet snack (they can even be breakfast fare if you're feeling indulgent). To make them as easy as they are versatile, we started with store-bought puff pastry and a simple precooked filling of blueberries flavored with cinnamon and lemon zest. Freezing the pastries before baking allowed the pastry enough time to crisp up without the risk of the filling overcooking or bubbling out in the oven. Even still, cutting sufficient steam vents—we found we needed three 1-inch-long slits in the tops—was key to preventing the turnovers from bursting open and leaking blueberry. Brushed with egg wash and sprinkled with sugar, our turnovers were crispy and flaky on the outside and full of luscious blueberry filling. To thaw frozen puff pastry, let it sit either in the refrigerator for 24 hours or on the counter for 30 minutes to 1 hour.

---

**1** Cook blueberries, ½ cup sugar, lemon zest, salt, and cinnamon in medium saucepan over medium heat, stirring occasionally, until blueberries begin to break down and release their juices, about 8 minutes. Reduce heat to medium-low and continue to cook until mixture thickens and spatula starts to leave trail when pulled through, 8 to 10 minutes.

**2** Whisk cornstarch and water together in bowl, then stir into blueberry mixture. Cook until mixture has thickened to jam-like consistency, about 1 minute (you should have about 1¼ cups filling). Let cool completely, about 30 minutes.

**3** Adjust oven rack middle position and heat oven to 400 degrees. Line rimmed baking sheet with parchment paper. Working with 1 sheet of pastry at a time, roll into 10-inch square on floured counter. Cut pastry into four 5-inch squares. Place 2 tablespoons blueberry filling in center of each square.

**4** Brush edges of squares with egg wash, then fold dough over filling to form rectangle. Using fork, crimp edges of dough to seal. Transfer pies to prepared sheet and cut three 1-inch slits on top (do not cut through filling). Freeze pies until firm, about 15 minutes. (Once frozen, pies can be transferred to airtight container and stored in freezer for up to 1 month.)

**5** Brush tops of pies with remaining egg wash and sprinkle with remaining 1 tablespoon sugar. Bake until well browned, about 25 minutes, rotating sheet halfway through baking. Transfer pies to wire rack and let cool slightly, about 15 minutes. Serve warm or at room temperature.

## Making Blueberry Hand Pies

**1** Place 2 tablespoons blueberry filling in center of each square.

**2** Brush edges of squares with egg wash, then fold dough over filling to form rectangle.

**3** Using fork, crimp edges of dough to seal. Transfer pies to prepared sheet and cut three 1-inch slits on top (do not cut through filling).

# CARAMEL APPLE HAND PIES

Serves 8

2 (9½ by 9-inch) sheets puff
   pastry, thawed

1 large Granny Smith apple,
   peeled, cored, and cut into
   ½-inch pieces (1 cup)

½ cup Caramel Sauce (page 341)

1 large egg, lightly beaten with
   1 tablespoon water

2 tablespoons sugar

½ teaspoon ground cinnamon

**WHY THIS RECIPE WORKS** Caramel sauce and apples are a classic pairing, with the sweet, rich, buttery sauce balancing the tart, juicy fruit. We wanted to combine caramel and apples in a filling for hand pies, for an easy, versatile dessert that could be eaten out of hand or served as an elegant plated dessert at a dinner party. How easy? All we needed to do for our filling was chop up a Granny Smith apple (tasters liked its tart flavor and the pieces held their shape nicely through baking) and dollop on a tablespoon of our classic Caramel Sauce (page 341). Finishing our hand pies with a sprinkling of cinnamon sugar gave them a sweet sparkle and a superthin, shattering crust that looked beautiful and tasted great. To thaw frozen puff pastry, let it sit either in the refrigerator for 24 hours or on the counter for 30 minutes to 1 hour.

**1** Adjust oven rack to middle position and heat oven to 400 degrees. Line rimmed baking sheet with parchment paper.

**2** Working with 1 sheet of pastry at a time, roll into 10-inch square on floured counter. Cut pastry into four 5-inch squares. Place 2 tablespoons apple in center of each square and dollop 1 tablespoon caramel sauce over top.

**3** Brush edges of squares with egg wash, then fold 1 corner of each square diagonally over filling. Using fork, crimp edges of dough to seal. Transfer pies to prepared sheet and cut three 1-inch slits on top (do not cut through filling). Freeze pies until firm, about 15 minutes. (Once frozen, pies can be transferred to airtight container and stored in freezer for up to 1 month.)

**4** Combine sugar and cinnamon in bowl. Brush tops of pies with remaining egg wash and sprinkle with cinnamon sugar. Bake until well browned, 15 to 20 minutes, rotating sheet halfway through baking. Transfer pies to wire rack and let cool slightly, about 15 minutes. Serve warm or at room temperature.

# CHERRY HAND PIES

Serves 8

1 pound fresh or frozen sweet cherries, pitted and chopped

¼ cup (1¾ ounces) plus 1 tablespoon sugar, divided

½ teaspoon almond extract

½ teaspoon grated orange zest

⅛ teaspoon table salt

1 tablespoon cornstarch

1 tablespoon water

2 (9½ by 9-inch) sheets puff pastry, thawed

1 large egg, lightly beaten with 1 tablespoon water

**WHY THIS RECIPE WORKS** Summer cherry season is so fleeting that if you blink you can miss it. That's why we were thrilled to discover that fresh or frozen sweet cherries worked equally well in our cherry hand pies. We found the sweetness, deep color, and firm texture of sweet cherries more appealing than softer jarred or canned tart cherries (which are commonly used for pies) in this quick-baking pastry. Chopping the cherries gave the filling more body and ensured every bite of turnover had chunks of fruit. A little almond extract and orange zest deepened the cherry flavor without being distracting. We now had cherry hand pies that tasted like summer but could be made at any time of year. Weigh frozen cherries before thawing and draining. The three 1-inch slits are essential to prevent the pastries from bursting and leaking filling. To thaw frozen puff pastry, let it sit either in the refrigerator for 24 hours or on the counter for 30 minutes to 1 hour.

1 Cook cherries, ¼ cup sugar, almond extract, orange zest, and salt in medium saucepan over medium heat, stirring occasionally, until cherries release their juices, mixture thickens and spatula starts to leave trail when pulled through, 6 to 8 minutes.

2 Whisk cornstarch and water together in bowl, then stir into cherry mixture. Cook until mixture has thickened to jam-like consistency, about 1 minute (you should have about 1¼ cups filling). Let cool completely, about 30 minutes.

3 Adjust oven rack to middle position and heat oven to 400 degrees. Line rimmed baking sheet with parchment paper. Working with 1 sheet of pastry at a time, roll into 10-inch square on floured counter. Cut pastry into four 5-inch squares. Place 2 tablespoons cherry filling in center of each square.

4 Brush edges of squares with egg wash, then fold 1 corner of each square diagonally over filling. Using fork, crimp edges of dough to seal. Transfer pies to prepared sheet and cut three 1-inch slits on top (do not cut through filling). Freeze pies until firm, about 15 minutes. (Once frozen, pies can be transferred to airtight container and stored in freezer for up to 1 month.)

5 Brush tops of pies with remaining egg wash and sprinkle with remaining 1 tablespoon sugar. Bake until well browned, about 25 minutes, rotating sheet halfway through baking. Transfer pies to wire rack and let cool slightly, about 15 minutes. Serve warm or at room temperature.

# FRIED PEACH HAND PIES

Serves 8

4 ripe peaches, peeled, halved, pitted, and cut into ½-inch wedges

½ cup (3½ ounces) sugar

1 teaspoon table salt, divided

2 teaspoons lemon juice

2 cups (10 ounces) all-purpose flour

2 teaspoons baking powder

6 tablespoons unsalted butter, melted and cooled

½ cup whole milk

2 quarts peanut or vegetable oil for frying

**WHY THIS RECIPE WORKS** There's a lot of peach pie in the South, and it's not unusual to find it in the form of hand pies. But what's even better than a personal peach pie? A fried one from Alabama. These hand pies have it all: a crust that's delicate and tender yet crumbly wrapped around a thick filling that's purely peach in flavor. Starting with the filling, we cooked peeled, sliced peaches with sugar and a pinch of salt on the stovetop before gently mashing the fruit and letting it thicken. For the crust, we knew we couldn't use traditional pie pastry for frying; instead, we created a soft dough with melted butter and flour. The addition of baking powder and milk helped us achieve the dainty, almost cake-like crumble we wanted. After a quick fry in the hot oil, our pies emerged crisp, golden brown, and supremely satisfying. You can substitute 20 ounces frozen peaches for the fresh peaches; increase the cooking time in step 1 to 15 to 20 minutes. Use a Dutch oven that holds 6 quarts or more for frying.

1 Combine peaches, sugar, and ¼ teaspoon salt in medium saucepan. Cover and cook over medium heat, stirring occasionally and breaking up peaches with spoon, until tender, about 5 minutes.

2 Uncover and continue to cook, stirring and mashing frequently with potato masher to coarse puree, until mixture is thickened and measures about 1⅔ cups, 7 to 13 minutes. Off heat, stir in lemon juice and let cool completely.

3 Line rimmed baking sheet with parchment paper. Pulse flour, baking powder, and remaining ¾ teaspoon salt in food processor until combined, about 3 pulses. Add melted butter and pulse until mixture resembles wet sand, about 8 pulses, scraping down sides of bowl as needed. Add milk and process until no floury bits remain and dough looks pebbly, about 8 seconds.

4 Turn dough onto lightly floured counter, gather into disk, and divide into 8 equal pieces. Roll each piece between your hands into ball, then press to flatten into round. Place rounds on prepared sheet, cover with plastic wrap, and refrigerate for 20 minutes.

5 Working with 1 dough round at a time, roll into 6- to 7-inch circle about ⅛ inch thick on floured counter. Place 3 tablespoons filling in center of circle. Brush edges of dough with water and fold dough over filling to create half-moon shape, lightly pressing out air at seam. Trim any ragged edges and crimp edges with fork to seal. Return pies to prepared sheet, cover with plastic, and refrigerate until ready to fry. (Pies can be covered and refrigerated for up to 24 hours.)

6 Line platter with triple layer of paper towels. Add oil to large Dutch oven until it measures about 1½ inches deep and heat over medium-high heat to 375 degrees. Gently place 4 pies in hot oil and fry until golden brown, about 3 minutes, using slotted spatula or spider skimmer to flip halfway through frying. Adjust burner, if necessary, to maintain oil temperature between 350 and 375 degrees. Transfer pies to prepared platter. Return oil to 375 degrees and repeat with remaining 4 pies. Let cool for 10 minutes before serving.

# CHOCOLATE-CHERRY PIE POPS

Serves 8

1 cup cherry preserves

1 recipe single-crust pie dough (see pages 316–326)

2 tablespoons plus 2 teaspoons chocolate chips

8 (4- to 6-inch) lollipop or popsicle sticks

1 large egg, lightly beaten with 1 tablespoon water

½ cup (2 ounces) confectioners' sugar

**WHY THIS RECIPE WORKS** Pie pops—miniature pies on sticks—are festive, hand-held desserts perfect for parties or as a gift for pie lovers, young or old. (They're fun to assemble and eat with children, and they're flavor-packed for adults.) With their concentrated flavor, fruit preserves made an ideal filling for these two-bite treats. Tasters loved a cherry-chocolate combination, but loosely set cherry preserves leaked out of the pies during baking. Straining the preserves and using only the solids for the filling proved a successful fix. But we didn't let that glossy-pink liquid go to waste; we combined it with confectioners' sugar to create a glaze for drizzling. We found 3-inch circles of dough gave us the best filling-to-crust ratio. Quickly chilling the partially assembled pies set the filling enough to prevent it from squeezing out the sides when we pressed on the top crust. We had success using Bonne Maman cherry preserves here, but you can use any brand. You can find lollipop and popsicle sticks at most craft stores. This recipe can be easily doubled.

1 Microwave cherry preserves in bowl until fluid, 45 to 60 seconds, stirring halfway through microwaving. Strain preserves through fine-mesh strainer set over bowl, pressing on solids to extract as much liquid as possible; reserve solids (you should have about ⅓ cup) and liquid separately. Set aside to cool.

2 Roll dough into 15-inch circle on floured counter. Using 3-inch round biscuit or cookie cutter, cut 16 rounds from dough circle and transfer to parchment paper–lined rimmed baking sheet. Reserve dough scraps for another use. Cover rounds loosely with plastic wrap and refrigerate until firm but still pliable, about 10 minutes.

3 Line second rimmed baking sheet with parchment. Transfer 8 dough rounds to second prepared sheet, spaced evenly apart. Working with 1 dough round at a time, lay lollipop stick flat on top of dough with 1 end in center of dough round. Press stick firmly into dough. Mound 2 teaspoons cherry solids and 1 teaspoon chocolate chips in center of each dough round on top of stick. Transfer sheet with filled rounds to freezer and chill for 10 minutes.

4 Adjust oven rack to upper-middle position and heat oven to 375 degrees. Brush edges of filled dough rounds with egg wash, then top with remaining chilled dough rounds, pressing edges firmly to seal. Crimp edges of each pie with fork. Cut three ½-inch slits in top of each pie and brush with remaining egg wash. Bake until crusts are golden brown, 22 to 26 minutes, rotating sheet halfway through baking. Transfer sheet to wire rack and let pies cool for 10 minutes. Using spatula, carefully transfer pies to wire rack and let cool completely, about 1 hour.

5 Whisk 2 tablespoons reserved cherry preserve liquid and confectioners' sugar together in small bowl until smooth. Let glaze sit until slightly thickened but still able to be drizzled, about 10 minutes. Adjust thickness with up to 1 teaspoon extra cherry liquid as needed. Drizzle pies with glaze and let sit for 10 minutes. Serve.

# APPLE BUTTER PIE POPS

Serves 8

⅓ cup plus 2 tablespoons
apple butter

1 ounce cream cheese, softened

1 recipe single-crust pie dough
(see pages 316–326)

8 (4- to 6-inch) lollipop or popsicle
sticks

1 large egg, lightly beaten with
1 tablespoon water

**WHY THIS RECIPE WORKS** Apple pie is a winner no matter what form it takes, from the biggest (see our Apple Slab Pie on page 200) to the smallest (these pops). But making the best apple pie pops doesn't mean simply putting your favorite apple pie filling on a stick. For starters, peeling, chopping, and precooking were too much hassle for these petite pies. And leaking wasn't OK, whether in the oven or onto our shoes when taking a bite. Using apple butter for the filling addressed these concerns; it stayed thick through baking and offered warm-spiced, deep apple flavor that easily satisfied our apple pie cravings. But we found that apple butter was too sweet on its own; blending in a couple tablespoons of cream cheese added creaminess, richness, and tang. You can find lollipop and popsicle sticks at most craft stores. To soften cream cheese, microwave it for 10 to 15 seconds. This recipe can be easily doubled.

**1** Stir apple butter and cream cheese together in small bowl until fully combined. Refrigerate until ready to use.

**2** Roll dough into 15-inch circle on floured counter. Using 3-inch round biscuit or cookie cutter, cut 16 rounds from dough circle and transfer to parchment paper–lined rimmed baking sheet. Reserve dough scraps for another use. Cover rounds loosely with plastic wrap and refrigerate until firm but still pliable, about 10 minutes.

**3** Line second rimmed baking sheet with parchment. Transfer 8 dough rounds to second prepared sheet, spaced evenly apart. Working with 1 dough round at a time, lay lollipop stick flat on top of dough with 1 end in center of dough round. Press stick firmly into dough. Mound 1 tablespoon apple butter mixture in center of each dough round on top of stick. Transfer sheet with filled rounds to freezer and chill for 10 minutes.

**4** Adjust oven rack to upper-middle position and heat oven to 375 degrees. Brush edges of filled dough rounds with egg wash, then top with remaining chilled dough rounds, pressing edges firmly to seal. Crimp edges of each pie with fork. Cut three ½-inch slits in top of each pie and brush with remaining egg wash.

**5** Bake until crusts are golden brown, 22 to 26 minutes, rotating sheet halfway through baking. Transfer sheet to wire rack and let pies cool for 10 minutes. Using spatula, carefully transfer pies to wire rack and let cool completely, about 1 hour. Serve.

# ALL ABOUT MAKING PIE POPS

Pie pops are the ultimate party starter, party dessert, or party favor—and they're way more kid–friendly than a full–size pie. The process starts with good old pie dough and some rolling; after that it's a breeze. Follow our illus–trated steps below to learn how to turn rounds of dough and some pantry ingredients into something you'll love to make and share.

## MAKING PIE POPS

**1** Using 3-inch round cutter, cut 16 rounds from dough circle and transfer to baking sheet. Cover and refrigerate until firm but still pliable, about 10 minutes.

**2** Transfer 8 dough rounds to second sheet. Working with 1 round at a time, lay lollipop stick flat on top of dough with one end in center. Press stick firmly into dough.

**3** Mound 1 tablespoon filling in center of each dough round on top of stick. Transfer sheet with filled rounds to freezer and chill for 10 minutes.

**4** Brush edges of filled dough rounds with egg wash.

**5** Top with remaining chilled dough rounds, pressing edges firmly to seal.

**6** Crimp edges of each pie with fork. Cut three ½-inch slits in top of each pie and brush with remaining egg wash.

# ALL ABOUT DECORATING PIE POPS

In our pie pop recipes, we've shown distinct ways to finish these darling desserts: a cherry glaze or a classic egg wash. You can make pie pops party–pretty with other tricks, too. Below, find some other tips for decorating. A fun idea is to bake the pies plain or with egg wash and let guests (young or old) gussy them up. These treatments would work on hand pies, too.

## ICING ON THE PIE

In our Chocolate-Cherry Pie Pops (page 226), we make a glaze from the liquid drained from our preserves and confectioners' sugar. But you can make an all-purpose glaze for other pops, too. Whisk ½ cup (2 ounces) confectioners' sugar with 1 tablespoon of milk until smooth. Whisk in an additional 1 teaspoon of milk if needed to reach the right consistency. Drizzle or spread the glaze on the cooled pops and wait for it to set, about 10 minutes, before serving the pops. Substitute lemon, orange, or lime juice for the milk for a citrusy glaze, or add ¼ teaspoon of almond extract for a nutty, aromatic glaze. You can also top the wet glaze with sprinkles of any kind. Or add a couple drops of food coloring to the white glaze for something more vibrant.

## BETTER WITH CHOCOLATE

Most desserts are better with chocolate—and pie is no different. Melt any type of chocolate you like and drizzle away or pipe on a design. Let the chocolate set before serving. We think milky white chocolate would be a lovely pairing with our sweet-and-tangy Apple Butter Pie Pops (page 229). Or dress up everyday Cherry Hand Pies (page 222) with decadent dark chocolate.

## GREAT GRAINS OF SUGAR

Sometimes we finish pies with egg wash and a sprinkling of sugar for some extra shine and crackle. You can do the same with pie pops. Our standard is granulated sugar, but turbinado sugar or colored sugar will provide a different kind of shine and the former will have more crunch. Or make cinnamon sugar (or combine another spice with sugar), as in our Caramel Apple Hand Pies (page 221), for extra flavor.

## COOL CUTOUTS

We cut slits in the top crust of our pie pops so moisture can evaporate, but you can go a step further and make a cutout. Using a ½- to ¾-inch cutter, cut a shape out of the center of half the dough rounds before chilling. The cutout will be a window to the filling inside.

**Make Your Own Colored Sugar**

**1** Spread ½ cup granulated sugar into pie plate. Mix 5 drops food coloring into sugar.

**2** Push sugar through fine-mesh strainer and spread sugar back into plate. The sugar should dry thoroughly before you use it; this may take several hours.

# BANANA-CARAMEL PIE IN A JAR

Serves 12

5  ripe bananas, divided

4  tablespoons unsalted butter, divided

2½  cups half-and-half

⅛  teaspoon ground cinnamon

½  cup (3½ ounces) plus 2 tablespoons sugar

6  large egg yolks

¼  teaspoon table salt

2  tablespoons cornstarch

1  teaspoon vanilla extract

6  whole graham crackers, crushed into coarse crumbs, divided

1  cup Caramel Sauce (page 341), divided

1  recipe Whipped Cream (page 340)

**WHY THIS RECIPE WORKS**  Like pie pops, pie in a jar is another type of pie meant for individual enjoyment. Though relatively simple to make and assemble, this multi-layered pie makes for an impressive presentation. Preparing and enjoying cream pies in this manner works especially well as there is no precarious slicing and serving—and no fighting over who gets the biggest piece. For our banana-caramel pie in a jar, we combined a fresh-tasting banana pastry cream with crunchy crumbled graham crackers and gooey caramel sauce. We layered the elements in a clear Mason jar so each delicious component was visible; layers of lightly sweetened whipped cream, sliced bananas, a sprinkle of more cracker crumbs and a final drizzle of caramel made for an impressive finish. You will need twelve 4-ounce widemouthed Mason jars or eight 6-ounce ramekins for this recipe.

1  Peel and slice 2 bananas ½ inch thick. Melt 1 tablespoon butter in medium saucepan over medium-high heat. Add sliced bananas and cook until they begin to soften, about 2 minutes. Add half-and-half and cinnamon, bring to boil, and cook for 30 seconds. Remove from heat, cover, and let sit for 40 minutes.

2  Whisk sugar, egg yolks, and salt together in large bowl until smooth. Whisk in cornstarch. Strain cooled half-and-half mixture through fine-mesh strainer into yolk mixture (do not press on bananas) and whisk until incorporated; discard cooked bananas.

3  Transfer mixture to clean medium saucepan. Cook over medium heat, whisking constantly, until mixture is thickened and registers 180 degrees, 4 to 6 minutes (mixture should have consistency of thick pudding). Off heat, whisk in vanilla and remaining 3 tablespoons butter until smooth. Strain mixture through fine-mesh strainer into clean bowl. Spray piece of parchment paper with vegetable oil spray and press directly against surface of filling. Refrigerate until chilled, at least 1 hour or up to 24 hours.

4  Slice remaining 3 bananas ¼ inch thick on bias. Divide ¾ cup cracker crumbs evenly among twelve 4-ounce widemouthed glass jars, then divide banana cream filling and ¾ cup caramel sauce evenly among jars. Top jars evenly with whipped cream, remaining banana slices, remaining ¼ cup cracker crumbs, and remaining ¼ cup caramel sauce. Serve.

# CHOCOLATE CREAM PIE IN A JAR

Serves 12

2½ cups half-and-half

⅓ cup (2⅓ ounces) sugar, divided

Pinch table salt

6 large egg yolks

2 tablespoons cornstarch

6 tablespoons unsalted butter, cut into 6 pieces

6 ounces semisweet chocolate, chopped fine

1 ounce unsweetened chocolate, chopped fine

1 teaspoon vanilla extract

10 Oreo cookies, broken into coarse crumbs, divided

1 recipe Whipped Cream (page 340)

**WHY THIS RECIPE WORKS** While it can be hard to please everyone when it's time for dessert, we're betting our chocolate cream pies in a jar will get you pretty close. We made a rich chocolate custard with lots of semisweet (and a little bit of unsweetened) chocolate for deep, but not bitter, chocolate flavor that would please both kids and adults alike, making this a family-friendly treat. We layered our chocolate cream over crumbled Oreos (for more chocolate flavor and an irresistible crunchy-creamy texture) and topped it with lightly sweetened whipped cream for mini desserts that tasted as good—and chocolaty—as they looked. For a decidedly grown-up option, we also created a mocha variation by adding instant espresso powder and chocolate-covered espresso beans. We'd call that having your pie and eating it too. You will need twelve 4-ounce widemouthed Mason jars or eight 6-ounce ramekins for this recipe.

1 Bring half-and-half, 3 tablespoons sugar, and salt to simmer in medium saucepan over medium heat, stirring occasionally. Whisk egg yolks, cornstarch, and remaining sugar together in medium bowl until smooth. Slowly whisk 1 cup of half-and-half mixture into yolk mixture to temper, then slowly whisk tempered yolk mixture back into remaining half-and-half mixture in saucepan.

2 Cook half-and-half mixture over medium heat, whisking constantly, until mixture is thickened and registers 180 degrees, about 30 seconds. Off heat, whisk in butter, semisweet chocolate, unsweetened chocolate, and vanilla until smooth. Strain mixture through fine-mesh strainer into clean bowl. Spray piece of parchment paper with vegetable oil spray and press directly against surface of filling. Refrigerate until chilled, at least 1 hour or up to 24 hours.

3 Divide ¾ cup cookie crumbs evenly among twelve 4-ounce widemouthed glass jars, then divide chocolate filling evenly among jars. Top with whipped cream and remaining ¼ cup cookie crumbs. Serve.

### Mocha Cream Pie in a Jar

Add 2 teaspoons instant espresso powder to half-and-half mixture in step 1. Sprinkle 2 tablespoons coarsely chopped chocolate covered espresso beans evenly over top of whipped cream with cookie crumbs before serving.

# INDIVIDUAL FREE-FORM APPLE TARTLETS

**Serves 6**

1  recipe Free-Form Tart Dough for Tartlets (page 332)

2  McIntosh apples, peeled, cored, halved, and sliced ¼ inch thick

1  Granny Smith apple, peeled, cored, halved, and sliced ¼ inch thick

½  cup (3½ ounces) sugar, divided

1½  teaspoons lemon juice

Pinch ground cinnamon

**WHY THIS RECIPE WORKS** Since we had already had success supersizing galettes to serve a crowd, we decided to go in the opposite direction and try our hand at making individual free-form tarts. Here we surround a combination of sweet and tart apples with flaky, buttery dough to form tartlets that are just the right size for one person. We sliced the apples thin enough to cook through in a short amount of time and tossed them with sugar, a little lemon juice, and a pinch of cinnamon. After we divided our standard free-form tart dough into 6 portions and rolled them into circles, all that was left was to pile in the apple mixture and fold the dough around it before baking these tartlets to crisp, golden-brown perfection. We like to serve the tartlets with Caramel Sauce (page 341).

1  Working with 1 disk of dough at a time, roll into 6½-inch circle on floured counter; stack on baking sheet, separated by 7-inch-square sheets of parchment paper. Cover with plastic wrap and refrigerate until firm but pliable, about 10 minutes.

2  Adjust oven racks to upper-middle and lower-middle positions and heat oven to 375 degrees. Toss apples with 7 tablespoons sugar, lemon juice, and cinnamon. Arrange dough circles with parchment squares on 2 baking sheets. Mound apple mixture evenly in center of each circle, leaving 1-inch border around edge. Fold dough over apples, pleating every 2 to 3 inches as needed. Gently pinch pleated dough to secure, but do not press dough into fruit.

3  Brush top and sides of tartlets lightly with water and sprinkle with remaining 1 tablespoon sugar. Bake until crusts are golden brown and apples are tender, about 45 minutes, switching and rotating sheets halfway through baking.

4  Transfer sheets to wire rack and let tartlets cool for 10 minutes. Using metal spatula, loosen tartlets from parchment and carefully slide onto wire rack; let tartlets cool until apple juices have thickened, about 25 minutes. Serve slightly warm or at room temperature.

# LEMON TARTLETS

Serves 6

## crust

- 2 cups (10 ounces) all-purpose flour
- ½ cup (3½ ounces) granulated sugar
- ¾ teaspoon table salt
- 14 tablespoons unsalted butter, melted

## filling

- 3 large eggs plus 9 large yolks
- 1 cup (7 ounces) granulated sugar
- 3 tablespoons grated lemon zest plus ¾ cup juice (4 lemons)
- ¼ teaspoon table salt
- 6 tablespoons unsalted butter, cut into 6 pieces
- 3 tablespoons heavy cream, chilled

  Confectioners' sugar

**WHY THIS RECIPE WORKS** Our classic Lemon Tart (page 154) is an elegant dessert, but individual tartlets are the darlings of pastry cases and the thought of enjoying a sleek fluted tart all our own was undeniably appealing. However, we didn't love the thought of rolling out six dough rounds and then carefully fitting them into small intricate pans, so we made a dough that we could easily press into the bottoms and flutes of our pans with our hands. We simply melted butter and stirred it into our dry ingredients (flour, sugar, and salt) to create a soft—but not melty or greasy—dough. We blind-baked these crusts so they wouldn't shrink and would remain crisp under the traditional lemon curd filling after baking. You will need six 4-inch tart pans with removable bottoms for this recipe. Once the lemon curd ingredients have been combined, cook the curd immediately; otherwise, its finished texture will be grainy. It is important to add the filling to the tart shells while it is still warm; if the shells have cooled, rewarm them in the oven for 5 minutes before adding the filling.

---

**1** *For the crust* Adjust oven racks to middle and lowest positions and heat oven to 350 degrees. Spray six 4-inch tart pans with removable bottoms with vegetable oil spray. Whisk flour, sugar, and salt together in bowl. Add melted butter and stir with wooden spoon until dough forms.

**2** Divide dough into 6 equal pieces. Working with 1 piece of dough at a time, press two-thirds of dough into bottom of 1 prepared pan using your fingers. Press remaining dough into fluted sides of pan. Press and smooth dough with your fingers to even thickness. (See page 243.)

**3** Line tart pans with double layer of aluminum foil, covering edges to prevent burning, and fill with pie weights. Place pans on wire rack set in rimmed baking sheet and bake on lower rack until edges are beginning to turn golden, about 25 minutes. Carefully remove foil and weights, rotate sheet, and continue to bake until tart shells are golden brown and firm to touch, 10 to 15 minutes; set aside (tart shells must still be warm when filling is added).

**4** *For the filling* Whisk eggs and yolks together in medium saucepan. Whisk in sugar until combined, then whisk in lemon zest and juice and salt. Add butter and cook over medium-low heat, stirring constantly, until mixture thickens slightly and registers 170 degrees, about 5 minutes. Immediately pour mixture through fine-mesh strainer into bowl. Stir in cream.

**5** With tarts still on wire rack, divide warm lemon filling evenly among warm tart shells. Bake on upper rack until filling is shiny and opaque and centers jiggle slightly when shaken, about 10 minutes, rotating sheet halfway through baking.

**6** Let tartlets cool completely on wire rack in sheet, about 2 hours. Remove outer ring of tart pans, slide thin metal spatula between tartlets and pan bottoms, and carefully slide tartlets onto serving platter or individual plates. Dust with confectioners' sugar. Serve.

# PECAN TARTLETS

**Serves 6**

## crust

- 2 cups (10 ounces) all-purpose flour
- ½ cup (3½ ounces) granulated sugar
- ¾ teaspoon table salt
- 14 tablespoons unsalted butter, melted

## filling

- ¾ cup packed (5¼ ounces) dark brown sugar
- ½ cup plus 1 tablespoon light corn syrup
- 6 tablespoons unsalted butter
- 3 large egg yolks
- 1½ teaspoons vanilla extract
- ¼ teaspoon table salt
- 1½ cups pecans, toasted and chopped coarse

**WHY THIS RECIPE WORKS** The higher ratio of crust to filling in pecan tartlets automatically makes them the perfect dessert for those who love the nutty flavor of pecan pie, with more of an emphasis on its buttery nature rather than on the sweetness. To start, we simply scaled down our regular pecan pie recipe to fit these smaller packages. Some pecan tartlets feature whole pecan halves, but while we wanted ours to be ultranutty, we found that pecan halves were too difficult to cut through with a fork when we dug in. Coarsely chopped nuts still offered plenty of pecan flavor and texture but made our mini tarts much easier to eat. We love the pecans here, but you can substitute walnuts, if desired. You will need six 4-inch tart pans with removable bottoms for this recipe.

---

**1** *For the crust* Adjust oven racks to middle and lowest positions and heat oven to 350 degrees. Spray six 4-inch tart pans with removable bottoms with vegetable oil spray. Whisk flour, sugar, and salt together in bowl. Add melted butter and stir with wooden spoon until dough forms.

**2** Divide dough into 6 equal pieces. Working with 1 piece of dough at a time, press two-thirds of dough into bottom of 1 prepared pan using your fingers. Press remaining dough into fluted sides of pan. Press and smooth dough with your fingers to even thickness. (See page 243.)

**3** Line tart pans with double layer of aluminum foil, covering edges to prevent burning, and fill with pie weights. Place pans on wire rack set in rimmed baking sheet and bake on lower rack until edges are beginning to turn golden, about 25 minutes. Carefully remove foil and weights, rotate sheet, and continue to bake until tart shells are golden brown and firm to touch, 10 to 15 minutes; let cool completely, about 1 hour.

**4** *For the filling* Heat sugar and corn syrup in medium saucepan over medium heat, stirring occasionally, until sugar has dissolved, about 2 minutes. Off heat, whisk in butter until melted. Whisk in egg yolks, vanilla, and salt until combined. Stir in pecans.

**5** With tarts still on wire rack, divide warm pecan mixture evenly among cooled tart shells, smoothing tops with clean spatula into even layer. Bake on upper rack until centers jiggle slightly when gently shaken, 10 to 15 minutes, rotating sheet halfway through baking.

**6** Let tartlets cool completely on wire rack in sheet, about 2 hours. Remove outer ring of tart pans, slide thin metal spatula between tartlets and pan bottoms, and carefully slide tarts onto serving platter or individual plates. Serve.

# NUTELLA TARTLETS

Serves 6

## crust

2 **cups (10 ounces) all-purpose flour**

½ **cup (3½ ounces) sugar**

¾ **teaspoon table salt**

14 **tablespoons unsalted butter, melted**

## filling

1 **cup hazelnuts, toasted and skinned**

1½ **cups Nutella**

½ **cup plus 1 tablespoon heavy cream**

3 **ounces bittersweet chocolate, chopped**

3 **tablespoons unsalted butter**

**WHY THIS RECIPE WORKS** Nutella is an ideal tartlet filling because with just a few more simple ingredients, you can create a decadent—and easy—dessert. In order to transform Nutella into a creamy filling, we knew we'd have to amp up its richness and transform its thick texture. We started with 1½ cups of Nutella—just the right amount for six 4-inch tarts—and then added heavy cream and butter for richness and creaminess and 3 ounces of bittersweet chocolate for a deeper, more intense flavor. We then microwaved the mixture, stirring it often, until it formed a homogeneous filling—essentially a ganache that just needed some time in the fridge to set up. Once chilled, the luscious truffle-like chocolate-hazelnut filling perfectly complemented the crisp, buttery crust. But we wanted even more contrast: A sprinkling of chopped hazelnuts in the bottom of each tart shell added welcome crunch to the smooth, creamy filling, while adorning the top with whole hazelnuts hinted at what was inside. You will need six 4-inch tart pans with removable bottoms for this recipe.

1 *For the crust* Adjust oven rack to lowest position and heat oven to 350 degrees. Spray six 4-inch tart pans with removable bottoms with vegetable oil spray. Whisk flour, sugar, and salt together in bowl. Add melted butter and stir with wooden spoon until dough forms.

2 Divide dough into 6 equal pieces. Working with 1 piece of dough at a time, press two-thirds of dough into bottom of 1 prepared pan using your fingers. Press remaining dough into fluted sides of pan. Press and smooth dough with your fingers to even thickness.

3 Line tart pans with double layer of aluminum foil, covering edges to prevent burning, and fill with pie weights. Place pans on wire rack set in rimmed baking sheet and bake until edges are beginning to turn golden, about 25 minutes. Carefully remove foil and weights, rotate sheet, and continue to bake until crust is golden brown and firm to touch, 10 to 15 minutes; let cool completely, about 1 hour.

4 *For the filling* Reserve 48 whole hazelnuts for garnish, then chop remaining hazelnuts coarse. Sprinkle chopped hazelnuts evenly among cooled tart shells.

5 Microwave Nutella, cream, chocolate, and butter together in covered bowl at 30 percent power, stirring often, until mixture is smooth and glossy, about 1 minute (do not overheat). Divide warm Nutella filling evenly among cooled tart shells, smoothing tops with clean spatula into even layer.

6 Refrigerate tarts until filling is just set, about 15 minutes. Arrange reserved whole hazelnuts evenly around edge of tarts and continue to refrigerate until filling is firm, about 1½ hours. Remove outer ring of tart pans, slide thin metal spatula between tartlets and pan bottoms, and carefully slide tartlets onto serving platter or individual plates. Serve.

## Forming the Crust for Tartlets

**1** Whisk flour, sugar, and salt together in bowl. Add melted butter and stir with wooden spoon until dough forms.

**2** Divide dough into 6 equal pieces.

**3** Working with 1 piece of dough at a time, press two-thirds of dough into bottom of 1 prepared pan using your fingers.

**4** Press remaining dough into fluted sides of pan. Press and smooth dough with your fingers to even thickness.

NUTELLA TARTLETS

# PORTUGUESE EGG TARTS

**Serves 12**

1½ (9½ by 9-inch) sheets puff pastry, thawed

1½ cups whole milk

1 cup (7 ounces) granulated sugar

¾ cup heavy cream

2 (3-inch) strips lemon zest

¼ cup (1¼ ounces) all-purpose flour

½ teaspoon table salt

8 large egg yolks

1½ teaspoons vanilla extract

Confectioners' sugar

Ground cinnamon

**WHY THIS RECIPE WORKS** The sweet, creamy vanilla- and lemon-scented custard filling and crisp pastry shell of petite Portuguese egg tarts leave many a tourist yearning for these iconic pastries upon returning home. Store-bought puff pastry, parbaked in muffin tin cups, gave us the most shattering crust beneath the custard filling. But to get the classic swirled pastry layers, we needed to roll the puff pastry dough into logs, slice it into rounds and press it into the muffin tin cups. While many of our custard recipes use cornstarch as a thickener, we found that flour helped this custard withstand the high oven heat necessary to achieve the spotty brown surface found on traditional tarts. Serve these tarts warm or at room temperature with a sprinkle of cinnamon and powdered sugar as they do in Portugal. To thaw frozen puff pastry, let it sit either in the refrigerator for 24 hours or at room temperature for 30 minutes to 1 hour.

**1** Unfold puff pastry sheets on clean counter. Brush tops lightly with water. Roll full pastry sheet into tight log and pinch seam to seal. Roll short side of half pastry sheet into tight log and pinch seam to seal. Transfer to rimmed baking sheet, cover loosely with plastic wrap, and refrigerate until firm, at least 30 minutes.

**2** Spray 12-cup muffin tin with vegetable oil spray. Using serrated knife, trim off uneven ends of each dough log and discard. Cut twelve 1-inch slices from dough logs and place 1 slice in each muffin tin cup, cut side up. Using moistened fingers, press dough into bottom and up sides of muffin cups so dough reaches top of cups (dough should be very thin). Prick shells all over with fork and refrigerate muffin tin until dough is firm, about 20 minutes.

**3** Adjust oven racks to upper-middle and lower-middle positions and heat oven to 350 degrees. Line tart shells with muffin tin liners and fill with pie weights. Place muffin tin on lower rack and bake until pastry is puffed but still pale, about 10 minutes. Cover muffin tin with aluminum foil and continue to bake until pastry is just blond at edges, about 5 minutes. Transfer muffin tin to wire rack, discard foil, and let tart shells cool slightly, 10 to 15 minutes. Remove liners and weights. Increase oven temperature to 500 degrees.

**4** Combine milk, granulated sugar, cream, and lemon zest in medium saucepan and cook over medium-low heat, stirring occasionally, until steaming, about 6 minutes. Off heat, let mixture steep for 15 minutes; discard zest. Whisk flour and salt together in bowl, then gradually whisk in egg-milk mixture. Whisk in egg yolks and vanilla until smooth. Return egg mixture to saucepan and cook over medium-low heat, whisking constantly, until mixture begins to thicken, 6 to 8 minutes. Strain mixture through fine-mesh strainer into clean bowl.

**5** Divide custard evenly among pastry shells. Bake on upper rack until shells are dark golden brown and crisp and custard is puffed and spotty brown, 8 to 11 minutes. Let tarts cool in muffin tin on wire rack for 10 minutes. Remove tarts from muffin tin and let cool on wire rack for 15 minutes. Dust with confectioners' sugar and cinnamon and serve warm or at room temperature.

## Making Portuguese Egg Tarts

**1** Roll full pastry sheet into tight log and pinch seam to seal. Roll short side of half pastry sheet into tight log and pinch seam to seal. Refrigerate until firm.

**2** Using serrated knife, trim off uneven ends of each dough log and discard. Cut twelve 1-inch slices from dough logs.

**3** Place 1 slice in each muffin tin cup, cut side up. Using moistened fingers, press dough into bottom and up sides of muffin cups so dough reaches top of cups (dough should be very thin).

**4** Prick shells all over with fork and refrigerate muffin tin until dough is firm, about 20 minutes.

**5** Line tart shells with muffin tin liners and fill with pie weights. Place muffin tin on lower rack and bake until pastry is puffed, but pale, about 10 minutes.

**6** Cover muffin tin with aluminum foil and continue to bake until pastry is just blond at edges, about 5 minutes.

**7** Transfer muffin tin to wire rack, discard foil, and let tart shells cool slightly, 10 to 15 minutes. Remove liners and weights.

**8** Divide custard evenly among pastry shells.

**9** Bake on upper rack until shells are dark golden brown and crisp and custard is puffed and spotty brown, 8 to 11 minutes.

# regional
# FAVORITES

# OREGON BLACKBERRY PIE

Serves 8

1 recipe double-crust pie dough (see pages 320–327)

¾ cup (5¼ ounces) sugar plus 1 teaspoon, divided

5 tablespoons (1¼ ounces) cornstarch

¼ teaspoon table salt

20 ounces (4 cups) blackberries

2 tablespoons lemon juice

2 tablespoons unsalted butter, cut into ½-inch pieces

1 large egg, lightly beaten with 1 tablespoon water

**WHY THIS RECIPE WORKS** In high summer, blackberry brambles blanket the Pacific Northwest and a slice of blackberry pie is never far from reach. One typically knows what kind of texture to expect from a berry pie filling—something a little looser and juicier than, say, an apple or pear pie, both of which hold together slices of lower-moisture fruit. But Oregon blackberry pie (known to natives as marionberry pie) is different. Its hallmark is its surprisingly sturdy filling; no soupy, oozy slices here. A good amount of cornstarch seamlessly thickened our version so the filling retained its shape without dulling the lively berry flavor. We wanted a lattice topping to show off the filling and to allow moisture to evaporate, but summertime heat and humidity don't provide ideal conditions for intricate dough-weaving. Instead, we went with a lazy lattice for lazy summer days: We created the illusion of a lattice by laying the dough strips over each other in a perpendicular pattern. Be sure to rinse the berries and dry them thoroughly before using. Do not use frozen berries in this recipe.

**1** Roll 1 disk of dough into 12-inch circle on floured counter. Loosely roll dough around rolling pin and gently unroll it onto 9-inch pie plate, letting excess dough hang over edge. Ease dough into plate by gently lifting edge of dough with your hand while pressing into plate bottom with your other hand. Leave any dough that overhangs plate in place. Wrap dough-lined plate loosely in plastic wrap and refrigerate until firm, about 30 minutes.

**2** Roll other disk of dough into 12-inch circle on floured counter, then transfer to parchment paper–lined baking sheet. Using pizza cutter, cut dough into twelve 1-inch strips. Discard 4 short end pieces, then cover remaining 8 long strips loosely with plastic and refrigerate until firm, about 30 minutes. Adjust oven rack to lower-middle position and heat oven to 400 degrees.

**3** Whisk ¾ cup sugar, cornstarch, and salt together in large bowl. Add blackberries and toss gently to coat. Add lemon juice and toss until no dry sugar mixture remains. (Blackberries will start to exude some juice.)

**4** Spread blackberry mixture into dough-lined plate and scatter butter over top. Space 4 strips evenly across top of pie, parallel to counter edge. Brush strips with egg wash, leaving ½ inch at ends unbrushed. Space 4 strips evenly across pie, perpendicular to first layer of strips. (If dough becomes too soft to work with, refrigerate pie and dough strips to firm up.)

**5** Trim overhang to ½ inch beyond lip of plate. Pinch edges of lattice strips and bottom crust firmly together. Tuck overhang under itself; folded edge should be flush with edge of plate. Crimp dough evenly around edge of plate. Brush surface with egg wash and sprinkle with remaining 1 teaspoon sugar. Place pie on aluminum foil–lined rimmed baking sheet and bake until crust is golden brown and juices bubble evenly along surface, 45 to 50 minutes, rotating sheet halfway through baking. Let pie cool on wire rack until filling is set, about 4 hours. Serve.

# MARLBOROUGH APPLE PIE

Serves 8

1  recipe single-crust pie dough (see pages 316–326)

4  tablespoons unsalted butter

2  Granny Smith apples, peeled and shredded (2 cups)

2  Fuji, Gala, or Golden Delicious apples, peeled and shredded (2 cups)

½  cup (3½ ounces) sugar

¼  teaspoon ground cinnamon

¼  teaspoon ground mace

¼  teaspoon table salt

3  large eggs, lightly beaten

½  cup heavy cream

5  tablespoons dry sherry

1  teaspoon grated lemon zest

1  teaspoon vanilla extract

**WHY THIS RECIPE WORKS** Marlborough pie, an almost-forgotten New England apple pie (the first recipe appeared in the United States in 1796), combines the comforting apple-and-spice flavors of traditional apple pie with rich, creamy custard. Pre–Civil War bakers turned out these pies as a tasty way to use up the bruised, aging apples from their root cellars. They grated the apples to disguise the imperfections and added lemon juice—often liberally—to balance the very sweet nature of old apples before stirring the apples into a custard base. Looking for balanced flavors straight from the supermarket, we worked with a mix of Granny Smith (for tartness) and Fuji, Gala, or Golden Delicious (for contrasting sweetness). This mix needed only a bit of complementary lemon zest rather than a distracting amount of juice. We grated our apples and then sautéed them; this step eliminated moisture that could make the custard wet and weepy and also concentrated the apple flavor. Additional flavors of sherry, cinnamon, and mace rounded out the pie's profile. Shred the apples on the large holes of a box grater. The pie can be refrigerated for up to 24 hours.

1  Roll dough into 12-inch circle on floured counter. Loosely roll dough around rolling pin and gently unroll it onto 9-inch pie plate, letting excess dough hang over edge. Ease dough into plate by gently lifting edge of dough with your hand while pressing into plate bottom with your other hand.

2  Trim overhang to ½ inch beyond lip of plate. Tuck overhang under itself; folded edge should be flush with edge of plate. Crimp dough evenly around edge of plate. Wrap dough-lined plate loosely in plastic wrap and refrigerate until firm, about 30 minutes. Adjust oven rack to middle position and heat oven to 350 degrees.

3  Line chilled pie shell with double layer of aluminum foil, covering edges to prevent burning, and fill with pie weights. Bake on foil-lined rimmed baking sheet until edges are set and just beginning to turn golden, 25 to 30 minutes, rotating sheet halfway through baking. Remove foil and weights, rotate sheet, and continue to bake crust until golden brown and crisp, 10 to 15 minutes longer. Transfer sheet to wire rack. (Crust must still be warm when filling is added.) Adjust oven rack to lower-middle position and reduce oven temperature to 325 degrees.

4  Meanwhile, melt butter in 12-inch skillet over medium heat. Add apples and cook, stirring frequently, until pan is dry and apples have softened, 12 to 14 minutes. Transfer apples to bowl and let cool completely, about 20 minutes.

5  Whisk sugar, cinnamon, mace, and salt together in large bowl. Add eggs, cream, sherry, lemon zest, and vanilla and whisk until smooth. Add cooled apples and stir to combine. With pie still on sheet, pour mixture into warm crust. Bake until center is just set, about 40 minutes. Let pie cool completely on wire rack, about 4 hours. Serve.

# NORTH CAROLINA LEMON PIE

Serves 8

## crust

- 6 ounces saltines
- ⅛ teaspoon table salt
- 10 tablespoons unsalted butter, melted
- ¼ cup light corn syrup

## filling

- 1 (14-ounce) can sweetened condensed milk
- 4 large egg yolks
- ¼ cup heavy cream
- 1 tablespoon grated lemon zest plus ½ cup juice (3 lemons)
- ⅛ teaspoon table salt

- ½ recipe Whipped Cream (page 340)

**WHY THIS RECIPE WORKS** Along the North Carolina coast, many menus feature a pie often called simply "lemon pie." What is it more specifically? A light, bright delight with the perfect balance of sweet, salty, and sour flavors. The salty comes from a crunchy saltine cracker crust, and the filling is an opaque lemon custard, usually made with sweetened condensed milk. A layer of whipped cream covers the top. Saltines lack the moisture of cookies, so we added a little bit of corn syrup to our crust to give the crackers elasticity and ensure a pliable crust. Simple is the name of the game with this pie, so we stuck with a filling that didn't require stovetop cooking. Lemon juice alone didn't provide quite enough lemon flavor after baking; adding a tablespoon of lemon zest contributed the missing citrus zing. In addition to the sweetened condensed milk, we added ¼ cup of heavy cream to soften the lemon's sharper edges. A bit of salt in the filling, in addition to that in the saltines, helped give the pie its classic saline note. Whisk, bake, cool, spread with whipped cream, and you're done with this delicious North Carolina pie.

**1** *for the crust* Adjust oven rack to middle position and heat oven to 350 degrees. Combine saltines and salt in food processor and pulse to coarse crumbs, about 15 pulses. Add melted butter and corn syrup and pulse until crumbs are broken down into oat-size pieces, about 15 pulses.

**2** Transfer saltine mixture to greased 9-inch pie plate. Using bottom of dry measuring cup, press crumbs into even layer on bottom and sides of plate, using your hand to keep crumbs from spilling over plate edge. Bake on aluminum foil–lined rimmed baking sheet until light golden brown and fragrant, 17 to 19 minutes. Transfer sheet to wire rack.

**3** *for the filling* Whisk condensed milk, egg yolks, cream, lemon zest, and salt in bowl until fully combined. Whisk in lemon juice until fully incorporated.

**4** With pie plate still on sheet, pour filling into crust. Bake until edges are beginning to set but center still jiggles when shaken, 15 to 17 minutes. Let pie cool completely on wire rack, about 2 hours. Refrigerate pie until fully chilled, about 4 hours.

**5** Spread whipped cream evenly over pie. Serve.

# SWEET POTATO PIE

Serves 8

1 recipe single-crust pie dough
(see pages 316–326)

1¼ cups packed (8¾ ounces)
light brown sugar, divided

1¾ pounds sweet potatoes,
unpeeled

½ teaspoon table salt

4 tablespoons unsalted butter

½ teaspoon ground cinnamon

¼ teaspoon ground nutmeg

1 cup sour cream

3 large eggs plus 2 large yolks

2 tablespoons bourbon (optional)

1 teaspoon vanilla extract

**WHY THIS RECIPE WORKS** Sweet potatoes grow abundantly in the American South, and they star commonly in pie. It's a delicious tradition when done right, but too often recipes for sweet potato pie feature heavy, grainy, cloying fillings. To fix the heaviness problem, we "baked" the sweet potatoes in the microwave. This approach to cooking the potatoes not only yielded a fluffy puree, it also dramatically reduced the cooking time (unlike another shortcut, boiling, which resulted in dense, soggy potatoes). Like pumpkin pie, sweet potato pie is a custard pie; for the dairy component, we liked sour cream for its smoothness and subtle tang. Cinnamon and nutmeg are classic flavorings, and we briefly cooked them with butter to bloom their flavors before adding them—along with some bourbon and vanilla—to the pie. For a final layer of interest, we sprinkled brown sugar over the crust before pouring in the filling; it melted into a gooey faux caramel for a decadent touch.

1 Roll dough into 12-inch circle on floured counter. Loosely roll dough around rolling pin and gently unroll it onto 9-inch pie plate, letting excess dough hang over edge. Ease dough into plate by gently lifting edge of dough with your hand while pressing into plate bottom with your other hand.

2 Trim overhang to ½ inch beyond lip of plate. Tuck overhang under itself; folded edge should be flush with edge of plate. Crimp dough evenly around edge of plate. Wrap dough-lined plate loosely in plastic wrap and refrigerate until firm, about 30 minutes. Adjust oven rack to middle position and heat oven to 375 degrees.

3 Line chilled pie shell with double layer of aluminum foil, covering edges to prevent burning, and fill with pie weights. Bake on foil-lined rimmed baking sheet until lightly golden around edges, 18 to 25 minutes, rotating sheet halfway through baking. Remove foil and weights, rotate sheet, and continue to bake until center begins to look opaque and slightly drier, 3 to 6 minutes. Transfer sheet to wire rack and let cool completely, about 45 minutes. Sprinkle ¼ cup sugar over bottom of crust. Reduce oven temperature to 350 degrees.

4 Meanwhile, prick potatoes all over with fork. Microwave on large plate until potatoes are very soft and surface is slightly wet, 15 to 20 minutes, flipping every 5 minutes. Immediately slice potatoes in half to release steam. When cool enough to handle, scoop flesh into bowl of food processor. Add salt and remaining 1 cup sugar and process until smooth, about 1 minute, scraping down sides of bowl as needed. Microwave butter, cinnamon, and nutmeg in small bowl until melted, 15 to 30 seconds; stir to combine. Add spiced butter; sour cream; eggs and yolks; bourbon, if using; and vanilla to potatoes and process until incorporated, about 10 seconds, scraping down sides of bowl as needed.

5 With pie still on sheet, pour potato mixture into cooled crust. Bake until filling is set around edges but center registers 165 degrees and jiggles slightly when pie is shaken, 35 to 40 minutes. Let pie cool completely on wire rack, about 4 hours. Serve.

# BUTTERMILK PIE

Serves 8

| | |
|---|---|
| 1 | recipe single-crust pie dough (see pages 316–326) |
| ¾ | cup (5¼ ounces) plus 2 teaspoons sugar, divided |
| 1 | tablespoon cornstarch |
| ¾ | teaspoon table salt |
| 2 | large eggs plus 5 large yolks |
| 1¾ | cups buttermilk |
| ¼ | cup heavy cream |
| 4 | tablespoons unsalted butter, melted |
| 2 | teaspoons distilled white vinegar |
| 1½ | teaspoons vanilla extract |

**WHY THIS RECIPE WORKS** In the South, buttermilk pie holds its own against pecan, sweet potato, and peach pies, thanks to its creamy texture, tangy-sweet flavor, and irresistibly crunchy sugar top. To make ours stand out, we looked to the texture we love in flans and *pots de crème* for the filling. Custards get their richness from egg and heavy cream, so we started by whisking these ingredients together with the standard buttermilk pie components: sugar, vinegar, butter, vanilla, cornstarch, and, of course, plenty of buttermilk. The cornstarch and yolks provided a perfectly wobbly structure, and the vinegar backed up the buttermilk's pleasant tang. Baking the pie at a gentle 300 degrees cooked the filling evenly, but we also wanted a crackly, lightly browned top. A sprinkling of sugar 10 minutes into baking got us on the right track, and increasing the temperature for the last few minutes sealed the deal—the almost-melted sugar caramelized quickly. From its delicately crunchy sugar crust to its rich, creamy filling, our buttermilk pie was simple but full of Southern charm. Use commercial cultured buttermilk (avoid nonfat), as some locally produced, artisanal buttermilks that we tested were prone to curdling during baking.

1 Roll dough into 12-inch circle on floured counter. Loosely roll dough around rolling pin and gently unroll it onto 9-inch pie plate, letting excess dough hang over edge. Ease dough into plate by gently lifting edge of dough with your hand while pressing into plate bottom with your other hand.

2 Trim overhang to ½ inch beyond lip of plate. Tuck overhang under itself; folded edge should be flush with edge of plate. Crimp dough evenly around edge of plate. Wrap dough-lined plate loosely in plastic wrap and refrigerate until firm, about 30 minutes. Adjust oven racks to middle and upper-middle positions and heat oven to 350 degrees.

3 Line chilled pie shell with double layer of aluminum foil, covering edges to prevent burning, and fill with pie weights. Bake on foil-lined rimmed baking sheet on lower rack until edges are set and just beginning to turn golden, 25 to 30 minutes, rotating sheet halfway through baking. Remove foil and weights, rotate sheet, and continue to bake crust until golden brown and crisp, 10 to 15 minutes longer.

4 Meanwhile, whisk ¾ cup sugar, cornstarch, and salt together in large bowl. Whisk eggs and yolks into sugar mixture until well combined. Whisk buttermilk, cream, melted butter, vinegar, and vanilla into sugar-egg mixture until incorporated. Reduce oven temperature to 300 degrees. Whisk buttermilk mixture to recombine and, leaving pie shell in oven, carefully pour buttermilk mixture into hot pie shell. Bake on lower rack for 10 minutes.

5 Sprinkle remaining 2 teaspoons sugar evenly over top of pie. Continue to bake until center jiggles slightly when pie is shaken, 30 to 40 minutes. Remove pie from oven and increase oven temperature to 450 degrees. Once oven comes to temperature, place pie on upper rack and bake until golden brown on top, 5 to 7 minutes. Let pie cool on wire rack for 2 hours. Refrigerate for 3 hours. Serve.

# NEW ENGLAND MINCEMEAT PIE

Serves 8

1½ pounds Granny Smith apples, peeled, cored, halved, and cut into ¼-inch pieces

1½ pounds McIntosh apples, peeled, cored, halved, and cut into ¼-inch pieces

1½ cups apple cider, divided, plus extra as needed

1 cup golden raisins

1 cup dried currants

¾ cup packed (5¼ ounces) dark brown sugar

8 tablespoons unsalted butter

¼ cup diced candied orange peel (optional)

1½ tablespoons grated orange zest plus ½ cup juice

1 tablespoon grated lemon zest plus 3 tablespoons juice

1 teaspoon ground cinnamon

½ teaspoon ground allspice

½ teaspoon ground ginger

¼ teaspoon ground cloves

¼ teaspoon table salt

⅓ cup rum or brandy

1 recipe double-crust pie dough (see pages 320–327)

1 large egg, lightly beaten with 1 tablespoon water

**WHY THIS RECIPE WORKS** Mincemeat—a thick, spiced, fruit-filled compote of English origin—is a common pie filling in New England. But most of the mincemeat pies we've tried have been murky-tasting and overly rich; more than a bite or two is too much. We love the complex fruit flavors of the rich preserve, but we wanted to bring it into the modern age by giving it a cleaner, lighter spin. First stop: dropping the meat (yes, very traditional recipes do, in fact, include fall-apart braised meat and/or beef suet). Second, and related: replacing the suet with butter. Without the beef, we focused on making the fruit flavor come through loud and clear. A combination of McIntosh and Granny Smith apples provided an ideal fruit foundation, while golden raisins, currants, and candied orange peel completed the mix. To intensify the flavor of the filling, we simmered the fruit for 3 hours in apple cider.

1 Bring apples; 1 cup cider; raisins; currants; sugar; butter; orange peel, if using; orange zest and juice; lemon zest and juice; cinnamon; allspice; ginger; cloves; and salt to boil in large saucepan over medium-low heat. Reduce to simmer and cook gently, stirring occasionally to prevent scorching, until mixture thickens and darkens in color, about 3 hours, adding extra cider as needed to prevent scorching. Continue to cook, stirring mixture every 1 or 2 minutes, until it has jam-like consistency, about 20 minutes. Stir in remaining ½ cup cider and rum and cook until liquid in pan is thick and syrupy, about 10 minutes; let filling cool completely. (At this point, mincemeat can be refrigerated for up to 4 days.)

2 Meanwhile, roll 1 disk of dough into 12-inch circle on floured counter. Loosely roll dough around rolling pin and gently unroll it onto 9-inch pie plate, letting excess dough hang over edge. Ease dough into plate by gently lifting edge of dough with your hand while pressing into plate bottom with your other hand. Leave any dough that overhangs plate in place. Wrap dough-lined plate loosely in plastic wrap and refrigerate until firm, about 30 minutes. Roll other disk of dough into 12-inch circle on floured counter, then transfer to parchment paper–lined rimmed baking sheet; cover with plastic and refrigerate until firm, about 30 minutes.

3 Adjust oven rack to lowest position and heat oven to 400 degrees. Spread mincemeat into dough-lined plate. Loosely roll remaining dough round around rolling pin and gently unroll it onto filling. Trim overhang to ½ inch beyond lip of plate. Pinch edges of top and bottom crusts firmly together. Tuck overhang under itself; folded edge should be flush with edge of plate. Crimp dough evenly around edge of plate. Cut four 2-inch slits in top of dough. Brush surface with egg wash.

4 Place pie on aluminum foil–lined rimmed baking sheet and bake until crust is light golden brown, about 25 minutes. Reduce oven temperature to 350 degrees, rotate sheet, and continue to bake until juices are bubbling and crust is deep golden brown, 30 to 35 minutes longer. Let pie cool on wire rack until filling has set, about 4 hours. Serve.

# PENNSYLVANIA DUTCH APPLE PIE

**Serves 8**

### pie

2½  pounds apples, peeled, cored, halved, and sliced ¼ inch thick

½  cup melted vanilla ice cream

½  cup raisins (optional)

½  cup (3½ ounces) granulated sugar

1  tablespoon lemon juice

1  teaspoon vanilla extract

1  teaspoon ground cinnamon

½  teaspoon table salt

1  recipe single-crust pie dough (see pages 316–326)

### topping

1  cup (5 ounces) all-purpose flour

½  cup packed (3½ ounces) light brown sugar

6  tablespoons unsalted butter, melted

½  teaspoon table salt

**WHY THIS RECIPE WORKS** Bakers in Pennsylvania Dutch country are voracious, turning out a delicious assortment of pies: shoofly, butterscotch, mixed berry, and our favorite, Dutch apple. The hallmark of this pie, aside from its crumbly topping, is its creamy apple filling. But we didn't rely on the traditional cream to achieve it. Instead, we cleverly added melted vanilla ice cream to the filling for creaminess with more body (melted ice cream is essentially custard) and a rich vanilla flavor that nicely complemented the apples. After slicing the apples, we let them sit in the melted ice cream along with cinnamon, sugar, and lemon juice until they were soft and pliable; this way, they packed easily into the pie plate and created a cohesive interior that cooked evenly. Before baking, we sprinkled a mixture of melted butter, flour, brown sugar, and a good dose of salt over the top of the pie for a supremely buttery crumble. Letting the pie cool completely before slicing into it allowed it to firm up so that we could produce beautifully clean wedges with neat stacks of apple. We prefer sweet Golden Delicious or Gala apples here, but Fuji, Braeburn, or Granny Smith varieties also work well. You may substitute ½ cup of heavy cream for the melted ice cream, if desired. This pie is best when baked a day ahead of time and allowed to rest overnight.

1 *for the pie* Toss all ingredients in large bowl until apples are evenly coated. Let sit at room temperature for at least 1 hour or up to 2 hours.

2 Roll dough into 12-inch circle on floured counter. Loosely roll dough around rolling pin and gently unroll it onto 9-inch pie plate, letting excess dough hang over edge. Ease dough into plate by gently lifting edge of dough with your hand while pressing into plate bottom with your other hand.

3 Trim overhang to ½ inch beyond lip of plate. Tuck overhang under itself; folded edge should be flush with edge of plate. Crimp dough evenly around edge of plate. Wrap dough-lined plate loosely in plastic wrap and refrigerate until firm, about 30 minutes. Adjust oven rack to lower-middle position and heat oven to 350 degrees.

4 *for the topping* Stir all ingredients in bowl until no dry spots remain and mixture forms clumps. Refrigerate until ready to use.

5 Working with 1 large handful at a time, distribute apple mixture in plate, pressing into even layer and filling in gaps before adding more. Take care not to mound apple mixture in center of plate. Pour any remaining liquid from bowl into pie. Break topping (it will harden in refrigerator) into pea-size crumbs and distribute evenly over apple mixture. Pat topping lightly to adhere.

6 Place pie on aluminum foil–lined rimmed baking sheet. Bake until top is golden brown and paring knife inserted in center meets no resistance, about 1 hour 10 minutes, rotating sheet halfway through baking. Let pie cool on wire rack for at least 4 hours or preferably 8 to 12 hours. Serve.

# SOUTHERN PRALINE PECAN PIE

Serves 8

1 recipe single-crust pie dough (see pages 316—326)

¾ cup packed (5¼ ounces) dark brown sugar

8 tablespoons unsalted butter, cut into 8 pieces

1 teaspoon table salt

3 large eggs

¾ cup dark corn syrup

1 tablespoon vanilla extract

2 tablespoons bourbon

2 cups pecans, toasted and chopped fine

**WHY THIS RECIPE WORKS** There's traditional pecan pie, comprised of its namesake nut and a sticky-sweet custard, and then there's the souped-up version many Southerners know well: rich, buttery, dark praline pecan pie flavored with more than a hint of bourbon. We wanted to create a pie with true Southern flavor. Dark brown sugar and dark corn syrup combined to give the filling a deep, rich, molasses flavor. Hefty shots of vanilla and bourbon brought out the complex earthiness of the brown sugar for perfect praline flavor. A generous amount of salt helped cut through the sweetness of our pie. Finally, we created a variation that turns things up a notch with an extra 2 tablespoons of bourbon in the filling for those so inclined.

1 Roll dough into 12-inch circle on floured counter. Loosely roll dough around rolling pin and gently unroll it onto 9-inch pie plate, letting excess dough hang over edge. Ease dough into plate by gently lifting edge of dough with your hand while pressing into plate bottom with your other hand.

2 Trim overhang to ½ inch beyond lip of plate. Tuck overhang under itself; folded edge should be flush with edge of plate. Crimp dough evenly around edge of plate. Wrap dough-lined plate loosely in plastic wrap and refrigerate until firm, about 30 minutes. Adjust oven rack to middle position and heat oven to 350 degrees.

3 Line chilled pie shell with double layer of aluminum foil, covering edges to prevent burning, and fill with pie weights. Bake on foil-lined rimmed baking sheet until edges are set and just beginning to turn golden, 25 to 30 minutes, rotating sheet halfway through baking. Remove foil and weights, rotate sheet, and continue to bake crust until golden brown and crisp, 10 to 15 minutes longer. Transfer sheet to wire rack. (Crust must still be warm when filling is added.) Decrease oven temperature to 275 degrees.

4 Meanwhile, cook sugar, butter, and salt in medium saucepan over medium heat until sugar is melted and butter is absorbed, about 2 minutes. Off heat, whisk in eggs, one at a time; whisk in corn syrup, vanilla, and bourbon. Return pan to medium heat and stir constantly until mixture is glossy and warm to touch and registers about 130 degrees, about 4 minutes. (Do not overheat; remove pan from heat if mixture starts to steam or bubble.) Off heat, stir in pecans.

5 With pie still on sheet, pour mixture into warm crust. Bake until center looks set but yields like gelatin when gently pressed with back of spoon, 45 minutes to 1 hour, rotating sheet halfway through baking. Let pie cool on wire rack until filling has set, about 4 hours. Serve.

*After-Hours Southern Praline Pecan Pie*
Increase bourbon to ¼ cup.

# FLORIDA SOUR ORANGE PIE

Serves 8

*crust*

- 5 ounces animal crackers
- 3 tablespoons sugar

  Pinch table salt
- 4 tablespoons unsalted butter, melted

*filling*

- 1 (14-ounce) can sweetened condensed milk
- 6 tablespoons thawed orange juice concentrate
- 4 large egg yolks
- 2 teaspoons grated lemon zest plus 6 tablespoons juice (2 lemons)
- 1 teaspoon grated orange zest

  Pinch table salt

  Orange Whipped Cream (page 340)

**WHY THIS RECIPE WORKS** Sour orange pie, with its custard-like filling featuring the juice of wild sour oranges, is northern Florida's answer to Key lime pie. Sour oranges pack a tart punch, and incorporating their juice into a custard pie makes for a refreshing and bright dessert. Unfortunately, it's not easy to find these oranges outside of Florida and some tropical locations. For a sour orange pie that would be accessible to cooks in any part of the country, we made a comparable substitute for the tart juice by combining lemon juice and orange juice concentrate. We thought a sweet, vanilla-scented crust would provide a pleasant contrast to the creamy, tangy citrus filling, and animal crackers were the perfect cookie to get us there. Orange whipped cream provided the perfect finishing touch. If sour oranges are available, use ¾ cup of strained sour orange juice in place of the lemon juice and orange juice concentrate. Minute Maid Original Frozen is our favorite orange juice concentrate. Depending on the brand, 5 ounces is between 80 and 90 animal crackers.

1 *for the crust* Adjust oven rack to middle position and heat oven to 325 degrees. Process crackers, sugar, and salt in food processor to fine, even crumbs, about 30 seconds. Sprinkle melted butter over crumbs and pulse to incorporate, about 8 pulses.

2 Sprinkle mixture into 9-inch pie plate. Using bottom of dry measuring cup, press crumbs into even layer on bottom and sides of pie plate. Bake on aluminum foil–lined rimmed baking sheet until crust is fragrant and beginning to brown, 12 to 14 minutes. Transfer sheet to wire rack and let cool completely, about 30 minutes.

3 *for the filling* When crust is cool, whisk condensed milk, orange juice concentrate, egg yolks, lemon zest and juice, orange zest, and salt in bowl until fully combined. With pie still on sheet, pour filling into cooled crust.

4 Bake until center of pie jiggles slightly when shaken, 15 to 17 minutes. Let pie cool completely on wire rack, about 2 hours. Refrigerate for at least 3 hours or up to 24 hours. (If refrigerating for more than 3 hours, cover with greased plastic wrap before chilling.) Serve with whipped cream.

# MAPLE SYRUP PIE

Serves 8

1 recipe single-crust pie dough
(see pages 316–326)

1¾ cups maple syrup

⅔ cup heavy cream

¼ teaspoon salt

5 tablespoons unsalted butter,
cut into 5 pieces

2 tablespoons cornstarch

3 large eggs plus 2 large yolks

2 teaspoons cider vinegar

**WHY THIS RECIPE WORKS** Maple syrup pie was once common in the syrup-producing northern regions of this country and in Canada. No mystery there; if you have a surplus of syrup, why not make a pie with it? The best versions are sweetened with nothing but real maple. But we wanted pie, not candy. For a pie that truly tasted of maple we found that a hefty dose of syrup was in order—a full 1¾ cups of dark amber syrup, in fact. But with maple flavor comes maple sweetness, so we added just a touch of cider vinegar to balance all the sweetness and introduce a subtle tang. Some cornstarch, in addition to the custard's eggs, helped the pie slice neatly. Make sure to use pure maple syrup in this recipe. We like to serve this rich pie with crème fraîche for sophistication and tang or unsweetened whipped cream.

---

**1** Roll dough into 12-inch circle on floured counter. Loosely roll dough around rolling pin and gently unroll it onto 9-inch pie plate, letting excess dough hang over edge. Ease dough into plate by gently lifting edge of dough with your hand while pressing into plate bottom with your other hand.

**2** Trim overhang to ½ inch beyond lip of plate. Tuck overhang under itself; folded edge should be flush with edge of plate. Crimp dough evenly around edge of plate. Wrap dough-lined plate loosely in plastic wrap and refrigerate until firm, about 30 minutes. Adjust oven rack to middle position and heat oven to 350 degrees.

**3** Line chilled pie shell with double layer of aluminum foil, covering edges to prevent burning, and fill with pie weights. Bake on foil-lined rimmed baking sheet until edges are set and just beginning to turn golden, 25 to 30 minutes, rotating sheet halfway through baking. Remove foil and weights, rotate sheet, and continue to bake until center begins to look opaque and slightly drier, 3 to 6 minutes. Transfer sheet to wire rack and let cool completely, about 30 minutes.

**4** Bring maple syrup, cream, and salt to boil in medium saucepan. Add butter and whisk until melted. Reduce heat to medium-low and whisk in cornstarch. Bring to simmer and cook for 1 minute, whisking frequently. Transfer to large bowl and let cool for at least 30 minutes. Whisk in eggs and yolks and vinegar until smooth. (Cooled filling can be refrigerated for up to 24 hours. Whisk to recombine and proceed with step 5, increasing baking time to 55 minutes to 1 hour 5 minutes.)

**5** With pie still on sheet, pour filling into cooled crust. Bake until just set, 35 to 45 minutes. Let pie cool completely on wire rack, about 2 hours. Refrigerate pie until fully set, at least 2 hours or up to 24 hours. Serve cold or at room temperature.

# APPLE PIE WITH CHEDDAR CHEESE CRUST

Serves 8

## dough

2½ cups (12½ ounces) all-purpose flour

1 tablespoon granulated sugar

1 teaspoon table salt

1 teaspoon dry mustard

⅛ teaspoon cayenne pepper

8 ounces extra-sharp cheddar cheese, shredded (2 cups)

8 tablespoons unsalted butter, cut into ¼-inch pieces and frozen for 15 minutes

⅓ cup ice water, plus extra as needed

## filling

2 pounds Granny Smith, Empire, or Cortland apples, peeled, cored, halved, and sliced ¼ inch thick

2 pounds Golden Delicious, Jonagold, or Braeburn apples, peeled, cored, halved, and sliced ¼ inch thick

6 tablespoons (2⅔ ounces) granulated sugar

¼ cup packed (1¾ ounces) light brown sugar

½ teaspoon grated lemon zest plus 1 tablespoon juice

¼ teaspoon table salt

⅛ teaspoon ground cinnamon

**WHY THIS RECIPE WORKS** While mostly foreign to folks in other parts of the country, serving a slice of warm apple pie with a wedge of cheddar on top is commonplace in New England and the Midwest. If a nibble of rich, salty cheese eaten with a forkful of sweet pie is so satisfying, we thought it would be even better to bake the cheese right into the crust. The right ratio of fat to flour to liquid is essential to a good pie crust, but for ample cheese flavor we found that we had to cut back a bit on butter or the crust would crumble. Reducing the butter in our double crust to 8 tablespoons allowed us to load half a pound of cheese—extra-sharp packed the most punch—into the dough. Two unlikely ingredients boosted the cheese flavor even more without throwing off the fat balance: dry mustard and cayenne. Good choices for tart apples are Granny Smiths, Empires, or Cortlands; for sweet, we recommend Golden Delicious, Jonagolds, or Braeburns. Be sure to use extra-sharp cheddar here. Freezing the butter for 15 minutes promotes flakiness in the crust; do not skip this step.

---

**1** *for the dough* Process flour, sugar, salt, mustard, and cayenne in food processor until combined, about 5 seconds. Scatter cheddar and butter over top and pulse until butter is size of large peas, about 10 pulses.

**2** Pour half of ice water over flour mixture and pulse until incorporated, about 3 pulses. Repeat with remaining ice water. Pinch dough with your fingers; if dough feels dry and does not hold together, sprinkle 1 to 2 tablespoons extra ice water over mixture and pulse until dough forms large clumps and no dry flour remains, 3 to 5 pulses.

**3** Using spatula, divide dough into 2 equal portions. Transfer each portion to sheet of plastic wrap and form each into 4-inch disk. Wrap each piece tightly in plastic and refrigerate for at least 1 hour or up to 2 days. Let chilled dough sit on counter to soften slightly, about 10 minutes, before rolling. (Wrapped dough can be frozen for up to 1 month. If frozen, let dough thaw completely on counter before rolling.)

**4** *for the filling* Toss apples, granulated sugar, brown sugar, lemon zest, salt, and cinnamon together in Dutch oven. Cover and cook over medium heat, stirring frequently, until apples are tender when poked with fork but still hold their shape, 10 to 15 minutes. Off heat, stir in lemon juice. Spread apples and their juices on rimmed baking sheet and let cool completely, about 30 minutes. (Filling can be refrigerated for up to 24 hours.)

**5** Roll 1 disk of dough into 12-inch circle between 2 sheets of parchment paper. Loosely roll dough around rolling pin and gently unroll it onto 9-inch pie plate, letting excess dough hang over edge. Ease dough into plate by gently lifting edge of dough with your hand while pressing into plate bottom with your other hand. Leave any dough that overhangs plate in place. Wrap dough-lined plate loosely in plastic and refrigerate until firm, about 15 minutes.

**6** Adjust oven rack to lowest position and heat oven to 425 degrees. Spread apple mixture into dough-lined plate. Roll other disk of dough into 12-inch circle between 2 sheets of parchment. Loosely roll dough around rolling pin and gently unroll it onto filling.

**7** Trim overhang to ½ inch beyond lip of plate. Pinch edges of top and bottom dough firmly together. Tuck overhang under itself; folded edge should be flush with edge of plate. Crimp dough evenly around edge of plate. Cut four 2-inch slits in top of dough.

**8** Place pie on aluminum foil–lined rimmed baking sheet and bake for 20 minutes. Reduce oven temperature to 375 degrees, rotate sheet, and continue to bake until juices are bubbling and crust is deep golden brown, 35 to 45 minutes longer. Let pie cool on wire rack until filling has set, about 4 hours. Serve.

# CHOCOLATE HAUPIA CREAM PIE

Serves 8

1 recipe single-crust pie dough (see pages 316–326)

4 ounces semisweet chocolate, chopped

1 (14-ounce) can coconut milk

1 cup whole milk

½ cup (3 ½ ounces) sugar

¼ cup (1 ounce) cornstarch

⅛ teaspoon table salt

1 recipe Whipped Cream (page 340)

**WHY THIS RECIPE WORKS** The name takes some sounding out, but once we'd developed our recipe, this Hawaiian pie was the talk of the test kitchen. The defining characteristic of this popular dessert is its firm haupia (pronounced how-PEE-ah), or coconut pudding, filling. Not the rich, ploppable stuff you usually think of as pudding, haupia is stable and slices cleanly: ¼ cup of cornstarch and a can of coconut milk with plenty of fat produced pudding with the perfect consistency. Combining just 1 cup of the hot pudding mixture with some chopped chocolate melted the chocolate and allowed us to spread a layer of chocolate pudding under the coconut pudding. We prefer Chaokoh or Thai Kitchen coconut milk for this recipe. Do not use "lite" coconut milk or any coconut milk that has less than 12 grams of fat and/or greater than 3 grams of sugar per ⅓-cup serving. If you do, the pudding will be too runny and sweet.

1 Roll dough into 12-inch circle on floured counter. Loosely roll dough around rolling pin and gently unroll it onto 9-inch pie plate, letting excess dough hang over edge. Ease dough into plate by gently lifting edge of dough with your hand while pressing into plate bottom with your other hand.

2 Trim overhang to ½ inch beyond lip of plate. Tuck overhang under itself; folded edge should be flush with edge of plate. Crimp dough evenly around edge of plate. Wrap dough-lined plate loosely in plastic wrap and refrigerate until firm, about 30 minutes. Adjust oven rack to middle position and heat oven to 350 degrees.

3 Line chilled pie shell with double layer of aluminum foil, covering edges to prevent burning, and fill with pie weights. Bake on rimmed baking sheet until edges are set and just beginning to turn golden, 25 to 30 minutes, rotating sheet halfway through baking. Remove foil and weights, rotate sheet, and continue to bake crust until golden brown and crisp, 10 to 15 minutes longer. Transfer sheet to wire rack and let cool completely, about 30 minutes.

4 *for the filling* Once crust has cooled completely, place chocolate in bowl; set aside. Whisk coconut milk, milk, sugar, cornstarch, and salt in medium saucepan until no lumps of cornstarch remain. Cook over medium heat, stirring and scraping saucepan corners constantly with rubber spatula, until mixture thickens to glue-like consistency and large bubbles break surface, about 6 minutes.

5 Quickly pour 1 cup coconut pudding over chocolate in bowl and whisk until smooth. Spread chocolate pudding evenly in cooled crust. Using clean, dry whisk, vigorously rewhisk remaining coconut pudding in saucepan, then gently pour on top of chocolate pudding and spread into even layer. Refrigerate, uncovered, until set, at least 3 hours or up to 24 hours.

6 Once pie is fully chilled, transfer whipped cream to pastry bag fitted with medium open or closed star tip (about ½-inch diameter). Pipe whipped cream stars onto top of pie until completely covered. Serve.

# FRENCH COCONUT PIE

Serves 8

1 recipe single-crust pie dough (see pages 316–326)

1¼ cups (3¾ ounces) unsweetened shredded coconut

½ cup buttermilk

1 teaspoon vanilla extract

1 cup (7 ounces) sugar

8 tablespoons unsalted butter, melted and cooled

2 large eggs plus 1 large yolk

2 tablespoons all-purpose flour

¼ teaspoon table salt

**WHY THIS RECIPE WORKS** French coconut pie is a custard pie that has been popular across the American South (no, not France) for generations. Many recipes we tried were unpopular in the test kitchen, however: They were simply too sweet and lacking in coconut flavor. We set out to tackle these issues, starting with the coconut itself. All of the recipes we found called for sweetened shredded coconut, so we decided to try unsweetened shredded coconut. This was an easy way to fix both problems: The unsweetened variety automatically decreased sweetness and also contributed serious coconut flavor. But unsweetened coconut lacks moisture and wasn't fully softening as the pie baked. Soaking it in buttermilk and vanilla before adding it to the filling tenderized the coconut in advance and further offset sweetness. The finished pie was golden brown, from the crust to the lovely sugar topping that formed on the custard. Look for shredded unsweetened coconut, about ¼ inch in length, in the natural foods section of the supermarket. It sometimes goes by the name "coconut flakes." Do not use large flaked coconut.

**1** Roll dough into 12-inch circle on floured counter. Loosely roll dough around rolling pin and gently unroll it onto 9-inch pie plate, letting excess dough hang over edge. Ease dough into plate by gently lifting edge of dough with your hand while pressing into plate bottom with your other hand.

**2** Trim overhang to ½ inch beyond lip of plate. Tuck overhang under itself; folded edge should be flush with edge of plate. Crimp dough evenly around edge of plate. Wrap dough-lined plate loosely in plastic wrap and refrigerate until firm, about 30 minutes. Adjust oven rack to middle position and heat oven to 325 degrees.

**3** Line chilled pie shell with double layer of aluminum foil, covering edges to prevent burning, and fill with pie weights. Bake on foil-lined rimmed baking sheet until lightly golden around edges, 18 to 25 minutes, rotating sheet halfway through baking. Transfer sheet to wire rack and remove foil and weights. (Crust must still be warm when filling is added.)

**4** Meanwhile, combine coconut, buttermilk, and vanilla in bowl. Cover with plastic and let sit for 15 minutes.

**5** Whisk sugar, melted butter, eggs and yolk, flour, and salt together in large bowl. Stir in coconut mixture until fully incorporated. With pie still on sheet, pour coconut mixture into warm crust. Bake until custard is set and golden-brown crust forms on top of pie, 40 to 55 minutes. Let pie cool completely on wire rack, about 4 hours. Serve.

# THOROUGHBRED PIE

Serves 8

1 recipe single-crust pie dough (see pages 316–326)

3 ounces bittersweet chocolate, chopped fine

8 tablespoons unsalted butter, cut into 8 pieces

3 tablespoons bourbon

¾ cup (5¼ ounces) granulated sugar

½ cup packed (3½ ounces) light brown sugar

2 tablespoons cornstarch

½ teaspoon salt

2 large eggs plus 1 large yolk, lightly beaten

1 teaspoon vanilla extract

1½ cups walnuts, toasted and chopped

**WHY THIS RECIPE WORKS** The original recipe for Derby Pie—the chocolate-walnut-bourbon pie served at Kentucky Derby parties—is the closely guarded secret of the Kern family of Prospect, Kentucky. After tasting the real thing, we were jockeying to re-create this top-secret trademarked pie at home. We kept the filling's sweetness in check with a combination of brown and white sugars, and used cornstarch for thickening. Browned butter added depth, and a hit of bourbon gave the filling a nutty, boozy flavor that paired well with the toasted walnuts. Parbaking the shell ensured a crisp crust under the filling, but the warm crust was also an opportunity to sprinkle the bottom with chopped bittersweet chocolate chunks, which melted so we could spread them into an even layer. We knew we had a Triple Crown winner—a sweet, deeply nutty filling baked in a golden crust, with an intense jolt of chocolate in every bite. We like this pie served with our Brown Sugar and Bourbon Whipped Cream (page 340).

1 Roll dough into 12-inch circle on floured counter. Loosely roll dough around rolling pin and gently unroll it onto 9-inch pie plate, letting excess dough hang over edge. Ease dtough into plate by gently lifting edge of dough with your hand while pressing into plate bottom with your other hand.

2 Trim overhang to ½ inch beyond lip of plate. Tuck overhang under itself; folded edge should be flush with edge of plate. Crimp dough evenly around edge of plate. Wrap dough-lined plate loosely in plastic wrap and refrigerate until firm, about 30 minutes. Adjust oven racks to middle and lower-middle positions and heat oven to 350 degrees.

3 Line chilled pie shell with double layer of aluminum foil, covering edges to prevent burning, and fill with pie weights. Bake on foil-lined rimmed baking sheet on upper rack until edges are set and just beginning to turn golden, 25 to 30 minutes, rotating sheet halfway through baking. Remove foil and weights, rotate sheet, and continue to bake crust until golden brown and crisp, 10 to 15 minutes longer. Transfer sheet to wire rack. Sprinkle chocolate evenly over hot pie crust and let sit until softened, about 5 minutes; smooth into even layer. Decrease oven temperature to 325 degrees.

4 Melt butter in small saucepan over medium-low heat. Cook, stirring constantly, until butter is nutty brown, 5 to 7 minutes. Off heat, slowly stir in bourbon (mixture will bubble vigorously). Let mixture cool for 5 minutes.

5 Whisk granulated sugar, brown sugar, cornstarch, and salt in large bowl until combined. Whisk in eggs and yolk and vanilla until smooth. Slowly whisk in butter mixture until incorporated. Stir in walnuts. With pie still on sheet, pour mixture into chocolate-lined crust. Bake on lower rack until filling is puffed and center jiggles slightly when pie is gently shaken, 35 to 40 minutes, rotating sheet halfway through baking. Let pie cool completely on wire rack, about 4 hours. Serve.

# FUDGY TAR HEEL PIE

**Serves 8**

1 recipe single-crust pie dough (see pages 316–326)

1 cup (6 ounces) semisweet chocolate chips, divided

4 tablespoons unsalted butter

¼ cup vegetable oil

2 tablespoons unsweetened cocoa powder

¾ cup packed (5¼ ounces) dark brown sugar

2 large eggs

1 tablespoon vanilla extract

¾ teaspoon table salt

¼ cup (1¼ ounces) all-purpose flour

1¼ cups pecans, toasted and chopped coarse

**WHY THIS RECIPE WORKS** Some think the moniker "tar heel" stems from an incident during the Revolutionary War when North Carolinians poured tar into a river to slow British troops; others point to the Civil War, when soldiers from that state threatened to tar the heels of retreating comrades. Whatever its origins, tar heel pie serves up the best of elements of both pie and gooey, fudgy brownie in one decadent dessert. However, this turned out to be a tough pie to tackle: Whenever we got the texture right, the flavor went south—and vice versa. To correct the cloying sweetness of this brownie pie without sacrificing its fudgy texture, we replaced the white sugar with dark brown sugar, which introduced depth. Upping the vanilla and salt and adding cocoa powder finished the job. To make the pie gooey and fudgy but not runny, we backed the flour down to just ¼ cup (half of what most recipes call for) and we used a combination of butter and oil for the fat (oil makes for a softer, chewier crumb). Toasting the nuts before adding them to the batter ensured they stayed crisp. We like to serve this pie with ice cream.

---

**1** Roll dough into 12-inch circle on floured counter. Loosely roll dough around rolling pin and gently unroll it onto 9-inch pie plate, letting excess dough hang over edge. Ease dough into plate by gently lifting edge of dough with your hand while pressing into plate bottom with your other hand.

**2** Trim overhang to ½ inch beyond lip of plate. Tuck overhang under itself; folded edge should be flush with edge of plate. Crimp dough evenly around edge of plate. Wrap dough-lined plate loosely in plastic wrap and refrigerate until firm, about 30 minutes. Adjust oven rack to middle position and heat oven to 350 degrees.

**3** Line chilled pie shell with double layer of aluminum foil, covering edges to prevent burning, and fill with pie weights. Bake on foil-lined rimmed baking sheet until lightly golden around edges, 18 to 25 minutes. Remove foil and weights, rotate sheet, and continue to bake crust until center begins to look opaque and slightly drier, 3 to 6 minutes. Transfer sheet to wire rack and let cool completely, about 30 minutes. Reduce oven temperature to 325 degrees.

**4** Microwave ⅔ cup chocolate chips and butter in bowl at 50 percent power, stirring often, until melted, about 90 seconds. Whisk in oil and cocoa until smooth.

**5** Whisk sugar, eggs, vanilla, and salt in second bowl until smooth. Whisk chocolate mixture into sugar mixture until incorporated. Stir in flour and remaining ⅓ cup chocolate chips until just combined.

**6** With pie still on sheet, spread pecans in bottom of cooled crust, then pour batter over top, spreading into even layer with spatula. Bake until toothpick inserted in center comes out with thin coating of batter attached, 30 to 35 minutes. Let pie cool on wire rack until barely warm, about 1½ hours. Serve warm. (Pie can be reheated, uncovered, in a 300-degree oven until warm throughout, 10 to 15 minutes.)

# VIRGINIA PEANUT PIE

Serves 8

1    recipe single-crust pie dough (see pages 316–326)

¾   cup light corn syrup

¾   cup packed (5¼ ounces) brown sugar

3    large eggs

6    tablespoons unsalted butter, melted

1    tablespoon vanilla extract

½   teaspoon table salt

2    cups salted dry-roasted peanuts

**WHY THIS RECIPE WORKS** One bite and you'll go nuts for this Old Dominion pie. The contrasting flavors and textures of this pie—a specialty of the bustling Virginia Diner in Wakefield, Virginia—are easy to love. The pie is simultaneously sweet and salty, with a creamy filling tucked beneath a crunchy top. It's a lot like pecan pie but easier to make. The recipes we tried turned out pies that were too busy with added flavors and spices, were too sweet, or had nuts that weren't really incorporated into the filling. For our version, we settled on a mix of light corn syrup and brown sugar as the sweeteners, limited our flavorings to just vanilla and salt, and doubled the amount of peanuts called for in most recipes. We also found a way around precooking the filling and prebaking the crust: superchilling the dough and baking the pie on the lowest rack for more than an hour. Salted dry-roasted, cocktail, or honey-roasted peanuts can be used in this recipe. Do not use Spanish red skin peanuts. Inspect the peanut packaging to be sure the ingredient list includes only peanuts, salt, and oil (plus sweetener if using honey-roasted peanuts). Crush the peanuts in a zipper-lock bag using a rolling pin or meat pounder; you want peanut pieces, not dust. Do not use a Pyrex pie plate in this recipe.

1 Adjust oven rack to lowest position and heat oven to 350 degrees. Roll dough into 12-inch circle on floured counter. Loosely roll dough around rolling pin and gently unroll it onto 9-inch pie plate, letting excess dough hang over edge. Ease dough into plate by gently lifting edge of dough with your hand while pressing into plate bottom with your other hand.

2 Trim overhang to ½ inch beyond lip of plate. Tuck overhang under itself; folded edge should be flush with edge of plate. Crimp dough evenly around edge of plate. Wrap dough-lined plate loosely in plastic wrap and freeze until firm, about 15 minutes.

3 Whisk corn syrup, sugar, eggs, melted butter, vanilla, and salt in large bowl until fully combined. Stir in peanuts until incorporated.

4 Place chilled pie shell on aluminum foil–lined rimmed baking sheet. Pour filling into shell. Bake until filling is puffed and set but still jiggles slightly when pie is shaken, 1 hour 5 minutes to 1 hour 10 minutes. Transfer pie to wire rack and let cool completely, at least 4 hours or up to 8 hours. Serve.

# HOOSIER PIE

Serves 8

1 recipe single-crust pie dough (see pages 316–326)
1 cup (7 ounces) sugar
¼ cup (1 ounce) cornstarch
¼ teaspoon table salt
3 cups heavy cream
5 tablespoons unsalted butter, cut into 5 pieces
1 tablespoon vanilla extract
Whole nutmeg

**WHY THIS RECIPE WORKS** Hoosier pie, also known as sugar cream pie, was born in Indiana as a "desperation dessert" in the 1800s, when fresh fruit was scarce and eggs weren't always easy to come by. In dreary winter months, innovative home cooks turned to the basics: sugar, cream, flour, and, whenever it was available, a tiny hit of nutmeg. They'd gently stir the handful of modest ingredients together right in the pie shell before baking it to produce a custardy, pudding-like pie. To stay true to its humble roots, we decided to use only basic ingredients. But while we loved the simplicity of this pie and its ingredients, we found that each one we baked had a slightly different texture—and it wasn't always good. To eliminate inconsistency, we opted to cook the eggless custard and the pie crust separately and then marry the two. We also switched from flour to cornstarch; this allowed us to use less starch overall and prevented a stodgy filling. And for a bit of luxury, we incorporated 5 tablespoons of butter into the filling. With a little extra work, we had a crisp, never-soggy crust and a creamy yet sliceable filling—every time.

1  Roll dough into 12-inch circle on floured counter. Loosely roll dough around rolling pin and gently unroll it onto 9-inch pie plate, letting excess dough hang over edge. Ease dough into plate by gently lifting edge of dough with your hand while pressing into plate bottom with your other hand.

2  Trim overhang to ½ inch beyond lip of plate. Tuck overhang under itself; folded edge should be flush with edge of plate. Crimp dough evenly around edge of plate. Wrap dough-lined plate loosely in plastic wrap and refrigerate until firm, about 30 minutes. Adjust oven rack to middle position and heat oven to 350 degrees.

3  Line chilled pie shell with double layer of aluminum foil, covering edges to prevent burning, and fill with pie weights. Bake on foil-lined rimmed baking sheet until edges are set and just beginning to turn golden, 25 to 30 minutes, rotating sheet halfway through baking. Remove foil and weights, rotate sheet, and continue to bake crust until golden brown and crisp, 10 to 15 minutes longer. Transfer sheet to wire rack.

4  Whisk sugar, cornstarch, and salt together in large saucepan. Whisk in cream until combined. Add butter and cook over medium heat, whisking constantly, until mixture is thick and large bubbles appear at surface, 6 to 8 minutes. Continue to whisk 20 seconds longer. Off heat, whisk in vanilla. Pour custard into pie shell and smooth top with rubber spatula. Let pie cool completely, about 2 hours. Refrigerate pie until cold, about 2 hours. Grate nutmeg over pie and serve.

# MISSISSIPPI MUD PIE

**Serves 10 to 12**

*brownie layer*

4 ounces bittersweet chocolate, chopped fine

3 tablespoons unsalted butter

3 tablespoons vegetable oil

1½ tablespoons Dutch-processed cocoa powder

⅔ cup packed (4⅔ ounces) dark brown sugar

2 large eggs

2 teaspoons vanilla extract

¼ teaspoon table salt

3 tablespoons all-purpose flour

1 recipe Chocolate Cookie Crust (page 335), baked and cooled

*topping*

10 chocolate wafer cookies (2 ounces)

2 tablespoons confectioners' sugar

1 tablespoon Dutch-processed cocoa powder

⅛ teaspoon table salt

2 tablespoons unsalted butter, melted

*mousse*

6 ounces milk chocolate, chopped fine

1 cup heavy cream, chilled, divided

2 tablespoons Dutch-processed cocoa powder

2 tablespoons confectioners' sugar

⅛ teaspoon table salt

**WHY THIS RECIPE WORKS** The different layers of this intense—and we mean intense—chocolate pie are said to be named for the Mississippi River's silty bottom. But there's nothing muddy about its flavor or texture. This pie is pure chocolate and boasts crunch, chew, and creaminess. We started by baking a chewy brownie layer in a chocolate cookie crust. To achieve the perfect gooey texture for this layer, we relied on a mixture of melted bittersweet chocolate and moisture-rich dark brown sugar and baked it until it was slightly underdone. Once this layer was fully chilled, we added the mousse, essentially a mixture of melted and cooled milk chocolate, sugar, and cocoa powder folded into whipped cream. Our first couple of tests produced mousse that was a far cry from the fluffy-yet-sliceable mixture we eventually ended up with. Two key changes helped us get the right texture. First, we replaced the granulated sugar with starchier confectioners' sugar for more stability. Second, we made sure to let the chocolate cool to between 90 and 100 degrees before incorporating it—any warmer and it deflated the mousse. For a crunchy topping, we toasted chocolate wafer cookie pieces with melted butter, cocoa, and sugar and sprinkled them over the mousse layer to form a cookie streusel. Be sure to use milk chocolate in the mousse, as bittersweet chocolate will make the mousse too firm.

1 *for the brownie layer* Adjust oven rack to middle position and heat oven to 325 degrees. Combine chocolate, butter, oil, and cocoa in bowl and microwave at 50 percent power, stirring often, until melted, about 1½ minutes. Whisk sugar, eggs, vanilla, and salt in second bowl until smooth. Whisk in chocolate mixture until incorporated. Whisk in flour until just combined.

2 Pour brownie batter into crust. Bake pie until edges begin to set and toothpick inserted in center comes out with thin coating of batter attached, about 15 minutes. Transfer to wire rack and let cool for 1 hour, then refrigerate until fully chilled, about 1 hour longer.

3 *for the topping* Meanwhile, line rimmed baking sheet with parchment paper. Place cookies in zipper-lock bag, press out air, and seal bag. Using rolling pin, crush cookies into ½- to ¾-inch pieces. Combine sugar, cocoa, salt, and crushed cookies in bowl. Stir in melted butter until mixture is moistened and clumps begin to form. Spread crumbs in even layer on prepared sheet and bake until fragrant, about 10 minutes, shaking sheet to break up crumbs halfway through baking. Transfer sheet to wire rack and let cool completely.

4 *for the mousse* Once brownie layer has fully chilled, microwave chocolate in large bowl at 50 percent power, stirring often, until melted, 1½ to 2 minutes. Let cool until just barely warm and registers between 90 and 100 degrees, about 10 minutes.

**5** Microwave 3 tablespoons cream in small bowl until it registers between 105 and 110 degrees, about 15 seconds. Whisk in cocoa until combined. Combine cocoa-cream mixture, sugar, salt, and remaining cream in bowl of stand mixer. Fit mixer with whisk attachment and whip cream mixture on medium speed until beginning to thicken, about 30 seconds, scraping down bowl as needed. Increase speed to high and whip until soft peaks form, 30 seconds to 1 minute.

**6** Using whisk, fold one-third of whipped cream mixture into melted chocolate to lighten. Using rubber spatula, fold in remaining whipped cream mixture until no dark streaks remain. Spoon mousse into chilled pie and spread evenly from edge to edge. Sprinkle with cooled topping and refrigerate for at least 3 hours or up to 8 hours. Serve.

## Making the Topping

**1** Place cookies in zipper-lock bag, press out air, and seal bag. Using rolling pin, crush cookies into ½- to ¾-inch pieces.

**2** Combine sugar, cocoa, salt, and crushed cookies in bowl. Stir in melted butter until mixture is moistened and clumps begin to form.

**3** Spread crumbs in even layer on prepared sheet.

**4** Bake until fragrant, about 10 minutes, shaking sheet to break up crumbs halfway through baking.

MISSISSIPPI MUD PIE

SWEET POTATO SONKER

# SWEET POTATO SONKER

**Serves 12**

## sonker

| | |
|---|---|
| 1 | recipe double-crust pie dough (see pages 320–327) |
| 1 | recipe single-crust pie dough (see pages 316–326) |
| 2 | cups apple cider |
| 4 | pounds sweet potatoes, peeled, quartered lengthwise, and sliced ¼ inch thick |
| 1 | cup packed (7 ounces) light brown sugar |
| 4 | tablespoons unsalted butter, softened |
| 2½ | tablespoons all-purpose flour |
| 2 | tablespoons lemon juice |
| 1 | teaspoon vanilla extract |
| ¾ | teaspoon ground cinnamon, divided |
| ½ | teaspoon ground allspice |
| ¼ | teaspoon table salt |
| 1 | tablespoon granulated sugar |

## custard dip

| | |
|---|---|
| 2 | cups whole milk |
| ¼ | cup (1¾ ounces) granulated sugar |
| 2 | teaspoons cornstarch |
| ¼ | teaspoon ground cinnamon |
| ⅛ | teaspoon table salt |
| 1½ | teaspoons vanilla extract |

**WHY THIS RECIPE WORKS** From its funny name to its starring ingredient, the little-known sweet potato sonker baffles food historians. Where more familiar sweet potato pie delivers a creamy filling of mashed sweet potatoes in a single crust, the much larger sonker serves up sliced sweet potatoes in a double crust and is drizzled with a sweet, spiced, custard "dip." For soft, flavorful sweet potatoes that held their shape, we steamed the slices over apple cider until almost tender; we then reduced the cider and tossed the sweets with the concentrated liquid and flavorings. Once cooled, we spread the slices in a dough-lined baking dish and covered it all with a lattice top. Cornstarch, not eggs, thickened our dip. After we took just one bite of this pie, its unusual name was no laughing matter.

---

**1** *for the sonker* Line rimmed baking sheet with parchment paper. Roll each piece of dough into 16 by 11-inch rectangle on floured counter; stack on prepared sheet, separated by additional sheets of parchment. (You should have 3 rectangles.) Cover loosely with plastic wrap and refrigerate until firm but still pliable, about 10 minutes.

**2** Using parchment as sling, transfer 2 chilled dough rectangles to counter and return remaining dough rectangle on sheet to refrigerator. Starting at short side of 1 piece of dough, loosely roll around rolling pin, then gently unroll over half of long side of 13 by 9-inch baking dish. Repeat with second piece of dough, overlapping first piece of dough by ½ inch in center of dish. Ease dough into dish by gently lifting edges of dough with your hand while pressing into dish bottom with your other hand (you should have about 1½ inches overhang on each side of sheet). Brush overlapping edge of dough rectangles with water and press to seal. Cover loosely with plastic and refrigerate until firm, about 30 minutes.

**3** Using parchment as sling, transfer remaining dough rectangle to counter. Using pizza cutter or sharp knife, cut chilled dough rectangle into ten 1-inch-wide by 16-inch-long strips, saving scraps for another use. Return strips to sheet, cover loosely with plastic, and refrigerate until firm, about 30 minutes.

**4** While dough chills, adjust oven rack to middle position and heat oven to 375 degrees. Bring cider to boil in Dutch oven. Place steamer basket in pot and fill with potatoes. Reduce heat to medium and cook, covered, until potatoes are nearly tender, about 10 minutes. Remove potatoes. Cook cider over high heat until reduced to ½ cup, about 5 minutes. Combine potatoes, reduced cider, brown sugar, butter, flour, lemon juice, vanilla, ½ teaspoon cinnamon, allspice, and salt in large bowl. Spread potato mixture over clean rimmed baking sheet and let cool completely, about 20 minutes.

**5** Remove dough strips from refrigerator; if too stiff to be workable, let sit at room temperature until softened slightly but still very cold. Transfer cooled potato mixture to dough-lined dish and press into even layer. Space 4 dough strips evenly across length of dish, parallel to counter edge. Fold back first and third strips almost completely. Lay 1 strip across pie, perpendicular to second and fourth strips, keeping it snug to folded edges of dough strips, then unfold first and third strips over top. Fold back second and fourth strips and add second perpendicular strip. Repeat laying remaining strips evenly across pie, alternating between folding back first and third strips and second and fourth strips to create lattice pattern. Shift strips as needed so they are evenly spaced over top of pie. (If dough become too soft to work with, refrigerate pie and dough strips to firm up.)

**6** Trim overhang to ½ inch beyond edge of dish. Pinch edges of lattice strips and bottom crust together firmly to seal. Tuck overhang under itself; folded edge should be flush with edge of dish. Crimp dough evenly around edge of dish. (If dough is very soft, refrigerate for 10 minutes before baking.) Combine granulated sugar and remaining

¼ teaspoon cinnamon in bowl. Brush surface with water and sprinkle with cinnamon sugar. Cover dish with aluminum foil and bake for 15 minutes. Uncover and bake until deep golden brown, 55 minutes to 1 hour, rotating dish halfway through baking. Let sonker cool on wire rack for at least 1½ hours. (Completely cooled sonker can be refrigerated for up to 24 hours. Bring sonker to room temperature before serving.)

**7** *for the custard dip* While sonker cools, bring milk, sugar, cornstarch, cinnamon, and salt to simmer in medium saucepan over medium heat. Reduce heat to medium-low and cook, whisking frequently, until slightly thickened, about 15 minutes. Off heat, add vanilla. Transfer dip to bowl and let cool completely, about 30 minutes. Serve sonker slightly warm or at room temperature with dip.

## Forming a Sonker

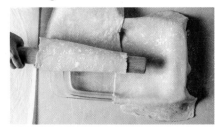

**1** Loosely roll 1 dough rectangle around rolling pin, then gently unroll over half of 13 by 9-inch baking dish. Repeat with second piece of dough, overlapping first by ½ inch in center. Ease dough into dish.

**2** Brush edge where doughs overlap with water, pressing to seal.

**3** Cut remaining chilled dough rectangle into ten 1-inch-wide by 16-inch-long strips. Refrigerate until firm, about 30 minutes.

**4** Space 4 dough strips evenly across length of potato-filled dish, parallel to counter edge. Fold back first and third strips almost completely.

**5** Lay 1 strip across pie, perpendicular to second and fourth strips, keeping it snug to folded edges of dough strips, then unfold strips over top.

**6** Fold back second and fourth strips and add second perpendicular strip. Repeat laying remaining strips evenly across pie to create lattice pattern.

# *icebox and*
# ICE CREAM PIES

# LEMON ICEBOX PIE

**Serves 8**

2 (14-ounce) cans sweetened condensed milk, divided

3 large egg yolks

¾ cup plus 2 tablespoons lemon juice (5 lemons)

1 recipe Graham Cracker Crust (page 334), baked and cooled

1 cup heavy cream

½ teaspoon vanilla extract

**WHY THIS RECIPE WORKS** Much like Key lime pie, lemon icebox pie boasts a buttery graham cracker crust that holds a tart, citrusy filling made with sweetened condensed milk and egg yolks. Older versions are no-bake pies that are served chilled: cool, oh-so-creamy, sweet yet tart, and easy to make. Many Americans, however, are nervous about eating raw eggs, so modern recipes call for a brief bake time. Food safety worries aside, we found that the baking innovation was a good one: Baked pies set up and sliced much better than unbaked pies. After a few tests, we settled on baking for 15 minutes at a relatively gentle 325 degrees. Now we just needed to figure out the right amount of lemon. Recipes called for as little as 2 tablespoons of lemon juice (these pies were bland) and as much as 2 cups (these pies were inedibly sour). The perfect pucker appeared at 1 cup. We were going to sweeten the whipped cream with sugar but we realized we could get the same effect from using some of the sweetened condensed milk from the filling. Stealing 3 tablespoons threw off the pie's balance, so we decreased the lemon juice slightly to reestablish harmony.

---

1 Adjust oven rack to middle position and heat oven to 325 degrees. Set aside 3 tablespoons condensed milk. Whisk egg yolks and remaining condensed milk in bowl until smooth. Slowly whisk in lemon juice.

2 Pour filling into cooled crust. Bake until edges are beginning to set but center still jiggles when shaken, about 15 minutes. Let pie cool on wire rack for 1 hour. Refrigerate until chilled and set, at least 3 hours or up to 24 hours.

3 Using stand mixer fitted with whisk attachment, whip cream, vanilla, and reserved condensed milk on medium-low speed until foamy, about 1 minute. Increase speed to high and whip until stiff peaks form, 1 to 3 minutes. Spread whipped cream attractively over pie. Serve.

# FRESH STRAWBERRY PIE

Serves 8

1 recipe single-crust pie dough (see pages 316–326)

3 pounds strawberries, hulled (9 cups)

¾ cup (5¼ ounces) sugar

2 tablespoons cornstarch

1½ teaspoons fruit pectin

Pinch table salt

1 tablespoon lemon juice

**WHY THIS RECIPE WORKS** This pie of high-piled gleaming strawberries is an iconic diner dessert. What's the secret to preventing the berry mountain from tumbling? The thickener has to be just right; or rather, thickeners, as we soon discovered. Together, pectin and cornstarch—combined with a puree of some of the strawberries—produced a supple, lightly clingy glaze that held the berries together. To account for imperfect fruit, we call for several more ounces than will be used in the pie. If possible, seek out local, in-season berries. For fruit pectin, we recommend both Sure-Jell for Less or No Sugar Needed Recipes and Ball RealFruit Low or No-Sugar Needed Pectin. The pie is at its best after 2 hours of chilling; longer and the glaze becomes softer and wetter, though the pie will taste good.

1 Roll dough into 12-inch circle on floured counter. Loosely roll dough around rolling pin and gently unroll it onto 9-inch pie plate, letting excess dough hang over edge. Ease dough into plate by gently lifting edge of dough with your hand while pressing into plate bottom with your other hand.

2 Trim overhang to ½ inch beyond lip of plate. Tuck overhang under itself; folded edge should be flush with edge of plate. Crimp dough evenly around edge of plate. Wrap dough-lined plate loosely in plastic wrap and refrigerate until firm, about 30 minutes. Adjust oven rack to middle position and heat oven to 350 degrees.

3 Line chilled pie shell with double layer of aluminum foil, covering edges to prevent burning, and fill with pie weights. Bake on foil-lined rimmed baking sheet until edges are set and just beginning to turn golden, 25 to 30 minutes, rotating sheet halfway through baking. Remove foil and weights, rotate sheet, and continue to bake crust until golden brown and crisp, 10 to 15 minutes longer. Transfer sheet to wire rack and let cool completely, about 45 minutes.

4 Select 6 ounces misshapen, underripe, or otherwise unattractive berries, halving those that are large; you should have about 1½ cups. Process berries in food processor to smooth puree, 20 to 30 seconds, scraping down bowl as needed (you should have about ¾ cup puree). Whisk sugar, cornstarch, pectin, and salt together in medium saucepan. Stir in berry puree, making sure to scrape corners of pan. Bring to boil over medium-high heat, stirring constantly. Boil, scraping bottom and sides of pan to prevent scorching, for 2 minutes (mixture will appear frothy when it first reaches boil, then will darken and thicken with further cooking). Transfer glaze to large bowl and stir in lemon juice; let cool completely.

5 Meanwhile, pick over remaining berries and measure out 2 pounds of most attractive ones; halve only extra-large berries. Add berries to bowl with glaze and fold gently with rubber spatula until berries are evenly coated. Scoop berries into cooled crust, piling into mound. Turn any cut sides face down. If necessary, rearrange berries so that holes are filled and mound looks attractive. Refrigerate until chilled and set, at least 2 hours or up to 5 hours. Serve.

# RASPBERRY CHIFFON PIE

**Serves 8**

1 recipe single-crust pie dough (see pages 316–326)

*fruit*

12 ounces (2½ cups) frozen raspberries

3 tablespoons fruit pectin

1½ cups (10½ ounces) sugar

Pinch table salt

5 ounces (1 cup) fresh raspberries

*chiffon*

3 tablespoons raspberry-flavored gelatin

3 tablespoons boiling water

3 ounces cream cheese, softened

1 cup heavy cream, chilled

1 recipe Whipped Cream (page 340)

**WHY THIS RECIPE WORKS** Raspberry chiffon pie features a frothy confection of berries, whipped egg whites or cream, sugar, and gelatin surrounded by a crisp crust. It's an old-fashioned sort of pie that really appealed to us—in theory. In reality, we were turned off by wan, saccharine foam fillings. For a chiffon pie that was creamy, light, and packed with raspberry flavor, we started by including an extra layer. We made a thickened puree of frozen raspberries, stirred in whole fresh raspberries, and spread it on the crust beneath the chiffon. We stiffened our chiffon filling by using plenty of (raspberry-flavored) gelatin and a little cream cheese. This thicker chiffon was able to hold a liberal amount of raspberry puree (we reserved some from our bottom layer) for even more fruit flavor. Whipped cream spread on top kept the pie light and lovely. For fruit pectin, we recommend both Sure-Jell for Less or No Sugar Needed Recipes and Ball RealFruit Low or No-Sugar Needed Pectin. For an accurate measurement of boiling water, bring a full kettle of water to a boil and then measure out the desired amount.

---

**1** Roll dough into 12-inch circle on floured counter. Loosely roll dough around rolling pin and gently unroll it onto 9-inch pie plate, letting excess dough hang over edge. Ease dough into plate by gently lifting edge of dough with your hand while pressing into plate bottom with your other hand.

**2** Trim overhang to ½ inch beyond lip of plate. Tuck overhang under itself; folded edge should be flush with edge of plate. Crimp dough evenly around edge of plate. Wrap dough-lined plate loosely in plastic wrap and refrigerate until firm, about 30 minutes. Adjust oven rack to middle position and heat oven to 350 degrees.

**3** Line chilled pie shell with double layer of aluminum foil, covering edges to prevent burning, and fill with pie weights. Bake on foil-lined rimmed baking sheet until edges are set and just beginning to turn golden, 25 to 30 minutes, rotating sheet halfway through baking. Remove foil and weights, rotate sheet, and continue to bake crust until golden brown and crisp, 10 to 15 minutes longer. Transfer sheet to wire rack and let cool completely, about 30 minutes.

**4** *for the fruit* Cook frozen raspberries in medium saucepan over medium-high heat, stirring occasionally, until berries begin to give up their juices, about 3 minutes. Stir in pectin and bring to boil, stirring constantly. Stir in sugar and salt and return to boil. Cook, stirring constantly, until slightly thickened, about 2 minutes. Strain mixture through fine-mesh strainer into bowl, pressing on solids to extract as much puree as possible. Scrape puree off underside of strainer into bowl.

**5** Transfer ⅓ cup raspberry puree to small bowl and let cool completely. Gently fold fresh raspberries into remaining puree and spread evenly over bottom of cooled crust; set aside.

**6** *for the chiffon* Dissolve gelatin in boiling water in bowl of stand mixer. Fit stand mixer with paddle, add cream cheese and reserved ⅓ cup raspberry puree, and beat on high speed, scraping down bowl once or twice, until smooth, about 2 minutes. Add cream and beat on medium-low speed until incorporated, about 30 seconds. Scrape down bowl. Increase speed to high and beat until cream holds stiff peaks, 1 to 2 minutes. Spread evenly over fruit in pie shell. Cover pie with plastic. Refrigerate until set, at least 3 hours or up to 2 days. Spread whipped cream attractively over pie before serving.

# RUM PUMPKIN CHIFFON PIE

**Serves 8**

### crust

9   **whole graham crackers, broken into 1-inch pieces**

3   **tablespoons granulated sugar**

½   **teaspoon ground ginger**

5   **tablespoons unsalted butter, melted**

### filling

1   **tablespoon unflavored gelatin**

¼   **cup dark rum**

1   **(15-ounce) can unsweetened pumpkin puree**

⅓   **cup packed (2⅓ ounces) dark brown sugar**

1   **teaspoon ground cinnamon**

¾   **teaspoon table salt**

½   **cup heavy cream**

4   **large egg whites**

⅓   **cup (2⅓ ounces) granulated sugar**

1   **recipe Whipped Cream (page 340)**

4   **gingersnap cookies, crushed into ¼-inch pieces**

**WHY THIS RECIPE WORKS** Pumpkin chiffon pie is a lighter, more elegant, and—as we found out—incredibly delicious version of the old Thanksgiving standard. It consists of a gelatin-stabilized pumpkin custard lightened by meringue and sometimes whipped cream. The result is a fluffy, mousse-like, flavor-packed pie. Preparing this pumpkin pie takes a bit more time than a traditional one, so we wanted to make sure our version was truly foolproof. To do this, we eliminated the cooked egg custard step found in many chiffon recipes. Instead, we simply whipped up a meringue and folded it into a smooth (thanks to the food processor) mixture of pumpkin, sugar, and cinnamon. Crunchy gingersnap cookies sprinkled over the whipped cream–covered pie and a healthy glug of rum turned this dessert into a festive showstopper. The filling for this pie is not cooked; if you prefer to use pasteurized egg whites, use ½ cup and increase the whipping time in step 4 to 5 to 6 minutes. For a well-mounded pie, be sure to fully whip the egg whites to glossy, stiff peaks in step 4.

---

**1** *for the crust* Adjust oven rack to middle position and heat oven to 325 degrees. Process cracker pieces, sugar, and ginger in food processor to fine, even crumbs, about 30 seconds. Sprinkle melted butter over crumbs and pulse to incorporate, about 8 pulses. Sprinkle mixture into 9-inch pie plate. Using bottom of dry measuring cup, press crumbs into even layer on bottom and sides of pie plate. Bake until crust is fragrant and beginning to brown, 12 to 18 minutes. Let crust cool completely on wire rack, about 30 minutes.

**2** *for the filling* Sprinkle gelatin over rum in large bowl and let sit until gelatin softens, about 5 minutes. Microwave until mixture is bubbling around edges and gelatin dissolves, about 30 seconds. Let cool until slightly warm, about 110 degrees. (It will be syrupy.)

**3** Meanwhile, microwave pumpkin in bowl until heated to 110 degrees, 30 seconds to 1 minute. Process warm pumpkin, brown sugar, cinnamon, and salt in food processor until completely smooth, about 1 minute. Scrape down sides of bowl; process until no streaks remain, 10 to 15 seconds. Transfer pumpkin mixture to bowl with gelatin mixture; stir to combine. Stir in cream.

**4** Using stand mixer fitted with whisk attachment, whip egg whites on medium-low speed until foamy, about 1 minute. Increase speed to medium-high and whip whites to soft, billowy mounds, about 1 minute. Gradually add granulated sugar and whip until glossy, stiff peaks form, 2 to 3 minutes. Whisk one-third of meringue into pumpkin mixture until smooth. Using rubber spatula, fold remaining meringue into pumpkin mixture until only few white streaks remain.

**5** Spoon filling into center of crust. Gently spread filling to edges of crust, leaving mounded dome in center. Refrigerate pie for at least 4 hours or up to 24 hours. Spread whipped cream evenly over pie, following domed contours. Sprinkle gingersnaps over top. Serve.

## Making Rum Pumpkin Chiffon Filling

**1** Sprinkle gelatin over rum in large bowl and let sit until gelatin softens, about 5 minutes.

**2** Microwave until mixture is bubbling around edges and gelatin dissolves, about 30 seconds. Let cool until slightly warm, about 110 degrees. (It will be syrupy.)

**3** Meanwhile, microwave pumpkin until heated to 110 degrees, 30 seconds to 1 minute.

**4** Process warm pumpkin, brown sugar, cinnamon, and salt in food processor until completely smooth, about 1 minute. Scrape down sides of bowl and process until no streaks remain, 10 to 15 seconds.

**5** Transfer pumpkin mixture to bowl with gelatin mixture and stir to combine. Stir in cream.

**6** Whisk one-third of meringue into pumpkin mixture until smooth.

**7** Using rubber spatula, fold remaining meringue into pumpkin mixture until only few white streaks remain.

**8** Spoon filling into center of crust. Gently spread filling to edges of crust, leaving mounded dome in center. Refrigerate pie for at least 4 hours or up to 24 hours.

RUM PUMPKIN CHIFFON PIE

FRENCH SILK CHOCOLATE PIE

# FRENCH SILK CHOCOLATE PIE

Serves 8

1 recipe single-crust pie dough (see pages 316–326)

1 cup heavy cream, chilled

3 large eggs

¾ cup (5¼ ounces) sugar

2 tablespoons water

8 ounces bittersweet chocolate, melted and cooled

1 tablespoon vanilla extract

8 tablespoons unsalted butter, cut into ½-inch pieces and softened

**WHY THIS RECIPE WORKS** Don't let the name fool you: The recipe for French silk pie—a retro pie that's lighter and less dense than chocolate cream pie (the filling literally melts in your mouth) but silky-smooth and packed with richness—was born in America. Created by Betty Cooper in 1951 for the third annual Pillsbury Bake-Off, this old-fashioned icebox pie isn't made enough today, perhaps due to the filling's reliance on raw eggs for volume and richness. We wanted to change that. Cooper's original recipe called for whipping butter, sugar, three squares of melted-and-cooled unsweetened chocolate, and eggs until the mixture was light and fluffy. She chilled the filling in a pie crust until it was firm—no baking required. For our updated version, we cooked the eggs with sugar on the stovetop—whipping them in the process—until the mixture was light and thick. Once removed from the heat, we continued whipping the mixture until it was fully cooled. However, this filling was much too dense when we beat in the two sticks of softened butter called for in the original recipe. Cutting the amount of butter in half gave our filling a silkier texture. Bittersweet chocolate, folded into the cooled egg and sugar mixture, boosted the chocolate flavor better than milder varieties. And to lighten the pie, we incorporated whipped cream into the filling before spooning it into the pie shell. We like to serve this pie with more Whipped Cream (page 340) and chocolate curls.

1 Roll dough into 12-inch circle on floured counter. Loosely roll dough around rolling pin and gently unroll it onto 9-inch pie plate, letting excess dough hang over edge. Ease dough into plate by gently lifting edge of dough with your hand while pressing into plate bottom with your other hand.

2 Trim overhang to ½ inch beyond lip of plate. Tuck overhang under itself; folded edge should be flush with edge of plate. Crimp dough evenly around edge of plate. Wrap dough-lined plate loosely in plastic wrap and refrigerate until firm, about 30 minutes. Adjust oven rack to middle position and heat oven to 350 degrees.

3 Line chilled pie shell with double layer of aluminum foil, covering edges to prevent burning, and fill with pie weights. Bake on foil-lined rimmed baking sheet until edges are set and just beginning to turn golden, 25 to 30 minutes, rotating sheet halfway through baking. Remove foil and weights, rotate sheet, and continue to bake crust until golden brown and crisp, 10 to 15 minutes longer. Transfer sheet to wire rack and let cool completely, about 30 minutes.

4 Using handheld mixer set at medium-high speed, whip cream to stiff peaks, 2 to 3 minutes. Refrigerate until ready to use.

**5** Combine eggs, sugar, and water in large heatproof bowl set over saucepan filled with 1 inch barely simmering water, making sure that water does not touch bottom of bowl. Using handheld mixer on medium speed, beat until egg mixture is thickened and registers 160 degrees, 7 to 10 minutes. Remove bowl from heat and continue to beat until egg mixture is fluffy and cooled completely, about 8 minutes.

**6** Add chocolate and vanilla to egg mixture and beat until incorporated. Beat in butter, few pieces at a time, until incorporated. Using rubber spatula, fold in refrigerated whipped cream until no white streaks remain. Transfer filling to cooled crust, smoothing top with spatula. Refrigerate, uncovered, until set, at least 3 hours. Serve.

---

## Making French Silk Chocolate Pie

**1** Combine eggs, sugar, and water in large bowl set over saucepan filled with 1 inch barely simmering water. Beat on medium speed until egg mixture is thickened and registers 160 degrees, 7 to 10 minutes.

**2** Remove bowl from heat and continue to beat until egg mixture is fluffy and cooled completely, about 8 minutes.

**3** Add melted and cooled chocolate and vanilla to egg mixture and beat until incorporated.

**4** Beat in butter, few pieces at a time, until incorporated.

**5** Using rubber spatula, fold in refrigerated whipped cream until no white streaks remain.

# CARAMEL TURTLE ICEBOX PIE

Serves 8 to 10

1 recipe Caramel-Chocolate-Pecan Sauce (page 342)

1 recipe Chocolate Cookie Crust (page 335), baked and cooled

8 ounces cream cheese, softened

1 cup marshmallow crème

½ cup heavy cream

½ cup creamy peanut butter

2 tablespoons unsalted butter, softened

**WHY THIS RECIPE WORKS** Turtles showcase the ultimate combination of contrasting flavors and textures—smooth, deep chocolate; sweet, chewy caramel; and rich, crunchy nuts—and to us, they are candy perfection. But these contrasts are qualities we like in any dessert, so we decided to make a turtle in pie form. For the base we opted for a chocolate cookie crust, which was only mildly sweet so the pie could handle a rich filling and a thick pecan-caramel sauce. Rather than reserve the sauce for the top, we decided to pour a generous layer right onto the baked crust so it was more integrated into the pie. On top of the sauce we spread our filling: a combination of marshmallow crème, cream cheese, heavy cream, peanut butter, and butter. The cream cheese tempered the sweetness of the marshmallow, while the heavy cream ensured our filling was fluffy and light—rather than sticky and thick—so we could (more than) easily finish a slice. We developed this recipe with Fluff brand marshmallow crème, but any brand of marshmallow crème will work; do not use products labeled marshmallow sauce or marshmallow topping. When working with the marshmallow crème, grease both the inside of your measuring cup and a spatula with vegetable oil spray to prevent sticking. The sauce will need to be warm so that it is pourable.

1 Pour 1 cup sauce into bottom of crust and refrigerate, uncovered, until set, about 30 minutes.

2 Using stand mixer fitted with paddle, beat cream cheese, marshmallow crème, heavy cream, peanut butter, and butter on medium-high speed until light and fluffy, about 5 minutes, scraping down sides of bowl as needed. Transfer filling to cooled crust, smoothing top with spatula. Cover pie and refrigerate until filling is chilled and set, at least 2 hours or up to 24 hours. Drizzle remaining sauce attractively over top of pie and serve.

# PEANUT BUTTER PIE

Serves 8

½ cup honey roasted peanuts, chopped, divided

1 recipe Graham Cracker Crust (page 334), baked and cooled

¾ cup (3 ounces) plus 2 tablespoons confectioners' sugar, divided

¾ cup creamy peanut butter

6 ounces cream cheese, softened

1¾ cups heavy cream, divided

1 teaspoon vanilla extract

**WHY THIS RECIPE WORKS** Smooth, creamy peanut butter seems like a natural filling for pie, but keeping its flavor strong while creating a light, almost airy texture took some finessing. For a pie with the intense, nutty flavor of peanut butter but without its dense texture, we started by whipping smooth peanut butter with cream cheese (for tang and to aid sliceability), confectioners' sugar, and a touch of cream, which loosened the mixture just enough for a light and fluffy consistency; folding in some whipped cream lightened the filling even further. Our pie now had undeniable peanut flavor but it lacked peanut texture. Peanuts sprinkled directly onto the crust gave it crunch but they didn't really stand out, so we upgraded to sweet, crunchier honey roasted peanuts before layering in the filling and then topping the whole thing with still more whipped cream. Before serving, a second dose of crunchy nuts was the perfect finishing touch. All-natural peanut butters will work in this recipe. You can use our homemade Candied Nuts (page 345) with peanuts in place of the honey roasted peanuts for even deeper flavor and more crunch.

**1** Spread ⅓ cup peanuts evenly over bottom of crust.

**2** Using stand mixer fitted with whisk attachment, mix ¾ cup sugar, peanut butter, cream cheese, and 3 tablespoons cream on low speed until combined, about 1 minute. Increase speed to medium-high and whip until fluffy, about 1 minute. Transfer to large bowl; set aside.

**3** In now-empty mixer bowl, whip ¾ cup cream on medium-low speed until foamy, about 1 minute. Increase speed to high and whip until stiff peaks form, 1 to 3 minutes. Gently fold whipped cream into peanut butter mixture in 2 additions until no white streaks remain. Spoon filling into crust and spread into even layer with spatula.

**4** In now-empty mixer bowl, whip vanilla, remaining cream, and remaining 2 tablespoons sugar on medium-low speed until foamy, about 1 minute. Increase speed to high and whip until stiff peaks form, 1 to 3 minutes. Spread whipped cream attractively over pie. Refrigerate until set, about 2 hours. Sprinkle with remaining peanuts. Serve.

# GRASSHOPPER PIE

Serves 8

3 large egg yolks

2 cups heavy cream, divided

½ cup (3½ ounces) sugar

Pinch table salt

2 teaspoons unflavored gelatin

¼ cup green crème de menthe

¼ cup white crème de cacao

1 recipe Mint Chocolate Cookie Crust (page 335), baked and cooled

**WHY THIS RECIPE WORKS** Named after the minty, creamy cocktail first shaken up in New Orleans, grasshopper pie is one of the fluffiest, creamiest (and greenest) pies you'll ever eat, with enough mint and chocolate flavor to shame a Peppermint Pattie. While ice cream pie often comes to mind now at the mention of this dessert, we wanted to make the original: mint chiffon in a cookie crust. We started by softening gelatin in cream—along with some sugar and salt—over medium heat and then whisking the heated mixture into beaten egg yolks. We returned the gelatin-egg mixture to the stove to thicken and then incorporated the cordials: minty green crème de menthe and chocolaty white crème de cacao. After letting the filling firm up in the refrigerator, we added whipped cream for an ultrafluffy texture, carefully whisking in 1 cup before folding the gelatin mixture into the rest. A simple cookie crust of minty Oreos, in place of classic chocolate wafers, mirrored the filling's mint-chocolate flavor. We like to top the pie with chocolate curls.

1 Beat egg yolks together in bowl. Combine ½ cup cream, sugar, and salt in medium saucepan. Sprinkle gelatin over cream mixture and let sit until gelatin softens, about 5 minutes. Cook over medium heat until gelatin dissolves and mixture is very hot but not boiling, about 2 minutes. Whisking vigorously, slowly add gelatin mixture to egg yolks. Return mixture to saucepan and cook, stirring constantly, until slightly thickened, about 2 minutes. Remove from heat and add crème de menthe and crème de cacao. Pour into clean bowl and refrigerate, stirring occasionally, until filling is wobbly but not set, about 20 minutes.

2 Using stand mixer fitted with whisk attachment, whip remaining 1½ cups cream on medium-low speed until foamy, about 1 minute. Increase speed to high and whip until stiff peaks form, 1 to 3 minutes. Whisk 1 cup whipped cream into gelatin mixture until completely incorporated. Using rubber spatula, fold gelatin mixture into remaining whipped cream until no white streaks remain. Transfer filling to cooled crust, smoothing top with spatula. Refrigerate until firm, at least 6 hours or preferably 12 hours. (Pie can be refrigerated for up to 2 days.) Serve.

# COOKIES AND CREAM ICE CREAM PIE

Serves 8

12 sugar cones

5 tablespoons unsalted butter, melted

2 tablespoons sugar

2 pints vanilla ice cream

2 cups coarsely chopped Oreo cookies

2 cups Whipped Cream (page 340)

**WHY THIS RECIPE WORKS** When done right, cookies and cream ice cream pie is sure to be a crowd-pleaser. But all too often this dessert—frequently featured on restaurant menus—tastes stale and as if it has freezer burn. For a fresher take on this pie, we used crushed sugar cones to make the crust, turning an ice cream cone into a plated affair. The flavor was a better match for the ice cream than the more conventional graham cracker crust, and it didn't overshadow the texture of the cookies in the pie the way a chocolate cookie crust would. Instead of using prepared cookies-and-cream ice cream, we made our own by adding our favorite crushed chocolate sandwich cookies to ice cream that we softened in a bowl with a spatula. (Leaving the container out to soften resulted in an unevenly melted mess.) This allowed us to control the size of the cookie pieces for appealing texture. We like to serve the pie with Hot Fudge Sauce (page 343) for a sundae-like effect.

1 Adjust oven rack to middle position and heat oven to 350 degrees. Process sugar cones in food processor to fine crumbs, about 30 seconds. (You should have 1⅓ cups.) Transfer crumbs to bowl and stir in melted butter and sugar until crumbs are moistened. Press crumb mixture evenly against bottom and sides of 9-inch pie plate, compacting it with your fingertips. Bake crust until crisp, 6 to 8 minutes. Let crust cool completely on wire rack, about 30 minutes. (Crust can be wrapped in plastic wrap and frozen for up to 1 month.)

2 Scoop ice cream into bowl and work with rubber spatula to soften. Add Oreos to bowl and mash mixture with back of spoon until well combined. Spread ice cream mixture into crust in even layer. Place plastic directly on surface of ice cream and freeze until completely frozen, at least 4 hours or up to 1 week.

3 Cut pie into wedges and dollop each piece with whipped cream. Serve.

# COCONUT-RASPBERRY GELATO PIE

Serves 8

1 cup raspberry sorbet

1 recipe Graham Cracker Crust (page 334), baked and cooled

1 pint coconut gelato

7½ ounces (1½ cups) raspberries, divided

½ cup macadamia nuts, toasted and chopped

**WHY THIS RECIPE WORKS** Our Cookies and Cream Ice Cream Pie (page 311) is a fun cross between an ice cream cone and an ice cream sundae in sliceable form. But ice cream pie isn't just for kids; we wanted to make an easy yet sophisticated version using store-bought ingredients, for a layered ice cream pie with complex flavors. Our graham cracker crust was an easy starting point. And for a refreshing twist, we decided to use sweet-tart sorbet paired with coconut gelato for contrasting richness. We spread an even layer of sorbet into the crust followed by the gelato; mashing some fresh raspberries into the gelato before layering it into our pie allowed the two flavors to meld. Toasted and chopped macadamia nuts sprinkled on top gave a nod to the tropical and contributed crunch. We like the rich texture and bold flavor of coconut gelato in this recipe. You can use coconut ice cream in place of gelato in this recipe, but it may be a little icy. Serve the pie with Hot Fudge Sauce (page 343), if desired.

1 Scoop raspberry sorbet into bowl and work with rubber spatula to soften. Spread raspberry sorbet into crust in even layer. Transfer to freezer while making coconut layer.

2 Scoop coconut gelato into clean bowl and work with rubber spatula to soften. Stir in 1 cup raspberries, mashing mixture with spatula until well combined. Remove pie from freezer and spread gelato mixture over sorbet in even layer. Place plastic wrap directly on surface of gelato and freeze until filling is completely frozen, at least 4 hours or up to 1 week.

3 Let pie sit at room temperature for 30 minutes. Halve remaining ½ cup raspberries, then sprinkle raspberries and macadamia nuts over top of pie. Serve.

# pie and tart
# DOUGHS

# PAT-IN-PAN PIE DOUGH

**Makes one 9-inch single crust**

1¼   cups (6¼ ounces) all-purpose
     flour

2   tablespoons sugar

¼   teaspoon table salt

8   tablespoons unsalted butter,
    softened

2   ounces cream cheese, softened

Anyone can make this simple pat-in-pan pie dough—it requires no rolling and eliminates the step of transferring the dough to a dish. The addition of cream cheese helped make this dough easy to handle and ensured a tender crust. Make sure you press the dough evenly into the pie plate. If you're using a glass pie plate, you can hold the dough-lined plate up to the light to see any thick or thin spots. If you're using this dough in our pie recipes, skip the steps of rolling the dough and fitting it into the pan; move directly to parbaking or filling.

**1** Lightly spray 9-inch pie plate with vegetable oil spray. Whisk flour, sugar, and salt together in bowl.

**2** Using stand mixer fitted with paddle, beat butter and cream cheese on medium-high speed until completely homogeneous, about 2 minutes, stopping once or twice to scrape down paddle and bowl. Add flour mixture and mix on medium-low speed until mixture resembles coarse cornmeal, about 20 seconds. Scrape down bowl. Increase mixer speed to medium-high and beat until dough begins to form large clumps, about 30 seconds. Set aside 3 tablespoons of dough. Transfer remaining dough to lightly floured counter, gather into ball, and form into 6-inch disk. Transfer disk to pie plate.

**3** Using heel of your hand, press dough evenly over bottom of plate toward sides, making sure it is evenly distributed. Using your fingertips, continue to work dough over bottom of plate and up sides until evenly distributed.

**4** Roll reserved dough into 12-inch rope on lightly floured counter. Divide rope into 3 pieces and roll each piece into 8-inch rope. Arrange ropes, evenly spaced, around top of pie plate, pressing and squeezing to join them with dough in plate and form uniform edge. Crimp dough evenly around edge of plate. Wrap dough-lined plate loosely in plastic wrap and refrigerate until dough is firm, about 1 hour, before using.

## Making Pat-in-Pan Pie Dough

**1** Beat butter and cream cheese on medium-high speed until completely homogeneous, about 2 minutes, stopping once or twice to scrape down paddle and bowl.

**2** Add flour mixture and mix on medium-low speed until mixture resembles coarse cornmeal, about 20 seconds. Scrape down bowl.

**3** Increase mixer speed to medium-high and beat until dough begins to form large clumps, about 30 seconds. Set aside 3 tablespoons of dough.

**4** Transfer remaining dough to lightly floured counter, gather into ball, and form into 6-inch disk. Transfer disk to greased pie plate.

**5** Using heel of your hand, press dough evenly over bottom of plate toward sides, making sure it is evenly distributed.

**6** Using your fingertips, continue to work dough over bottom of plate and up sides until evenly distributed.

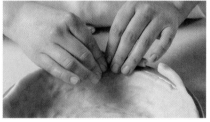

**7** Roll reserved dough into 12-inch rope on lightly floured counter. Divide rope into 3 pieces and roll each piece into 8-inch rope.

**8** Arrange ropes, evenly spaced, around top of pie plate, pressing and squeezing to join them with dough in plate and form uniform edge.

**9** Crimp dough evenly around edge of plate. Wrap dough-lined plate loosely in plastic wrap and refrigerate until dough is firm, about 1 hour, before using.

# FOOLPROOF ALL-BUTTER PIE DOUGH

This is our go-to dough: It's supremely supple and extremely easy to roll out. Even better, it bakes up buttery, tender, and flaky. How did we do it? First we used the food processor to coat two-thirds of the flour with butter, creating a water-resistant paste-like mixture. Next we broke that dough into pieces, coated the pieces with the remaining flour, and tossed in grated butter. By doing this, the water we folded in was absorbed only by the dry flour that coated the butter-flour chunks. Since gluten can develop only when flour is hydrated, this waterproofing method resulted in a crust that was supertender but had enough structure to support flakes. After a 2-hour chill, the dough was completely hydrated and easy to roll out. Be sure to weigh the flour. If your recipe requires rolling your dough piece(s) to a rectangle after chilling, form the dough into a 5-inch square instead of a disk. This dough will be moister than most pie doughs, but it will absorb a lot of excess moisture as it chills. Roll out the dough on a well-floured counter.

## FOOLPROOF ALL-BUTTER SINGLE-CRUST PIE DOUGH

**Makes one 9-inch single crust**

| 10 | tablespoons unsalted butter, chilled, divided |
| 1¼ | cups (6¼ ounces) all-purpose flour, divided |
| 1 | tablespoon sugar |
| ½ | teaspoon table salt |
| ¼ | cup ice water, divided |

**1** Grate 2 tablespoons butter on large holes of box grater and place in freezer. Cut remaining 8 tablespoons butter into ½-inch cubes.

**2** Pulse ¾ cup flour, sugar, and salt in food processor until combined, 2 pulses. Add cubed butter and process until homogeneous paste forms, about 30 seconds. Using your hands, carefully break paste into 2-inch chunks and redistribute evenly around processor blade. Add remaining ½ cup flour and pulse until mixture is broken into pieces no larger than 1 inch (most pieces will be much smaller), 4 to 5 pulses. Transfer mixture to bowl. Add grated butter and toss until butter pieces are separated and coated with flour.

**3** Sprinkle 2 tablespoons ice water over mixture. Toss with rubber spatula until mixture is evenly moistened. Sprinkle remaining 2 tablespoons ice water over mixture and toss to combine. Press dough with spatula until dough sticks together. Transfer dough to sheet of plastic wrap. Draw edges of plastic over dough and press firmly on sides and top to form compact, fissure-free mass. Wrap in plastic and form into 5-inch disk. Refrigerate dough for at least 2 hours or up to 2 days. Let chilled dough sit on counter to soften slightly, about 10 minutes, before rolling. (Wrapped dough can be frozen for up to 1 month. If frozen, let dough thaw completely on counter before rolling.)

### Herb Single-Crust Pie Dough
Add 1½ tablespoons minced fresh sage or thyme to flour-sugar mixture.

### Lemon Single-Crust Pie Dough
*This also works well with orange or lime zest.*
Add 4 teaspoons grated lemon zest to flour-sugar mixture.

### Nut Single-Crust Pie Dough
*Do not use toasted nuts in this recipe.*
Reduce cubed butter to 6 tablespoons and reduce first addition of flour to 6 tablespoons. Add ½ cup pecans, walnuts, hazelnuts, almonds, or peanuts, chopped and frozen, to food processor with flour, sugar, and salt and process until finely ground, about 30 seconds.

### Whole-Grain Single-Crust Pie Dough
Substitute ¾ cup whole-wheat or rye flour for first addition of all-purpose flour, using ½ cup all-purpose flour for second addition of flour.

## Mixing Foolproof All-Butter Single-Crust Pie Dough

**1** Pulse ¾ cup flour, sugar, and salt in food processor until combined, 2 pulses. Add cubed butter and process until homogeneous paste forms, about 30 seconds.

**2** Using your hands, carefully break paste into 2-inch chunks and redistribute evenly around processor blade.

**3** Add remaining ½ cup flour and pulse until mixture is broken into pieces no larger than 1 inch (most pieces will be much smaller), 4 to 5 pulses. Transfer mixture to bowl.

**4** Add grated butter and toss until butter pieces are separated and coated with flour.

**5** Sprinkle 2 tablespoons ice water over mixture. Toss with rubber spatula until mixture is evenly moistened. Sprinkle remaining 2 tablespoons ice water over mixture and toss to combine.

**6** Transfer dough to sheet of plastic wrap. Draw edges of plastic over dough and press firmly on sides and top to form compact, fissure-free mass. Wrap in plastic and form into 5-inch disk.

## Rolling Single-Crust Pie Dough

**1** Roll dough into 12-inch circle on floured counter.

**2** Loosely roll dough around rolling pin and gently unroll it onto 9-inch pie plate, letting excess dough hang over edge.

**3** Ease dough into plate by gently lifting edge of dough with your hand while pressing into plate bottom with your other hand.

**4** Trim overhang to ½ inch beyond lip of plate.

**5** Tuck overhang under itself; folded edge should be flush with edge of plate.

**6** Crimp dough evenly around edge of plate.

# FOOLPROOF ALL-BUTTER DOUBLE-CRUST PIE DOUGH

**Makes one 9-inch double crust**

20   tablespoons (2½ sticks) unsalted butter, chilled, divided

2½   cups (12½ ounces) all-purpose flour, divided

2   tablespoons sugar

1   teaspoon table salt

½   cup (4 ounces) ice water, divided

**1** Grate 4 tablespoons butter on large holes of box grater and place in freezer. Cut remaining 16 tablespoons butter into ½-inch cubes.

**2** Pulse 1½ cups flour, sugar, and salt in food processor until combined, 2 pulses. Add cubed butter and process until homogeneous paste forms, 40 to 50 seconds. Using your hands, carefully break paste into 2-inch chunks and redistribute evenly around processor blade. Add remaining 1 cup flour and pulse until mixture is broken into pieces no larger than 1 inch (most pieces will be much smaller), 4 to 5 pulses. Transfer mixture to bowl. Add grated butter and toss until butter pieces are separated and coated with flour.

**3** Sprinkle ¼ cup ice water over mixture. Toss with rubber spatula until mixture is evenly moistened. Sprinkle remaining ¼ cup ice water over mixture and toss to combine. Press dough with spatula until dough sticks together. Using spatula, divide dough into 2 equal portions. Transfer each portion to sheet of plastic wrap. Working with 1 portion at a time, draw edges of plastic over dough and press firmly on sides and top to form compact, fissure-free mass. Wrap in plastic and form into 5-inch disk. Refrigerate dough for at least 2 hours or up to 2 days. Let chilled dough sit on counter to soften slightly, about 10 minutes, before rolling. (Wrapped dough can be frozen for up to 1 month. If frozen, let dough thaw completely on counter before rolling.)

### Herb Double-Crust Pie Dough
Add 3 tablespoons minced fresh sage or thyme to flour-sugar mixture.

### Lemon Double-Crust Pie Dough
*This also works well with orange or lime zest.*
Add 2½ tablespoons grated lemon zest to flour-sugar mixture.

### Nut Double-Crust Pie Dough
*Do not use toasted nuts in this recipe.*
Reduce cubed butter to 12 tablespoons and reduce first addition of flour in step 2 to ¾ cup. Add 1 cup pecans, walnuts, hazelnuts, almonds, or peanuts, chopped and frozen, to food processor with flour, sugar, and salt and process until finely ground, about 30 seconds.

### Whole-Grain Double-Crust Pie Dough
Substitute 1½ cup (8¼ ounces) whole-wheat or rye flour for first addition of all-purpose flour, using 1 cup all-purpose flour (5 ounces) for second addition of flour.

## Rolling Double-Crust Pie Dough

**1** Roll 1 disk of dough into 12-inch circle on floured counter.

**2** Loosely roll dough around rolling pin and gently unroll it onto 9-inch pie plate, letting excess dough hang over edge.

**3** Ease dough into plate by gently lifting edge of dough with your hand while pressing into plate bottom with your other hand. Leave any dough that overhangs plate in place.

**4** Wrap dough-lined plate loosely in plastic wrap and refrigerate until dough is firm, about 30 minutes.

**5** Roll other disk of dough into 12-inch circle on well-floured counter, then transfer to parchment paper–lined baking sheet.

**6** Fill dough-lined plate; loosely roll remaining dough round around rolling pin and gently unroll it onto filling.

**7** Trim overhang to ½ inch beyond lip of plate. Pinch edges of top and bottom dough firmly together.

**8** Tuck overhang under itself; folded edge should be flush with edge of plate.

**9** Crimp dough evenly around edge of plate.

# CLASSIC PIE DOUGH

We love the flavor of a buttery pie dough, and we achieved that with our Foolproof All-Butter Pie Dough (page 318). It's a breeze to work with and our recommended dough for those who fear pie dough. But if you have experience, the process might not be intuitive—and you might not need that reassurance. For bakers who want to cut fat into flour and bring it together with water like their grandparents did (but with a food processor), we're providing a classic pie dough. It employs a tried-and-true combination of butter (for flavor and flakiness) and shortening (for tenderness and workability). If your recipe requires rolling your dough piece(s) to a rectangle after chilling, form the dough into a 5-inch square instead of a disk.

## CLASSIC SINGLE-CRUST PIE DOUGH

**Makes one 9-inch single crust**

- 1¼ cups (6¼ ounces) all-purpose flour
- 1 tablespoon sugar
- ½ teaspoon table salt
- 4 tablespoons vegetable shortening, cut into ½-inch pieces and chilled
- 6 tablespoons unsalted butter, cut into ¼-inch pieces and chilled
- 3 tablespoons ice water, plus extra as needed

**1** Process flour, sugar, and salt in food processor until combined, about 5 seconds. Scatter shortening over top and process until mixture resembles coarse cornmeal, about 10 seconds. Scatter butter over top and pulse until mixture resembles coarse crumbs, about 10 pulses.

**2** Transfer mixture to bowl. Sprinkle ice water over mixture. Stir and press dough with spatula until dough sticks together. If dough does not come together, stir in up to 1 tablespoon ice water, 1 teaspoon at a time, until it does.

**3** Transfer dough to sheet of plastic wrap and form into 4-inch disk. Wrap tightly in plastic and refrigerate for at least 1 hour or up to 2 days. Let chilled dough sit on counter to soften slightly, about 10 minutes, before rolling. (Wrapped dough can be frozen for up to 1 month. If frozen, let dough thaw completely on counter before rolling.)

## CLASSIC DOUBLE-CRUST PIE DOUGH

**Makes one 9-inch double crust**

- 2½ cups (12½ ounces) all-purpose flour
- 2 tablespoons sugar
- 1 teaspoon table salt
- 8 tablespoons vegetable shortening, cut into ½-inch pieces and chilled
- 12 tablespoons unsalted butter, cut into ¼-inch pieces and chilled
- 6 tablespoons ice water, plus extra as needed

**1** Process flour, sugar, and salt in food processor until combined, about 5 seconds. Scatter shortening over top and process until mixture resembles coarse cornmeal, about 10 seconds. Scatter butter over top and pulse until mixture resembles coarse crumbs, about 10 pulses.

**2** Transfer mixture to large bowl. Sprinkle ice water over mixture. Stir and press dough with spatula until dough sticks together. If dough does not come together, stir in up to 2 tablespoons ice water, 1 tablespoon at a time, until it does.

**3** Using spatula, divide dough into 2 equal portions. Transfer each portion to sheet of plastic wrap and form each into 4-inch disk. Wrap each piece tightly in plastic and refrigerate for at least 1 hour or up to 2 days. Let chilled dough sit on counter to soften slightly, about 10 minutes, before rolling. (Wrapped dough can be frozen for up to 1 month. If frozen, let dough thaw completely on counter before rolling.)

## Mixing Classic Single-Crust Pie Dough

**1** Process flour, sugar, and salt in food processor until combined, about 5 seconds. Scatter shortening over top and process until mixture resembles coarse cornmeal, about 10 seconds.

**2** Scatter butter over top and pulse until mixture resembles coarse crumbs, about 10 pulses.

**3** Transfer mixture to bowl. Sprinkle ice water over mixture. Stir and press dough with spatula until dough sticks together.

**4** Transfer dough to sheet of plastic wrap and form into 4-inch disk.

### TIPS FOR BLIND BAKING

**1** Most recipes call for blind-baking a single crust on a baking sheet on the middle rack in a 350-degree oven.

**2** Don't completely enclose the crust edge with foil; it will stick to or steam the dough. Fill the pie with 1 quart of pie weights.

**3** To avoid accidents, take the crust out of the oven to remove the pie weights, even if a recipe calls for returning the crust to the oven.

**4** Remember to adjust the oven temperature if called for in a recipe after the crust is done parbaking.

## Blind-Baking Any Single-Crust Pie Dough

**1** Line chilled pie shell with double layer of aluminum foil, covering edges to prevent burning, and fill with pie weights.

**2** Bake on rimmed baking sheet until edges are set and just beginning to turn golden, 25 to 30 minutes, rotating sheet halfway through baking.

**3** Remove foil and weights, rotate sheet, and continue to bake crust until golden brown and crisp, 10 to 15 minutes longer.

# VEGAN PIE DOUGH

A tender, flaky, and crisp crust with rich baked flavor—this is the aspiration of any pie maker, vegan or not. Since butter (along with flour, sugar, salt, and maybe shortening) is a key ingredient in traditional pie dough, we thought veganizing this workhorse would be a challenge. But many pie fillings—especially fruit varieties—are naturally vegan, so it made sense to develop a vegan crust we could incorporate into our repertoire. Baking with all shortening gave us a tender crust, but it lacked structure and was greasy. Vegetable oil was a failure, delivering a cracker-like crust. We'd hesitated to try coconut oil as it's very hard when chilled—too hard to roll. But when we substituted room-temperature coconut oil for the chilled butter (and passed on chilling the dough itself), we achieved a flaky, nicely browned, rich crust. If you're not a strict vegan, feel free to use conventional sugar. If your recipe requires rolling your dough piece(s) to a rectangle, form the dough into a 4-inch square instead of a disk.

## VEGAN SINGLE-CRUST PIE DOUGH

**Makes one 9-inch single crust**

1½ cups (7½ ounces) all-purpose flour, divided

1 tablespoon organic sugar

½ teaspoon table salt

½ cup plus 1 tablespoon coconut oil

¼ cup ice water, plus extra as needed

**1** Process ¾ cup flour, sugar, and salt in food processor until combined, about 5 seconds. Pinch off ½-inch pieces of oil into flour mixture and pulse until sticky and dough just begins to clump, 10 to 16 pulses. Redistribute dough evenly around processor blade, add remaining ¾ cup flour, and pulse until just incorporated, 3 to 6 pulses; transfer to large bowl.

**2** Sprinkle ice water over mixture. Stir and press dough with spatula until dough sticks together, being careful not to overmix. If dough does not come together, stir in up to 1 tablespoon ice water, 1 teaspoon at a time, until it does. Transfer dough to sheet of plastic wrap and form into 4-inch disk. (Dough can be wrapped tightly in plastic wrap and refrigerated for up to 2 days or frozen for up to 1 month. Let dough sit at room temperature to soften completely before rolling out, about 2 hours if refrigerated or 4 hours if frozen.)

## VEGAN DOUBLE-CRUST PIE DOUGH

**Makes one 9-inch double crust**

3 cups (15 ounces) all-purpose flour, divided

2 tablespoons organic sugar

1 teaspoon table salt

1 cup plus 2 tablespoons coconut oil

½ cup ice water, plus extra as needed

**1** Process 1½ cups flour, sugar, and salt in food processor until combined, about 5 seconds. Pinch off ½-inch pieces of oil into flour mixture and pulse until sticky and dough just begins to clump, 12 to 16 pulses. Redistribute dough evenly around processor blade, add remaining 1½ cups flour, and pulse until just incorporated, 3 to 6 pulses; transfer to large bowl.

**2** Sprinkle ice water over mixture. Stir and press dough with spatula until dough sticks together, being careful not to overmix. If dough doesn't come together, stir in up to 2 tablespoons ice water, 2 teaspoons at a time, until it does. Using spatula, divide dough into 2 equal portions. Transfer each portion to sheet of plastic wrap and form each into 4-inch disk. (Dough can be wrapped tightly in plastic wrap and refrigerated for up to 2 days or frozen for up to 1 month. Let dough sit at room temperature to soften completely before rolling out, about 2 hours if refrigerated or 4 hours if frozen.)

# GLUTEN-FREE PIE DOUGH

If you've bought or made a gluten-free pie before and been less than pleased when you ate it, you're not alone. Pie dough's structure comes from gluten—the long protein chains that form when flour mixes with water—so any dough without it is going to be at a disadvantage. Without enough gluten, the dough won't stick together (although if too much gluten develops, the crust will be tough). So we assumed we'd face a structural issue when developing a gluten-free crust, and we did; but flavor was lacking, too. Some xanthan gum added to the dry ingredients helped bind the dough and provide structure, giving it the feel of a traditional crust once baked. We used all butter (along with a little sour cream for tenderness) rather than a mix of butter and shortening for rich flavor that stood up to the starchiness of the gluten-free flour. The dough needed still more tenderness, however. We added a bit of vinegar, a known tenderizer, and it was just right. If your recipe requires rolling your dough piece(s) to a rectangle after chilling, form the dough into a 5-inch square instead of a disk. Use the steps that follow to roll out the dough for your recipe. We strongly recommend that you weigh your ingredients, as the ratios of ingredients are integral to successful gluten-free baking.

## GLUTEN-FREE SINGLE-CRUST PIE DOUGH

**Makes one 9-inch single crust**

-  3   tablespoons ice water
-  1½  tablespoons sour cream
-  1½  teaspoons rice vinegar
-  6½  ounces (¾ cup plus ⅔ cup) all-purpose gluten-free flour blend
-  1½  teaspoons sugar
-  ½   teaspoon table salt
-  ¼   teaspoon xanthan gum
-  8   tablespoons unsalted butter, cut into ¼-inch pieces and frozen for 10 to 15 minutes

**1** Combine ice water, sour cream, and vinegar in bowl. Process flour blend, sugar, salt, and xanthan gum in food processor until combined, about 5 seconds. Scatter butter over top and pulse until crumbs look uniform and distinct pieces of butter are no longer visible, 20 to 30 pulses.

**2** Pour sour cream mixture over flour mixture and pulse until dough comes together in large pieces around processor blade, about 20 pulses.

**3** Transfer dough to sheet of plastic wrap and form into 5-inch disk. Wrap tightly in plastic and refrigerate for at least 1 hour or up to 2 days. Let chilled dough sit on counter to soften slightly, about 30 minutes, before rolling. (Dough cannot be frozen.)

### GLUTEN-FREE FLOUR BLENDS

Each store-bought gluten-free flour blend relies on a different mix of ingredients, yielding pies and other baked goods with varying textures, colors, and flavors. Some work well, while others carry off-flavors or result in less-than-satisfactory textures. We've had good luck with and recommend **King Arthur Gluten-Free All-Purpose Flour** and **Betty Crocker All-Purpose Gluten Free Rice Flour Blend**, which both turned out tender but sturdy pie crusts. Bob's Red Mill Gluten Free All-Purpose Baking Flour also works, but it will add a noticeable bean flavor in most instances.

# GLUTEN-FREE DOUBLE-CRUST PIE DOUGH

**Makes one 9-inch double crust**

- 6   tablespoons ice water
- 3   tablespoons sour cream
- 1   tablespoon rice vinegar
- 13  ounces (2¾ cups plus 2 tablespoons) all-purpose gluten-free flour blend
- 1   tablespoon sugar
- 1   teaspoon table salt
- ½  teaspoon xanthan gum
- 16  tablespoons unsalted butter, cut into ¼-inch pieces and frozen for 10 to 15 minutes

**1** Combine ice water, sour cream, and vinegar in bowl. Process flour blend, sugar, salt, and xanthan gum in food processor until combined, about 5 seconds. Scatter butter over top and pulse until crumbs look uniform and distinct pieces of butter are no longer visible, 20 to 30 pulses.

**2** Pour half of sour cream mixture over flour mixture and pulse to incorporate, about 3 pulses. Add remaining sour cream mixture and pulse until dough comes together in large pieces around processor blade, about 20 pulses.

**3** Using spatula, divide dough into 2 equal portions. Transfer each portion to sheet of plastic wrap and form each into 5-inch disk. Wrap each piece tightly in plastic and refrigerate for at least 1 hour or up to 2 days. Let chilled dough sit on counter to soften slightly, about 30 minutes, before rolling. (Dough cannot be frozen.)

## Rolling Gluten-Free Pie Dough

**1** Roll dough into 12-inch circle between 2 large sheets of plastic wrap.

**2** Remove top plastic and gently invert dough over 9-inch pie plate.

**3** Working around circumference, ease dough into plate by gently lifting plastic wrap with 1 hand while pressing dough into plate bottom with other hand.

# CLASSIC TART DOUGH

**Makes one 9-inch tart crust**

1    large egg yolk

1    tablespoon heavy cream

½    teaspoon vanilla extract

1¼    cups (6¼ ounces) all-purpose flour

⅔    cup (2⅔ ounces) confectioners' sugar

¼    teaspoon table salt

8    tablespoons unsalted butter, cut into ¼-inch pieces and chilled

While regular pie crust is tender and flaky, classic tart crust should be fine-textured, buttery-rich, crisp, and crumbly. (It's often described as shortbread-like.) A tart typically features less filling than a traditional pie, so we needed a top-notch crust that could handle the spotlight. We found that using a whole stick of butter made tart dough that tasted great and was easy to handle, yet still had a delicate crumb. Instead of using the hard-to-find superfine sugar and pastry flour that many recipes call for, we used confectioners' sugar (the finest of the fine) combined with all-purpose flour to achieve a crisp texture. Rolling the dough and fitting it into the tart pan was easy, and we had ample dough to patch any holes. You need only to lightly flour the counter when rolling out this supple dough.

1   Whisk egg yolk, cream, and vanilla together in bowl. Process flour, sugar, and salt together in food processor until combined, about 5 seconds. Scatter butter over top and pulse until mixture resembles coarse cornmeal, about 15 pulses. With processor running, add egg yolk mixture and continue to process until dough just comes together around processor blade, about 12 seconds.

2   Transfer dough to sheet of plastic wrap and form into 6-inch disk. Wrap tightly in plastic and refrigerate for at least 1 hour or up to 2 days. Let chilled dough sit on counter to soften slightly, about 10 minutes, before rolling. (Wrapped dough can be frozen for up to 1 month. If frozen, let dough thaw completely on counter before rolling.)

### Chocolate Tart Dough
Substitute ¼ cup Dutch-processed cocoa powder for ¼ cup flour.

## Making and Rolling Classic Tart Dough

**1** Whisk egg yolk, cream, and vanilla together in bowl.

**2** Process flour, sugar, and salt together in food processor until combined, about 5 seconds. Scatter butter over top and pulse until mixture resembles coarse cornmeal, about 15 pulses.

**3** With processor running, add egg yolk mixture and continue to process until dough just comes together around processor blade, about 12 seconds.

**4** Transfer dough to sheet of plastic wrap and form into 6-inch disk. Wrap tightly in plastic and refrigerate for at least 1 hour or up to 2 days.

**5** Let chilled dough sit on counter to soften slightly, about 10 minutes, before rolling. Roll dough into 11-inch circle on floured counter.

**6** Transfer dough circle to parchment paper–lined baking sheet, cover with plastic, and refrigerate for 30 minutes.

**7** Loosely roll dough around rolling pin and gently unroll it onto 9-inch tart pan with removable bottom, letting excess dough hang over edge.

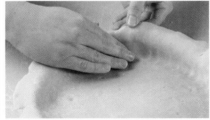

**8** Lift dough and gently press it into corners and fluted sides of pan.

**9** Run rolling pin over top of pan to remove any excess dough. Wrap loosely in plastic, place on large plate, and freeze until dough is fully chilled and firm, about 30 minutes.

# GLUTEN-FREE TART DOUGH

**Makes one 9-inch tart crust**

1   **large egg yolk**

½   **teaspoon vanilla extract**

7   **ounces (1⅓ cups plus ¼ cup) all-purpose gluten-free flour blend**

2⅓   **ounces (⅓ cup packed) light brown sugar**

1   **ounce (¼ cup) confectioners' sugar**

1   **teaspoon xanthan gum**

¼   **teaspoon table salt**

8   **tablespoons unsalted butter, cut into ¼-inch pieces and chilled**

2   **teaspoons ice water**

Simply substituting a gluten-free flour blend for all-purpose flour made a tart dough that was too sweet (the rice flour found in these blends has a distinct sweetness) and, as with our pie dough, too fragile. Adding xanthan gum helped reinforce the structure, but our tart shell was still too crumbly and too sweet. Reducing the amount of sugar was an obvious first step. Next we enriched the dough with an additional egg and extra cream—but the crust was crumbly and sweet still. In the end we found that using a mix of confectioners' sugar and brown sugar did the trick. We also learned that we didn't need the cream at all—just a very small amount of water was all that was required to bind the dough. Because our gluten-free tart dough is softer than traditional dough, you will need to roll it out between sheets of plastic wrap; follow the rolling steps on page 331. We strongly recommend that you weigh your ingredients, as the ratios of ingredients are integral to successful gluten-free baking.

**1**  Whisk egg yolk and vanilla together in bowl. Process flour blend, brown sugar, confectioners' sugar, xanthan gum, and salt in food processor until combined, about 5 seconds. Scatter butter over top and pulse until mixture resembles coarse cornmeal, about 10 pulses.

**2**  With processor running, add egg yolk mixture and continue to process until dough just comes together around processor blade, about 15 seconds. Add 1 teaspoon ice water and pulse until dough comes together. If dough does not come together, add remaining 1 teaspoon ice water and pulse until dough comes together.

**3**  Transfer dough to sheet of plastic wrap and form into 6-inch disk. Wrap tightly in plastic and refrigerate for at least 1 hour or up to 2 days. (Wrapped dough can be frozen for up to 2 months. If frozen, let dough thaw completely on counter before rolling.)

## Rolling Gluten-Free Tart Dough

**1** Roll dough into 12-inch circle between 2 sheets of plastic wrap. Slide onto baking sheet, then carefully remove top sheet of plastic.

**2** Place tart pan, bottom side up, in center of dough and press gently so that sharp edge of tart pan cuts dough.

**3** Holding tart pan in place, pick up baking sheet and carefully flip it over so that tart pan is right side up on counter. Remove baking sheet and peel off remaining plastic.

**4** Run rolling pin over edges of tart pan to cut dough completely. Gently ease and press dough into bottom of pan, reserving scraps.

**5** Roll dough scraps into ½-inch-thick rope, line edge of tart pan with rope, and gently press into fluted sides.

**6** Line tart pan with plastic and, using measuring cup, gently press and smooth dough to even thickness (sides should be ¼ inch thick). Trim any excess dough with paring knife.

# FREE-FORM TART DOUGH

**Makes enough for one 9-inch tart**

1½  cups (7½ ounces) all-purpose
     flour

½  teaspoon table salt

10  tablespoons unsalted butter,
     cut into ½-inch cubes and
     chilled

3–6  tablespoons ice water

A free-form tart—a single layer of buttery pie dough folded up and around fresh fruit—is a simpler take on pie that has a rustic elegance all its own. But without the support of a pie plate, the ultratender crust for this tart is prone to leaking juice, resulting in a soggy tart bottom. For our crust, we used a high proportion of butter to flour, which provided the most buttery flavor and tender texture without compromising structure the way shortening might. But the real answer to satisfying structure was found in a French method for making pastry called *fraisage*; with this technique, chunks of butter are pressed into the flour in long, thin sheets which creates lots of long, flaky layers when the dough is baked. These long layers are tender for eating yet sturdy and impermeable, making this crust ideal for supporting a generous filling of fresh, juicy fruit.

**1** Process flour and salt in food processor until combined, about 5 seconds. Scatter butter over top and pulse until mixture resembles coarse sand and butter pieces are about size of small peas, about 10 pulses. Continue to pulse, adding ice water 1 tablespoon at a time, until dough begins to form small curds that hold together when pinched with fingers, about 10 pulses.

**2** Transfer mixture to lightly floured counter and gather into rectangular-shaped pile. Starting at farthest end, use heel of hand to smear small amount of dough against counter. Continue to smear dough until all crumbs have been worked. Gather smeared crumbs together in another rectangular-shaped pile and repeat process.

**3** Form dough into 6-inch disk, wrap tightly in plastic wrap, and refrigerate for at least 1 hour or up to 2 days. Let chilled dough sit on counter to soften slightly, about 10 minutes, before rolling. (Wrapped dough can be frozen for up to 1 month. If frozen, let dough thaw completely on counter before rolling.)

### Free-Form Tartlet Dough
Using spatula, divide dough into 6 equal portions and form each into 4-inch disk. Wrap tightly in plastic wrap and refrigerate as directed in step 3.

## Making Free-Form Tart Dough

**1** Process flour and salt in food processor until combined, about 5 seconds. Scatter butter over top and pulse until mixture resembles coarse sand and butter pieces are size of small peas, about 10 pulses.

**2** Continue to pulse, adding ice water 1 tablespoon at a time, until dough begins to form small curds that hold together when pinched with fingers, about 10 pulses.

**3** Turn mixture onto lightly floured counter and gather into rectangular-shaped pile.

**4** Starting at farthest end, use heel of hand to smear small amount of dough against counter. Continue to smear dough until all crumbs have been worked.

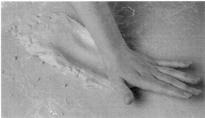

**5** Gather smeared crumbs together in another rectangular-shaped pile and repeat process.

**6** Form dough into 6-inch disk, wrap tightly in plastic wrap, and refrigerate for at least 1 hour or up to 2 days.

# GRAHAM CRACKER CRUST

**Makes one 9-inch crust**

8 **whole graham crackers, broken into 1-inch pieces**

3 **tablespoons sugar**

5 **tablespoons unsalted butter, melted and cooled**

We wanted a fresh-tasting homemade graham cracker crust that wasn't too sweet and featured a crisp texture. This one couldn't be easier to make: After combining crushed crumbs with sugar and a little melted butter to bind them, we simply used a measuring cup to pack the crumbs into the pie plate. Producing a perfect graham cracker crust has a lot to do with the type of graham crackers used. After experimenting with the three leading brands, we discovered subtle but distinct differences among them and found that these differences carried over into crumb crusts made with each kind of cracker. In the end, we preferred Keebler Grahams Crackers Original in our crust. We don't recommend using store-bought graham cracker crumbs here, as they can often be stale.

1 Adjust oven rack to middle position and heat oven to 325 degrees. Process graham cracker pieces and sugar in food processor to fine, even crumbs, about 30 seconds. Sprinkle melted butter over crumbs and pulse to incorporate, about 5 pulses.

2 Sprinkle mixture into 9-inch pie plate. Using bottom of dry measuring cup, press crumbs into even layer on bottom and sides of pie plate. Bake until crust is fragrant and beginning to brown, 12 to 18 minutes; transfer to wire rack. Following particular pie recipe, use crust while it is still warm or let it cool completely.

# COCONUT COOKIE CRUST

**Makes one 9-inch crust**

2 **cups (4½ ounces) Nilla Wafer cookies (34 cookies)**

½ **cup (1½ ounces) sweetened shredded coconut**

2 **tablespoons sugar**

1 **tablespoon all-purpose flour**

¼ **teaspoon table salt**

4 **tablespoons unsalted butter, melted**

Coconut is a great crust mix-in because, once processed, it doesn't disrupt the texture and it adds a fragrance that permeates the entire crust. Nilla Wafers were our cookie of choice; they added complementary vanilla flavor without detracting from the coconut. A hearty dash of salt enhanced all the flavors.

1 Adjust oven rack to middle position and heat oven to 325 degrees. Process cookies, coconut, sugar, flour, and salt in food processor until finely ground, about 30 seconds. Sprinkle melted butter over crumbs and pulse to incorporate, about 6 pulses.

2 Sprinkle mixture into 9-inch pie plate. Using bottom of dry measuring cup, press crumbs firmly into bottom and up sides of plate. Bake until crust is fragrant and set, 18 to 22 minutes. Following particular pie recipe, use crust while it is still warm or let it cool completely.

# CHOCOLATE COOKIE CRUST

**Makes one 9-inch crust**

16 Oreo cookies, broken into rough pieces

4 tablespoons unsalted butter, melted and cooled

Sometimes it's nice to have a chocolaty alternative to a graham cracker pie crust. Looking for just the right source for the crumbs, we found our answer right in the cookie aisle. Oreo cookies, the childhood favorite, offered just the right balance of dark, rich chocolate crumbs and a texture that was neither too dry nor too moist once processed. Other brands of chocolate sandwich cookies may be substituted, but avoid "double-filled" cookies as the proportion of cookie to filling won't be correct.

1 Adjust oven rack to middle position and heat oven to 325 degrees. Pulse cookies in food processor until coarsely ground, about 15 pulses, then process to fine, even crumbs, about 15 seconds. Sprinkle melted butter over crumbs and pulse to incorporate, about 5 pulses.

2 Sprinkle mixture into 9-inch pie plate. Using bottom of dry measuring cup, press crumbs into even layer on bottom and sides of pie plate. Bake until crust is fragrant and appears set, 13 to 18 minutes; transfer to wire rack. Following particular pie recipe, use crust while it is still warm or let it cool completely.

*Mint Chocolate Cookie Crust*
Substitute 16 Cool Mint Creme Oreo cookies for Oreo cookies.

*Nutter Butter Cookie Crust*
Substitute 16 Nutter Butter cookies for Oreo cookies.

### Pressing Cracker or Cookie Crumbs into a Pie Plate

Sprinkle crumb mixture into 9-inch pie plate. Using bottom of dry measuring cup, press crumbs into even layer on bottom and sides of pie plate.

# SLAB PIE DOUGH

**Makes one 18 by 13-inch single crust**

24 tablespoons (3 sticks) unsalted butter, divided

2¾ cups (13¾ ounces) all-purpose flour, divided

2 tablespoons sugar

1 teaspoon table salt

½ cup ice water, divided

This slab pie dough is simply a larger yield of our Foolproof All-Butter Pie Dough (page 318). The dough is very workable, which made it ideal for rolling into large rectangles that would fit into a baking sheet to make these large-scale pies. Be sure to weigh the flour for this recipe. In the mixing stage, this dough will be moister than most pie doughs, but as it chills it will absorb much of the excess moisture. Be sure to roll the dough on a well-floured counter.

---

**1** Grate 5 tablespoons butter on large holes of box grater and place in freezer. Cut remaining 19 tablespoons butter into ½-inch cubes.

**2** Pulse 1¾ cups flour, sugar, and salt in food processor until combined, 2 pulses. Add cubed butter and process until homogeneous paste forms, 40 to 50 seconds. Using your hands, carefully break paste into 2-inch chunks and redistribute evenly around processor blade. Add remaining 1 cup flour and pulse until mixture is broken into pieces no larger than 1 inch (most pieces will be much smaller), 4 to 5 pulses. Transfer mixture to bowl. Add grated butter and toss until butter pieces are separated and coated with flour.

**3** Sprinkle ¼ cup ice water over mixture. Toss with rubber spatula until mixture is evenly moistened. Sprinkle remaining ¼ cup ice water over mixture and toss to combine. Press dough with spatula until dough sticks together. Using spatula, divide dough into 2 equal portions. Transfer each portion to sheet of plastic wrap. Working with 1 portion at a time, draw edges of plastic over dough and press firmly on sides and top to form compact, fissure-free mass. Wrap in plastic and form into 5 by 6-inch rectangle. Refrigerate dough for at least 2 hours or up to 2 days. Let chilled dough sit on counter to soften slightly, about 10 minutes, before rolling. (Wrapped dough can be frozen for up to 1 month. If frozen, let dough thaw completely on counter before rolling.)

## Making and Rolling Slab Pie Dough

**1** Use spatula to divide dough into 2 portions.

**2** Transfer each portion to sheet of plastic wrap.

**3** Working with 1 portion at a time, draw edges of plastic over dough and press firmly on sides and top to form compact, fissure-free mass.

**4** Wrap in plastic and form into 5 by 6-inch rectangle. Refrigerate dough for at least 2 hours or up to 2 days.

**5** Line rimmed baking sheet with parchment paper. Roll each piece of dough into 16- by 11-inch rectangle on well-floured counter.

**6** Stack dough on prepared sheet, separated by parchment. Cover sheet loosely with plastic wrap and refrigerate until dough is firm but still pliable, about 10 minutes.

**7** Using parchment as sling, transfer chilled dough rectangles to counter and wipe sheet clean with paper towels.

**8** Starting at short side of 1 piece of dough, loosely roll around rolling pin, then gently unroll over half of long side of sheet, leaving about 2 inches of dough overhanging 3 edges of sheet.

**9** Repeat with second piece of dough, overlapping first piece of dough by ½ inch in center of sheet.

**10** Ease dough into sheet by gently lifting edges of dough with your hand while pressing into sheet bottom with your other hand.

**11** Brush edge where doughs overlap with water, pressing to seal.

**12** Cover loosely with plastic and refrigerate until dough is firm, about 30 minutes.

# toppings, sauces, AND MORE

# TOP IT OFF

---

Pie à la mode is classic, but you can enhance pies and tarts with more than just ice cream (although we do have a recipe for it!). Here we've included our favorite pie accompaniments. There's nary a pie that doesn't benefit from a dollop of whipped cream (in many flavors and variations). Sauces can dress up a classic or rustic pie, highlight the elegance of sophisticated tarts, or add appealing richness to fun icebox or ice cream pies. And crunchy toppings such as candied nuts or brittles can bring texture to creamy fillings or cap off your whipped cream. Have fun making your own pie pairings.

## WHIPPED CREAM

---

**Makes about 2 cups**

Whipped cream may be a simple topping, but it's often just the right addition to a slice of pie. Whipping the ingredients on medium-low speed to start ensured the sugar, vanilla, and salt were evenly dispersed in the cream before we increased the mixer speed to achieve soft peaks (our preference for a decadent dollop). Lightly sweetened whipped cream goes with just about everything, but occasionally we want to add another layer of flavor. Creating a maple or orange whipped cream was as simple as stirring in a few flavorings, while chilling the cream mixture for Brown Sugar and Bourbon Whipped Cream gave the heavier, wetter brown sugar time to dissolve and the flavors to blend. Yogurt Whipped Cream offers a thicker, tangier alternative to plain. And Peanut Butter Whipped Cream required a slower whipping speed; when whipped on high, the peanut butter–cream mixture went from runny to curdled in an instant. For a vegan whipped cream, we turned to the creamy top layer in canned coconut milk; it whipped just like heavy cream into velvety billows, and its mild coconut flavor complements most any pie.

1 **cup heavy cream, chilled**

1 **tablespoon sugar**

1 **teaspoon vanilla extract**

   **Pinch table salt**

Using stand mixer fitted with whisk attachment, whip cream, sugar, vanilla, and salt on medium-low speed until foamy, about 1 minute. Increase speed to high and whip until soft peaks form, 1 to 3 minutes. (Whipped cream can be refrigerated in fine-mesh strainer set over small bowl and covered with plastic wrap for up to 8 hours.)

### Maple Whipped Cream

Substitute 2 tablespoons maple syrup for sugar. Reduce vanilla to ½ teaspoon.

### Brown Sugar and Bourbon Whipped Cream

Omit vanilla. Substitute ½ cup packed light brown sugar for granulated sugar. Increase salt to ⅛ teaspoon. Add ½ cup sour cream and 2 teaspoons bourbon. Whisk all ingredients together in bowl of stand mixer, cover with plastic wrap, and refrigerate for at least 4 hours or up to 24 hours. Whisk to combine before whipping.

### Orange Whipped Cream

Substitute 2 tablespoons orange juice for vanilla. Add 1 teaspoon grated orange zest to stand mixer with cream before whipping.

### Peanut Butter Whipped Cream

Add ¼ cup creamy peanut butter to stand mixer with cream before whipping. Once mixture is foamy, continue to whip on medium-low speed until soft peaks form, 1 to 3 minutes.

### Vegan Coconut Whipped Cream

*You will need 4 (14-ounce) cans coconut milk for this recipe.*

Omit heavy cream. Increase sugar to 2 tablespoons and increase vanilla to 2 teaspoons. Refrigerate 4 (14-ounce) unopened cans of coconut milk for at least 24 hours to ensure that distinct layers form. Skim top layer of cream from each can and measure out 2 cups (save any extra cream for another use). Using stand mixer fitted with whisk attachment, whip all ingredients on low speed until well combined, about 30 seconds. Increase speed to high and whip until mixture thickens and soft peaks form, about 2 minutes. (Whipped cream can be refrigerated for up to 4 days.)

### Yogurt Whipped Cream

Omit sugar, vanilla, and salt. Reduce heavy cream to ¾ cup. Add ½ cup plain Greek yogurt to stand mixer with cream before whipping.

# MIXED BERRY COULIS

**Makes about 1½ cups**

For a traditional coulis—a fruit-based sauce that's pureed and strained to give it a silky-smooth texture—we turned to juicy berries, cooking them only briefly to release some pectin which thickened the sauce without dampening the fresh berry flavor. This vibrant sauce balances and brightens sweet, rich pies or tarts such as Rich Chocolate Tart (page 192). The type and ripeness of berries used will affect the sweetness of the coulis, so the amount of sugar is variable; start with 5 tablespoons, then add more to taste in step 2 if necessary. Additional sugar should be stirred into the warm coulis immediately after straining so that the sugar will readily dissolve.

- 15 ounces (3 cups) fresh or thawed frozen blueberries, blackberries, and/or raspberries
- ¼ cup water
- 5 tablespoons sugar, plus extra for seasoning
- ⅛ teaspoon table salt
- 2 teaspoons lemon juice

**1** Bring berries, water, sugar, and salt to gentle simmer in medium saucepan over medium heat and cook, stirring occasionally, until sugar is dissolved and berries are heated through, about 1 minute.

**2** Process mixture in blender until smooth, about 20 seconds. Strain through fine-mesh strainer into bowl, pressing on solids to extract as much puree as possible. Stir in lemon juice and season with extra sugar as needed. Cover and refrigerate until well chilled, about 1 hour. Adjust consistency with extra water as needed. (Sauce can be refrigerated for up to 4 days; stir to recombine before using.)

### Blueberry-Cinnamon Coulis
Use all blueberries and add ⅛ teaspoon ground cinnamon to saucepan with blueberries.

### Raspberry-Lime Coulis
Use all raspberries and substitute 1 tablespoon lime juice for lemon juice.

# CARAMEL SAUCE

**Makes about 2 cups**

When sugar is heated to a high enough temperature, it undergoes an array of chemical reactions that create new flavor compounds—and the result is a nutty, buttery dessert sauce. But caramel can intimidate: Too blonde and it lacks flavor; turn away for a second and it's too dark and bitter. We made our recipe foolproof by adding water to ensure that the sugar fully dissolved; this helped us avoid the common pitfalls of burning and crystallization (which occur when the sugar cooks unevenly). We prefer an instant-read thermometer for measuring the temperature of caramel. To ensure an accurate reading, swirl the caramel to even out hot spots and then tilt the pot so that the caramel pools 1 to 2 inches deep. Move the thermometer back and forth for about 5 seconds before taking a reading. Try drizzling this sauce on Deep-Dish Apple Pie (page 28) or anything with chocolate.

- 1¾ cups (12¼ ounces) sugar
- ½ cup water
- ¼ cup light corn syrup
- 1 cup heavy cream
- 1 teaspoon vanilla extract
- ¼ teaspoon table salt

**1** Bring sugar, water, and corn syrup to boil in large saucepan over medium-high heat. Cook, without stirring, until mixture is straw-colored, 6 to 8 minutes. Reduce heat to low and continue to cook, swirling saucepan occasionally, until caramel is amber-colored, 2 to 5 minutes. (Caramel should register between 360 and 370 degrees.)

**2** Off heat, carefully stir in cream, vanilla, and salt; mixture will bubble and steam. Continue to stir until sauce is smooth. Let cool slightly. (Sauce can be refrigerated for up to 2 weeks; gently warm in microwave, stirring every 10 seconds, until pourable, before using.)

### Dark Rum Caramel Sauce
Whisk 3 tablespoons dark rum into caramel with cream.

### Orange-Espresso Caramel Sauce
Stir 3 tablespoons Kahlúa, 1 tablespoon instant espresso powder, and 2 teaspoons finely grated orange zest in bowl until espresso dissolves. Stir Kahlúa mixture into caramel with cream.

### Salted Caramel Sauce
Increase salt to 1 teaspoon.

## CARAMEL-CHOCOLATE-PECAN SAUCE

**Makes about 1½ cups**

The addition of bittersweet chocolate and pecans to caramel creates a turtle-inspired sauce. This smooth sauce studded with crunchy bits is a key component of our Caramel Turtle Icebox Pie (page 304), but you can use to add luxury to ice cream pies or any other pie that caramel or chocolate complements, such as Banana Cream Pie (page 50) or even Cherry Hand Pies (page 222). We prefer an instant-read thermometer for measuring the temperature of caramel. To ensure an accurate reading, swirl the caramel to even out hot spots, then tilt the pot so that the caramel pools 1 to 2 inches deep. Move the thermometer back and forth for about 5 seconds before taking a reading.

- 1 cup (7 ounces) sugar
- ⅓ cup water
- 3 tablespoons light corn syrup
- ¾ cup heavy cream
- 2 ounces bittersweet chocolate, chopped
- 1 tablespoon unsalted butter, chilled
- ½ cup pecans, toasted and chopped
- 1 teaspoon vanilla extract
- ⅛ teaspoon table salt

**1** Bring sugar, water, and corn syrup to boil in large saucepan over medium-high heat. Cook, without stirring, until mixture is straw-colored, 6 to 8 minutes. Reduce heat to low and continue to cook, swirling saucepan occasionally, until caramel is amber-colored, 2 to 5 minutes. (Caramel should register between 360 and 370 degrees.)

**2** Off heat, carefully stir in cream; mixture will bubble and steam. Stir in chocolate and butter and let sit for 3 minutes. Whisk sauce until smooth and chocolate is fully melted. Stir in pecans, vanilla, and salt. Let cool slightly. (Sauce can be refrigerated for up to 2 weeks; gently warm in microwave, stirring every 10 seconds, until pourable, before using.)

## BUTTERSCOTCH SAUCE

**Makes about 1½ cups**

Cooking brown sugar and butter gives butterscotch its complexity without the precision of cooking caramel. In addition to serving butterscotch alongside pies, we fold it into the filling of our Pear-Butterscotch Slab Pie (page 206).

- 1 cup packed (7 ounces) brown sugar
- 2 teaspoons light corn syrup
- 8 tablespoons unsalted butter
- 1 tablespoon water
- ½ cup heavy cream
- 1 teaspoon vanilla extract

Heat sugar, corn syrup, butter, and water in medium saucepan over medium-high heat, stirring often, until sugar is fully dissolved, about 2 minutes. Continue to cook, without stirring, until mixture begins to bubble, 1 to 2 minutes. Off heat, carefully stir in cream and vanilla; mixture will bubble and steam. Continue to stir until sauce is smooth. Let cool slightly. (Sauce can be refrigerated for up to 2 weeks; gently warm in microwave, stirring every 10 seconds, until pourable, before using.)

## DULCE DE LECHE

**Makes about 2 cups**

Dulce de leche is a traditional Latin American dessert sauce made by cooking sweetened condensed milk until it thickens, for something lighter in flavor but richer than caramel. The microwave made our recipe foolproof; cooking the milk gently (and stirring) in this environment ensured it heated and caramelized evenly. Serve warm or at room temperature; we love it on Banana Cream Pie (page 50).

- 1 (14-ounce) can sweetened condensed milk
- 1 cup heavy cream
- 1 teaspoon vanilla extract

Microwave condensed milk in large covered bowl at 50 percent power, whisking every 3 minutes, until slightly darkened and thickened, 12 to 15 minutes. (Mixture may look curdled while microwaving, but will smooth out after whisking.) Slowly whisk in cream and vanilla until incorporated. (Sauce can be refrigerated for up to 1 week; gently warm in microwave, stirring every 10 seconds, until pourable, if desired, before using.)

# HOT FUDGE SAUCE

**Makes about 2 cups**

Intense and complex, a luxurious chocolate sauce can transform a simple pie into a decadent dessert. Our classic hot fudge sauce relies on cocoa powder and unsweetened chocolate for complexity and richness. Using milk rather than cream helped preserve the intense chocolate flavor; butter imparted an attractive sheen. It's the perfect topping for ice cream pies.

1¼  cups (8¾ ounces) sugar

⅔  cup whole milk

¼  teaspoon table salt

⅓  cup (1 ounce) unsweetened cocoa powder, sifted

3  ounces unsweetened chocolate, chopped fine

4  tablespoons unsalted butter, cut into 8 pieces and chilled

1  teaspoon vanilla extract

**1** Heat sugar, milk, and salt in medium saucepan over medium-low heat, whisking gently, until sugar has dissolved and liquid starts to bubble around edges of saucepan, about 6 minutes. Reduce heat to low, add cocoa, and whisk until smooth.

**2** Off heat, stir in chocolate and let sit for 3 minutes. Whisk sauce until smooth and chocolate is fully melted. Whisk in butter and vanilla until fully incorporated and sauce thickens slightly. (Sauce can be refrigerated for up to 1 month; gently warm in microwave, stirring every 10 seconds, until pourable, before using.)

*Mexican Hot Fudge Sauce*
Add ¼ teaspoon ground cinnamon and ¼ teaspoon chipotle chile powder to saucepan with milk.

*Orange Hot Fudge Sauce*
Bring milk and 8 (3-inch) strips orange zest to simmer in medium saucepan over medium heat. Off heat, cover, and let sit for 15 minutes. Strain milk mixture through fine-mesh strainer into bowl, pressing on orange zest to extract as much liquid as possible. Return milk to now-empty saucepan and proceed with recipe as directed.

*Peanut Butter Hot Fudge Sauce*
Increase salt to ½ teaspoon. Whisk ¼ cup creamy peanut butter into sauce after butter.

# CRÈME ANGLAISE

**Makes about 1½ cups**

Crème anglaise is a classic pourable custard sauce that's typically flavored with vanilla bean. It's ideal for upping the elegance of your dessert when you want the creamy richness that ice cream provides but not the icy cold contrast. A vanilla bean gives the deepest flavor, but 1 teaspoon of vanilla extract can be used instead; skip the steeping stage in step 1 and stir the extract into the sauce after straining it in step 2. Drizzle it on fruit pies such as Ginger Cranberry-Pear Streusel Pie (page 101) or set a slice of tart such as Blood Orange and Chocolate Tart (page 195) on a pool of it.

½  vanilla bean

1½  cups whole milk

Pinch table salt

4  large egg yolks

¼  cup (1¾ ounces) sugar

**1** Cut vanilla bean in half lengthwise. Using tip of paring knife, scrape out seeds. Bring vanilla bean and seeds, milk, and salt to simmer in medium saucepan over medium-high heat, stirring occasionally. Remove from heat, cover, and let steep for 20 minutes.

**2** Whisk egg yolks and sugar together in large bowl until smooth, then slowly whisk in hot milk mixture to temper. Return milk mixture to saucepan and cook over low heat, stirring constantly with rubber spatula, until sauce thickens slightly, coats back of spoon, and registers 180 degrees, 5 to 7 minutes. Immediately strain sauce through fine-mesh strainer into clean bowl; discard vanilla bean. Cover and refrigerate until cool, about 45 minutes. (Sauce can be refrigerated, with plastic wrap pressed directly on surface, for up to 3 days.)

*Coffee Crème Anglaise*
Add 1½ teaspoons instant espresso powder to saucepan with vanilla bean and seeds.

*Earl Grey Crème Anglaise*
Substitute 1 Earl Grey tea bag for vanilla bean. Remove tea bag after steeping in step 1.

*Orange Crème Anglaise*
Substitute 2 (3-inch) strips orange zest for vanilla bean. Stir 1 tablespoon Grand Marnier into finished sauce after straining.

# VANILLA ICE CREAM

**Makes about 1 quart**

Pie and ice cream are an irresistible combination. Who doesn't love a scoop melting slowly over a warmed slice of pie? You can pick up a pint at the store, but making it yourself is a surefire way to impress your guests. For completely smooth ice cream it is necessary to reduce the size of the ice crystals; the smaller they are, the less perceptible they are. We replaced some of the sugar in our custard base with corn syrup; the syrup interfered with crystal formation and resulted in a supersmooth texture. To speed up the freezing process—another way to ensure smaller ice crystals—we froze a portion of the custard prior to churning and then mixed it with the remaining chilled custard. Two teaspoons of vanilla extract can be substituted for the vanilla bean; stir the vanilla into the cold custard in step 3. An instant-read thermometer is critical for best results. If using a canister-style ice cream maker, be sure to freeze the empty canister at least 24 hours and preferably 48 hours before churning. For self-refrigerating ice cream makers, prechill the canister by running the machine for 5 to 10 minutes before pouring in the custard.

| | |
|---|---|
| 1 | vanilla bean |
| 1¾ | cups heavy cream |
| 1¼ | cups whole milk |
| ½ | cup plus 2 tablespoons (4⅓ ounces) sugar, divided |
| ⅓ | cup light corn syrup |
| ¼ | teaspoon table salt |
| 6 | large egg yolks |

**1** Place 8- or 9-inch square metal baking pan in freezer. Cut vanilla bean in half lengthwise. Using tip of paring knife, scrape out vanilla seeds. Combine vanilla bean and seeds, cream, milk, ¼ cup plus 2 tablespoons of sugar, corn syrup, and salt in medium saucepan. Heat over medium-high heat, stirring occasionally, until mixture is steaming steadily and registers 175 degrees, 5 to 10 minutes. Remove saucepan from heat.

**2** While cream mixture heats, whisk egg yolks and remaining ¼ cup sugar in bowl until smooth, about 30 seconds. Slowly whisk 1 cup heated cream mixture into egg yolk mixture to temper. Return mixture to saucepan and cook over medium-low heat, stirring constantly, until mixture thickens and registers 180 degrees, 7 to 14 minutes. Immediately pour custard into large bowl and let cool until no longer steaming, 10 to 20 minutes. Transfer 1 cup of custard to small bowl. Cover both bowls with plastic wrap. Place large bowl in refrigerator and small bowl in freezer and chill for at least 4 hours or up to 24 hours. (Small bowl of custard will freeze solid.)

**3** Remove custards from refrigerator and freezer. Scrape frozen custard from small bowl into large bowl of custard. Stir occasionally until frozen custard has fully dissolved. Strain custard through fine-mesh strainer and transfer to ice cream maker. Churn until mixture resembles thick soft-serve ice cream and registers about 21 degrees, 15 to 25 minutes. Transfer ice cream to frozen baking pan and press plastic wrap on surface. Return to freezer until firm around edges, about 1 hour.

**4** Transfer ice cream to airtight container, pressing firmly to remove any air pockets, and freeze until firm, at least 2 hours, before serving.

## SUPERMARKET VANILLA ICE CREAM

We love to make homemade ice cream and find it to be a satisfying accomplishment. But if you just want to purchase the ice cream for your pie, we highly recommend **Turkey Hill Original Vanilla Premium Ice Cream.** Its rich vanilla flavor and spoonable, velvety texture means it's great over the finest pies, but also nice on its own.

# CANDIED NUTS

**Makes about 1 cup**

Many single-crust pies could benefit from a little crunch to top things off. A very easy way to achieve this is to sprinkle on some toasted nuts, but to take this topping to the next level we like to candy the nuts for a toasty, sweet, salty treat that's much easier to achieve than you'd think. You can use any nut you'd like in this recipe. Try candied almonds on Vanilla Cream Pie (page 46).

|     |                       |
| --- | --------------------- |
| 1   | cup nuts, toasted     |
| ¼   | cup (1¾ ounces) sugar |
| ¼   | cup water             |
| ½   | teaspoon table salt   |

**1** Line rimmed baking sheet with parchment paper. Bring all ingredients to boil in medium saucepan over medium heat. Cook, stirring constantly, until water evaporates and sugar appears dry, opaque, and somewhat crystallized and evenly coats nuts, about 5 minutes.

**2** Reduce heat to low and continue to stir nuts until sugar is amber-colored, about 2 minutes longer. Transfer nuts to prepared sheet and spread in even layer. Let cool completely, about 10 minutes.

# CANDIED COFFEE BEANS

**Makes about ¼ cup**

Nuts aren't the only thing you can candy. Coffee beans are a crunchy alternative that add interest to pies. We chopped the beans in the food processor first so they would be easier to eat. These beans are potent—a small amount goes a long way. Use them to add an extra jolt to Banoffee Pie (page 60) or to give Butterscotch Cream Pie (page 64) a bit of crunch.

|      |                   |
| ---- | ----------------- |
| ¼    | cup coffee beans  |
| 1    | tablespoon sugar  |
| 1½   | teaspoons water   |
|      | Pinch table salt  |

**1** Line rimmed baking sheet with parchment paper. Pulse coffee beans in food processor until coarsely chopped, 6 to 8 pulses. Bring all ingredients to boil in medium saucepan over medium heat. Cook, stirring constantly, until water evaporates and sugar appears dry, opaque, and somewhat crystallized and evenly coats coffee beans, about 5 minutes.

**2** Reduce heat to low and continue to stir coffee beans until sugar turns amber-colored, about 2 minutes longer. Transfer coffee beans to prepared sheet and spread in even layer. Let cool completely, about 10 minutes.

# SESAME BRITTLE

**Makes about 2 cups**

Sesame brittle gives our Chocolate-Tahini Tart (page 193) a stunning patterned top. But you can break this brittle into shards of any size and top your desired pie any way you like—if you can resist eating it straight off the baking sheet. The thin brittle tastes of toasted sesame and caramel. When pouring and rolling out the hot mixture, you will need to work quickly to prevent it from setting before it reaches the right thickness.

|     |                            |
| --- | -------------------------- |
| 2   | tablespoons water          |
| 2   | tablespoons sugar          |
| 2   | tablespoons light corn syrup |
| 1   | tablespoon unsalted butter |
| ⅓   | cup sesame seeds, toasted  |
| ⅛   | teaspoon table salt        |

**1** Place large sheet parchment on cutting board. Heat water, sugar, corn syrup, and butter in small saucepan over medium-high heat, stirring often, until butter is melted and sugar is fully dissolved, about 1 minute. Bring to boil and cook, without stirring, until mixture has faint golden color and registers 300 degrees, 4 to 6 minutes.

**2** Reduce heat to medium-low and continue to cook, gently swirling pan, until syrup is amber-colored and registers 350 degrees, 1 to 2 minutes. Off heat, stir in sesame seeds and salt. Working quickly, transfer mixture to prepared parchment, top with second layer of parchment and carefully smooth into ¹⁄₁₆-inch-thick layer using rolling pin.

**3** Remove top sheet parchment and let cool completely, about 45 minutes. Break into rough 1-inch pieces before using. (Brittle can be stored in airtight container for up to 1 month.)

# NUTRITIONAL INFORMATION FOR OUR RECIPES

To calculate the nutritional values of our recipes per serving, we used The Food Processor SQL by ESHA research. When using this program, we entered all the ingredients, using weights for important baking ingredients such as flour for crusts and fruit for pie fillings. We also used our preferred brands in these analyses. Any ingredient listed as "optional" was excluded from the analyses. If there is a range in the serving size, we used the highest number of servings to calculate the nutritional values.

| | CALORIES | TOTAL FAT (G) | SAT FAT (G) | CHOL (MG) | SODIUM (MG) | TOTAL CARB (G) | DIETARY FIBER (G) | TOTAL SUGARS (G) | PROTEIN (G) |
|---|---|---|---|---|---|---|---|---|---|
| **Mastering the Classics** | | | | | | | | | |
| Skillet Apple Pie | 350 | 17 | 11 | 45 | 150 | 48 | 3 | 26 | 3 |
| Deep-Dish Apple Pie | 630 | 28 | 18 | 75 | 370 | 91 | 6 | 50 | 5 |
| Blueberry Pie | 590 | 31 | 19 | 85 | 310 | 75 | 3 | 35 | 5 |
| Summer Berry Pie | 220 | 8 | 4.5 | 20 | 60 | 39 | 5 | 28 | 1 |
| Sweet Cherry Pie | 590 | 31 | 19 | 85 | 330 | 75 | 3 | 35 | 6 |
| Free-Form Fruit Tart with Plums and Raspberries | 380 | 18 | 12 | 50 | 190 | 48 | 3 | 19 | 4 |
| Free-Form Fruit Tart with Apricots and Blackberries | 370 | 19 | 12 | 50 | 190 | 47 | 2 | 19 | 5 |
| Free-Form Fruit Tart with Peaches and Blueberries | 370 | 19 | 12 | 50 | 200 | 46 | 3 | 18 | 5 |
| Pumpkin Pie | 530 | 29 | 18 | 195 | 520 | 58 | 2 | 37 | 8 |
| Pecan Pie | 690 | 43 | 16 | 130 | 350 | 71 | 3 | 52 | 7 |
| Maple Pecan Pie | 580 | 36 | 14 | 120 | 320 | 60 | 2 | 39 | 7 |
| Chocolate Cream Pie | 660 | 49 | 28 | 235 | 220 | 48 | 1 | 36 | 11 |
| **Cream, Custard, and Curd Pies** | | | | | | | | | |
| Vanilla Cream Pie | 510 | 33 | 20 | 205 | 240 | 44 | 0 | 24 | 8 |
| Coconut Cream Pie | 470 | 30 | 18 | 175 | 290 | 45 | 1 | 34 | 6 |
| Golden Milk Coconut Cream Pie | 470 | 30 | 18 | 175 | 310 | 45 | 1 | 34 | 6 |
| Banana Cream Pie | 530 | 30 | 18 | 215 | 270 | 58 | 2 | 30 | 7 |
| Chocolate–Peanut Butter Banana Cream Pie | 660 | 39 | 22 | 220 | 280 | 69 | 3 | 38 | 11 |
| Black Bottom Pie | 570 | 36 | 20 | 160 | 150 | 57 | 0 | 46 | 7 |
| Mocha Cream Pie | 580 | 37 | 23 | 95 | 290 | 52 | 1 | 29 | 9 |
| Key Lime Pie | 400 | 25 | 15 | 160 | 95 | 38 | 0 | 36 | 6 |
| Banoffee Pie | 510 | 32 | 20 | 90 | 220 | 52 | 1 | 28 | 5 |
| Lemon Chess Pie | 530 | 28 | 17 | 185 | 260 | 64 | 0 | 46 | 6 |
| Butterscotch Cream Pie | 680 | 51 | 32 | 280 | 270 | 46 | 0 | 28 | 7 |
| Lemon Meringue Pie | 450 | 20 | 12 | 185 | 220 | 61 | 0 | 39 | 6 |

| | CALORIES | TOTAL FAT (G) | SAT FAT (G) | CHOL (MG) | SODIUM (MG) | TOTAL CARB (G) | DIETARY FIBER (G) | TOTAL SUGARS (G) | PROTEIN (G) |
|---|---|---|---|---|---|---|---|---|---|
| **Cream, Custard, and Curd Pies (cont.)** | | | | | | | | | |
| Chocolate Angel Pie | 610 | 44 | 27 | 160 | 220 | 49 | 2 | 35 | 8 |
| Rhubarb Custard Pie | 550 | 29 | 18 | 120 | 460 | 64 | 1 | 29 | 7 |
| Ricotta Lemon-Thyme Pie | 540 | 32 | 20 | 165 | 330 | 45 | 0 | 29 | 15 |
| Holiday Eggnog Custard Pie | 640 | 41 | 26 | 190 | 300 | 56 | 0 | 37 | 9 |
| Lavender Crème Brûlée Pie | 470 | 28 | 17 | 145 | 280 | 45 | 0 | 27 | 7 |
| Orange-Chocolate Custard Pie | 680 | 48 | 29 | 180 | 250 | 55 | 2 | 25 | 10 |
| Chocolate Chess Pie | 530 | 28 | 17 | 195 | 330 | 61 | 2 | 40 | 8 |
| Passion Fruit Curd Pie | 520 | 24 | 13 | 180 | 220 | 75 | 9 | 53 | 5 |
| **Upping Your Game** | | | | | | | | | |
| Salted Caramel Apple Pie | 580 | 28 | 17 | 145 | 390 | 75 | 2 | 53 | 7 |
| Pumpkin Praline Pie | 520 | 28 | 12 | 115 | 380 | 61 | 3 | 40 | 9 |
| Peanut Butter and Concord Grape Pie | 880 | 57 | 24 | 95 | 590 | 84 | 4 | 60 | 16 |
| Sour Cherry–Hazelnut Pie | 580 | 27 | 11 | 45 | 330 | 81 | 3 | 38 | 7 |
| Ginger Cranberry-Pear Streusel Pie | 510 | 21 | 13 | 55 | 190 | 78 | 6 | 40 | 4 |
| Butternut Squash Pie with Browned Butter and Sage | 550 | 36 | 22 | 190 | 480 | 50 | 2 | 24 | 7 |
| Apple-Cranberry Pie | 640 | 28 | 18 | 75 | 440 | 94 | 6 | 52 | 5 |
| Crab Apple Rose Pie | 740 | 31 | 19 | 85 | 370 | 113 | 2 | 46 | 5 |
| Mulled Wine Quince Pie | 730 | 28 | 18 | 75 | 380 | 101 | 3 | 40 | 5 |
| Plum-Ginger Pie | 570 | 29 | 18 | 75 | 360 | 75 | 5 | 36 | 7 |
| Apricot, Vanilla Bean, and Cardamom Pie | 600 | 29 | 18 | 75 | 370 | 80 | 6 | 41 | 8 |
| Pecan Peach Pie | 540 | 27 | 11 | 45 | 360 | 70 | 4 | 33 | 7 |
| Blueberry Earl Grey Pie | 650 | 31 | 19 | 85 | 310 | 89 | 3 | 49 | 6 |
| Cape Gooseberry Elderflower Meringue Pie | 400 | 15 | 9 | 40 | 290 | 62 | 0 | 29 | 6 |
| Red Currant and Fig Pie | 590 | 28 | 18 | 75 | 330 | 79 | 5 | 38 | 6 |
| Strawberry-Rhubarb Pie | 610 | 28 | 18 | 75 | 300 | 84 | 3 | 43 | 6 |
| Chai Blackberry Pie | 570 | 28 | 18 | 75 | 370 | 74 | 5 | 33 | 6 |
| **Elegant Tarts** | | | | | | | | | |
| Fresh Fruit Tart | 460 | 28 | 16 | 90 | 100 | 49 | 4 | 28 | 6 |
| Poached Pear and Almond Tart | 450 | 19 | 9 | 65 | 115 | 55 | 3 | 37 | 5 |
| Easy Berry Tart | 350 | 16 | 9 | 25 | 210 | 53 | 4 | 28 | 5 |
| Lemon Tart | 370 | 20 | 11 | 230 | 95 | 42 | 0 | 28 | 6 |
| French Apple Tart | 450 | 17 | 10 | 65 | 160 | 74 | 6 | 45 | 3 |
| Classic Apple Tarte Tatin | 480 | 24 | 15 | 85 | 110 | 65 | 4 | 44 | 3 |
| Peach Tarte Tatin | 350 | 18 | 11 | 50 | 220 | 44 | 2 | 26 | 3 |
| Easy Pear Tarte Tatin | 470 | 32 | 19 | 70 | 115 | 50 | 4 | 30 | 4 |
| Free-Form Apple Tart | 530 | 25 | 16 | 65 | 260 | 72 | 3 | 33 | 5 |

| | CALORIES | TOTAL FAT (G) | SAT FAT (G) | CHOL (MG) | SODIUM (MG) | TOTAL CARB (G) | DIETARY FIBER (G) | TOTAL SUGARS (G) | PROTEIN (G) |
|---|---|---|---|---|---|---|---|---|---|
| **Elegant Tarts (cont.)** | | | | | | | | | |
| Strawberry Galette with Candied Basil and Balsamic | 410 | 19 | 12 | 50 | 270 | 56 | 2 | 25 | 4 |
| Roasted Plum and Mascarpone Tart | 420 | 31 | 17 | 65 | 160 | 32 | 2 | 17 | 6 |
| Sablé Breton Tart with Cranberry Curd | 400 | 21 | 13 | 120 | 110 | 47 | 2 | 25 | 5 |
| Linzertorte | 400 | 21 | 8 | 45 | 105 | 48 | 2 | 31 | 5 |
| Baked Raspberry Tart | 330 | 18 | 11 | 85 | 130 | 36 | 2 | 20 | 4 |
| Baked Blackberry Tart | 320 | 18 | 11 | 85 | 130 | 36 | 1 | 20 | 4 |
| Baked Blueberry-Raspberry Tart | 320 | 18 | 11 | 85 | 130 | 36 | 2 | 20 | 4 |
| Fig, Cherry, and Walnut Tart | 340 | 18 | 7 | 45 | 65 | 37 | 3 | 19 | 5 |
| Rustic Walnut Tart | 440 | 28 | 10 | 75 | 190 | 42 | 1 | 27 | 6 |
| Chocolate-Hazelnut Raspberry Mousse Tart | 380 | 24 | 13 | 30 | 210 | 41 | 4 | 22 | 5 |
| Cranberry-Pecan Tart | 450 | 29 | 13 | 70 | 95 | 45 | 2 | 29 | 4 |
| Raspberry Streusel Tart | 450 | 20 | 11 | 45 | 75 | 64 | 3 | 37 | 5 |
| Rich Chocolate Tart | 440 | 33 | 20 | 110 | 120 | 33 | 2 | 8 | 5 |
| Chocolate-Tahini Tart | 510 | 37 | 18 | 100 | 150 | 41 | 2 | 17 | 8 |
| Blood Orange and Chocolate Tart | 320 | 21 | 13 | 60 | 150 | 33 | 1 | 18 | 3 |
| Chocolate, Matcha, and Pomegranate Tart | 390 | 26 | 16 | 70 | 125 | 39 | 1 | 23 | 5 |
| **Pies Big and Small** | | | | | | | | | |
| Apple Slab Pie | 460 | 23 | 14 | 60 | 240 | 60 | 2 | 30 | 4 |
| Peach Slab Pie | 410 | 22 | 14 | 60 | 190 | 47 | 2 | 20 | 4 |
| Pear-Butterscotch Slab Pie | 580 | 33 | 21 | 90 | 250 | 67 | 4 | 34 | 4 |
| Nectarine and Raspberry Slab Galette | 210 | 11 | 7 | 30 | 120 | 26 | 2 | 11 | 2 |
| Triple Berry Slab Pie with Ginger-Lemon Streusel | 350 | 16 | 10 | 45 | 150 | 48 | 3 | 23 | 3 |
| Key Lime Meringue Slab Pie | 290 | 13 | 8 | 125 | 90 | 38 | 0 | 35 | 6 |
| Pear-Rosemary Muffin Tin Pies | 410 | 22 | 12 | 50 | 300 | 51 | 4 | 24 | 4 |
| Blueberry Hand Pies | 330 | 15 | 7 | 0 | 280 | 53 | 3 | 21 | 5 |
| Caramel Apple Hand Pies | 330 | 17 | 9 | 10 | 230 | 49 | 2 | 20 | 5 |
| Cherry Hand Pies | 300 | 15 | 7 | 0 | 240 | 45 | 2 | 14 | 5 |
| Fried Peach Hand Pies | 410 | 23 | 7 | 25 | 410 | 47 | 1 | 20 | 5 |
| Chocolate-Cherry Pie Pops | 350 | 15 | 9 | 40 | 150 | 53 | 0 | 34 | 3 |
| Apple Butter Pie Pops | 250 | 15 | 10 | 40 | 160 | 24 | 0 | 7 | 3 |
| Banana-Caramel Pie in a Jar | 400 | 22 | 13 | 155 | 140 | 47 | 1 | 38 | 4 |
| Chocolate Cream Pie in a Jar | 370 | 27 | 16 | 145 | 105 | 28 | 0 | 21 | 5 |
| Mocha Cream Pie in a Jar | 370 | 27 | 16 | 145 | 105 | 29 | 0 | 22 | 5 |
| Individual Free-Form Apple Tartlets | 400 | 18 | 12 | 50 | 200 | 55 | 2 | 26 | 4 |
| Lemon Tartlets | 840 | 49 | 28 | 480 | 440 | 88 | 0 | 51 | 12 |
| Pecan Tartlets | 970 | 59 | 29 | 190 | 420 | 105 | 3 | 67 | 9 |
| Nutella Tartlets | 1180 | 81 | 37 | 110 | 330 | 104 | 3 | 58 | 13 |
| Portuguese Egg Tarts | 300 | 17 | 9 | 145 | 220 | 36 | 1 | 19 | 6 |

| | CALORIES | TOTAL FAT (G) | SAT FAT (G) | CHOL (MG) | SODIUM (MG) | TOTAL CARB (G) | DIETARY FIBER (G) | TOTAL SUGARS (G) | PROTEIN (G) |
|---|---|---|---|---|---|---|---|---|---|
| **Regional Favorites** | | | | | | | | | |
| Oregon Blackberry Pie | 560 | 31 | 19 | 85 | 360 | 65 | 4 | 26 | 6 |
| Marlborough Apple Pie | 440 | 27 | 16 | 140 | 250 | 44 | 2 | 24 | 5 |
| North Carolina Lemon Pie | 520 | 30 | 18 | 170 | 170 | 54 | 0 | 38 | 8 |
| Sweet Potato Pie | 530 | 27 | 16 | 185 | 380 | 64 | 2 | 36 | 7 |
| Buttermilk Pie | 440 | 27 | 16 | 225 | 450 | 42 | 0 | 24 | 8 |
| New England Mincemeat Pie | 840 | 39 | 25 | 105 | 380 | 112 | 5 | 70 | 6 |
| Pennsylvania Dutch Apple Pie | 520 | 23 | 15 | 65 | 450 | 75 | 3 | 41 | 5 |
| Southern Praline Pecan Pie | 700 | 47 | 18 | 135 | 510 | 63 | 3 | 44 | 7 |
| After-Hours Southern Praline Pecan Pie | 710 | 47 | 18 | 135 | 510 | 63 | 3 | 44 | 7 |
| Florida Sour Orange Pie | 360 | 15 | 8 | 125 | 180 | 50 | 0 | 40 | 7 |
| Maple Syrup Pie | 570 | 31 | 19 | 195 | 260 | 67 | 0 | 45 | 6 |
| Apple Pie with Cheddar Cheese Crust | 540 | 21 | 13 | 60 | 550 | 79 | 5 | 38 | 12 |
| Chocolate Haupia Cream Pie | 560 | 40 | 28 | 75 | 210 | 47 | 0 | 26 | 6 |
| French Coconut Pie | 490 | 31 | 20 | 140 | 260 | 47 | 1 | 28 | 5 |
| Thoroughbred Pie | 630 | 45 | 20 | 135 | 310 | 47 | 2 | 21 | 8 |
| Fudgy Tar Heel Pie | 650 | 46 | 18 | 100 | 390 | 56 | 2 | 33 | 8 |
| Virginia Peanut Pie | 690 | 42 | 17 | 130 | 350 | 69 | 3 | 47 | 14 |
| Hoosier Pie | 690 | 53 | 34 | 160 | 240 | 49 | 0 | 29 | 5 |
| Mississippi Mud Pie | 470 | 32 | 17 | 80 | 220 | 44 | 1 | 29 | 5 |
| Sweet Potato Sonker | 720 | 33 | 21 | 90 | 470 | 96 | 5 | 37 | 8 |
| **Icebox and Ice Cream Pies** | | | | | | | | | |
| Lemon Icebox Pie | 390 | 24 | 15 | 140 | 95 | 38 | 0 | 34 | 6 |
| Fresh Strawberry Pie | 340 | 14 | 9 | 40 | 170 | 51 | 3 | 29 | 3 |
| Raspberry Chiffon Pie | 640 | 39 | 25 | 120 | 240 | 67 | 4 | 46 | 6 |
| Rum Pumpkin Chiffon Pie | 380 | 24 | 15 | 70 | 310 | 35 | 2 | 28 | 4 |
| French Silk Chocolate Pie | 660 | 49 | 30 | 170 | 180 | 52 | 2 | 21 | 7 |
| Caramel Turtle Icebox Pie | 610 | 42 | 21 | 85 | 270 | 56 | 2 | 42 | 7 |
| Peanut Butter Pie | 600 | 49 | 24 | 105 | 250 | 30 | 2 | 23 | 11 |
| Grasshopper Pie | 510 | 36 | 20 | 150 | 140 | 46 | 0 | 37 | 4 |
| Cookies and Cream Ice Cream Pie | 580 | 40 | 24 | 115 | 220 | 50 | 0 | 33 | 6 |
| Coconut-Raspberry Gelato Pie | 290 | 18 | 8 | 35 | 45 | 29 | 2 | 23 | 3 |
| **Pie and Tart Doughs** | | | | | | | | | |
| Pat-in-Pan Pie Dough | 210 | 13 | 8 | 40 | 100 | 20 | 0 | 3 | 3 |
| Foolproof All-Butter Single-Crust Pie Dough | 210 | 14 | 9 | 40 | 150 | 18 | 0 | 2 | 2 |
| Herb Single-Crust Pie Dough | 210 | 14 | 9 | 40 | 150 | 18 | 0 | 2 | 2 |
| Lemon Single-Crust Pie Dough | 210 | 14 | 9 | 40 | 150 | 18 | 0 | 2 | 2 |
| Nut Single-Crust Pie Dough | 200 | 13 | 6 | 25 | 150 | 19 | 1 | 2 | 3 |
| Whole-Grain Single-Crust Pie Dough | 210 | 14 | 9 | 40 | 150 | 19 | 2 | 2 | 3 |

| | CALORIES | TOTAL FAT (G) | SAT FAT (G) | CHOL (MG) | SODIUM (MG) | TOTAL CARB (G) | DIETARY FIBER (G) | TOTAL SUGARS (G) | PROTEIN (G) |
|---|---|---|---|---|---|---|---|---|---|
| **Pie and Tart Doughs (cont.)** | | | | | | | | | |
| Foolproof All-Butter Double-Crust Pie Dough | 410 | 28 | 18 | 75 | 290 | 35 | 0 | 3 | 5 |
| Herb Double-Crust Pie Dough | 420 | 28 | 18 | 75 | 290 | 35 | 0 | 3 | 5 |
| Lemon Double-Crust Pie Dough | 420 | 28 | 18 | 75 | 290 | 36 | 0 | 3 | 5 |
| Nut Double-Crust Pie Dough | 410 | 26 | 11 | 45 | 290 | 37 | 1 | 4 | 6 |
| Whole-Grain Double-Crust Pie Dough | 420 | 28 | 18 | 75 | 290 | 37 | 3 | 3 | 6 |
| Classic Single-Crust Pie Dough | 210 | 15 | 7 | 25 | 150 | 18 | 0 | 2 | 2 |
| Classic Double-Crust Pie Dough | 430 | 29 | 14 | 45 | 290 | 35 | 0 | 3 | 5 |
| Vegan Single-Crust Pie Dough | 230 | 16 | 15 | 0 | 150 | 21 | 0 | 2 | 3 |
| Vegan Double-Crust Pie Dough | 470 | 31 | 29 | 0 | 290 | 42 | 0 | 3 | 5 |
| Gluten-Free Single-Crust Pie Dough | 190 | 12 | 7 | 30 | 160 | 19 | 1 | 1 | 1 |
| Gluten-Free Double-Crust Pie Dough | 380 | 23 | 14 | 65 | 320 | 39 | 1 | 2 | 2 |
| Classic Tart Dough | 230 | 12 | 8 | 55 | 75 | 26 | 0 | 9 | 3 |
| Chocolate Tart Dough | 210 | 13 | 8 | 55 | 75 | 21 | 0 | 9 | 2 |
| Gluten-Free Tart Dough | 240 | 12 | 7 | 55 | 100 | 32 | 1 | 12 | 2 |
| Free-Form Tart Dough | 290 | 18 | 12 | 50 | 190 | 26 | 0 | 0 | 4 |
| Free-Form Tartlet Dough | 290 | 18 | 12 | 50 | 190 | 26 | 0 | 0 | 4 |
| Graham Cracker Crust | 100 | 7 | 4.5 | 20 | 20 | 7 | 0 | 6 | 0 |
| Coconut Cookie Crust | 170 | 11 | 6 | 20 | 150 | 18 | 0 | 11 | 1 |
| Chocolate Cookie Crust | 160 | 10 | 5 | 15 | 95 | 17 | 0 | 9 | 1 |
| Mint Chocolate Cookie Crust | 190 | 13 | 6 | 15 | 100 | 21 | 0 | 13 | 1 |
| Nutter Butter Cookie Crust | 180 | 11 | 5 | 15 | 105 | 18 | 0 | 10 | 2 |
| Slab Pie Dough | 480 | 33 | 21 | 90 | 290 | 38 | 0 | 3 | 5 |
| **Toppings, Sauces, and More** | | | | | | | | | |
| Whipped Cream | 110 | 11 | 7 | 35 | 25 | 2 | 0 | 2 | 1 |
| Maple Whipped Cream | 120 | 11 | 7 | 35 | 25 | 4 | 0 | 4 | 1 |
| Brown Sugar and Bourbon Whipped Cream | 180 | 13 | 8 | 40 | 50 | 15 | 0 | 15 | 1 |
| Orange Whipped Cream | 110 | 11 | 7 | 35 | 25 | 3 | 0 | 3 | 1 |
| Peanut Butter Whipped Cream | 160 | 15 | 8 | 35 | 65 | 4 | 0 | 3 | 3 |
| Vegan Coconut Whipped Cream | 130 | 12 | 11 | 0 | 25 | 5 | 0 | 3 | 1 |
| Yogurt Whipped Cream | 100 | 10 | 7 | 30 | 10 | 1 | 0 | 1 | 2 |
| Mixed Berry Coulis | 80 | 0 | 0 | 0 | 50 | 19 | 2 | 17 | 0 |
| Blueberry-Cinnamon Coulis | 80 | 0 | 0 | 0 | 50 | 19 | 2 | 17 | 0 |
| Raspberry-Lime Coulis | 80 | 0 | 0 | 0 | 50 | 19 | 5 | 14 | 1 |

| | CALORIES | TOTAL FAT (G) | SAT FAT (G) | CHOL (MG) | SODIUM (MG) | TOTAL CARB (G) | DIETARY FIBER (G) | TOTAL SUGARS (G) | PROTEIN (G) |
|---|---|---|---|---|---|---|---|---|---|
| **Sauces, Toppings, and More (cont.)** | | | | | | | | | |
| Caramel Sauce | 300 | 11 | 7 | 35 | 90 | 53 | 0 | 53 | 1 |
| Dark Rum Caramel Sauce | 310 | 11 | 7 | 35 | 90 | 53 | 0 | 53 | 1 |
| Orange-Espresso Caramel Sauce | 320 | 11 | 7 | 35 | 90 | 56 | 0 | 55 | 1 |
| Salted Caramel Sauce | 300 | 11 | 7 | 35 | 310 | 53 | 0 | 53 | 1 |
| Caramel-Chocolate-Pecan Sauce | 290 | 17 | 8 | 30 | 50 | 37 | 1 | 32 | 2 |
| Butterscotch Sauce | 250 | 16 | 10 | 45 | 10 | 26 | 0 | 26 | 0 |
| Dulce de Leche | 260 | 15 | 10 | 50 | 70 | 28 | 0 | 28 | 5 |
| Hot Fudge Sauce | 260 | 12 | 7 | 15 | 85 | 37 | 2 | 32 | 3 |
| Mexican Hot Fudge Sauce | 260 | 12 | 7 | 15 | 85 | 37 | 2 | 32 | 3 |
| Orange Hot Fudge Sauce | 260 | 12 | 7 | 15 | 85 | 37 | 2 | 32 | 3 |
| Peanut Butter Hot Fudge Sauce | 310 | 16 | 8 | 15 | 190 | 39 | 2 | 33 | 4 |
| Crème Anglaise | 80 | 3.5 | 1.5 | 95 | 40 | 9 | 0 | 8 | 3 |
| Coffee Crème Anglaise | 80 | 3.5 | 1.5 | 95 | 40 | 9 | 0 | 8 | 3 |
| Earl Grey Crème Anglaise | 80 | 3.5 | 1.5 | 95 | 40 | 9 | 0 | 8 | 3 |
| Orange Crème Anglaise | 80 | 3.5 | 1.5 | 95 | 40 | 40 | 0 | 9 | 3 |
| Vanilla Ice Cream | 340 | 24 | 14 | 200 | 120 | 31 | 0 | 30 | 5 |
| Candied Nuts | 130 | 9 | 1.5 | 0 | 150 | 10 | 2 | 7 | 4 |
| Candied Coffee Beans | 80 | 2.5 | 0 | 0 | 85 | 15 | 3 | 6 | 2 |
| Sesame Brittle | 70 | 4.5 | 1.5 | 5 | 40 | 9 | 1 | 7 | 1 |

# CONVERSIONS AND EQUIVALENTS

Baking is a science and an art, but geography has a hand in it, too. Flours and sugars manufactured in the United Kingdom and elsewhere will feel and taste different from those manufactured in the United States. So we cannot promise that a pie you bake in Canada or England will taste the same as a pie baked in the States, but we can offer guidelines for converting weights and measures. We also recommend that you rely on your instincts when making our recipes. Refer to the visual cues provided. If the dough hasn't "come together in a ball" as described, you may need to add more flour—even if the recipe doesn't tell you to. You be the judge.

The recipes in this book were developed using standard U.S. measures following U.S. government guidelines. The charts below offer equivalents for U.S. and metric measures. All conversions are approximate and have been rounded up or down to the nearest whole number.

### example
1 teaspoon = 4.9292 milliliters, rounded up to 5 milliliters
1 ounce = 28.3495 grams, rounded down to 28 grams

## VOLUME CONVERSIONS

| U.S. | METRIC |
| --- | --- |
| 1 teaspoon | 5 milliliters |
| 2 teaspoons | 10 milliliters |
| 1 tablespoon | 15 milliliters |
| 2 tablespoons | 30 milliliters |
| ¼ cup | 59 milliliters |
| ⅓ cup | 79 milliliters |
| ½ cup | 118 milliliters |
| ¾ cup | 177 milliliters |
| 1 cup | 237 milliliters |
| 1¼ cups | 296 milliliters |
| 1½ cups | 355 milliliters |
| 2 cups (1 pint) | 473 milliliters |
| 2½ cups | 591 milliliters |
| 3 cups | 710 milliliters |
| 4 cups (1 quart) | 0.946 liter |
| 1.06 quarts | 1 liter |
| 4 quarts (1 gallon) | 3.8 liters |

## WEIGHT CONVERSIONS

| OUNCES | GRAMS |
| --- | --- |
| ½ | 14 |
| ¾ | 21 |
| 1 | 28 |
| 1½ | 43 |
| 2 | 57 |
| 2½ | 71 |
| 3 | 85 |
| 3½ | 99 |
| 4 | 113 |
| 4½ | 128 |
| 5 | 142 |
| 6 | 170 |
| 7 | 198 |
| 8 | 227 |
| 9 | 255 |
| 10 | 283 |
| 12 | 340 |
| 16 (1 pound) | 454 |

# CONVERSIONS FOR COMMON BAKING INGREDIENTS

Because measuring by weight is far more accurate than measuring by volume, and thus more likely to produce reliable results, in our recipes we provide ounce measures in addition to cup measures for many ingredients. Refer to the chart below to convert these measures into grams.

| INGREDIENT | OUNCES | GRAMS |
|---|---|---|
| **Flour** | | |
| 1 cup all-purpose flour* | 5 | 142 |
| 1 cup cake flour | 4 | 113 |
| 1 cup whole-wheat flour | 5½ | 156 |
| **Sugar** | | |
| 1 cup granulated (white) sugar | 7 | 198 |
| 1 cup packed brown sugar (light or dark) | 7 | 198 |
| 1 cup confectioners' sugar | 4 | 113 |
| **Cocoa Powder** | | |
| 1 cup cocoa powder | 3 | 85 |
| **Butter†** | | |
| 4 tablespoons (½ stick or ¼ cup) | 2 | 57 |
| 8 tablespoons (1 stick or ½ cup) | 4 | 113 |
| 16 tablespoons (2 sticks or 1 cup) | 8 | 227 |

\* U.S. all-purpose flour, the most frequently used flour in this book, does not contain leaveners, as some European flours do. These leavened flours are called self-rising or self-raising. If you are using self-rising flour, take this into consideration before adding leaveners to a recipe.

† In the United States, butter is sold both salted and unsalted. We recommend unsalted butter. If you are using salted butter, take this into consideration before adding salt to a recipe.

# OVEN TEMPERATURE

| FAHRENHEIT | CELSIUS | GAS MARK |
|---|---|---|
| 225 | 105 | ¼ |
| 250 | 120 | ½ |
| 275 | 135 | 1 |
| 300 | 150 | 2 |
| 325 | 165 | 3 |
| 350 | 180 | 4 |
| 375 | 190 | 5 |
| 400 | 200 | 6 |
| 425 | 220 | 7 |
| 450 | 230 | 8 |
| 475 | 245 | 9 |

# CONVERTING TEMPERATURES FROM AN INSTANT-READ THERMOMETER

We include doneness temperatures in many of the recipes in this book. We recommend an instant-read thermometer for the job. Refer to the table above to convert Fahrenheit degrees to Celsius. Or, for temperatures not represented in the chart, use this simple formula:

Subtract 32 degrees from the Fahrenheit reading, then divide the result by 1.8 to find the Celsius reading.

### example

"Cook caramel until it registers 160 degrees."

**To convert:**
$160°F - 32 = 128°$
$128° ÷ 1.8 = 71.11°C$, rounded down to $71°C$

# INDEX

Note: Page references in *italics* indicate photographs.

# Q

# R

# S